INSTRUCTIONAL DESIGN

PRINCIPLES AND APPLICATIONS

*CONTRIBUTING
AUTHORS*

Amy S. Ackerman

Ronald E. Bassett

Richard C. Boutwell

Robert K. Branson

John K. Burton

James Carey

Walter Dick

Robert M. Gagné

Robert J. Kibler

David G. Markle

Karen Medsker

Paul F. Merrill

Walter Wager

INSTRUCTIONAL DESIGN

PRINCIPLES AND APPLICATIONS

LESLIE J. BRIGGS, EDITOR

EDUCATIONAL TECHNOLOGY PUBLICATIONS
ENGLEWOOD CLIFFS, NEW JERSEY 07632

Library of Congress Cataloging in Publication Data
Main entry under title:

Instructional design.
  Includes index.
    1. Teaching. 2. Lesson planning. I. Briggs,
Leslie J.
LB1025.2.1645   371 3   77-23216
ISBN 0-87778-098-6

Printed in the United States of America.

Library of Congress Catalog Card Number:
77-23216.

International Standard Book Number:
0-87778-098-6.

First Printing: April, 1977.
Second Printing: January, 1979.
Third Printing: September, 1981.
Fourth Printing: January, 1985.

Preface

The authors of this book have perceived a need for a *comprehensive* treatment of the design of instruction. The desired book, it was thought, should be broad in coverage (from needs and goals analysis to summative evaluation of newly designed instruction), and consistent in viewpoint and recommendations for application.

The reading audience intended for this book includes teachers, teachers-in-training, curriculum personnel, military and industrial training personnel, and persons desiring to become professional instructional designers. It is thought that the book may also find use in educational psychology courses and in various courses relating to both educational theory and practice, at both the undergraduate and graduate levels.

The instructor should note that the absence of "instructional features," such as Chapter objectives, self-tests, and practice exercises, is not an oversight, but a very deliberate decision. The reason for this decision is that the book is intended for use in theory courses, in practicum courses, and for courses relating to research and needed research in the design of instruction. Therefore, no one set of objectives or exercises would be appropriate for all these purposes. That being the case, we have given examples of objectives for a practicum course in the form of four "assignment sheets" placed at the close of "Transition to Chapter 16." Instructors may find those pages useful in planning their own courses. Then, following those pages, Chapter 16 is a completed student project illustrating how the objectives of that

vii

course can be (and have been) met. Chapter 16 is a product from an advanced design course, and Chapter 17 is a similar product from an introductory course.

It was in connection with the introductory course just mentioned that this book came to be written. This writer was first assigned to teach this new introductory course in the Winter of 1975. No faculty member in the program of which that course is a part could suggest a textbook having the desired breadth of coverage. Thus, scattered readings were used, and guest lecturers gave presentations on each course topic, the writer serving in a "tie-in" role. The students expressed the need for a text that would enable them to learn more from the guest lectures. The writer then produced a 60-page "overview of instructional design," which during 1976 served as a brief interim text, and as an outline for the Chapter authors of this book. In the meantime the guest lectures were repeated, this time on videotape. Most of those guest lecturers are Chapter authors for this book.

During the 1976 offerings of the introductory course, Dr. Richard Boutwell served twice as a team teacher with the writer, and he conducted the course twice by himself. During one quarter an "outside formative evaluator" was brought in to help pinpoint needed course improvements. Data were gathered from students five times during the academic quarter. The need for this book was reiterated, even though a larger accumulation of books and videotapes was by then available. Since our opinion agreed with the feedback from students, a decision was made to undertake the preparation of this book.

It was originally intended that this writer would prepare only one or two Chapters, but as other faculty members faced the problem of prior commitments, the number of Chapters by this writer increased. Still, a total of 14 persons have contributed to the book, thus adding to the authoritativeness, since each writer is a specialist in the Chapter he or she contributed.

The majority of authors are faculty members at Florida State University; three are faculty members at other universities; one is self-employed; and two are students at the time of this writing. This writer served as local editor. We believe that, considering the number of authors, the book may be judged by others to be both authoritative and internally consistent.

The rationale for the sequence of Chapters in the book is given at many different points in the book. In Chapter 1, suggestions are given for how instructors and students may wish to deviate from this Chapter sequence for various purposes.

L.J.B.
October, 1976
Tallahassee, Florida

Table of Contents

Glossary

achievement — how well a learner performs a required course objective or set of such objectives, usually as measured by a test; performance of individuals and groups can then be judged as either satisfactory or unsatisfactory, based on a predetermined standard, or, performance may be stated in reference to norms describing how other groups scored on the test.

action verb — that part of a performance objective which describes the learner behavior taken as an indicator that the intended capability has been learned.

adjunct auto-instruction — the procedure, pioneered by Pressey, of providing practice tests for each chapter in a textbook, along with a simple device to give immediate automatic feedback to each student response to the practice test.

advance organizer — the practice of providing a brief, highly abstract summary at the beginning of a lecture or textbook chapter, to enable the learner to profit from the more detailed presentation to follow.

assessment — evaluation of the learning status of students for various purposes: (a) to determine readiness for a course; (b) to monitor progress during the course; (c) to measure achievement at the end of a year. Involves use of diagnostic tests, objective-referenced tests, and norm-referenced tests.

behavioral objectives — (*see* performance objectives)

candidate media — those media which can present the desired type of stimuli, without regard for which may be most effective or least costly. The distinction is from non-candidate media—e.g., a book *cannot* present spoken words—not from the ideal media.

CIPP Model — a model of summative evaluation, by Stufflebeam, which includes analysis of context, input, process, and product. A similar model by Gagné and Briggs examines support, aptitude, process, and outcomes.

competency-based instruction — (*see* mastery learning)

conditions of learning (external) — those features of the detailed tactics of instruction which are *special* to each domain of learning; these features are incorporated into the *instructional events*, which are common to all domains, when planning a lesson.

conditions of learning (internal) — those tendencies and memories within the learner which facilitate learning of an objective—motivation, readiness, and recall of essential prerequisites.

consortium — a voluntary association of several institutions or organizations to perform a specific task, such as the design, development, and evaluation of an instructional system.

contingency management — the practice of offering a favored activity as an inducement to first complete a non-favored activity. Example, "When you finish writing your paragraph, you may go play in the sand box."

cost-effectiveness — analysis of both the outcomes of instruction and the costs to reach the outcomes, so that management decisions as to the future use of the system can be made (possibly in comparison with alternate systems available.)

course (of instruction) — the total instruction being planned by a single design effort, whether it consists of a few days of instruction or an entire year. In elementary schools, a year of instruction may include all subjects taught; in high school a course may represent one semester of geometry or social studies.

course design objective — the practice of setting a definite criterion for the success of a course, such as "80% of the learners will master at least 80% of the objectives of the course."

courseware — (*see* software)

crew training — training conducted for several persons who are later to perform as a team or crew; the success of the performance depends both on individual skills and cooperative skills; often follows individual (skill) training; may or may not involve operation of equipment, as in an aircraft crew.

criterion — (1) the desired level of achievement of a learner on a performance objective; (2) the desired achievement of an entire class, taken as a "course design criterion" or goal of the instructional design effort.

criterion-referenced test — (*see* objective-referenced test)

cue — an indirect prompt given to help a learner complete a recitation or solve a problem; an indirect form of "guidance" stopping short of supplying the missing word or solution.

curriculum analysis — an overall, comprehensive view of the courses included in a program of studies, showing interrelationships among courses (or years of study) and an analysis of desirable or undesirable overlap; also a continuing review of the curriculum to spot gaps or other evidence of need for changes.

decision flow charting — a method of identifying and checking decisions to be made in a given job or task by reducing each decision to a binary (yes-no) decision (Chapter 15), as would be necessary for a computer program.

decision level analysis — an analysis of all decisions made in performing a job, including the rating of decisions in terms of time, complexity, and nature. For example, in Chapter 15, first aid training was analyzed as to topic (flesh wounds), type of decision (probable actions to be taken), and sequence of action (probable nature of injury before action decision). This results in a matrix of type of behavior (discrimination, rule, problem solving) and topic (wounds, sunstroke, etc.).

delivery system — the *form* in which an instructional system is developed and turned over to the user. Usually several *media* comprise a delivery system, such as: teachers, books, films; the media are chosen to suit the assumed learning environment—a classroom, a learning center, or home study.

Delphi technique — a procedure for predicting the future based on a series of mailed questionnaires addressed to experts (or, in some cases, the general public); the technique seeks consensus without face-to-face pressure to change or conform.

didactic teaching — methods in which the teacher or the materials present definitions, relationships, conclusions, etc., rather than having the learners discover them for themselves. Often employed in deductive teaching methods.

diffusion — the process by which new processes, data, techniques, products, or instructional systems come to be adopted by persons and organizations other than those which developed those items initially. The design team may initiate the diffusion effort, or it may be accomplished by others. The main obstacle is resistance to change in established institutions.

discovery learning — methods of teaching designed to permit the learner to induce relationships for himself rather than being "told." Often accomplished by inductive rather than deductive methods.

distortion (in a test) — a test or test item which is faulty because the student can answer it from use of a different kind of information processing than that intended—e.g., the wrong domain of learning outcome is brought into play.

domain (of learning outcome) — a major type of learning outcome differentiated from other domains in a taxonomy by (a) the kind of mental processing involved in learning, (b) the relevant conditions of learning and (c) the type of learned performance exhibited following learning. In Gagné's taxonomy, the domains are:

    1. Information learning
    2. Intellectual skills
    3. Cognitive strategies
    4. Motor skills
    5. Attitudes

There are sub-domains for domains 1 and 2 above.

    Taxonomies by Bloom and others list cognitive, affective, and psychomotor domains, also with sub-domains identified.

    Gagné's taxonomy began with a consideration of instruction while Bloom's began with outcomes to be measured.

empirical specification of objectives — a method of defining course objectives which employs extensive testing of untrained personnel to determine what they already know, so as to keep course objectives to a minimum; distinct from purely logical or rational methods or consensus methods.

enabling objective — a learned capability that facilitates the learning of a larger performance objective (*see* essential prerequisite and supportive prerequisite).

error data — using item analyses of responses of tryout students on a test (or responses to frames in programmed instruction) for the purpose of identifying needed improvements in the instruction (*see* formative evaluation; response-time data).

essential prerequisite — a performance capability that is essential to the learning of another capability because it is not possible to perform the second one unless the first one has been learned (and can be recalled); example: knowing how to "borrow" is essential to learning to subtract when borrowing is required. Synonym: essential enabling objective.

feedback — (1) in teaching, the confirmation or correction, to a student response, supplied by the teacher or by an "answer key" to a test or exercise (one of the nine instructional events); (2) in course design, the gathering of information from the learners as a basis for improving the instruction (formative evaluation).

field trial — the first use of a new delivery system in the actual operational (school) environment, as distinct from tryouts with a few students only. Often the field trial is a first test of both the delivery system and the installation procedures.

formative evaluation — tryouts and revisions of components (or all) of an instructional system before operational use. Includes tryouts of materials with individual learners and small groups, as well as with entire classes in the school situation. Such evaluations can also apply to teacher guides, teacher training, etc.

front-end analysis — accomplishment of the early stages of the design process, such as analysis of needs, goals, and objectives, and organizing the course units. Especially important in military and industrial training is the process of excluding unnecessary course content, in order to save training time.

Gantt chart — used to compare promised completion dates with actual performance of a team; consists of a list of tasks to be accomplished and the time allowed for each; some tasks are sequential in time and others are overlapping in time. *See* PERT.

goal — a statement of what "ought to be" with respect to learners' attainments, as distinct from present attainments.

goal analysis — the process of collecting a wide range of goals from resource persons, then sorting them to eliminate duplications, then converting the statements to measurable form, as in stating performance objectives.

goal-based evaluation — a model of instructional system evaluation that is based on comparing stated goals with actual learner attainments; this is a deductive model—desired behaviors are inferred from stated goals.

goal-free evaluation — a model of instructional system evaluation which ignores the *stated* goals of the designer in favor of *inferring* the goals that the behaviors demanded of the learners *indicate* were intended; this is an inductive model—goals are inferred from behaviors of pupils encouraged by the school. This model has been emphasized by Scriven, who also provides a comprehensive checklist for use in evaluating both the instruction and the evaluation data themselves.

"halo" effect — distortions in ratings or scoring of tests due to unintended extraneous factors considered by the rater or scorer. Examples: grading a student on basis of what the instructor thinks the student knows rather than on what was written on a test; including ratings of personality in what is intended as an achievement test.

hardware — mechanical and/or electrical (or electronic) devices used for instruction, such as computers, teaching machines, projectors, recorders, etc.

individual training (skill training) — training designed to establish competencies for individual trainees who may perform on the job either as an individual or as a crew member (see crew training).

individualized instruction — delivery systems which permit one or more of the following: (a) each learner chooses his objectives; (b) several media are provided for each objective; (c) each learner progresses at his own rate.

information processing analysis — an analysis of a performance objective to reveal the sequence of mental operations it requires.

instructional delivery system — the entire set of components needed to reach a set of instructional goals and objectives; such components include instructional materials and activities; assessments of learner performance; entry tests and remedial instruction; in short, all resources needed for the learners to reach the goals.

instructional design — the entire process of analysis of learning needs and goals and the development of a delivery system to meet the needs; includes development of instructional materials and activities; and tryout and revision of all instruction and learner assessment activities.

instructional designer — a person who engages in the planning, analysis, and development of instruction and instructional materials, in contrast to a person who operates the instructional system; a teacher may be both designer and system operator, while a curriculum developer may be only the designer.

instructional events (teaching steps) — those distinct teaching steps in a lesson which are supplied by the teacher, by the materials and activities, or by the learner himself. These events are common to all domains of learning outcomes; nine such events are listed and discussed (in Chapter 7). Within each domain, however, one refers to the appropriate *conditions of learning* so they may be implemented by the instruction.

instructional features (of software, or courseware) — as distinct from the content contained in books, films, and other instructional materials, these features refer to objectives, self-tests, practice exercises, etc.

instructional map — an arrangement of objectives for a course in such a way as to show how the various domains of outcomes interact in enabling the learner to achieve the course objective. Thus "triads" or clusters may show for each course unit, how information objectives, intellectual skill objectives, and attitude objectives are needed to accomplish the unit objective. A map thus shows relationships *among* objectives, while a *hierarchy* shows relationships *within a single intellectual skill objective* only.

instructional system — the total "package" of materials, tests, student guides, and teacher guides that is needed to reach the goals for any instructional unit, course, or curriculum, along with all supporting activities and processes required to operate the system as it was designed to be operated.

instructional systems design — a systematic approach to the planning and development of a means to meet instructional needs and goals; all components of the system (objectives, instructional materials, tests, etc.) are considered in relation to each other in an orderly but flexible sequence of processes; the resulting delivery system is tried out and improved before widespread use is encouraged.

instructional technology — (1) the process of instructional systems design; (2) the hardware used in instruction; (3) both (1) and (2).

job analysis — a process of arriving at a description of all the performance elements (tasks) that make up a job. Tasks are often clustered into "duties," or major parts of the job. Analysis is done by questionnaires, observations of performance, and interviews of incumbents and supervisors.

job evaluation — in industry, this often is a matter of setting pay or salary rates for various job classifications.

learned capability — an outcome of instruction; defined in terms of standard verbs describing various domains of learning outcomes; called the "capability verb" in written objectives.

learning — a change in behavior and performance capability that results from study, instruction, or practice, as distinct from behavior changes due to maturation, fatigue, or other influences such as drugs.

learning hierarchy — a format for identifying and arranging the essential prerequisites of an objective in the intellectual skill domain in such a way as to aid in determining the sequencing of the instruction for that objective; the hierarchy is the end product of a learning task analysis for objectives in the *intellectual skill domain only*. Analysis of other objectives may be called "instructional maps" when the purpose is to show relationships *among* objectives, and a "sequence chart" when sequencing, say, for an information objective, is being planned.

learning style — an individual's typically best way to learn; e.g., from reading, listening, viewing audio-visual presentations, etc.

learning task analysis — a process of identifying the elements of mental process and performance that should represent parts of a teaching sequence needed for mastery of the objective. This analysis reveals enabling objectives and essential skills that are needed to learn the objective; it may also reveal supportive prerequisites (enabling objectives).

lesson — the smallest unit for which instruction is usually planned, consisting of about an hour of instruction or study time.

lesson plan — a written outline of instruction to be conducted, usually for a single hour of instruction corresponding to one enabling objective. As recommended here, it lists the objective, the media, materials, and activities, and a prescription for how each instructional event (teaching step) will be conducted.

levels (or layers) of objectives — a way of organizing a course, working from general goals and purposes on down to increasingly detailed objectives. Seven such levels are described in Chapter 4:
1. needs
2. goals
3. life-long objectives

4. end-of-course objectives
5. unit objectives
6. specific performance objectives
7. enabling objectives supporting specific objectives.

mastery — (a) mastery learning is a flexible schedule plan in which each student uses as much study time as is needed to reach criterion on each objective; (b) a mastery criterion refers to *absolute* ability to perform the task, with no gradations below this considered acceptable.

mathemagenic behavior — the phenemonon in which use of practice tests in conjunction with reading of textual material enhances learning both for material covered in the practice tests and also *materials not so covered.*

media — the physical means of conveying instructional content—books, films, videotapes, slide-tape presentations, etc., including the teacher's voice and non-verbal behavior. (Earlier definitions viewed media only as aids to the teacher; the current concept is that all media teach.) Some definitions refer to the sense organ stimulated (eye, ear), and some to a general type of stimuli (e.g., spoken words, whether "live" or recorded).

"media trap" — this trap is encountered when one pays more attention to the delivery system than to the objectives when designing instruction; that is to say, when use of media *per se* overrides any rationale for using those particular media.

"mediation of instruction" — increased use of media other than the teacher to present the instructional stimulus (information). The mere mediation of a course, however, does not mean that a systems design model was followed.

mode of instruction — (*see* media; delivery systems)

model — a set of coherent procedures for actually carrying out a process, such as needs assessment, media selection, or evaluation.

module — usually a self-instructional package of material covering a small portion of a course, corresponding to a "lesson" in conventional instruction.

need — a discrepancy or gap between the way things "ought to be" and the way they "are." Needs and goals for elementary and secondary schools may be established by public concensus. Needs in industry may be established by job analysis. Needs in higher education are often established by precedent.

needs assessment — a systematic process for determining goals, identifying discrepancies between goals and the status quo, and establishing priorities for action; in education, needs are identified by consensus of the community; in military and industrial training, a job analysis may reveal training needs.

object — that part of a performance objective which shows the result of the action taken by the learner; examples—make a *speech*, write a *poem*, paint a *picture*.

objective-referenced tests — tests designed to measure performance on the objectives of a course; such tests may be scored simply as "satisfactory" or "unsatisfactory" using a pre-determined standard (criterion of performance). Commonly known as criterion-referenced tests. Different criteria can be set for different letter grades when grades are required.

occupational survey — an investigation of the relevance of a job analysis for a large number of workers by use of mailed questionnaires; of special importance to determine the most frequently performed duties and tasks.

operational use — when an instructional system has been installed in several schools, and when summative evaluation has been made, further adoptions or use of the system can be termed "operational use."

peer tutoring — (1) in education, the practice in which one student who has mastered an objective is assigned (or volunteers) to help another student learn the same task; (2) in military training, one trainee first observes, then practices and learns a task, then demonstrates it to another trainee (or serves as an instructor).

performance objectives — statements of what the learners will be able to do or how they will be expected to behave after completing a prescribed unit or course of instruction; may be stated either in terms of an observable action or in terms of a product which results from an action.

PERT (Program Evaluation and Review Technique) — a method of project management. PERT diagrams are sometimes called networks because of the type of visual display of tasks to be completed in various time periods.

posttest — a test given after instruction in a unit of a course or the entire course. Such tests are used to:
    1. monitor pupil progress.
    2. issue reports to parents
    3. measure gains for each learner
    4. evaluate the instruction
    5. pinpoint needed changes in the instruction.

predictive validity (of training) — the degree of correlation between performance on a test taken immediately after training and a later test of job performance.

presentation form — (*see* media; delivery systems)

pretest — a test given before instruction begins; the purposes for such tests include:
    1. to measure basic skills relevant to *all* instruction, such as reading and ability to interpret graphical data.
    2. to measure knowledge and skill relevant to the course to determine if some students should skip parts or all of the course.
    3. to determine each learner's "entry point" in an individualized instructional program.

4. to provide an "entry baseline" for an entire group so that gains resulting from the instruction may be measured as a step to improving the instruction.

5. to provide a baseline for evaluation of pupil progress and for course evaluation.

problem analysis — when evidence exists that there is a failure in performance of people, an analysis is done to determine whether the problem should be solved by training, by administrative action, or by buying new equipment, etc.

prompting — giving the learner the word or phrase he is trying to recall, as in reciting a poem; a direct form of "guidance"; providing a strong hint on how to solve a problem.

rationale — in the design model presented in this book, the rationale shows how the designer incorporated appropriate conditions of learning into the way the instructional events are to be accomplished, as summarized in the prescriptions for work to be done by media specialists.

reliability (of a test) — for an objective-referenced test, reliability refers to the *adequacy* of the test—does it require enough performance to represent the learner's true achievement on the objective? Reliability is enhanced by *length* of test and by *freedom from distortion*. (For reliability of norm-referenced tests, consult a measurement textbook.)

replicable media — forms of instruction which do not "vanish" after first use, as is the case with a lecture or discussion (unless they are recorded). In contrast, printed materials, films, or recordings do not vanish; they remain for analysis, evaluation, and further use. Thus capability of repeated use in the original form and content are features of a replicable medium. They can be expected to repeatedly produce the same results.

resources and constraints — the practical boundary conditions under which a design team operates. A detailed analysis considers budget, time, personnel, facilities, equipment, supplies, and institutional characteristics of the agencies concerned with the development and use of the delivery system.

response-time data — using automated recording equipment to record the time tryout students take to answer test questions. The results are used to identify ambiguities in the test or in the instructional material.

scope and sequence — an overall curriculum outline showing the year-by-year and subject-by-subject attainments to be accomplished.

simulator (trainer) — usually a complex training device, such as for training of pilots for either a one-person aircraft or a crew-served aircraft; the simulator requires realistic responses to realistic situations, but is less costly and less dangerous than training in an actual aircraft.

situation — used to refer to the "given" in a performance objective; e.g., "given a slide rule and 10 multiplication problems, the learner will . . . ."

software — instructional materials such as books, films, and recordings; the instructional part of hardware used in learning, such as a 16mm film used in a projector; a programmed instruction unit or materials presented and displayed by a computer or a teaching machine.

spiral sequencing — (1) a method of sequencing of instruction in which the same topic, concept, or objective is "returned to" several times during a course to enhance retention and generalization; this is distinct from teaching it in its entirety in one time period, without return to it during the course; (2) a method of sequencing intended to enhance motivation and learning by teaching a few concepts and rules to quickly arrive at one class of problem solving; then a few more related rules and concepts lead to problem solving for another topic or objective, etc. Often called "re-cycling."

strategy of instruction — as treated here, this consists of (a) determining the sequencing of enabling objectives within an objective, and (b) deciding how to implement the instructional events for individual lessons.

subordinate competencies — (*see* enabling objectives; essential prerequisites; supportive prerequisites)

successive approximation — a procedure of course design which begins with a series of test questions, carefully sequenced, to serve as a "bare bones" program. Then teaching materials are gradually added only when learner performance indicates the need. Response-time data and error data are used to judge when and where to add instructional content. This method avoids inclusion of unneeded material. (*See* Chapter 15.)

summative evaluation — the process of gathering, combining, and interpreting data in order to make a decision about a new instructional product or delivery system. This evaluation comes after all formative evaluations have been completed.

supportive prerequisite — a performance capability which *facilitates* the learning of another capability but which is not *essential* for such learning. Synonym: a supporting enabling objective.

system installation — when an instructional system is designed by a group outside the schools for which the system is developed, the completed system is said to be installed in the schools when it is first in full operation. There may follow periods of adjustment and adaptation before (1) system evaluation, and (2) "operational use."

tactics of instruction — as treated here, the tactics are reflected in the prescriptions for each instructional event for a lesson, with particular reference to how the needed conditions of learning are incorporated.

task analysis — an analysis of each performance objective prior to determining the teaching strategy for that objective. This analysis may consist of three steps:
   1. information processing analysis
   2. task classification
   3. learning task analysis.

task classification — categorizing the type of learning outcome represented by a performance objective as to domain in a taxonomy, as a means of identifying necessary conditions of learning to be incorporated into the instructional events for a lesson plan.

taxonomy of learning outcomes — a system for categorizing performance objectives and their enabling objectives into *domains* of learning and learning outcomes. (*See* Chapter 5.)

teaching steps — (*see* instructional events)

terminal objective — a troublesome term, used by some to mean "end-of-course" objective, but used here to mean a "performance objective" within a course or unit of instruction. It is "terminal" only in the sense that its performance is preceded by the learning of all essential prerequisites (enabling objectives) for that objective.

test — as used here, any means of assessing progress of learners, including written tests, observation of behavior, or evaluation of a student product such as a composition.

time line analysis — setting time schedules for completion of the many design stages which may overlap in time; *see* Gantt and PERT.

tools and constraints — that part of a performance objective which describes aids or references the learner may or may not use when demonstrating mastery of an objective; examples—dictionary, slide rule, calculator, etc.; also any time limits for the performance.

trade associations — affiliations of several industrial firms in the same line of business to support their mutual needs, such as needs for training programs.

training aids — pieces of equipment used by an instructor to illustrate the working relationship within some type of mechanical device; may consist of actual equipment with parts cut away for better visibility.

training devices — pieces of equipment on which a trainee practices some operation related to a job in maintenance or operation of equipment.

type of stimulus — statement of the *form* of desired presentation without identification of the specific medium. Examples: (1) spoken words represent a *type* of stimulus; potential media are "live speech by teacher" or "recorded speech"; (2) moving pictures may be presented by TV, ITV, or 16mm projection.

validity (of a test) — for an objective-referenced test, validity is determined by checking to see that the performance required by the test is the same as that described in the objective (for validity of norm-referenced tests, consult a standard test and measurements textbook).

INSTRUCTIONAL DESIGN

PRINCIPLES AND APPLICATIONS

Part I

Principles of Instructional Design

Chapter 1

Introduction

Leslie J. Briggs
Florida State University

It is the thesis of this book that instruction can be designed more systematically than has traditionally been the case. At a minimum, this means that objectives, methods, and evaluation procedures can all be designed to support each other.

When materials for the learners have already been chosen, as in the prior adoption of a textbook, for example, the teacher can state appropriate chapter objectives for the learners to use to focus their study efforts appropriately. Then the test given over the chapter can be a test intended to measure the announced objectives rather than some other, unannounced objectives.

When the learning materials have not already been chosen, the teacher can determine the objectives first, and then seek out materials and learning activities by which the objectives can be attained by the learners. Then, appropriate evaluations of the learning can be devised. (Chapter 8 was written especially for teachers working under either of the above circumstances.)

When a team of designers is to *develop* whatever learning materials and activities are needed, the same principles apply, although the total design effort required is then much greater. (Chapter 9 was written especially for such team members.)

So, whether a teacher is working alone to plan the instruction, or whether a large group of people is developing an entire new course or curriculum, this basic principle of achieving *congruence* among objectives, teaching strategy, and evaluation of student performance still applies.

Curriculum-development teams may include teachers,

administrators, subject-matter experts, evaluation specialists, media specialists, instructional designers, and many other specialist personnel. Teams for designing industrial and military training courses would consist of a similar range of personnel.

In short, whatever the size of unit of instruction to be developed (whether a single lesson, or a course, or an entire curriculum), and whether the design effort falls upon the shoulders of a single person or a large group of persons, the principles and procedures in this book can be utilized, at least to some degree. A minimal degree of utilization is represented by congruence among objectives, methods and materials, and evaluation.

Greater degrees of utilization of the theory and procedures outlined in this book can be achieved by continued study and practice of the procedures recommended here. An instructor, supervisor, or colleague may assist the reader in achieving added expertise, as study and efforts in application of these principles continue.

Instructional Systems

The phrase "instructional systems design" has come into usage in recent years. This phrase is a specific application of "general systems theory," which means a number of things when applied to instructional design.

First of all, a "system," in the present context, is an integrated plan of operation of all components (sub-systems) of a system, designed to solve a problem or meet a need. We have already given a very simple example of this concept when we noted that objectives, methods, and evaluation should be designed to be mutually supportive of each other. The three components should not be designed "piecemeal," but as parts of an integrated plan. Thus, a systems approach to the design of instruction can be implemented by one teacher planning one lesson, by 50 people developing a new curriculum, or by 500 people planning a new university. In the latter case, "instruction" would be a sub-system of the university system; other subsystems would include buildings and maintenance, food services, student and faculty recruiting, etc.

Second, the planning represented by a systems approach implies an analysis of components in a logical order, and careful coordination of the total effort among the planners. Imagine what might result if three teachers were to work independently to plan the three components for a unit of instruction on "oriental culture." Teacher A, assigned to write the objectives, might focus upon learning of facts about education in China; teacher B, assigned to write or choose the instructional materials, might focus on principles relating to the political system in Japan; and teacher C, assigned to make the tests, might focus on "how to solve industrial problems in Korea." The result, obviously, would be complete chaos. Learners could appropriately complain that there was no agreement among objectives, materials, and evaluation. Even in a course designed by a single instructor, have you ever had the experience of being led to believe that the purpose of the course was to learn to solve a particular type of problem, while the instruction focused only on concepts, and the examination required recall of isolated facts from the textbook? If so, you were the victim of a failure to use an integrated plan to make the three components compatible with each other.

Third, the *process* of planning follows an orderly but flexible sequence. Part I of this book contains chapters arranged in an orderly, logical sequence, but with frequent reminders that there is much "backtracking" as well as "looking ahead" during the actual practice of this total series of steps. So, while there *is* an overall logical order of design steps or stages, one step in the listed sequence is not always completed before the next, in a fixed linear order, and never returned to again. Actually, there is a "spiral sequence," in which one returns to an earlier step and makes corrections, due to a new insight gained while taking a later step. This cyclical or "iterative" nature of this instructional design model is one of its greatest strengths—it is open to "self-correction." A glance at the chapter titles for Part I of the book, reveals, in effect, the outline of the major steps in this design procedure.

Fourth, the design procedures recommended in this book are research based, in so far as possible. References to research data are made to show the extent to which the procedures illustrated are based on research, and the extent to which they are based on theory, experience, or common sense.

Fifth, the design model calls for empirical testing and improvement of the total instructional plan. Since instructional theory is at an early stage of development compared to theory in the physical sciences, heavy reliance must be placed on actual tryout and revision of the instruction; this is called *formative evaluation* (see Chapter 10).

Sixth, this design model requires comparison of the final version of the instruction with alternate instruction; or, in the absence of an alternative, the value of the final form of the instruction is to be determined. This is called *summative evaluation* (see Chapter 11).

The total set of design procedures represented in this book may be considered a "systems-oriented" model for instructional design.

Origins of Instructional Systems Design

The reader may already have one of several impressions—that the design procedures discussed here are new and strange, or only partly new, or "just common sense." In a way, all these reactions may be valid for different readers. There are many origins of influences from the past which have merged together in recent years to the extent that "Instructional Systems Design" is recognized in some universities as an area of specialization for degrees, and in industrial and military training as a job specialty. In some of these institutions, the term, "instructional technology" is used. We prefer "instructional systems design," because many persons associate technology with hardware (computers or audiovisual devices used for instruction). Our intent, by use of "instructional systems design," is to imply the total planning process necessary to deliver whatever instruction is needed, including hardware (if any) and software (books, films, and all instructional media, materials, and exercises). The entire package is called a delivery system (Chapter 9). Other books in this field have also adopted our meaning of instructional systems as broad enough to include both hardware and software, as well as the operations or processes required to install the system in a school or training facility.

Lumsdaine (1964) has identified some of the historical roots which have merged into the "tree" of instructional systems design: (a) a heritage from both psychology and education of interest in individual differences among learners, including use of self-paced instructional devices and teaching machines, and similar "job training" devices or simulators as used in military and industrial training; (b) behavioral science learning theory, emphasizing either reinforcement of correct responses or guidance for cognitive activities; (c) engineering technology compatible with self-paced, individualized learning; and (d) the audiovisual field as employed in education and elsewhere.

Another historical root was the military concept of training as a part of the personnel subsystem needed to support a new weapons system. In business and industry, systems theory was first applied to management procedures, then to training of personnel.

Instructional Systems Design
as Value Free

Some critics of such instructional systems design models as that presented in this book claim that instruction so designed focuses on trivial objectives and that the methods used are "mechanistic" rather than "humanistic." Our reply is that the design model advocated here determines only the methodology of problem-solving, not the nature of the goals, objectives, or outcomes to be sought, nor the method of instruction. We encourage the use of the recommended procedures for any desired attitudinal objectives as well as skill and knowledge objectives, and for planning a discovery as well as a didactic teaching style. In fact, the recommended model is compatible for either group-paced, teacher-conducted instruction, or for learner-paced, individualized instruction, whatever the objectives are for each learner.

In short, the procedures recommended here are usable by designers and teachers having an extremely wide range of preferences as to goals as well as to methods of instruction. In this sense, the model presented is "value free," although we encourage both "goal based evaluation of the outcomes of instruction" and "goal free evaluation of instruction" (Scriven, 1974).

By use of both these forms of evaluation, one can determine that the *intended* objectives were met, and can ascertain any *unexpected* outcomes from the instruction.

Alternate Models for the Design of Instruction

The word "model" has been used here without a formal definition. For practical purposes, a model is a suggested way to perform work, and it provides some guidelines as to dimensions. A dressmaker's model can be adjusted to fit the person for whom the dress is to be made. It is therefore a flexible model, but which uses consistently some standard concepts, such as neckline and hemline.

The reader is undoubtedly aware that not all educators or training directors approve of (to say nothing of using) the "systems" model presented here. In the past, much of curriculum and instructional design has been based on tradition, or on the structure of disciplines as seen by researchers in the disciplines, or as guided by preferred learning theories. There is also a widespread belief that there is nothing general about learning and instruction that is separate from the subject-matter being taught.

Our position is that there is, indeed, much generalizable knowledge about teaching and learning that can be applied to all areas of education and training. But we also agree that there is much to be learned from those who have taught their subject for many years. Thus, we believe, there are general principles common to all instruction, and special principles and insights especially suited to specific subject areas.

Various models for the design of teaching have been summarized in the book by Joyce and Weil (1972). Those models of teaching, as well as different learning theories, are not as unlike as they may seem if one allows for the fact that different domains of learning outcomes are being addressed. While there *are* differences in how teaching and learning are conceptualized, if all the experts were asked to address a single domain of learning, the differences would be reduced; thus, the importance of a taxonomy of learning outcomes, as presented in Chapter 5.

The authors of this book have paid serious attention to taxonomies of learning outcomes which enable a designer to *classify* the desired objectives for the purposes of (a) preparing appropriate *evaluation* instruments, and (b) designing the specific *conditions of learning* needed for the various types of desired outcomes into the appropriate teaching strategy for each objective.

Of the available taxonomies, we have chosen to utilize the taxonomy of Gagné (1970), which appears to us most useful for the design of instruction and for assessment of learner performance. This important aspect of instructional design has been utilized in other books (Briggs, 1970, 1972; Gagné and Briggs, 1974), which have been used as texts to produce such course designs as those reproduced in Chapters 16 and 17.

Another value of a taxonomy is that it enables one to avoid "either-or" decisions, and to see more alternatives in design strategy. That is to say, one need not feel forced to choose between a didactic method and a discovery method when one can see the many degrees of guidance to the learner's thinking that can be applied for various domains of outcomes (see Tables 1-3, Chapter 9). One degree of guidance is appropriate for acquiring information but a different degree is appropriate for problem-solving.

Thus, one may design many degrees of "guidance to learning," all the way from complete independence of the learner to discover all by himself, to complete "telling the learner the answers." An extensive research literature attempts to relate the optimum *degree of guidance* to the nature of the task to be learned and to the nature of the learners. Recommendations growing out of such research are given in Chapter 7 for various types of learning outcomes.

Organization of This Book

Part I Chapter Sequence

The writer faced a dilemma as to the sequence of the Chapters for Part I of this book. Three different rationales for the Chapter sequences were considered:

First, there is the question of how the reader can best learn from this book. This involves the order in which various concepts and design skills might be initially learned by the reader.

Second, there is the sequence used by experienced designers who have already mastered the skills discussed in the book.

Third, there is the order in which the instruction is conducted in the classroom after a course has been designed.

Table 1 serves as an example of the difference these considerations could have led to in organizing this book.

Table 1

Three Sequences of Importance

The Learning Sequence	The Design Sequence	The Classroom Sequence
1. Learn to identify goals	1. Identify goals	1. Give the objectives to the learners
2. Learn to write objectives	2. Organize the course	2. Conduct or monitor the instruction as planned
3. Learn to organize a course	3. Write objectives	3. Assess learner performance
4. Learn to analyze objectives	4. Prepare assessments of learner performance	
5. Learn to assess pupil performance	5. Analyze objectives	
6. Learn to design instructional strategies	6. Design strategy of instruction	
7. Learn to design lessons or module materials	7. Design lessons or modules	
8. Learn formative evaluation of materials and learner activities	8. Conduct formative evaluation	

The reader can perhaps easily discern which of the three alternatives we selected—the sequence for *learning* of the design skills that we believe will be best for you, the reader.

In preparing Table 1, we had no intention of minimizing the

complexity of the classroom operations. The reason why the classroom column of Table 1 looks skimpy is that this book is about *designing* instruction. We do not discuss here the classroom teaching skills that apply to the total classroom management aspect of teaching. We do, however, deal with design skills as they can be applied by the busy teacher (Chapter 8) and by design teams (Chapter 9). A major difference between the two situations is that teachers normally *select* instructional materials, whereas design teams *develop* such materials. Chapter 7 suggests that the *strategy* of design is the same for the two situations, even though the tactics differ. That is why the book "branches" at Chapter 8; the teacher can take that branch, and the design team can take Chapter 9.

All through Part I of the book, we give more details about our Chapter sequence rationale, so that you will fully understand why we present Chapters to you in a different order than if we were jointly conducting a design project, using the book as an outline of steps to be taken. So, we try, in Part I, to look at the task from your point of view as the reader and learner. Then, Chapter 9 gives the "project" flavor of how a design team operates, and Chapter 15 is a "project report" of a completed course design.

We hope that the foregoing explanation will not only convince you that we care whether the book is sequenced for your convenience, but also that the illustration in Table 1, showing the difference between the *learning* sequence and the *job* sequence, will have permanent value for you as a designer.

Having said all this, let us now recognize that different readers have different amounts of prior knowledge or experience in the matters discussed in Part I of this book. Also, your first applications of the knowledge you gain from this book may involve many different circumstances or starting points. Therefore, we next try to suggest reasons why some readers may want to read the Chapters somewhat out of sequence.

Starting point. It could be that your first application of what you learn from this book (or from a course in which the book is used), begins with a situation in which the needs and goals for the new or modified course of instruction are already known. In that case, you could skip Chapter 2.

If, in addition, you already know how to write objectives by the five-component method described in Chapter 3, you could very well begin your reading with Chapter 4 (organizing the course).

Personal goal. If your personal goal is to become a teacher (or to become a better teacher), you may not want to read the second part of Chapter 9, which deals with how design teams operate. If, on the other hand, you want to be a design team member or leader, by all means read that entire Chapter. If your interest is in theory or research, you may want to use this book as an advance organizer or "place keeper," and to read other sources cited in the volume.

Whatever your goal, we hope we have not "told you more than you want to know" about the rationale for Chapter sequence in Part I. But we made a deliberate decision to give you our rationale, and if we must err, we would prefer to say too much rather than too little. Thus, the "transition" pages between Chapters, as well as the Chapter content, will give you more detail about "where you are now" as you read along.

Part II Chapter Sequence

Part II turns from the design model itself, with all the theory and procedures discussed in Part I, to special applications of the model. The Chapters in Part II are of two distinct kinds: discursive and illustrative, as next discussed.

Chapters 12, 13, and 14 discuss how the design model is applied in higher education (including medical schools) and in military and industrial training. Chapter 12 is placed first because it addresses both education and training environments.

Then, since Chapter 15 deals with first aid training in an industrial situation, it is placed after the medical education Chapter. Another important difference is that Chapter 15 is a "project report," showing how the instruction was designed and what the results were. That Chapter thus documents in detail the design techniques employed. Those techniques are consistent with the overall model presented in Part I, but they also include some distinctive innovations deserving of more widespread publication. Chapter 15 is one of only three Chapters that were not originally written for this book. All other Chapters were originally written specifically for use here. Chapter 15 first appeard as a mimeo-graphed project report addressed to the client, American Telephone and Telegraph Company, by Dr. Markle as an employee of the American Institutes for Research. Appreciation is expressed to all of these for permission to reprint that report.

Finally, Chapters 16 and 17 are of a still different nature. They are neither theory nor model Chapters (as in Part I), nor are they like other Chapters in Part II. They are *sample, partial, course designs*, prepared by persons who were students at the time of this writing. More details about how and why these designs were undertaken are found in Part II.

Developing Design Skills

As discussed in the *Preface*, this book is intended for several different kinds of courses—theory courses, practicum courses, and research planning courses.

In the event that you intend to use this book to develop practical skills in design, these closing comments are offered.

1. *Begin practicing each skill early.* While reading each Chapter of Part I, you may wish to refer to the corresponding portions of Chapter 16 and 17 to see how two students took that step in the design process. After you have seen examples of the skill being discussed in a Chapter, try an example of your own, and compare it to our examples. If possible, ask an instructor or colleague to react to it.

2. *Don't expect to always get it right the first time.* Students in practicum courses often need a second attempt, using feedback from others.

3. *Conduct a self-evaluation of your efforts by using the "assignment sheets" placed just prior to Chapter 16.* They suggest specific criteria for checking your work.

4. *Do some tryouts.* Design a single lesson first, not an entire course. Give the objective and the instructional materials to one or more appropriate learners. Ask for reactions and give a brief test as described in Chapter 10 as a basis for revising your materials.

5. *Listen to those who criticize a systems design model*

such as the one presented in this book. The writer has learned a lot by listening to his critics.

6. *Try a team project.* Whether it is for pay or just for experience, it is good to work on a team effort while learning, even if your ultimate goal is to work alone as a designer and/or teacher.

7. *Try to accept criticism objectively.* This is often hard to do. The writer had several students read and react to his Chapters in this book, and most of their comments were useful.

8. *If you are a teacher, get some feedback from your students.* Ask them about specific features of the materials as well as about your own procedures. Again try to react to their comments as related to your *procedures,* not to "you" as a person.

9. *Discuss feedback you receive from students with your colleagues and with the students.*

10. *Never stop revising your course.* Even if you can't revise the books or other materials, use one-page handouts to update, correct, or add to existing materials. The more complete your materials are, the more you can use class time to add the latest information or to diagnose and remedy problems that individual students encounter. There may even be time for some interesting enrichment exercises or sharing of experiences. If revising your course becomes enjoyable to you, your students might begin to show a joy in learning.

Summary

This book presents a "systems approach" to the design of instruction, whether the design is accomplished by a teacher (or instructor) or by a design team. The theory of design presented can be employed by a teacher who selects instructional material or by teams that develop such materials.

The significance of the term "instructional system" was discussed, and features of a systems model were identified. Some origins of instructional technology were traced. The design model presented in this book is "value free," in that it is a problem-solving methodology, not a "position" on what the goals or methods of instruction should be.

Alternate models were seen as offering real alternatives to the systems model, but differences among teaching models and learning theories were seen as less sharp than they appear if it were realized that different theorists are addressing different domains of learning outcomes. A taxonomy of such outcomes can help clarify real differences among theorists, and help avoid exaggeration of differences. Considering alternate models is good for a designer to keep him or her flexible in practice. It is good to listen to our critics.

The taxonomy of learning outcomes by Gagné is selected for use in this book, since he has related it clearly to both conditions of learning and to assessment of learner performance. Such a taxonomy leads to flexibility in teaching methods, in which different degrees of guidance to the learner's thinking are appropriate for different types of outcomes. This is an important component in designing the strategy of instruction.

The organization of this book was discussed in some detail in order to help instructors and students (or trainees) use it for various purposes. Part I presents the design model, and Part II presents sample applications. Table 1 in this Chapter shows how the learning sequence for the reader is different from both the design sequence and the classroom sequence.

Finally, a list of suggestions was given for how to use this book in conjunction with other learning opportunities to develop design skills.

References

Briggs, L.J. *Handbook of Procedures for the Design of Instruction.* Pittsburgh: American Institutes for Research, 1970.

Briggs, L.J. *Student's Guide to Handbook of Procedures for the Design of Instruction.* Pittsburgh: American Institutes for Research, 1972.

Gagné, R.M. *The Conditions of Learning*, 2nd Edition. New York: Holt, Rinehart, and Winston, 1970.

Gagné, R.M., and Briggs, L.J. *Principles of Instructional Design.* New York: Holt, Rinehart, and Winston, 1974.

Joyce, B., and Weil, M. *Models of Teaching.* Englewood Cliffs,

N.J.: Prentice-Hall, 1972.

Lumsdaine, A.A. Educational Technology, Programmed Learning, and Instructional Science. In H.G. Richey (Ed.), *Theories of Learning and Instruction*. Chicago: University of Chicago Press, 1964.

Scriven, M. Evaluation Perspectives and Procedures. In W.J. Popham (Ed.), *Evaluation in Education: Current Applications*. Berkeley: McCutchan Publishing Co., 1974.

Transition to Chapter 2

The title of this book could have been "Instructional *Systems* Design." The word "systems," as used here, refers to a systematic approach to the design of instruction. This approach is to be used only when *instruction* is the chosen solution to an educational *problem*. Thus when an educational goal has been set, and when the indications are that the goal is not now being met, or is not being met well, a *need* has been identified. If new or modified instruction is deemed the appropriate way to meet the need, then the goal is further analyzed to spell out in detail the exact objectives needed to reach the goal. Thereafter, the instructional strategy is designed, and supporting instructional materials are developed.

Chapter 2 describes how to assess needs and goals, and how to set priorities as to which goals will receive attention by designing strategies to meet the needs. Some goals are best met by instruction; others may be met by other means, such as administrative action. This book concentrates on educational or training goals which can be met through *instruction*. Other goals, which might be met by political action, personnel policies, budgets, etc., are beyond the scope of this book.

This book advocates the *deductive* approach in relating pupil performance to goals. In this approach, *desired* pupil performance is outlined in the form of goals; after the instruction has been developed and carried on in the classroom, *actual* pupil performance is assessed. If the actual performance matches the desired performances, then the goal has been reached. This deductive

19

approach is ideal for *pre-designed* instruction, in which methods and materials are designed for the purpose of reaching the predetermined goals.

In the *inductive* approach, in contrast to the deductive, one first assesses pupil performance; and, on basis of those data, one next *infers* what the goals of the program were.

While the major thrust of this book is upon the pre-design of instruction for goals stated in advance, we also acknowledge the value of "goal-free evaluation"—looking at the *outcomes* of instruction to spot intended or unintended outcomes which "emerge" from the instruction and from pupil behavior. If these outcomes are deemed desirable and valuable, they can then be added to the goals for pre-designed instruction for the next group of learners.

Some needs and goals arise from attempts to predict what people will need to know how to do in the society of the future, not the society of the past or present. Other goals are continued on from educational traditions of the past, which may or may not be relevant for the present and the future society.

Chapter 2 discusses several ways of setting goals, emphasizing the deductive method mentioned above.

The remainder of this book deals with how to reach goals, and how to know that goals have been reached.

In military and industrial training, goals are often derived from a *job analysis* (see Chapter 12) rather than from a consensus of a varied group of citizens, as is the case in setting goals for education. Once the goals are determined, the theory and process of instructional design advocated in this book are the same for designing instruction for either educational or training purposes. The kinds of instructional strategies appropriate for various types of learning outcomes also apply equally to education and training, for, after all, *learning* is the purpose of both.

Chapter 2

Needs Assessment:
Goals, Needs, and Priorities

John K. Burton and Paul F. Merrill
University of Mid-America

The purpose of this book is to present a systematic approach to solving instructional problems. While it may seem trivial to mention, the first step in solving a problem is to decide that you have one. The needs assessment procedure presented in this chapter will help you decide if you have a problem, where you have a problem, how big a problem you have, and how important it is to solve the problem. Later chapters will deal with solutions to problems, techniques and materials, and evaluation of problem-solving effectiveness.

In recent years there has been a clamor on the part of the professional and the lay public alike for accountability and relevance in education. Roughly translated, these terms mean that what is taught should be useful to the individual, the community, and the country, and that educators and their systems are responsible for the success or failure of their efforts.

Needs assessment is a systematic process for determining goals, identifying discrepancies between goals and the status quo, and establishing priorities for action. With respect to education, needs assessment is a process for determining what should be taught. This process is based on the active involvement of those directly affected by the educational system (students, parents, and members of the community) in addition to professional educators.

Although needs assessment may be conducted at the national, state, and school district levels, the focus of this chapter will be on the application of needs assessment at the course level. Needs assessment should be the first step in a systematic approach to the development of instructional materials for a course or training program.

To understand needs assessment, however, we must first take a closer look at the concept of need.

The Concept of Need

The term need is used in many different ways: psychologists refer to primary needs and learned needs, physiologists study biological needs, economists identify consumer demand needs, while the general public has its own conception of needs. Educational need, however, draws heavily on the concept of social need. One social scientist, Bradshaw (1972), has enumerated four types of needs: normative need, felt need, expressed need, and comparative need. These four, as well as a fifth type of need, anticipated need, are described below.

Types of Needs

1. *Normative Need.* A normative need is present when an individual or group has less than some established standard. Thus, an individual whose diet is deficient when compared to the Food and Drug Administration's minimum daily adult requirements, or whose income is low when compared to the federal government's poverty level income standard, has a normative need. A normative need also exists if student performance in a given school system is less than state or national standards or averages. Unfortunately, it is sometimes difficult to get experts to agree on what the norm or standard actually is. Dietary need is certainly affected by such things as climate, work output, body size, and other individual differences. Financial standards may not be the same in New York City and Niangua, Missouri.

2. *Felt Need.* Felt need is synonymous with want. This type of need is usually identified by simply asking people what they need. Although this approach has a certain democratic appeal to most of us, it also has some inherent problems. What people say they want is affected by their perceptions of what is possible and socially acceptable as well as what they think is available. Some people may be so independent that they feel it would be

inappropriate to express their felt needs to others. On the other hand, some people may ask for help that they do not really need. In an educational community citizens may not express a felt need for sex education because they do not see the school as an appropriate instrument. Thus, they may see a "need" for young people to receive sex education but at the same time not "want" the school to be involved. In another situation, a teacher may see a "need" for a certain course when in fact he/she means that he/she "wants" to teach it.

3. *Expressed Need or Demand.* An expressed need is similar to the economic idea that if people need something they'll create a demand. A felt need for gasoline may also become an expressed need if people wait to have their automobile gasoline tanks filled. In other words, an expressed need exists when a person puts his or her money on the line for a product. If more college students sign up for a course than there are seats available, administrators will begin talking about the need for more sections and staff. If there is a long waiting list for public housing, then there is a need for more public housing, and so on. Certainly, there will be no demand unless people perceive a need. Does a need exist, however, if there is no public housing to be on the waiting list for, or if the course "in demand" is the lesser of several evils necessary to meet an outdated requirement that satisfies no current need from the student's perspective?

4. *Comparative Need.* A comparative need exists when the characteristics of a population that does not receive a service are similar to the characteristics of a population that does receive it. Thus, if East Side High School has a modern chemistry laboratory, and West Side High has no laboratory, then a comparative need may be said to exist. Unfortunately, the concept of comparative need does not take into consideration the fact that those receiving a service may still have a need for more service or that there may be needs for which no service has yet been established. Comparative need has been a favorite in higher education.

5. *Anticipated or Future Needs.* Anticipated needs have to do with the projected demands of the future. When a city plans new roads to be built over a number of years, the people doing the planning must take into consideration where growth will probably occur. At the time the roads are planned it may appear that a lot

of money is being spent to service only a few people, yet the roads are designed to meet future as well as present needs of the community. It is the lack of such assessment of future needs that causes roads, schools, etc., to be obsolete or overcrowded by the time they are completed. Identification of this type of need may help us to prepare students to cope with their environment as it will be, rather than the way it is. Anticipated needs are a necessary component in both social and educational planning to avoid what Toffler (1971) has called "future shock."

Definition of Need

Each of the types of need described above carry the same central idea: *a need is present when there is a discrepancy or gap between the way things "ought to be" and the way they "are."* Thus, a *normative* need is a discrepancy between an individual's or group's present state and a given norm or standard. A *felt* need is a discrepancy between what a person wants and what he/she has. A need is *expressed* when an individual takes action to remove the discrepancy between what he/she wants and has. A *comparative* need is a discrepancy between what one group has and what another group, with similar characteristics, has. Finally, if there is a discrepancy between what is presently available and the projected demands of the future, then there is an *anticipated* need.

The definition presented above has certain implications and difficulties that are of importance when considering methods of assessing needs. First, there must be a discrepancy for a need to be present. To say you need love when the love you have matches what you ought to have is incorrect in the language of needs assessment. However, if you were to experience a loss of love, then a discrepancy would exist, and you would have a *need* for love. Thus, according to the definition of need presented above, the basic needs of food, water, shelter, love, sex, etc., are only needs during a state of deprivation. They would not be considered needs during a state of satiation.

Second, the measurement of the way things "are" involves a degree of error which is related to the reliability and validity of instruments used.

Third, the way things "ought to be" is a value judgment which cannot be separated from the value structures woven into each of us by our experiences. Given different value structures, the determination of a consensus as to what "ought to be" is difficult. It we try to establish the way things "ought to be" in the future by extrapolating from existing conditions and trends, the error in our projections can be expected to increase as a function of how far into the future we predict.

Fourth, to eliminate a discrepancy or need, at least two alternatives are available—change the way things are to conform to what ought to be *or* change what ought to be to conform to the way things are. There is some question, for example, as to whether the American perception of how much fuel, food, fertilizer, etc., that there ought to be is a responsible perception in light of dwindling resources, growing population, etc. This is a problem of solutions rather than needs assessments, but it is raised here to serve as a caution not to assume that only one type of solution is possible.

Educational Needs

In educational needs assessment, one should try to consider all five types of needs by involving as many people as possible in the process. Professionals, business leaders, labor, and parents have access to *normative* data. ("The government indicates that 75 percent of all high school graduates seek a position within x miles of their home town." "A medical survey indicates that the average number of hospital beds for a city our size is . . . ." "The average salary for an assistant professor in the Big Ten is. . . .") Administrators and interested action groups usually have *demand* data. ("Our records indicate that more students signed up for introductory psychology than we had seats for." "Since this program for the aged began six months ago, we have had to turn away x people due to lack of space.") Many people can provide at least informal *comparative* information. ("When I lived in x we had two free health clinics." "When I worked for the x school system we had a student-teacher ratio of 10 to 1.") Government and research reports may provide data for projecting anticipated needs. ("This report says that when E.R.A. goes through we will have to spend equal monies for men's and women's athletics." "By the time my kids grow up, the Social Security system will have collapsed.") And everybody has *felt* needs. ("I wish we had a swimming pool

built into this school." "We need to have a course on karate.")
Hopefully, a broad spectrum of needs will be addressed by
involving a broad spectrum of the community in the needs
assessment process.

The Concept of Needs Assessment

We have stated that a need is a discrepancy between the way
things ought to be and the way things are. *A goal is a statement of
what ought to be.* It follows then that *needs assessment is the
process of determining what ought to be (goals) and measuring the
amount of discrepancy between what ought to be and what
actually is (needs).* It should be noted that neither goals nor needs
are solutions. Solution alternatives are identified during later
stages of the instructional development process, and will be
discussed in depth in succeeding chapters. It would appear that we
now have definitions for goals, needs, and needs assessment—but
have we? Are all goals equally important, and are all needs equally
important? The answer is, most assuredly not. Then, we must
modify our definition of needs assessment in this manner: *needs
assessment is the process of determining goals, measuring needs,
and establishing priorities for action.* Notice again that we have
avoided the determination of what *type* of action should be taken,
which would get us into the realm of solutions.

Why Needs Assessment?

We have tried to build a case for needs assessment on the
grounds of relevance and accountability. Klein (1971) has suggested the following additional rationale:
  (a) Needs assessment focuses the attention of program
      planners on salient problems. It can be used to facilitate
      planning decisions regarding the modification and devel-
      opment of educational programs. Needs assessment data
      can thus be used to ensure more efficient utilization and
      allocation of personnel time and resources.
  (b) Needs assessment justifies focusing attention on some

needs, and not others. Such justification must often be made in proposals and in reports to school boards and parents.

(c) Needs assessment provides valuable baseline information against which to assess subsequent changes in student performance.

In addition to the justifications cited above, we would ask that you consider again the concept of involving many people, not only educators, in the decision-making process—not just to make everyone feel better, but on the premise that they may, in fact, contribute something meaningful to the process.

Now that we have introduced the concept of needs assessment, perhaps we should discuss some "hows." Those hows are the various needs assessment models. The term model will be used here to refer to a set of coherent procedures for actually carrying out a process such as needs assessment.

General Models of Needs Assessment

If we define need as a discrepancy between the way things are and the way things ought to be, then obviously any model of needs assessment must make provisions for defining and measuring the "are" and "ought to be" variables. Kaufman (1972) identifies three general types of models, which differ largely in the focus of measuring these crucial variables: the inductive, deductive, and classic models.

The inductive (Type I) model measures the students' behaviors and then classifies them in terms of apparent or implicit goals. This model is similar to a "goal free" evaluation model (Scriven, 1972), which does not utilize the goals that a course, agency, or institution *claims* it is trying to attain but rather the goals that the behaviors demanded of the students *indicate* they are trying to implement.[1] For example, if in observing a school system in operation it is determined that a significant amount of teacher and administrative effort is directed towards getting students to behave quietly at their desks, then we can infer that this behavior is valued, and is in fact a goal of the system. This model does appear to have some utility in determining whether the goals established are in fact the goals towards which effort is being directed, but it does not appear to be a useful model for determining what could be or ought to be valued. The inductive model may be more useful in a research or follow-up effort to determine the effect of setting goals.

The deductive (Type D) model begins with some specific goal referents and then derives the appropriate behaviors for students. As opposed to the inductive model, which begins with behavior and induces goals, the deductive model begins with goals and deduces the behaviors that would demonstrate goal achievement. Note that both the inductive and the deductive models are concerned with student behavior.

The classic (Type C) model deals with educator-oriented goals rather than with learner-oriented goals. Educator-oriented goals refer to what teachers should present or do in the classroom rather than to what learners should be able to do as a result of teacher and learner effort. These are subgoals at best, however, and relate more to implementation than to needs assessment. As Kaufman (1972, 1976) points out, there is a strong distinction between things like providing higher salaries for teachers, or reducing class size (which are in fact *solutions*), and things like increasing students' reading level (which are learner-oriented goals). We will concede that in some situations institutional goals are necessary in the form of (a) process-oriented goals which denote general activities or functions to be accomplished, and (b) structure-oriented goals which denote general physical or administrative conformities. Clearly, our bias here, however, is for learner-oriented goals, which denote general[2] expectations in terms of learner outcomes generated in a deductive fashion.

Levels of Needs Assessment

It is possible, at least in theory, to conduct educational needs assessment on a global level down to the level of a module within a course. Most of the needs assessment programs reported in the literature seem to have been conducted at the state or school district level. Since the focus of this Chapter is on the application of needs assessment in the development of instructional materials for courses, we will not attempt to review the literature on the application of needs assessment at higher levels (national, state, district, or school). This literature has been reviewed extensively by others (Southard, 1974; Witkin, 1976).

The major difference between needs assessment at the course level and at higher levels is largely in the degree of specificity of goals. State and district goals tend to be broad and global and are often difficult to operationalize, while course goals tend to be more specific. Higher level needs assessment programs also will usually have, and require, more time and resources than a needs assessment at the course level. Obviously, limited resources will affect the amount and type of data that can be collected, the sophistication of the data analysis, the staff to type and mail questionnaires and supplies, etc.

Four Basic Phases of Needs Assessment

Needs assessment models at the course level and at higher levels all involve four common phases of activities as outlined by Klein (1971). These phases are described in detail below:

Phase 1. Identify a broad range of possible goals.

Phase 2. Rank goals in order of importance.

Phase 3. Identify discrepancies between expected and actual performance.

Phase 4. Set priorities for action.

Let us consider these four basic activities more closely in light of Kaufman's (1972) deductive model.

Phase 1. Identify a Broad Range of Possible Goals

In the deductive model the range of possible goals is generated independently of existing conditions. A small committee of students, non-educators, and educators should identify the relevant goals. The goals may be generated by a survey, by a group brainstorming session, by a Delphi[3] approach, or by utilizing any of several existing lists of goals. The purpose of this phase of the needs assessment process is not to place any value or priority on any goals, but merely to identify the total range of relevant goals. The emphasis should be on getting the widest possible array of relevant goals collected (quantity) rather than on making judgments as to practicality, appropriateness, value, or utility (quality).

The goals identified during this phase should be defined in measurable terms and should include performance criteria. If the goals (what ought to be) are not defined in measurable terms, and the performance criteria are not specified, it will be extremely difficult to determine the discrepancy between the goal and actual performance (Phase 3).

Phase 2. Rank Goals in Order of Importance

The purpose of this phase is to rank the goals identified in Phase 1 in some numerical fashion (either ranks or weights) for the geographic area and level (national, state, district, school, or course) with which you are concerned. This should be accomplished using a broad spectrum of input. An attempt should be made to involve individuals from each subgroup of the community that will be affected by the outcomes of the needs assessment. We have stated that needs assessment is based on the involvement of non-educators as well as educators in the decision process. Phase 2 is *the* principle place where this must occur. This phase may be accomplished by small-group meetings of various groups (i.e., students, faculty, administrators, parents, business, labor, etc.), surveys, card sorts, questionnaries, etc. The output from this phase should be a list of goals ranked in terms of the most important to the least important for a given level and geographic area. This list should represent a consensus of the community as to which educational goals are the most important to achieve. It is the "ought to be" portion of needs assessment.

Phase 3. Identify Discrepancies Between Expected and Actual Performance

This phase involves measuring the discrepancies between goals and performance. The success of this phase is directly related to the quality of the goals generated in Phase 1. Phase 3 is composed of two parts: (a) determining current performance levels on the goals in Phase 2, and (b) comparing this performance to the criterion level specified in the goals. The actual performance level of students from the target population should be determined by using instruments which measure behaviors indicative of goal achievement. Standardized tests are often used for this purpose at higher levels of needs assessment (state, district, school). However, several types of data may be used in this phase:

(1) performance ratings based on observations;

(2) paper-and-pencil tests;

(3) behavioral frequency counts; and

(4) extant data (i.e., attendance records, grades, etc.).

Phase 4. Set Priorities for Action

The prioritizing of needs is basically a subjective decision-making process. Therefore, a representative committee consisting of non-educators and students as well as educators should be used to determine these priorities. The subjective nature of the process can be somewhat reduced by using some agreed-upon criteria to rate the needs identified in Phase 3. The simplest criterion for setting priorities among needs would be to use the ranking of corresponding goals from Phase 2. This would place the highest priority on goals, however, not needs (recall that they are not the same). Another obvious criterion would be the magnitude of the discrepancy between the actual performance and the goal criteria. A combined rating for these two criteria may be obtained by multiplying the numerical rank of the goal assigned in Phase 2 (assuming that high priorities are assigned high numbers) by the magnitude of the discrepancy in standard scores. This combined rating would be most appropriate in higher-level needs assessment programs where standardized tests are used to measure actual performance.

Kaufman (1972) suggests that needs should be prioritized based on the relationships between the cost to meet the need and the cost to ignore the need. For example, if the cost of classroom laboratory equipment necessary to reduce a need is high, while the effect of not having the needed laboratory skills is low, then the need may be given a low priority.

Additional criteria that may be considered in setting priorities include the length of time the need has persisted, the proportion of learners exhibiting the need, the time required to reduce the need, and the utility of remediation. The reduction of a given need is considered to have greater utility if the actual performance related to the need is below the mean on some normative test. For example, if the magnitude of the discrepancies between expected performance and actual performance for math and reading are the same, but only the reading scores are below the mean of the norm group, then it is more useful to remediate the reading discrepancy than it is to remediate the math discrepancy, where actual scores are above the mean.

Priorities for action may also be set by utilizing a sophisticated decision rule which assigns differential weights to several criteria. However, decision rules can be very complex and may require the use of computers and psychometricians.

Course Level Needs Assessment

The phases described above can be applied at all levels. We will now turn to a detailed description of the specific steps to be used within each phase for performing a needs assessment at the course level. Since this section is intended to serve not only as a unit of instruction but also as a quick future reference, it has been written in an outline format. The *inputs, operators, operations,* and *outputs* are listed for each of the four phases. Operations refer to the steps that must be performed within a given phase, and operators are those persons who are to perform the steps.

Phase 1. Identify a Broad Range
of Possible Goals

Inputs:
1. Mager's *Goal Analysis* (1972)
2. Past course syllabi from other instructors or institutions
3. State, district, or school goal statements (if available)
4. Certification requirements (if appropriate)
5. Extant course materials (texts, handouts, etc.)
6. Entry level requirements for subsequent course(s)
7. Course level and learner characteristics
8. Needs assessments from similar courses
9. Any related literature available
10. Osborn's *Applied Imagination* (1957) (optional)

Operators:
1. Appropriate project staff[4] member(s)
2. Two or three of the following, who are not part of the project staff:
   a. one student (potential enrollee in the course)
   b. one instructor (responsible for course)
   c. one administrator (if course is part of a larger *program* or feeds into *several* courses)
   d. one parent (if course is to meet family or community goals)
   e. one employee (if course is job related)
   f. one additional instructor (if course feeds *only* into one other course)

Operations:
1. Select two or three of the persons listed under operators, and form a committee which includes appropriate project staff.
2. Review inputs (either individually or as a group) for background and perspective.
3. Brainstorm goals (if none of the operators are familiar with this technique, a review of Osborn's *Applied Imagination* may be necessary). Remember, the purpose of this phase is to generate a broad set of goals, so opt for quantity and withhold qualitative judgments.
4. Do a preliminary screening to combine related goals; break down goals that are too complex; eliminate redundancies and "solutions" disguised as goals.
5. Obtain consensus on final list of goals.
6. Perform goal analysis[5] (define goals in measurable terms).

Output:
   List of goals

**Phase 2: Rank Goals in Order
of Importance**
   Inputs:
   List of goals from Phase 1

Operators:
   Project staff measurement specialist
Operations:
   1. Select or generate an instrument[6] to rank the list of goals from Phase 1.
   2. Identify which of the following community subgroups should be involved in rating the goals:
      a. students who have taken the course
      b. students who will take the course
      c. students now taking the course
      d. instructors (past, present, and future)
      e. instructors from other institutions
      f. program faculty (especially those who teach pre-requisite and subsequent courses)
      g. non-major faculty (faculty of areas that send students to course or *might* do so)
      h. administrators
      i. parents (if course has community impact)
      j. employers (if course is job related)
      k. any other relevant "experts" or "wise people" not included above.
   3. Administer instrument to a sample of individuals drawn from each of the subgroups identified in step 2.
   4. Analyze the responses and determine the mean ranking for each goal. (You might also analyze your data by subgroup.)
Output:
   List of goals in rank order

Phase 3. Identify Discrepancies Between
Desired and Actual Performance
   Inputs:
      Goals listed in order of importance.
   Operators:
      Project staff measurement specialist
   Operations:
      1. Determine the type of data you will need to collect for each goal in order to assess the way things "are." If you cannot determine what type of data would be appro-

priate, your goals may not be defined in measurable terms. Remember that one or more of the following types of data may be used:

    a.   Performance ratings based on observations
    b.   Paper-and-pencil test scores
    c.   Behavioral frequency counts
    d.   Extant data

2. Develop or select instruments or records which will provide the required data. If you have the necessary expertise and resources, check your instruments for reliability and validity. Make sure that your instruments are not cumbersome to use or to administer. Pilot testing of new instruments may help identify unexpected problems.

3. Collect the appropriate data on students projected to enroll in the course. If the number of students is large, you may have to collect data on only a sample.

4. Compute the discrepancy between the expected and actual performance for each goal by subtracting the mean student performance obtained in step 3 from the criteria specified for the corresponding goal. If the difference is positive, then you have identified a *need.*[7]

5. Prepare a list of the needs identified in step 4. Each need should be stated so as to indicate:

    a.   the target population[8]
    b.   the discrepant behavior
    c.   the actual performance (what is)
    d.   the expected performance criteria (what ought to be)

Examples of needs statements may be found in Note 9.

Outputs:
    List of needs statements

Phase 4. Set Priorities for Action

Inputs:
    List of needs statements

Operators:

1. Project staff
2. Committee of community representatives. This com-

mittee should be similar to the one used in Phase 1.

Operations:

1. Rate each need according to some agreed upon criteria. The following are possible criteria:
    a. cost of meeting the need versus cost of ignoring the need (Kaufman, 1972)
    b. rank of corresponding goal (from Phase 2)
    c. magnitude of need (from Phase 3)
    d. utility of need reduction
    e. length of time need has existed
    f. number of students affected
2. Obtain a consensus on the needs priorities.
3. Set target date for resolution of priority needs.

Outputs:

List of needs statements in priority order. The needs statements should include the target date for need resolution. (See Note 9.)

Some General Problems and Considerations in Needs Assessment

All of the needs assessment models referred to in this Chapter, whether at the course or higher levels, recommend significant community involvement. Klein (1971), however, has pointed out that massive involvement from a very early stage often leads to frustration and may cause people to "burn out" before the long haul is completed. Thus, a good rule of thumb is to involve the community, but do so in such a way that respects their time. Inform and consult the community during each step, but do not burden them. Give them concise, accurate reports written in easily comprehensible form. It is important that they become involved early, not only because their input is valuable, but because once the process has progressed to later stages, those involved in the assessment have so much invested that they resent input to change. It should also be pointed out that when parents are not informed, and dislike the product enough to organize against it, they win in their opposition more often than not (Schaffarzick, 1976).

When dealing with groups outside education it may be necessary to provide some facts or background for them. Schaffarzick (1976) points out that people often are asked to make decisions in areas about which they have little or no information. Informed decisions obviously require information. Another problem is that educators, parents, business, and labor all have some preconceptions about the role of education. Thus, they may perceive a goal or need as being important, but outside the range of the school. Parents may feel that parenting skills and sex education are needed, but outside the realm of the school.

Finally, avoid being too complex or too simple. Witkin (1976) reports that there is an inverse relationship between the sophistication of a model and its acceptance and implementation in schools. There is also the well-established precedent of establishing broad goals in some simple fashion involving the general population and never defining or measuring things well enough to be of any real use. Thus, the parents feel they are cheated: they have spent time, but teachers can still do anything they want because the goals are too vague.

Research in Needs Assessment

Reviewing the *discursive* (or opinion) literature in needs assessment is becoming a more and more arduous task. Reviewing the *research* in the area is still sadly easy. As Witkin (1976) has said: "Although several models have been field tested during development, I have found no research that compares the effectiveness of one approach with another or the reliability or validity of disparate approaches." Neither have we. Southard (1974) and Witkin (1976), among others, have attempted to compare the various models on some pre-established criteria, but no empirical comparisons are available. Thus, the critical question of which model should be selected cannot be made on the basis of comparative results obtained to date.

While some assessments have stated needs that relate to minority students, few have attempted to study the effects, problems, or participation of minority groups. Schaffarzick (1976) has collected data that show that lower socioeconomic status

(SES) groups are less involved in needs assessment and decision-making than higher SES groups, and Moore and Senungetuck (1974) have reported some of the problems involved in multiethnic communities, but again the area is sadly lacking in data.

Cost-effectiveness seems to be a potentially fruitful area for needs assessment research, but little has been done in the area, possibly due to the difficulty of transforming educational benefits to the usual cost-benefit equation. Temkin (1970) has confronted this problem thoughtfully, proposing that the student be viewed as the consumer and that accounting by systems be changed to accounting by objectives or activities. This, of course, would make it possible to assess very quickly just how much money was spent on a given need versus how much progress was made in remediation. This approach has not yet been instituted.

At a minimum, research is needed to compare various processes of needs assessment and to determine what impact, if any, needs assessment has had. For example, Maryland, Texas, Michigan, and Wisconsin, among others, have run massive state-wide needs assessments. Fresno, California, Bucks County, Pennsylvania, and the Bay Area of San Francisco have conducted city or regional needs assessments. What impact have these data had? Does the closing of discrepancies tend to lower the ranking of goals in followup? Are discrepancies getting smaller? Larger? Does concentration on high-priority goals cause widening discrepancies in other areas? Do lower levels charged with implementation even use the data? If not, how could they be persuaded to? If so, do they burn out after a period of time and return to old techniques? Unfortunately, there are many questions, but few answers.

Where Do You Go from Here?

Needs assessment is only the beginning step in the instructional development process. Needs assessment will enable you to focus your efforts on the development of materials to meet high-priority needs. Once the needs have been identified, attention should be turned towards the identification of solution alternatives. However, you should not assume that all discrepancies in student performance can best be reduced by instruction. Some deficiencies in performance may be the result of circumstances other than lack of knowledge or skill. Mager and Pipe (1970) suggest several external conditions which may result in a performance discrepancy: the desired performance may be punishing; non-performance may be rewarding; desired performance may not really matter; or there may be obstacles which impede proper performance. Additional or better instruction will not reduce performance discrepancies caused by the external conditions listed above. Obviously, the appropriate solution would require a modification of the external conditions. If the individual could already do it if he really had to, then instruction is not a viable solution.

If instruction is identified as a solution, then the goals or terminal objectives (Chapters 3 and 4) for the course or training program may be derived directly from the needs statements generated by the needs assessment process. These terminal objectives may then be used as input to the task analysis procedure described in Chapter 5. Task analysis will facilitate the identification of subordinate objectives and the determination of appropriate sequencing of instructional units (Chapter 7).

Summary

This Chapter is concerned with the first step in the instructional design process: needs assessment. Needs assessment is the process of determining goals, measuring needs, and establishing priorities for action. Goals are defined as what "ought to be," and needs as discrepancies between goals and the current status. In educational needs assessment, input is solicited from all segments of the community affected by the educational system. This approach provides information on all five types of needs: normative, felt, demand, comparative, and anticipated.

From the various types of models of needs assessment discussed, a deductive approach which centers on learner-oriented goals is advocated. While needs assessments may be conducted on levels ranging from national to within-course modules, this Chapter focuses on needs assessment at the course level, using a four-phase approach. Phase 1 involves the identification of a broad range of possible course goals. Phase 2 involves the ranking of goals by a sample of those who would be affected by the course. Phase 3 involves the identification of discrepancies (needs) between the goals generated in Phase 1 and actual performance. Phase 4 involves the setting of priorities for need remediation.

The output of needs assessment at the course level is a prioritized list of need statements. If it is subsequently determined that the appropriate solution for reducing the need is to develop a course of instruction, then the needs statements may be used to generate the terminal objectives of the course.

Notes

[1] Kaufman does not see the inductive model quite the same way that we have described it here. He sees the distinction between deductive and inductive as largely temporal; that is, the time at which goals are collected and ranked differ for the two models. In the inductive models it is assumed that the identification of goals has already occurred before the model is initiated.

[2] *General* as used here refers to degree of specificity. General *does not* mean fuzzy.

[3] The Delphi technique is especially useful for futuristic planning. Usually a list of items is circulated to a group of experts such as career military officers and NCOs, or business and labor leaders, or school administrators and teachers. (It is, of course, possible and often desirable to use non-experts.) The responses to the items are then circulated to the group, and answers are solicited once again. The idea is to obtain a consensus while respecting dissent. Since the experts do not come face-to-face, they do not experience social pressure to conform. Justifications of all positions are welcome. Examples of Delphi items might be: What skills do you think a citizen of the United States will need in the year 2000? To what extent will computers play a role in military operations by the year 2000? How will the marketing of our product be accomplished by the year 2000?

[4] The project staff may consist of only one person (an instructional designer or instructor), or may consist of a team of individuals. If the team has a measurement and/or evaluation

specialist, that person should carry the major responsibility for Phases 2 and 3. An instructional designer should be involved in the preparation of the goals and needs statements.

[5] Briefly, goal analysis is the process of taking rather abstract goals and restating them in terms of the student performances that would indicate that the goal has been achieved. If you wish students to have a positive self-concept, then you must state your goal in terms of what the students must *do* to show you that they have a positive self-concept. Similarly, if your goals are to get students to "understand . . .," "appreciate . . .," "internalize . . .," etc., then you must state your goals in terms of performances that show you that these things have been achieved. Mager (1972) lists five steps for analyzing goals: 1. Write down the goal, using whatever words best describe the intent. 2. Write down the performances that would cause you to agree that the goal has been achieved, without regard for duplication or fuzzy language. 3. Sort out the list. Delete items that are duplications or are unwanted. Mark the statements that are in terms of performances; repeat the process for the remaining items until each is in terms of a performance. 4. Write a complete statement for each performance, describing the nature, quality, or amount of performance you will consider acceptable. 5. Test the statements with the question, if someone achieved or demonstrated each of these performances, would I be willing to say he has achieved the goal? When you can answer yes, the analysis is finished. Methods of writing goals and objectives are discussed in Chapter 3.

[6] *Goal-Rating Methods*:

1. *Survey*. This can be either a face-to-face survey, a telephone survey, or a questionnaire for mailing. The most common procedure is to design a Likert scale which causes your respondents to rate the goals on a five-point scale running from extremely important (5 points) to unimportant (one point).

Advantages: Easy to construct; may be recorded on "mark sense" forms and machine scored; easy to analyze.

Disadvantages: Mailed surveys often have low return rates; costs of mailing and followup are expensive; telephone surveys restricts sample to those with phones and often those that can be reached during working hours; face-to-face surveys are very time-consuming if sample is large.

2. *Card Sort.* This is a variety of the Likert scale that utilizes a deck of cards with one goal per card. The respondent is instructed to place the cards in piles or envelopes corresponding to the five-point process discussed above. *Q-Sort* is similar to card sort except that the respondent must place a certain number of cards in each category. The number to be placed in each category corresponds roughly to a normal distribution. Thus, most of the cards will be placed in the three-point category of moderate importance and the least cards will be placed in the one- and five-point extreme categories.

> *Advantages*: Cards may be recycled; most people enjoy the sorting task; easy to analyze; Q-sort gives more weight to extremely high and low goals.
>
> *Disadvantages*: Difficult if there is a large number of goals; time-consuming for respondent.

3. *Rank Order.* Respondents are asked to rank the goals from most to least important.

> *Advantages*: Easy to construct (may use cards or forms); may be recorded on "mark sense" forms and machine scored; easy to analyze; spreads out rankings more than Likert scale methods.
>
> *Disadvantages*: Difficult if there is a large number of goals; more boring than other techniques.

4. *Paired Weighting Procedures.* This process involves having the respondents rate the goals two at a time, selecting the most important. This method requires that all possible combinations of the goals taken two at a time be used.

> *Advantages*: More exact than previous methods; most people enjoy the task if not too long.
>
> *Disadvantages*: Number of comparisons increases astronomically as goals increase; not practical if there are more than 10 or 12 goals; respondents may feel they are being fooled when the "same" goal comparisons come up over and over; data analysis is more time-consuming.

5. *Equal Appearing Intervals.* Respondents are instructed to place goals into categories or positions such that the perceived differences between goal positions are equal. This may mean that some positions are empty if two adjacent goals are subjectively several intervals apart.

Advantages: Most precise in terms of data generated; interval scaling.

Disadvantages: Use of computer is a virtual *must*; sophistication will also probably require trained assistance; difficult to analyze.

For a more thorough discussion of response scaling, consult a scaling or psychometric theory text, such as Nunnally (1967).

If you are concerned with a large, expensive program, then you should take care that your sample is representative of the groups involved; also, the instrument you select should be piloted, with some attempt to establish the reliability and validity of the instrument. Discussion of reliability and validity is beyond the scope of this chapter. Interested students should read a measurement text such as Lemke and Wiersma (1976).

[7] This exercise in mathematics will depend on the type of data you select and your level of sophistication. Standard scores are the best transforms for most data. If you are using standardized tests, the standard deviation should appear in the scoring manual. Using the raw scores (rather than percentiles), you will use the following formula:

$$\frac{X - \overline{X}}{S.\,D.} = \text{standard score (z-score)},$$

where X is the score representing where you are or where you ought to be and $\overline{X}$ and S.D. are the mean and standard deviation, respectively, taken either from the manual or your own computations.

Example: One of your goals involves achieving a student average on some standardized reading test of 90 percentile. The scoring manual for the test lists a raw score of 75 as equivalent to the 90th percentile for your subject group with a mean at 50 and a standard deviation of 10. You can compute where you ought to be:

$$\frac{75 - 50}{10} = \frac{25}{10} = 2.5.$$

Assume now that you administer the test to your students and get a class mean of 65. Using the formula then

$$\frac{65 - 50}{10} = \frac{15}{10} = 1.5.$$

Thus, where you are is 1.5 and where you ought to be is 2.5. Your discrepancy is 2.5 - 1.5 = 1.0. The same process may be used for any data type that you can quantify. A simpler procedure is to simply subtract the percentiles and deal with the percentile difference.

Example: You want to reach the 90th percentile and you are now at the 80th percentile, thus 90 - 80 = 10 or a 10 percentile point difference. This is a quick and distorting method since percentiles are area transformations that tend to exaggerate differences near the mean and obscure those at the extremes. Use of percentile differences from different tests is a crude procedure but better than nothing.

[8] *Individual needs.* At the level of a course needs assessment, it is possible to deal in terms of need for a single student or at least for groups of students that share some common characteristics. In these cases, recognizing that the instructor's time is limited, it is possible to create a prioritized list for each student. This list can then serve to guide the instructor's effort with individual students.

[9] The following are examples of need statements:

1. An examination of library records revealed that only five percent of the entering freshmen at Moyer State College voluntarily checked out at least one unassigned book related to poetry from the library during their first three months of enrollment. By the next fall semester 60 percent of Moyer State freshmen will demonstrate an appreciation for poetry by voluntarily checking out at least one book related to poetry during the subsequent three-month period.

2. Observations of military tactics instructors at Ft. Samuelson revealed that an average of only two positive reinforcing responses were made by instructors to students during randomly selected 50-minute class periods. By a year from this date instructors will make an average of ten positive reinforcing responses during a given class period.

References

Bradshaw, J. The Concept of Social Need. *New Society*, March 30, 1972, 640-643.

Kaufman, R.A. *Educational System Planning*. Englewood Cliffs, N.J.: Prentice-Hall, 1972.

Kaufman, R.A. *Needs Assessment: What It Is and How to Do It*. San Diego, California: University Cousortium on Instructional Development and Technology, 1976.

Klein, S.P. Choosing Needs for Needs Assessment. *Procedures for Needs Assessment Education: A Symposium*. CSE Report No. 69. Los Angeles: Center for the Study of Evaluation, 1971.

Lemke, E., and Wiersma, W. *Principles of Psychological Measurement*. Chicago: Rand McNally, 1976.

Mager, R.F., and Pipe, P. *Analyzing Performance Problems ('You Really Oughta Wanna')*. Belmont, Ca.: Fearon Publishers, 1970.

Mager, R.F. *Goal Analysis*. Belmont, Ca.: Fearon Publishers, 1972.

Moore, V.R., and Senungetuck, J.E. Statewide Community Participation in Needs Assessment. Paper presented at the annual meeting of the AERA, Chicago, April, 1974. ERIC: ED 093 984.

Nunnally, J.C. *Psychometric Theory*. New York: McGraw-Hill Book Company, 1967.

Osborn, A. *Applied Imagination*. New York: Charles Scribner's Sons, 1957.

Schaffarzick, J. Teacher and Lay Participation in Curriculum Change Considerations. Paper presented at AERA, San Francisco, April, 1976.

Scriven, M. Pros and Cons About Goal-Free Evaluation. *Evaluation Comment*, December, 1972, *3*(4).

Southard, M. A Framework for Evaluating Needs Assessment Models. Unpublished. Tallahassee: The Florida State University, May, 1974.

Temkin, S. Comprehensive Planning for School Districts. Paper presented at AERA, Minneapolis, March, 1970. ERIC: ED 041 389.

Toffler, A. *Future Shock*. New York: Bantam Books, 1971.

Witkin, B.R. Needs Assessment Models: A Critical Analysis. Paper presented at AERA, San Francisco, April, 1976.

Transition to Chapter 3

Once the learning goals have been identified, either by a job analysis (industry) or by a consensus process (education), the next step is to further define the goals in detail; this is done by specifying the *performance objectives* (or behavioral objectives).

The lay public participates, along with educators, in selecting educational goals. These goals are stated in terms of the broad outcomes of instruction. But more detailed statements of objectives, that would support such goals, are needed. The total process, then, is one of working "from the top, downward"; broad goals are first defined, then more specific objectives, all arranged in several "layers" with respect to the "size of chunk" of instruction that each covers. Six such "levels" of goals and objectives are outlined in Chapter 4, ending with "specific performance objectives." After such objectives are stated, they are further analyzed into still smaller units called essential and supportive prerequisites for learning of the total objective, as discussed in Chapter 5. It will be seen that one purpose of this last analysis is to arrive at the sequencing of instruction, a major element in designing the instructional strategy.

In Chapter 3, two methods of writing objectives are described. Some purposes of objectives are: to serve as a guideline for developing assessments of learner performance (Chapter 6); to aid in the design of instruction (Chapters 7-9); and to help learners and the teacher.

But how does one work from general course goals to increasingly specific objectives? This involves the matter of organizing the course, discussed in Chapter 4.

We chose to show you *how to write* objectives before discussing *how to choose* objectives, when we arranged the sequencing of the Chapters in this book. This sequence, we believed, would be best for you to *learn* these skills; but in *practice*, of course, one chooses the objectives before one writes them down.

Chapter 3

Writing Performance Objectives

Robert J. Kibler
Florida State University
and
Ronald E. Bassett
University of Texas

This Chapter focuses on performance objectives and their relationship to the design of instruction. The first part of the Chapter provides a conceptual overview of the emergence of performance objectives and defines key concepts related to them. The next part discusses the reasons for writing performance objectives. Part three deals with writing performance objectives. The fourth part of the Chapter describes the present state of research findings related to performance objectives. We conclude the Chapter with a summary. With this overview of the Chapter, we begin our examination of performance objectives.

A Conceptual Overview of
Performance Objectives

The purpose of this first part of the Chapter is to provide a background concerning performance objectives. We begin by presenting an overview of factors that have contributed to the development of performance objectives. After this, we pick up where the last Chapter ended, by discussing the relationships among needs, goals, and objectives. Then, we distinguish between goals and objectives; and, finally, we define performance objectives.

An Overview of Forces Contributing
to the Development of Performance Objectives

It is important to gain some perspective on the process by

which performance objectives were integrated into the main stream of instructional practice. To do this in the space available, we will identify some key movements and people from recent history that contributed to our understanding of performance objectives.

Terms like "behavioral objective," "performance objective," and "learning objective" were not used by curriculum specialists early in the Twentieth Century. However, you only have to read through the work of Bobbitt (1918, 1924) and Charters (1923, 1929; Charters and Waples, 1929) to relieve any doubt that these educators would have been very comfortable with such terms. Ammons (1969) credits Charters and Bobbitt with formulating a method for determining educational objectives on a *scientific* basis. As a potential instructional designer, you owe it to yourself to spend a few evenings reading some of these early works. If you are not humbled by this experience, at least, you will be enlightened.

However, it is Tyler (1934, 1950, 1964) who is most often identified as the "father" of today's performance objective. Beginning in the 1920's (Dale, 1967; Lindvall, 1964), Tyler's behavioral approach to test construction undoubtedly stimulated his interest in behaviorally stated objectives for students. But Charters' influences on Tyler was also apparent somewhat earlier, in Tyler's dissertation (Dale, 1967). The linkage between behaviorally stated objectives and carefully constructed tests to measure those behaviors was one of the many contributions Tyler made to instructional systems analysis.

Following closely on the contributions of Tyler came those interested in developing types of learning outcomes, which will be discussed in Chapter 5. Kearney (1953) and French (1957) were part of this group. Kearney's efforts were directed towards describing the measurable goals of instruction for elementary schools. A few years later, French's (1957) companion volume appeared for general education in the high school.

Another effort at developing taxonomies had its beginning at the 1948 Convention of the American Psychological Association. University examiners and scholars interested in test development and construction gathered to give birth to taxonomies of educational objectives. These taxonomies were prepared because members expressed a need for standardized terminology regarding human behavioral characteristics which educators attempt to appraise. Taxonomies of educational objectives followed (Bloom *et al.*, 1956; Krathwohl, Bloom, and Masia, 1964). The taxonomies have proved useful to many educators as a framework for specifying performance objectives.

Another group of professionals who contributed to our understanding of performance objectives came from the training laboratories of the military, industry, and foundation "think tanks." There are too many of these people to mention, but examples of their contributions can be found by interested students in Gagné's *Psychological Principles in Systems Development* (1962). Particularly, they contributed to our understanding of systems analysis and its relationship to the design of instruction. Miller's pioneering work (1962a, 1962b) on task analysis is a prime example of such a contribution. Miller's procedures for describing and analyzing job tasks were both unique and systematic. Clearly, these procedures had implications for creating performance objectives. It is also probably fair to say that Miller's work influenced the thinking of some of the leading instructional designers today.

But it was Gagné's (Gagné and Fleishman, 1959; Gagné, 1962, 1965a, 1965b, 1970) work in learning, task analysis, and many related applications to instructional systems that have become landmarks in the field of instructional design. Gagné's (1970) analysis of eight types of learning within the domain of intellectual skills has had a far-reaching impact on our conceptualization of the learning process and the analysis of objectives.

Briggs' (1968) work in the sequencing of instruction and later work on procedures for the design of instruction (1970) have also provided invaluable insights into organizing and sequencing objectives, as well as for conceptualizing instructional systems. These contributions have helped lay the groundwork for the field of instructional design and the emergence of performance objectives as a key component in the instructional systems approach to the design of instruction.

Those working in programmed instruction also worried about performance objectives. Instructional designers who were developing programmed instruction had already developed a plethora of research in this area (Schramm, 1964) and had made advances in teaching machine technology (Stolurow, 1961). Stating performance objectives was recognized very early by those working in programmed instruction as a critical component of the instructional process (Lang, 1967; Lumsdaine and Glaser, 1960). But, equally important, the wide use of programmed instruction helped to diffuse the use of performance objectives and related instructional technology throughout our educational system (Lang, 1967). While programmed instruction was not the panacea some believed and others feared it to be, it did help make practitioners aware of instructional design principles—including performance objectives.

However, it was only after the publication of Mager's *Preparing Objectives for Programmed Instruction* (1961) that educators developed a full-scale interest in performance objectives. By then, the avalanche was in motion that changed all of us a little. Instructional and curricular packages on "behavioral" objectives flowed from publishers. Although there was a period when performance objectives were criticized widely, mostly by teachers, that day appears to be behind us. Performance objectives are now generally recognized as an integral part of the instructional design process. For this reason, we will examine them in detail in this and the next two Chapters.

An Overview of the Relationship
Among Needs, Goals, and Objectives

That which we do as instructional designers is ultimately linked to some perceived need, either on the part of learners, their parents, employers, teachers, instructional administrators, state or federal agencies, or society. The last Chapter discussed the basis of such needs, how to determine and verify them, and the value in so doing. You learned that needs are identified and placed in priority by procedures termed needs assessment. A need is identified when a *discrepancy* is found between an *ideal* or *acceptable* state of affairs and the *present status* or *observed* state of affairs. This condition might be characterized in an oversimplified manner as the difference between what a learner *can do* and *should be able to do*, usually based on some verifiable standard. With the background you have already acquired, you are ready to consider how we move from needs to goals, and then to objectives.

Once the needs have been identified, verified, and prioritized, you are ready to translate these needs into useful statements for the purpose of designing instruction. Needs identified from valid needs assessment procedures are first translated into goal statements, and then the goal statements are translated into statements of objectives. These translation tasks are often the responsibility of instructional designers. That is why it is important for you to learn how to translate need statements into goal statements, and goal statements into objectives. We will briefly discuss here how to translate need statements into goal statements, and later in this Chapter (and in Chapter 4) will consider procedures for translating goal statements into objectives.

Based on a formal needs assessment, let us assume that you have identified a set of needs and placed them in priority, and that you are now ready to formulate goals based on the prioritized needs. Let us also assume that the highest priority need statement deals with the discrepancy found between the extremely low performance of eighth grade students on a standardized composition test and national norms on that test for that grade level (i.e., the acceptable state of affairs for the school system). The need statement probably would reflect that this discrepancy should be reduced and/or eliminated. At this point, you begin to translate the need to a goal statement. This is probably a long-range need, and it would need to be converted into a series of goal statements, becoming more specific as you moved towards a performance objective. Each goal statement would then be defined and illustrated along with specifications of the knowledge and skills required to perform these goals. Eventually, you might end up with a terminal course goal for the eighth grade English class that was something like this: "The student can write appropriate topic sentences for paragraph development of a thesis statement."

This and other course goals must then be defined even further by breaking them down into specific performance objectives. There may be a number of intervening steps required to get from the need to the goal, to subsequent goals, and then to the performance objective. This probably will require a number of levels of analysis before all of the short-term performance objectives are identified. When all of these short-term objectives are combined, they may be perceived as satisfying a related goal.

Distinctions Between Goals and Objectives

You learned in the previous Chapter that goals and objectives can range widely with regard to specificity. While some educators prefer to use the two terms interchangeably, it is useful to distinguish between them for the purpose of instructional design. Educational goals refer to broad statements of the ultimate outcome of our educational enterprises, and frequently reflect social, political, and economic philosophies. Objectives are at the other end of the continuum. They are much more specific, as for use in a module of instruction. The distinction we have adopted here to differentiate goals and objectives rests in the level of generality of each kind of statement. Imbedded in this distinction, however, is the "purpose" for which each is to be used. Goals communicate general educational outcomes that are long-range, while objectives communicate specific outcomes that are short-range. The *Cardinal Principles of Secondary Education* (1937) contains a listing of general goals, and you will see they are *very* long-range in nature: "This commission, therefore, regards the following as the main objectives of education: 1. Health. 2. Command of fundamental processes. 3. Worthy home-membership. 4. Vocation. 5. Citizenship. 6. Worthy use of leisure. 7. Ethical character." Note that the Commission used the term "objective" here, not "goal." If you remember what was said in Chapter 2 about the relationship between goals and objectives, the use of "objective" to describe such global outcomes of education probably bothers you a little. You may think that "goal" would be a more precise term to characterize these broad outcomes, and we would agree with you.

As we use the term in this book, objectives are much more specific, much narrower in scope than goals. Objectives are also short-range and more precisely stated than goals, as in objectives for a course. You will see later in this Chapter that objectives can be stated very specifically in behavioral terms. Such objectives are stated to describe what behavior can be observed in the student, as a result of instruction, to demonstrate mastery of an objective.

Goals are logically stated first and then objectives are derived from goals. But it does not always work this easily. Sometimes there needs to be a step between the stated goal and the specific objective. Gagné and Briggs (1974) suggest that instructional designers go from goals to statements of course "purposes," and then to the statements of specific objectives. Gronlund (1970) similarly recommends that "general" learning outcomes be stated next. For example, you might state "Uses critical thinking skills in reading," as a general learning outcome and then state, "Distinguishes between fact and inferences" (Gronlund, 1970, p. 14) as a specific learning outcome. We think this "interim" step between stating goals and objectives is useful for instructional designers. Whatever procedure you use, your goals clearly serve as the overall framework for deriving narrower, more specific performance objectives, which we shall consider next.

Meaning of Performance Objectives

We will use *performance objectives* here to refer to statements of what students will be able to do or how they will be expected to behave after completing a prescribed unit or course of instruction. Performance objectives are often used to inform students what behaviors or performances they are expected to achieve to demonstrate that they have learned what is required of them as a result of instruction. As such, they are written, verbal descriptions of specific terminal behaviors or instructional outcomes required of students to signify successful completion of their study. Accordingly, performance objectives identify the end products or terminal performances of instruction in terms of observable, measurable behavior. Other terms used to describe this same type of objective include: specific instructional objective, behavioral objective, learning objective, measurable objective, and operationally defined objective. As you will see shortly, our present definition of a performance objective is derived primarily from the work of such instructional systems specialists as Tyler (1934, 1950), Mager (1962), Gagné and Briggs (1974), as well as from our own efforts (Kibler, Barker, and Miles, 1970; Kibler, Cegala, Miles, and Barker, 1974).

Terms like "behavioral" are used to describe this type of objective because they state what behaviors or performances (e.g., draw a circle, write a sentence) students are required to do or perform in order to demonstrate that they have mastered the prescribed instruction. We use *behavioral* to mean actions and movements which people can observe (e.g., see, hear). These "behavioral" objectives must identify the action that learners must *perform*, or the result of that behavior.

Performance is behavior or a response that produces a result. It refers to what you do when faced with a task. It is concerned with those activities or behaviors we go through, responses we make, to produce the result, product, or objective. Sometimes performance is just a response, but usually it produces a result. Your achievement is your performance evaluated with regard to its adequacy—typically assessed in terms of a specified criterion. We evaluate performance, usually in terms of a product, with respect to a criterion to determine achievement. To simplify the distinction, performance is what you do to produce a result; achievement is how well you do it in terms of some criterion.

For example, if an objective is to write a letter according to a set of prescribed specifications (i.e., criteria) and under certain constraints or conditions, then the letter that the student turns in is the product or result. What the student did (i.e., behavior to produce the letter) is the performance. The performance is evaluated by comparing the letter produced (i.e., result or product) against the set of prescribed specifications (i.e., criteria reflecting the model of adequacy).

These definitions should give you a preliminary understanding of what we mean when we use the term performance objective. Since a later section of this Chapter provides a more detailed definition of performance objectives and shows you how they should be written, we will wait until then to describe their characteristics and components.

Section Summary

A number of forces that contributed to the development of performance objectives were considered in this section. Bobbitt (1918, 1924) and Charters (1923, 1929) were probably responsible for formulating a method for determining educational objectives on a scientific basis. It was Tyler (1934, 1950), however, who is most often credited as being the "father" of today's performance objectives. The work of Kearney (1953), French (1957), Bloom *et al.*, (1956) and Krathwohl *et al.* (1964) followed closely to provide early frameworks for classifying objectives. It was the contributions from systems analysis by scholars like Gagné (1962, 1970), Miller (1962a, 1962b), and Briggs (1970) that have had an impact on the systems approach to instruction. It was Mager's (1961) book that diffused the concept and use of performance objectives across all education.

The relationship among needs, goals, and objectives was discussed. Needs are determined first. Next, these needs are translated into goals. Goals serve as the basis for deriving objectives. There may be a number of intervening steps required to get from the need to the goal, to subsequent goals, and then to performance objectives. It is also useful to distinguish between goals and objectives. Goals are general, long-range educational outcomes; objectives are specific, short-range outcomes.

Performance objectives are statements of what students must do to complete some prescribed instruction successfully. These "behavioral" objectives must identify/describe the action that the learners must perform or the result of that behavior. We will consider the implications of performance objectives in the next section as we examine the reasons for writing them.

Reasons for Writing Performance Objectives

In this section, we examine some of the salient reasons for writing performance objectives. The primary reason for writing performance objectives is so that teachers can use them to plan their instruction. Another fundamental reason is to give them to students to guide their learning. Performance objectives also facilitate effective discussion about course outcomes among those in the educational community. We will discuss each of these reasons briefly as a rationale for writing performance objectives.

Benefits of Performance Objectives
for Teachers

Specification of performance objectives requires teachers to make discrete decisions in which the goals of instruction are defined clearly in terms of behavioral outcomes. An early question which any instructional designer must answer is: "What do I want my students to be able to do as a result of the instruction?" Although some attention was given to this question in the previous Chapter, on the identification of goals and needs, we will continue to consider the implications of this question as a primary reason for writing performance objectives.

One of the difficulties all of us have as teachers is clarifying our instructional intent to ourselves. While we usually have a pretty good idea what our objectives are, it is necessary to state them in operational terms if they are to be useful for instructional planning. Implementing the procedures specified in the previous Chapter to determine goals and needs will certainly help us get started in this process. However, as an instructional designer you undoubtedly will achieve additional clarity during the process of stating your instructional intent in the precise terms required for performance objectives. We have observed that even experienced teachers gain insights into what they *really* have been teaching and *want* to teach as a result of writing performance objectives. It is also common for teachers to change their objectives, or other components in the instructional system, as a result of using performance objectives. Clearly, writing objectives requires teachers and other designers to make definite decisions concerning the behavioral outcomes of their instruction.

Gagné and Briggs (1974) have wisely suggested that the initial approach to defining performance objectives should begin with an attempt to identify the purposes of the instructional unit(s). This is a step that is omitted by many instructional designers, although Gronlund (1970) uses "general instructional objectives" similarly to the way Gagné and Briggs (1974) use purpose. Whatever it is labeled, this step probably should be a prerequisite to the actual writing of performance objectives. Since this step is designed primarily to satisfy the instructional designer, it is not necessary to use the precise terms required for a performance objective. Even so, Gagné and Briggs (1974) provide two useful guidelines which should help instructional designers to avoid problems as they identify their purposes for courses:

1.   Purposes should state what students will do *after* or *following* the instruction, not what they will be doing *during* the course.

2. Purposes should state the *current* or *present* outcomes which are expected of the instruction, not outcomes which are *extremely long-range* or well into the future.

After you have defined the purposes for your instructional unit, you are ready to begin writing your performance objectives. We will provide information to help you do this task in a later section of this Chapter.

Performance objectives also help teachers review their evaluation and testing procedures. When your test items do not match your objectives, you will hear about it if the students have been given performance objectives. Giving performance objectives to students means "going public," so your evaluation procedures must "match" items. By "match," we mean the two must correspond, be relevant, and be congruent with one another (see Chapter 6).

You use performance objectives to plan your instruction, too—every phase of it. They help define what resources you need in order to prepare and conduct instruction. They affect media selected, materials required, and activities. In addition, they can be used to help you *train* students to *use* performance objectives (Bassett and Kibler, 1975). Yes, performance objectives will be with you throughout every step of the instructional systems design listed in Table 1 of Chapter 1.

Benefits of Performance Objectives for Students

Providing students with performance objectives permits them to direct their learning activity towards the specific behaviors that must be mastered to complete the instructional requirements satisfactorily. You have undoubtedly encountered a course in which you were given only limited information about the teacher's instructional intent. You may have been told to read a particular text book and to attend lectures, and that you would be required to take tests over the materials. Quite likely, you were not given any course goals or performance objectives for this course. After suffering some frustration in the course, you probably tried to "psych" out the teacher, to predict what that teacher wanted you to do. Such school experiences still occur all too frequently. Even so, successful students have survived by mastering the game of "second-guessing" the teacher or professor involved.

Hopefully, you have also been involved in instruction in which the teacher clarified the instructional intent for the course by giving you the performance objectives you were required to master. We might say this increases the instructional fidelity. Simply providing you with the objectives may have helped to direct your learning activities towards the terminal behaviors or outcomes required to complete the course satisfactorily. You were able to select the relevant from the irrelevant for the course. Such goal-directed activity may not only have saved you time, it might also have reduced your anxiety and frustration throughout the learning process.

Instructional designers have assumed for some time that students will perform more efficiently and effectively as a result of being provided with performance objectives. Later in this Chapter, you will learn that the research evidence on this matter is still inconclusive. Does this mean we should not employ performance objectives in our instruction? It certainly does not. Until more complete and better research evidence is available to clarify the results of employing performance objectives, instructional designers are well advised to rely upon the sound logic that has guided them thus far. When students are informed through performance objectives of what they are expected to learn and how they will be required to demonstrate mastery of that learning, it seems reasonable to expect that both the efficiency and effectiveness of their learning will be facilitated. Accordingly, students presumably will benefit from the use of performance objectives; and, as instructional designers, we have an obligation to provide them to learners.

Students benefit from performance objectives by being informed of what they must do to demonstrate mastery. One of these benefits is that students are informed of how they will be evaluated. Performance objectives encourage students to conduct their own self-evaluation, because they can compare their performance against the specified criterion. When possible, as in a mastery learning system, performance objectives encourage students to progress at their own rate. Frequently, performance objectives encourage students to progress more rapidly because expectations/requirements are clearly defined, and obtainable goals are perceived by the student.

Benefits of Performance Objectives
for the Educational Community

Performance objectives facilitate effective communication about course outcomes and their sequencing among those involved in the educational enterprise. Participants in the educational community also find performance objectives useful for many other reasons, and we shall discuss some of these here.

Teachers benefit from the use of performance objectives in many ways. We mentioned earlier that performance objectives help teachers to plan their instruction, to evaluate student performance, and to improve communication with students regarding their instructional intent. Performance objectives also aid teachers in their communication with other teachers, curriculum planners, administrators, and parents. Efforts to justify new and current courses, and to defend the legitimacy of existing courses and curriculum, are facilitated through the use of performance objectives. The coordination and communication among different teachers instructing similar units or courses can be improved when performance objectives are available to them.

Student advisors find performance objectives extremely useful. Advisors can help students plan programs of study more effectively and efficiently when they have access to performance objectives for various courses. You have undoubtedly read a course title or description that seemed to meet your needs, signed up for it and, after attending class, discovered that it was different from the course description. With performance objectives, advisors can help students select courses that match determined needs. Performance objectives can also be used by advisors to stimulate student interest in new topics and areas, by showing students precisely what they will be required to do in various courses.

Curriculum planners find performance objectives a valuable tool in their work. Given clearly specified performance objectives, curriculum coordinators can communicate more effectively about the curriculum with one another, teachers, and administrators. There is more accuracy in their discussion of curriculum and individual courses, and less guessing about the substance of their deliberations. With clearly specified performance objectives, curriculum planners can also restructure instructional sequences more effectively, ranging from individual units to whole courses

(Bernabei and Leles, 1970). "Gaps" between and within both instructional units and courses can be identified and eliminated by curriculum coordinators. Curriculum planners can also reduce or eliminate unnecessary "overlap" between instructional units and courses, when they possess performance objectives required of students at the beginning and end of courses. Procedures to aid both teachers and curriculum coordinators in these efforts are described in Chapters 4 and 5.

Parents also benefit when performance objectives are available. Parents can be informed regarding the precise nature of the instruction their children are receiving. At the same time, parents can exercise pressure on the schools to be accountable for specific instructional outcomes. When what students are to learn is known, parents can become involved in determining the adequacy of the curriculum. Communication parents have with teachers and administrators over the substance of courses is improved when performance objectives are available.

Section Summary

In this section, we have presented some of the salient reasons for writing and using performance objectives. Teachers require them for use in planning instruction. Writing and using performance objectives also helps teachers clarify their instructional intent for themselves and for their students. In addition, performance objectives aid teachers in the review of their evaluation and testing procedures. By using performance objectives, students can direct their learning towards the specific behaviors required to complete the instruction successfully. Students are also informed regarding how they will be evaluated through performance objectives, and self-evaluation is facilitated by their use.

Others in the educational community also benefit from the availability and use of performance objectives. Performance objectives help teachers, curriculum planners, administrators, parents, and students communicate more effectively about the precise nature of instruction. Student advisors find performance objectives useful to aid students to plan their programs, to match courses to their needs, and to explore new areas of course work. Performance objectives help curriculum planners to communicate more effectively, to restructure instructional sequences, and to reduce gaps and overlaps in instructional units/courses. Parents benefit through improved communication with teachers and administrators.

Writing Performance Objectives

Different approaches can be taken to writing performance objectives, and, in fact, many volumes have been written which describe and illustrate the procedures. In this section, two of the most popular approaches, created by Mager (1962) and by Gagné and Briggs (1974), will be examined. While these authors disagree somewhat on what the final product (i.e., the ideal objective) should be, they do agree that the task of writing objectives begins with an examination of instructional goal statements. Using the Gagné-Briggs Model, we will conclude this section with an example of performance objectives for each of five major domains of human cognitive capabilities.

As you saw previously, goals refer to desired long-term outcomes of instruction. Goals are usually expressed in non-behavioral terms, such as "citizenship." In contrast, objectives refer to desired short-range outcomes, such as may be achieved in a day or a week of study, and are expressed in behavioral terms. When writing objectives the instructional designer studies goal statements and asks this question: "How can it be determined that a student has achieved this goal?" The "good" objective provides an answer to the question. This is to say that it gives a precise description of what students would be *doing* if they had mastered the learning implied by the goal statement.

With this orientation for writing objectives, we will now examine how the task of deriving precise statements of objectives from rather imprecise statements of goals can be accomplished.

The Mager Model

While teachers and instructional designers have been formulating objectives for many years, we noted earlier that Mager (1961, 1962) is generally credited with producing the classic set of instructions on the writing of objectives. Many books on the topic have appeared since Mager's original contribution. The value of

Mager's work is evident, however, in that succeeding approaches to the writing of objectives have, for the most part, continued to incorporate the basic components he identified.

For Mager, an objective is simply "a description of a pattern of behavior (performance) we want the learner to be able to demonstrate (1962, p. 3)." Mager suggests the use of three components in writing such descriptions:

(1) identify the *action* the learner will be taking when he has achieved the objective (e.g., to write; to speak);

(2) describe the relevant conditions under which the learner will be acting (e.g., "without the use of references"); and

(3) specify how well the learner must perform the action (e.g., 100 percent correct").

Each of the three components is identified in the following objective. The number of each part is identified above the appropriate portion of the objective:

$$/ \overset{2}{\text{Given 10 linear equations to solve (and no outside}}$$

references) $/ \, / $ the student will write both the steps in

$\overset{1}{\text{the solutions as well as the answers}} / \, / $ getting 8 out of

$\overset{3}{\text{10 answers correct, with no missing steps in the}}$

solution $/$.

The action. Mager argues effectively that objectives must describe what the learner will be doing, because only in this way can the learner's intellect or skill be assessed. Teachers, parents, and other interested persons cannot look inside students' heads to determine what they have learned. Hence, to say that a student "knows how to read French," or that a student "understands the operation of internal combustion engines," creates a great deal of ambiguity. What does it mean to "know," or to "understand"? These words are imprecise in that they may be interpreted in a variety of ways. However, to say that a student can "write" or "state orally" or "throw" is much less ambiguous. These actions can be observed and the capabilities a student possesses can be inferred from the achievement he is able to demonstrate. Mager (1962) offers the following contrasting lists of words to illustrate this point (p. 11):

Words Open to Many Interpretations	*Words Open to Fewer Interpretations*
to know	to write
to understand	to recite
to *really* understand	to identify
to appreciate	to differentiate
to fully appreciate	to solve
to grasp the significance of	to consult
to enjoy	to list
to believe	to compare
to have faith in	to contrast

Mager's first suggestion for writing objectives, then, is to take a statement of an instructional purpose or goal and rework it until it describes in the clearest way possible what the learner will be *doing* when he has achieved the goal.

Relevant conditions. To state performance objectives that convey the precise intent of the writer to others, Mager suggests that it may be helpful to describe the conditions imposed upon the learner when performing the action. For example, try to envision what you would be observing if a student were "obtaining the sum of five single digit numbers." Would the learner be making marks on paper with a pencil, punching the keys on a hand-held calculator, counting on his fingers and toes, or what? By stating the relevant conditions under which the learner demonstrates achievement, you may be more successful in helping others to understand accurately your instructional purpose. Here are some examples of some "givens," "limitations," and "restrictions" that might be profitably included in statements of performance objectives:

"With the use of notes and references. . ."

"Without the aid of an electronic calculator or other mechanical calculating device. . ."

"Given a hammer and saw. . ."

Kibler, Cegala, Barker, and Miles (1974) offer three suggestions for determining the conditions under which the learner will be expected to demonstrate achievement:

1. Specify the information, tools, equipment, source materials, and anything else *that will be available* to students to help them perform the terminal behavior required in the objective.

2. Specify the information, tools, equipment, source materials, and anything else that the student *cannot use* when demonstrating the terminal behavior.

3. List as many of the actual conditions as possible under which the student might be expected to demonstrate the terminal behavior in a real-life setting, and try to include as many of them in the objective as possible (p. 38).

Performance standard. The final component in Mager-type objectives is a statement describing how *well* the learner must perform the action. This component is the performance standard which is used to decide if the learner has or has not mastered the objective.

Standards for minimum acceptable achievement can be specified in a number of ways. For some behaviors it is appropriate to specify a time limit. For example, consider these statements:

". . .must be able to ride a bicycle one mile in *six* minutes."

". . .must be able to climb a 15 foot length of rope in *15 seconds.*"

". . .must be able to solve three quadratic equations within *one hour.*"

Kibler *et al.* (1974) have provided some examples of various types of performance standards. The list is not intended to be exhaustive, but it should help you understand alternative forms of the component:

Minimum Number:

". . .must list *four steps. . .*"

". . .write all *ten* words presented accurately. . ."

". . .distinguish *three main ideas. . .*"

Percent or Proportion:
> ". . .write (spell) accurately *100 percent* of the 10 words presented. . ."
> ". . .list *80 percent* of the verbs appearing in a 200 word message. . ."

Limitation of Departure from Fixed Standard:
> ". . .must be correct to the *nearest percent*. . ."
> ". . .must be within *five decibels* of. . ."

Distinguishing Features of Successful Performance:
> ". . .the radio plays within a *one-day period*. . ."
> ". . .all balls on the paper are *colored red*. . ." (p. 40)

Summary of Mager's Approach. For Mager, an objective is simply a set of words which describes instructional purposes. An objective will communicate clearly if it describes in unambiguous terms what the student will be doing when he has learned. The three parts of the Mager-type objective are:

(1) the *action* the learner will be taking when he has achieved the objective;

(2) the *relevant conditions* under which the learner will be acting; and

(3) the specification of *how well* the learner must do.

We recommend Mager's approach for the person without prior experience in writing objectives because it is relatively simple and easily mastered. We believe, however, that an alternative method for writing objectives proposed by Gagné and Briggs (1974) has significant advantages not found in Mager's approach. In the next section the Gagné-Briggs approach will be examined.

The Gagné-Briggs Model

Gagné and Briggs (1974) have proposed an alternative to Mager's model for performance objectives. Recall that Mager suggested a complete objective should specify (1) the action, (2) the relevant conditions, and (3) the criterion for performance. While you will see that the Gagné-Briggs model does not differ markedly from the Mager model, it does include some insightful and important distinctions that have not been identified or implemented elsewhere.

Gagné and Briggs propose that statements of performance objectives consist of the following five components:

1. *Action*: What will the learner be doing which can be observed by another person (e.g., running, writing, naming)?
2. *Object*: What will the learner produce as a result of the action performed (e.g., a sentence, a painting, a number)?
3. *Situation*: What are the circumstances in which the learner must demonstrate performance (e.g., given a column of four digit numbers, given an audio-tape recorded message, given an inoperative television set)?
4. *Tools and Other Constraints*: How must the action be carried out? This includes not only tools (e.g., pencil, artist's brush, baseball bat), but also sets limits to the performance (e.g., without the use of references, within 15 minutes).
5. *Capability to be learned*: What is the learned capability that the action gives evidence of having been acquired as indicated in Table 1?

This five-part model appears to differ in three ways from Mager's three-part model. The most important difference is that Gagné and Briggs distinguish between verbs which identify the *observable action the learner is performing* (the *indicator* verb) and verbs which identify the *learned capability which may be inferred from the action* (the intent of the objective). Another difference is that Gagné and Briggs include the component called "object of the performance," while Mager does not. The third difference is related to the performance criteria. To help you understand these distinctions we will consider each separately.

Action verbs and capability verbs. We stated earlier that the foremost requirement of an objective is that it convey precisely the instructional intent of the teacher or other designer. It was this concern for communicative accuracy—instructional fidelity, if you prefer—which led Mager and others to reject words such as "knows," "understands," and "appreciates" for describing the outcomes of instruction. In place of these relatively ambiguous or "fuzzy" terms, action words such as "sings," "writes," "draws," "matches," "names," and "selects" were substituted. Gagné and Briggs argue, however, that such action verbs are still too imprecise because they do not denote the *learned capability* which the

Table 1

Verbs to Describe Human Capabilities, with Examples of Phrases Incorporating Them*

Capability	Verb	Example
Intellectual Skill Discrimination	DISCRIMINATES	discriminates, by matching the French sounds of "u" and "ou"
Concrete Concept	IDENTIFIES	identifies, by naming, the root, leaf, and stem of representative plants
Defined Concept	CLASSIFIES	classifies, by using a definition, the concept "family"
Rule	DEMONSTRATES	demonstrates, by solving verbally stated examples, the addition of positive and negative numbers
Higher-order Rule (Problem-Solving)	GENERATES	generates, by synthesizing applicable rules, a paragraph describing a person's actions in a situation of fear
Cognitive Strategy	ORIGINATES	originates a solution to the reduction of air pollution, by applying model of gaseous diffusion
Information	STATES	states orally the major issues on the Presidential campaign of 1932
Motor Skill	EXECUTES	executes backing a car into driveway
Attitude	CHOOSES	chooses playing golf as a leisure activity

learner has acquired. Now if you think that such distinctions are designed to split subtle academic hairs or to play semantic games, guess again. This is an important distinction—for both conceptual and practical reasons.

To illustrate this point, Gagné and Briggs analyze the lesson purpose, "types a letter." It is their contention that using *only* the action description "types a letter" does not permit a precise definition of the instructional intent. To support their case, they offer two examples of objectives in which the action verb (i.e., typing) is the same, but in which the learned capability is quite different.

For the first objective, "the task set for the typist is that of answering a piece of correspondence concerned with orders and shipping, without help from anyone as to what the contents of the letter should be" (p. 80). The resulting objective is:

	Objective		*Element of Objective*
a.	Given a received letter inquiring about the shipping of an order,	a.	Situation
b.	the learner generates	b.	Learned Capability: Problem-Solving
c.	a letter in reply	c.	Object
d.	by typing	d.	Action
e.	using an electric type-writer, making one carbon of a one-page letter	e.	Tools and Constraints

While all parts of the above objective are necessary for precise communication of instructional intent, Gagné and Briggs demonstrate that the verb identifying the learned capability distinguishes this complex task from the much simpler task of merely reproducing a letter in typed form from a longhand copy. This simpler task is described in the following objective:

	Objective		*Element of Objective*
a.	Given a written long-hand letter,	a.	Situation

b. the learner executes

b. Learned Capability: Motor Skill

c. a copy

c. Object

d. by typing

d. Action

e. using an electric type-writer, making one carbon of a one-page letter

e. Tools and Constraints

While the situations specified in these two objectives differ, the most important distinction is the *learned capability*. Of course, the learner, in the first objective, may be increasing his motor skill, a *little* by typing one letter, but that is not the principal intent of the first objective—it is the intent of the second one. Composing and typing a letter is a much different capability than merely reproducing by typing. Moreover, you will see in Chapter 5, and in Chapters 7-9, that the identification of capabilities is critical to the planning of conditions of learning and the sequencing of learning.

Whereas there are a number of action verbs which convey meaning rather clearly (e.g., writing, running, naming orally), it is immediately apparent that verbs describing *capabilities* would be more abstract and hence potentially more ambiguous. Consequently, Gagné and Briggs (1974) propose that nine verbs be used to describe capabilities. The capabilities, verbs, and examples for each verb are shown in Table 1. The consistent use of this set of verbs by writers and users of performance objectives has obvious advantages for clarifying communication.*

Object of the performance. The second way in which the Gagné-Briggs Model for objectives differs from Mager's is that in the former there is a component called "object of the performance." Kibler, Barker, and Miles (1970) used the term "result" to refer to this part of an objective, defining it as "the product, ... or the 'what' the student is to do." The portion of the following statements which is italicized identifies the "object" of the behavior:

The student sings *a song.*

The student swims from *point A to point B.*

*Note carefully that it is the CAPABILITY verb, not the action verb, that is *standard*. Any appropriate action verb will do.

Whereas the specification of the "learned capability" is a new component not found in Mager-type objectives, such is not the case with the "object" component. The "object" is clearly present in Mager's model. However, Mager simply does not separate this part of the objective from the action verb. If this distinction appears trivial, it is not. Our experience in teaching instructors to write performance objectives, and in helping students to use them, clearly demonstrates both practical and conceptual advantages of this distinction.

Performance criteria. The third and final difference between Gagné-Briggs' objectives and Mager's is with respect to the specification of performance criteria. As you saw, Mager's model requires that the objective writer state *how effectively* the learner must perform the task to have the performance judged as acceptable. In contrast, Gagné and Briggs recommend that the performance standard *not* be included in statements of objectives. Their justification for omitting this element is that it is intimately related to assessment procedures. They argue that assessment concerns should rightfully be taken up at a later stage in the design process. To attempt to deal with them at the stage, where preliminary identification of objectives is being done, is to invite added difficulty and confusion to an already complex stage in the design process. Therefore, this criterion component is discussed in Chapter 6.

Summary of Gagné-Briggs Approach. The Gagné-Briggs Model for generating statements of performance objectives is composed of five components: (1) action, (2) object, (3) situation, (4) tools and constraints, and (5) capability to be learned. It is probably the most complete model for performance objectives that has been conceived to date. This model also has the added advantage of reflecting a strong linkage to the research on human capabilities.

We have identified three differences here between the Mager Model and the Gagné-Briggs Model. First, Gagné and Briggs distinguish between (a) verbs which identify the observable action the learner is performing (the indicator), and (b) verbs which identify the learned capability which may be inferred from the action (the intent), while Mager does not. Second, the component of "objective of performance" is included in the Gagné-Briggs

Model, but not as a separate component in the Mager Model. Third, while the performance standard is included in Mager's objectives, Gagné and Briggs suggest that it not be included in performance objectives, but that the standard be decided after the test over the objective has been prepared.

With this overview, you should now be able to identify the principal components of both the Mager Model and the Gagné-Briggs Model, and to distinguish the three primary differences between them.

Examples of Gagné-Briggs Performance Objectives

Now that the components of the Gagné-Briggs Model for objectives have been identified, we shall examine more closely the process of formulating such statements for each of the domains identified in Table 1.

Intellectual skill domain. One purpose of an introductory course in instructional design reasonably might be that students will "understand how to prepare performance objectives." In formulating an objective from this goal statement, the instructional designer has to decide what learners must be able to do to demonstrate "understanding." If you were the instructor, would you be satisfied if students were able to "list the five parts of performance objectives?" Probably not, because the act of "listing" would simply reveal that students had acquired some verbal information which they could repeat. What you might want the students to do is to show that they can actually produce (i.e., *generate*) performance objectives. The task, then, is a problem-solving one. As shown in Table 1, "problem-solving" is a sub-domain of the domain "intellectual skill." The objective might be stated in this way:

	Objective		*Element of Objective*
a.	Given a general statement of the scope and sequence of topics, concepts, or unit objectives for any course in the high school curriculum,	a.	Situation

b. the learner will *gener-*   b. Learned Capability:
    ate   Problem-Solving
c. appropriate student   c. Object
    objectives in each of
    the five domains of
    learning
d. by *writing* such objec-   d. Action
    tives
e. to include all five ele-   e. Tools, Constraints, and
    ments for each objec-   Special Requirements
    tive, within a one-week
    period.

Cognitive strategies domain. The example for this domain comes from a hypothetical course in advanced physics. A goal for such a course might be that students will "know how to solve novel problems." For our purposes, assume that the person formulating the goal intended that the learner would have to draw upon rules and information previously learned in the course and apply them to solve a problem not previously encountered by the learner. According to Gagné and Briggs (1974), when the learner draws upon rules and/or information, "formulates a general type of solution, and checks to see how such a solution applies to one or more specific instances" (p. 86), the process of "originating" is complete. An objective for this domain would take the following form:

	Objective		*Element of Objective*
a.	Having passed tests over earlier instruction on models of gaseous diffusion,	a.	Situation
b.	the pupil can *originate* a solution	b.	Learned Capability
c.	for the following ''problem'' (problem omitted: it requires the use of models of gaseous diffusion to re-	c.	Object

duce air pollution
caused by automobiles
and various types of
industrial combustion
operations)

d.	by explaining orally his strategy, showing his computation and the right answer to the instructor,	d.	Action
e.	within three hours.	e.	Constraint

Attitude domain. Suppose that a goal for fifth-grade children was "being kind to others." In examining this purpose you can readily determine that the statement is not concerned with intellectual skills. You wouldn't be satisfied, for example, if the student was able to "explain what it means to be kind to others." Rather, "being kind to others" suggests that the objective deals with personal *choices* the child makes about his interpersonal relationships. Hence, the learning goal lies within the attitude domain. There are, of course, many ways in which a child could demonstrate his willingness to be kind. Thus, one way to measure this choice is to *ask learners* what they would do (a "self-report" type of measure). Another way is to *watch* students in their daily classroom behavior (an unobtrusive measure). One way is identified in the objective stated below; an unobtrusive measure for a similar objective is found in Chapter 6.

	Objective		*Element of Objective*
a.	Given a series of short, unfinished stories to be completed by the child in terms of his own actions (e.g., "first person"), in which a clear choice exists between a kind and an unkind act as the conclusion to the story,	a.	Situation

b.	the child will more frequently *choose*	b.	Learned Capability
c.	kind rather than unkind acts	c.	Object
d.	by *writing the end* of the stories	d.	Action
e.	within one hour.	e.	Constraint

Motor skill domain. A purpose statement for a physical education course might be that students will "be able to play golf." To communicate precisely what the student would be doing when achieving this course purpose would require a number of objectives. To play golf, a person must be able to *execute* long fairway shots, short "chips" to the green, "blasts" from sand traps, and so on. All of these actions fall within the domain of motor skills. Here is an objective for one specific golf shot, the putt:

	Objective		*Element of Objective*
a.	Given prior verbal instruction and coaching on how to perform a putt, and given a putting green and balls placed at 4, 6, 10, and 20 feet from the cup at four compass directions chosen at random,	a.	Situation
b.	the student will *execute* (successfully)	b.	Learned Capability (Criterion added)
c.	putts	c.	Object
d.	with a standard putter	d.	Tools
e.	by *striking* the four balls	e.	Action
f.	in less than five minutes.	f.	Constraint

Information domain. Returning for this last example to the class in instructional design, consider that another purpose of the course might be that students would "understand the major steps in designing instructional systems." Now, what will be convincing evidence that the students "understand?" As in the previous example, there are numerous ways in which the students could be asked to demonstrate their learning. The designer might decide, for instance, that "understanding" meant being able to *state* the purposes and interrelationships among the steps in the design process. Hence, the required capability is in the information domain, and the following objective might be written:

	Objective		*Element of Objective*
a.	Given a list of the major steps in designing an instructional system, the student will be	a.	Situation
b.	able to *state*	b.	Learned Capability
c.	the purpose of and the interrelationships among any selected number of these steps	c.	Object
d.	in writing	d.	Action
e.	within one hour	e.	Constraint

Summary. Five examples of performance objectives were presented in this subsection. We followed the Gagné-Briggs Model in each case so that you could see how to generate objectives using their model. As you have seen, the model is reasonably easy to use and is an invaluable tool for the instructional designer. Using the information presented here, hopefully, you will begin to write performance objectives for your own use.

Since an example was formulated for each of the five domains, you should also have some notion of how performance objectives can be related to various human capabilities. An understanding of these human capabilities is critical to the instructional designer, as you shall see in the next two Chapters.

Section Summary

In this section, we introduced two of the most popular

models for writing objectives—the Mager Model and the Gagné-Briggs Model. After reading this section you may be unable to write perfect performance objectives using each of these models, but you do have the basic information required to begin writing objectives.

Mager requires that three components be included in each objective: (1) the *action* the learner will be performing when achieving the objective; (2) the *relevant conditions* under which the learner will be required to perform the action; (3) the minimum criterion for acceptable performance. If you have never written performance objectives, you may want to start by employing Mager's Model. It has proved to be an easy model for the uninitiated.

The Gagné-Briggs Model has five components: (1) action; (2) object; (3) situation; (4) tools and other constraints; (5) capability to be learned. Briggs (1975) has reported that he experienced no more difficulty teaching graduate students to write performance objectives with the five-component method than with Mager's three-component method. A principal advantage of Gagné and Briggs' method is that once the standard verbs reported in Table 1 (Gagné and Briggs, 1974, p. 85) are learned, classification of the objective is automatic—*if* the verbs are used correctly (Briggs, 1975). As we shall see in Chapters 4 and 5, this automatic classification of an objective facilitates subsequent steps in the instructional design process.

Research Related to Objectives

You saw in the first part of this Chapter that the emergence of performance objectives into the instructional design process has been long and arduous. Since the advent of Mager's (1961) book, teachers and scholars alike have devoted substantial energy to praising and damning performance objectives. Supporters of performance objectives have had to learn to be master polemicists.

Although the philosophical and functional bases for the use of performance objectives have been discussed at length (Kibler *et al.*, 1974; Kibler and Barker, 1970; Kibler, Barker, and Cegala, 1970; Popham, 1968), little effort has been made to examine the empirical literature systematically (e.g., Duchastel and Merrill, 1973). Perhaps the reason for this is that the principal empirical research dealing with the effects of objectives has appeared only within the last decade. This corpus of research must be used, in part, to determine the efficacy of incorporating objectives into the instructional design process. Accordingly, this section is devoted to a review of the literature on the use of objectives. First, we will describe the procedures employed for the review. Next, the results of the review of literature on objectives will be presented. The final subsection includes a summary and a cautionary note concerning the review.

Procedures Employed in Reviewing
Experimental Research on Objectives

The procedures employed for this review have been described in detail elsewhere (Kibler, Bassett, and Byers, 1976). However, we present a brief summary of them here to aid you in making judgments about the adequacy of the conclusions we have reached.

We began our research by identifying appropriate descriptors or key words for indices and catalogues containing experimental literature pertinent to objectives. A search was then conducted of the following indices: *CIJE/ERIC* (Descriptors: behavioral objectives, instructional technology, performance criteria, and criterion-referenced tests); *Psychological Abstracts* (Descriptors: teaching, cognitive development, and psychomotor development); and *Dissertation Abstracts International* (Key Words: behavioral objectives, performance objectives, instructional objectives, and objectives).

This effort produced over 150 experimental studies, which we subsequently examined. The resulting corpus was comprised of journal articles, convention papers, theses, and dissertations (or their abstracts). While our complete review (Kibler *et al.*, 1976) included a report on all of these types of research, the condensed review which follows here is limited to journal articles and convention papers.

We included all studies in which authors stated or implied that students were provided with statements identifying what they must do to demonstrate learning. These statements were variously labeled as "objectives," "instructional objectives," "performance objectives," and "learning objectives," as well as "behavioral objectives." The preponderance of these studies dealt with cognitive learning, but a few studies did deal with affective or psychomotor learning outcomes. We tried to conduct an exhaustive review of the defined literature, but we undoubtedly missed some relevant articles.

We eliminated studies from the primary body of literature which did not employ experimental procedures (i.e., the manipulation of at least one independent variable). In addition, we excluded any studies in which the authors did not provide an explicit statement of whether or not the stated or implied research hypotheses were supported.

The remaining body of literature included over 100 experimental investigations. (While all of these studies were cited in a review reported earlier [Kibler *et al.*, 1976], only 39 convention papers and published investigations are reported here.) The research reports were carefully read, analyzed, and classified by variables investigated. In particular cases, the classification of a given report under a particular variable was arbitrary. In other instances, classification was possible only after making inferences about procedures employed in a given investigation. The classified findings were then summarized as they appear in the next section. When the review was written, it was also sometimes necessary to cite a study one or more times under various independent or dependent variables. A summary of the salient conclusions resulting from these procedures is contained in the next subsection.

A Review of Research on Objectives

Following the procedures described earlier, the findings and related studies were found to cluster around four areas of concern. These areas included relationships between (a) student possession of objectives and learning, (b) student possession of objectives and learning efficiency, (c) the form in which the objectives were stated and student learning, and (d) teacher possession of objectives and student achievement. Each of these relationships has been cast in the form of a question. After each question is introduced, the major conclusion or answer is stated, along with pertinent findings and references.

Given the amount of space devoted to advocacy of the use of behavioral objectives, you would expect to find a plethora of experimental research findings carefully delineating the conditions under which objectives should be used to improve the efficiency and effectiveness of instruction. Unfortunately, our careful examination of the literature did not yield such results. Conversely, the acceptance and use of objectives appears to have surpassed the empirical research supporting such applications. With this overview, we will now review the literature on objectives.

Does possession of instructional objectives by students facilitate their learning as a result of using objectives? This basic question might well be regarded as the *sine qua non* of the controversy on objectives. To help you understand the importance of this question, it is necessary to consider the rapid rate at which influential instructional designers and some other educators have adopted performance objectives, and to identify some of the difficulties encountered in this adoption process. However, we must first review the contextual setting from which the concept of performance objectives emerged.

From the brief historical overview presented at the beginning of this Chapter, you will probably remember that the present impetus for the use of objectives came from many vantage points (Bloom *et al.*, 1956; Briggs, 1970; French, 1957; Gagné, 1965a, 1965b, 1970; Glaser, 1962, 1965; Kearney, 1953; Kibler *et al.*, 1970; Krathwohl, 1964; Lindvall, 1964; Mager, 1962; Miller, 1962a; Popham, 1969; Popham and Baker, 1970; Tyler, 1934, 1950, 1964). The publication of Mager's (1961) book probably initiated the rapid diffusion of the concept of behavioral or performance objectives across all levels of the educational arena. The reaction among educators to the concept of behavioral objectives as imbedded in Mager's book ranged widely—from complete rejection, to indifference, to complete acceptance. Although the notion of behavioral objectives did not escape criticism from the scholarly community (e.g., Ebel, 1963; Eisner, 1967), by the late 1960's many teachers began to write and use them.

It is equally important to understand that the decade of the 1960's was a period during which education at every level received unprecedented financial support. Both basic and applied educational research was funded richly. It was a seller's market for teachers, and higher education was turning out teachers in record numbers. Innovation and experimentation in education were the favored terms of the day. In short, the 1960's were a golden age for education in this country.

Against this background, the concept of behavioral objectives emanated and soon permeated virtually every level of educational endeavor. So, it was not surprising that both researchers and practitioners were curious about the efficacy of providing students with objectives. Accordingly, a substantial body of research emerged related to this matter.

Before discussing the findings of this research, it is necessary to clarify some key terms we selected to include in our basic question on the effects of students' use of objectives. Generally, the studies reported here deal with a comparison of students' learning with and without objectives. There appears to be an implicit assumption in most of these studies that when students were *given* objectives they *used* them. Stated another way, giving students objectives was equated with students' using them. We prefer to use "possession/nonpossession" to characterize the independent variable under investigation. Even though most of the researchers cited attributed effects of use/nonuse of objectives, we think possession/nonpossession more accurately reflects the variables studied.

With this background, we are now ready to examine the research on our basic question: Does possession of instructional objectives by students facilitate their learning as a result of using objectives? Based on our review of pertinent literature, we concluded that *investigations of the effects of students' possession of instructional objectives have not consistently demonstrated any differential effects on learning attributable to students' use of objectives.* We examined 77 studies related to this question, which was a greater number of studies than we found for any other question posed. Since the complete review of literature, including dissertations, is reported elsewhere (Kibler, Bassett, and Byers, 1976), only 20 studies are referenced here. Of the 20 studies cited here in which the experimental designs included a comparison of students' learning with and without objectives, 10 reported that objectives improved learning significantly (Blaney and McKie,

1969; Dalis, 1970; Duell, 1974; Glovatski, 1973; Hastings, 1972; Kaplan, 1974; Morse and Tillman, 1972; Olsen, 1973; Rothkopf and Kaplan, 1972). An additional 21 dissertation/thesis studies, which were included in our original review (Kibler *et al.*, 1976) but are not referenced here, reported similar findings. Six other studies reported no differential effects on learning attributable to students' use of objectives (Baker, 1969; Jenkins and Deno, 1971; Tobias and Duchastel, 1974). However, you should also note that the latter finding was corroborated by the results from 35 dissertations/theses not referenced here (cf., Kibler *et al.*, 1976).

The results of four additional investigations merit particular attention. Duell (1974) found that objectives directed towards items that students might consider unimportant improved performance on posttest and retention measures of those items. Cook (1969) found no difference in immediate posttest achievement scores between students given and those not given objectives, but did find that students provided with objectives performed significantly better than students not provided them, on a retention measure administered two weeks later. Finally, two studies (Miree and Rayburn, 1976; Yelon and Schmidt, 1971) produced findings which indicated that students who were not given objectives demonstrated greater learning than those who possessed objectives.

The prevailing logic of instructional systems design suggests that students provided with performance objectives should demonstrate superior learning to those not provided with objectives. While we expected our review of pertinent literature on this issue to support this position, it did not. We must be satisfied with the inconclusive results obtained—at least for the present. Hopefully, additional studies conducted in the future will reduce our uncertainty regarding the empirical bases for providing students with objectives. Until that time, it would be inappropriate to infer from this review that you should not provide students with objectives. Just because the findings reported here do not clearly support the efficacy of giving students objectives is no reason to reject other rational grounds for so doing.

Does possession of instructional objectives by students influence the efficiency of their learning as measured by time required for learning? With the increased usage of programmed instruction, self-paced instruction, mastery learning, independent study, and similar systematic efforts, there has been a renewed surge of interest in the instructional efficiency of learning. It was a natural extension of this effort to conduct research on the efficiency of learning for students with and without objectives. One of the major advantages espoused for giving students instructional objectives was that this procedure would help them to direct their learning towards the behaviors required for mastery or success in a course. If this assumption is accurate, it is reasonable to expect that an increase in the efficiency of learning (i.e., a reduction in time required to learn) would obtain.

We examined the experimental literature to determine the empirical basis for this generally accepted view among instructional designers—that providing students with performance objectives will increase learning efficiency. Based on our review, we concluded that *investigations of the effects of objectives on efficiency of learning (in terms of time) have not consistently demonstrated that student possession of objectives reduces time required for learning.* Of the seven studies found using learning time as a dependent variable, three reported that the use of objectives significantly reduced time spent in learning (Allen and McDonald, 1963; Boem, Duker, Haesloop, and White, 1974; Mager and McCann, 1961). Four studies, however, found no difference in learning time for students provided with objectives and those not given objectives (Duell, 1974; Kaplan, 1974; Merrill and Towle, 1971; Miree and Rayburn, 1976). This latter result is also supported by the findings from five disserations/theses which are not reported here (cf. Kibler *et al.*, 1976).

We started this review expecting to find that providing students with objectives would increase their learning efficiency. This expectation was not realized, and so we share some disappointment on this matter with other instructional designers. As additional research on these variables is published, the reasons for the present inconclusive results may become apparent. Meanwhile, we believe reason favors an expected increase in learning efficiency with the use of objectives, until such time as viable rival explanations are offered to the contrary.

Does the form (i.e., specific versus general statements) in which the objectives are stated facilitate student learning? You have probably already observed in this and previous Chapters that objectives range widely with regard to specificity. The matter of how specific an objective should be has received increased attention since the 1960's, and the concern about this issue has become even more intensified during the last decade.

The major proponents of specific objectives have been empirically oriented instructional designers and measurement specialists. They have advocated the use of objectives that reflect the teacher's instructional intent, behavioral outcomes which can be observed, and learner behavior which can be measured. At the other end of the issue, some educators have deplored the constraining nature of performance objectives, doubted the efficacy of their use, and/or questioned their value in terms of the time required to write sound objectives.

Interestingly, most of the discussion about how specific an objective should be has been based primarily on personal values and professional philosophies. Empirical data have generally been brought into such discussions infrequently and, even then, only studies that support a given position seem to be cited. With such uncertainty about the desired specificity of an objective, you would expect that a substantial body of empirical research would have been produced on the matter. Unfortunately, this is not the case, as we shall see.

In an effort to clarify the effects of stating objectives at different levels of specificity, we reviewed the literature systematically. One of the consistent problems we found in reading the studies was the limited information reported concerning the operational definitions for specific and general objectives.

We found only 14 studies related to the form of objectives in our review and seven of these were dissertations, which are not reported here. Based on these studies we concluded that *investigations of the effects of objective form (i.e., specific versus general statements) have not consistently demonstrated any differential effects on student learning attributable to the way in which objectives are stated.*

Seven studies are reviewed here in which the form of the objective served as an independent variable. In three of these (Dalis, 1970; Rothkopf and Kaplan, 1972; Tiemann, 1968), students provided with objectives stated in a specific behavioral form achieved significantly higher scores on the criterion measure than students given objectives stated in a general form. The remainder of the studies (Duell, 1974; Jenkins and Deno, 1971; Oswald and Fletcher, 1970; Stedman, 1972) revealed no differences between the learning effects of providing students with specific and general statements of objectives.

We would have preferred to conclude that specific performance objectives are superior to general objectives in facilitating student learning. Unfortunately, given the results of this review, it is not possible to do so. The results on the matter are inconclusive for the present, and so we must wait for additional studies to be reported. However, again we say there are convincing logical grounds stated throughout this book to support the continued use of performance objectives until more reliable data on the issue are available.

Does the possession of instructional objectives by teachers facilitate student achievement? We mentioned at the beginning of this Chapter that there are sound reasons for giving teachers behavioral objectives. Instructional designers have assumed that providing teachers with performance objectives should facilitate the learning process. While this may be a reasonable expectancy, the present body of experimental literature does not support this contention.

Based on our review of relevant literature on this matter, we concluded that *investigations of the effects of teachers' possessing objectives suggest that it makes little difference whether or not teachers have them.* Three studies were found in which the teacher's use of objectives served as a dependent variable (Baker, 1969; McNeil, 1967; Wittrock, 1962). All three failed to find significant effects on student achievement as a function of teachers' possession of objectives. Even though four additional dissertations/theses reported elsewhere (cf. Kibler *et al.*, 1976) revealed similar findings, it is obvious that there are too few studies available on this question to infer reliable and conclusive findings.

Once again, what we believed to be a reasonable expectancy did not obtain in our review. The pertinent literature revealed that student achievement did not increase as a function of providing teachers with objectives. Of course, these findings in no way suggest that teacher possession of objectives has any *debilitating* effect on student achievement. Unlike much of the other research reported in this section, all studies cited here were published prior to 1970. Perhaps this helps to explain why they were particularly plagued with methodological problems, and we will have more to say about this in our concluding remarks. What is equally distressing, though, is the conspicuous absence of recent experimental studies focused on the effects of teachers' possession of objectives. Until such studies are forthcoming, we will have to live with the present inconclusive results on the matter. The advice we offered previously applies here as well. We must rely on our present rational bases for providing teachers with objectives.

Section Summary and
Cautionary Note

This research review has examined the efficacy of providing students and teachers with objectives, and the specificity of form in which objectives should be cast. The results of this review may be summarized for each question posed in a single word: "inconclusive." The present state of findings on research with objectives indicates their current usage may be beyond their present empirically determined value. While objectives have been shown to facilitate learning in a limited number of studies, such a facilitating effect has not been consistent across the vast majority of investigations. Consequently, we are left with the conclusion that present experimental findings do not consistently demonstrate any advantages—*or* disadvantages—for employing objectives in instruction. Even so, we have noted throughout this section that there are viable logical and practical grounds for the use of objectives in instruction.

We conclude this section with a note of caution. There are serious methodological problems apparent in the literature we have reviewed in this section. Although it is beyond the scope of this Chapter to consider these deficiencies here, we do suggest that you study our discussion of these problems reported elsewhere (Kibler *et al.*, 1976). Particularly, we urge you to examine these methodological defects prior to attributing any detrimental effects to the use of performance objectives or rejecting their value for the purpose of instructional design.

Chapter Summary

We began this Chapter with a conceptual overview of performance objectives. After providing a historical prospective on the forces that contributed to the development of performance objectives, we considered the relationships among needs, goals, and objectives. Needs are a principal source for determining our course goals, and these goals are the basis from which we ultimately derive performance objectives. Our next section distinguished between goals and objectives. Goals are global and long-term, while objectives are precise and short-term. Performance objectives were defined as statements of what students are required to do as a result of instruction to complete a course successfully.

The second section dealt with the reasons for writing objectives. We indicated that with performance objectives the learner's behavior can be directed more efficiently, the teacher can plan instruction more effectively, and that communication about what is to be learned is facilitated in the educational community.

Writing performance objectives was the topic of the third section. We introduced two popular models for writing performance objectives—the Mager Model and the Gagné-Briggs Model. Mager's Model includes three components: (1) the action; (2) the relevant conditions; (3) the performance standard. The Gagné-Briggs Model has five components: (1) action; (2) object; (3) situation; (4) tools and constraints; and (5) capability to be learned.

The fourth and final section discussed the research related to objectives. Four areas of research on objectives were reviewed. These included relationships between (1) student possession of objectives and learning; (2) student possession of objectives and learning efficiency; (3) the form in which the objective is stated and student learning; (4) teacher possession of objectives and student achievement. For each of the four relationships, the results were inconclusive. We concluded that the present experimental findings do not consistently demonstrate any advantages—or disadvantages—for employing objectives in instruction. Given this quandary, we urge instructional designers to rely on rational arguments based on systems analysis and logic as the foundation for determining the efficacy of using objectives. We believe sound logic presently favors the use of objectives.

This Chapter is only the first of three in this book dealing with objectives. The next focuses on organizing objectives, and Chapter 5 describes procedures for analyzing objectives. Both Chapter 2 and this Chapter should provide a sound orientation for the next two chapters you will encounter. Needs, goals, and objectives can guide organizing, sequencing, and analyzing for both objectives and the learning sequences required within an objective.

Finally, no research was uncovered relating to the value of performance objectives for *teams which design* instructional systems. Therefore, experience in managing such team operations is one source of guidance. Such team operations are discussed in Chapter 9.

References

Allen, D.W., and McDonald, F.J. The Effects of Self-Selection on Learning in Programmed Instruction. Paper presented at the annual meeting of the American Educational Research Association, Chicago, 1963.

Ammons, M. Objectives and Outcomes. In R.L. Ebel (Ed.), *Encyclopedia of Educational Research*. Toronto, Ontario: The Macmillan Company, 1969.

Baker, E.L. *Social Sciences Research Methods: An Experimental Instructional Unit*. Los Angeles: University of California, Department of Education, 1967.

Baker, E.L. Effects on Student Achievement of Behavioral and Nonbehavioral Objectives. *Journal of Experimental Education*, 1969, *38*, 5-8.

Bassett, R.E., and Kibler, R.J. Effects of Training in the Use of Behavioral Objectives on Student Achievement. *Journal of Experimental Education*, 1975, *44*, 12-16.

Bernabei, R., and Leles, S. *Behavioral Objectives in Curriculum and Evaluation*. Dubuque: Kendall/Hunt Publishing Company, 1970.

Blaney, J.P., and McKie, D. Knowledge of Conference Objectives and Effect Upon Learning. *Adult Education Journal*, 1969, *19*, 98-105.

Bloom, B.S. (Ed.), Engelhart, M.D., Furst, E.J., Hill, W.H., and Krathwohl, D.R. *Taxonomy of Educational Objectives—The Classification of Educational Goals. Handbook I: Cognitive Domain*. New York: David McKay Company, Inc., 1956.

Bobbitt, F. *The Curriculum*. Boston: Houghton-Mifflin, 1918.

Bobbitt, F. *How to Make a Curriculum*. Boston: Houghton-Mifflin, 1924.

Boehm, E.E., Duker, J., Haesloop, M.D., and White, M.A. Behavioral Objectives in Training for Competence in the Administration of Individual Intelligence Tests. *Journal of School Psychology*, 1974, *12*, 150-57.

Briggs, L.J. *Sequencing of Instruction in Relation to Hierarchies of Competence*. Pittsburgh: American Institutes for Research, 1968.

Briggs, L.J. *Handbook of Procedures for the Design of Instruction*. Pittsburgh: American Institutes for Research, 1970.

Briggs, L.J. *An Overview of Instructional Systems Design*. Tallahassee: Florida State University, 1975.

Cardinal Principles of Secondary Education (Bulletin No. 35). Washington, D.C.: United States Government Printing Office, 1937.

Charters, W.W. *Curriculum Construction*. New York: Macmillan, 1923.

Charters, W.W. *The Teaching of Ideals*. New York: Macmillan, 1929.

Charters, W.W., and Waples, D. *The Commonwealth Teacher-Training Study*. Chicago: University of Chicago Press, 1929.

Cook, J.M. *Learning and Retention by Informing Students of Behavioral Objectives and Their Place in the Hierarchical Learning Sequence*. Final Report. Office of Education (DHEW), Washington, D.C. Bureau of Research, No. BR-9-C-018, November, 1969. (ERIC Document Reproduction Service No. ED 036 869.)

Dale, E. Historical Setting of Programed Instruction. In P.C. Lange (Ed.), *Programed Instruction*. Chicago, Illinois: University of Chicago Press, 1967.

Dalis, G.T. Effect of Precise Objectives Upon Student Achievement in Health Education. *Journal of Experimental Education*, 1970, *39*, 20-23.

Duchastel, P.C., and Merrill, P.F. The Effects of Behavioral Objectives on Learning: A Review of Empirical Studies. *Review of Educational Research*, 1973, *43*, 53-69.

Duell, O.K. Effect of Type of Objective, Level of Test Questions, and the Judged Importance of Tested Materials Upon Posttest Performance. *Journal of Educational Psychology*, 1974, *66*, 225-232.

Ebel, R.L. The Relation of Testing Programs to Educational Goals, in the Impact and Improvement of School Testing Programs. In *The Impact and Improvement of School Testing Programs*, Part 2 of the 62nd Yearbook of the National Society for the Study of Education. Chicago: University of Chicago Press, 1963.

Eisner, E.W. Educational Objectives: Help or Hindrance? *School Review*, 1967, *75*, 250-260.

French, W., and Associates. *Behavioral Goals of General Education in High School*. New York: Russell Sage Foundation, 1957.

Gagné, R.M. (Ed.). *Psychological Principles in Systems Development*. New York: Holt, Rinehart, and Winston, 1962.

Gagné, R.M. Educational Objectives and Human Performances. In J.D. Krumboltz (Ed.), *Learning and the Educational Process*. Chicago: Rand McNally, 1965a.

Gagné, R.M. The Analysis of Instructional Objectives for the Design of Instruction. In R. Glaser (Ed.), *Teaching Machines and Programed Learning, II*. Washington, D.C.: National Education Association of the U.S., 1965b.

Gagné, R.M. *The Conditions of Learning*. New York: Holt, Rinehart, and Winston, Inc., 1970.

Gagné, R.M., and Briggs, L.J. *Principles of Instructional Design*. New York: Holt, Rinehart, and Winston, 1974.

Gagné, R.M., and Fleishman, E.A. *Psychology and Human Performance*. New York: Holt, Rinehart, and Winston, 1959.

Glaser, R. (Ed.). *Training Research and Education*. Pittsburgh: University of Pittsburgh Press, 1962.

Glaser, R. (Ed.). *Teaching Machines and Programed Learning, II*. Washington, D.C.: National Education Association of the U.S., 1965.

Glovatski, E.A. Behavioral Objectives for Geography Facilitate Communication and Increase Test Performance. *Journal of Geography*, 1973, *72*, 36-44.

Gronlund, N.E. *Stating Behavioral Objectives for Classroom Instruction*. Toronto, Ontario: The Macmillan Company, 1970.

Hastings, G.R. Independent Learning Based on Behavioral Objectives. *Journal of Educational Research*, 1972, *65*, 411-416.

Jenkins, J.R., and Deno, S.L. Influence of Knowledge and Type of Objectives on Subject-Matter Learning. *Journal of Educational Psychology*, 1971, *62*, 67-70.

Kaplan, R. Effects of Learning Prose with Part Versus Whole Presentations of Instructional Objectives. *Journal of Educational Psychology*, 1974, *66*, 787-792.

Kearney, N.C. *Elementary School Objectives*. New York: Russell Sage Foundation, 1953.

Kibler, R.J., and Barker, L.L. Stating Objectives in Speech Communication. *The Bulletin of The National Association of Secondary School Principals*, 1970, *54*, 30-39.

Kibler, R.J., Barker, L.L., and Cegala, D.J. A Rationale for Using Behavioral Objectives in Speech-Communication Instruction. *The Speech Teacher*, 1970, *19*, 245-256.

Kibler, R.J., Barker, L.L., and Miles, D.T. *Behavioral Objectives and Instruction*. Boston: Allyn and Bacon, Inc., 1970.

Kibler, R.J., Bassett, R.E., and Byers, J.P. Behavioral Objectives and Communication Instruction: State of the Research. Paper presented at the Annual Meeting of the International Communication Association, Portland, Oregon, April 13-17, 1976.

Kibler, R.J., Cegala, D.J., Barker, L.L., and Miles, D.T. *Objectives for Instruction and Evaluation*. Boston: Allyn and Bacon, Inc., 1974.

Kibler, R.J., Cegala, D.J., Miles, D.T., and Barker, L.L. *Instructional Objectives and Evaluation*. Boston: Allyn and Bacon, 1974.

Krathwohl, D.R., Bloom, B.S., and Masia, B.B. *Taxonomy of Educational Objectives—The Classification of Educational Goals. Handbook II: Affective Domain*. New York: David McKay Company, Inc., 1964.

Lange, P.C. (Ed.). *Programed Instruction.* Chicago, Illinois: The University of Chicago Press, 1967.

Lindvall, C.M. (Ed.). *Defining Educational Objectives.* Pittsburgh: University of Pittsburgh Press, 1964.

Lumsdaine, A.E., and Glaser, R. (Eds.). *Teaching Machines and Programed Learning.* Washington, D.C.: National Education Association of the United States, 1960.

Mager, R.F. *Preparing Objectives for Programmed Instruction.* San Francisco: Fearon Publishers, 1961.

Mager, R.F. *Preparing Instructional Objectives.* Palo Alto: Fearon Publishers, 1962.

Mager, R.F., and McCann, J. Learner-Controlled Instruction. Palo Alto: Varian Associates, 1961.

McNeil, J.D. Concomitants of Using Behavioral Objectives in the Assessment of Teacher Effectiveness. *Journal of Experimental Education*, 1967, *36*, 69-74.

Merrill, P.F., and Towle, N.J. The Effects of the Availability of Objectives on Performance in a Computer-Managed Graduate Course. Pre-publication paper, Florida State University, 1971.

Miller, R.B. Analysis and Specification of Behavior for Training. In R. Glaser (Ed.), *Training Research and Education.* Pittsburgh: University of Pittsburgh Press, 1962a.

Miller, R.B. Task Description and Analysis. In R.M. Gagné (Ed.), *Psychological Principles in Systems Development.* New York: Holt, Rinehart, and Winston, 1962b.

Miree, L.M., and Rayburn, M.D. Accountability in Instruction: The Efficiency of Instructional Objectives in a Mastery Learning System. Paper presented at the Annual Meeting of the International Communication Association, Portland, Oregon, April 13-17, 1976.

Morse, J.A., and Tillman, M.H. Effects on Achievement of Possession of Behavioral Objectives and Training Concerning Their Use. Paper presented at the annual meeting of the American Educational Research Association, Chicago, 1972.

Olsen, R.C. A Comparative Study of the Effect of Behavioral Objectives on Class Performance and Retention in Physical Science. *Journal of Research in Science Teaching*, 1973, *10*, 271-277.

Oswald, J.M., and Fletcher, J.D. Some Measured Effects of Specificity and Cognitive Level of Explicit Instructional Objectives Upon Test Performance Among Eleventh Grade Social Science Students. Paper presented at the annual meeting of the American Educational Research Association, Minneapolis, 1970.

Popham, W.J. Probing the Validity of Arguments Against Behavioral Goals. Paper presented at the annual American Educational Research Association meeting, Chicago, 1968.

Popham, W.J. (Ed.). *Instructional Objectives*. Chicago: Rand-McNally, 1969.

Popham, W.J., and Baker, E. *Establishing Instructional Goals*. Englewood Cliffs, New Jersey: Prentice-Hall, 1970.

Rothkopf, E.Z., and Kaplan, R. Exploration of the Effect of Density and Specificity of Instructional Objectives on Learning from Text. *Journal of Educational Psychology*, 1972, *63*, 295-302.

Schramm, W. *The Research on Programed Instruction*. Washington, D.C.: U.S. Government Printing Office, 1964.

Stedman, C.H. Is Providing Students with Behavioral Objectives Incorporated into Programmed Materials Efficient? *Journal of Experimental Education*, 1972, *41*, 73-77.

Stolurow, L.M. *Teaching by Machine*. Washington, D.C.: U.S. Government Printing Office, 1961.

Tiemann, P.W. Student Use of Behaviorally-Stated Objectives to Augment Conventional and Programmed Revisions of Televised College Economics Lectures. Paper presented at the annual meeting of the American Educational Research Association, Chicago, 1968.

Tobias, S., and Duchastel, P.C. Behavioral Objectives, Sequences, and Anxiety in CAI. *Instructional Science*, 1974, *3*, 231-242.

Tyler, R.W. *Constructing Achievement Tests*. Columbus, Ohio: Ohio State University, 1934.

Tyler, R.W. *Basic Principles of Curriculum and Instruction*. Chicago: University of Chicago Press, 1950.

Tyler, R.W. Some Persistent Questions on the Defining of Objectives. In C.M. Lindvall (Ed.), *Defining Educational Objectives*. Pittsburgh: University of Pittsburgh Press, 1964.

Wittrock, M.C. Set Theory Applied to Student Teaching. *Journal of Educational Psychology*, 1962, *53*, 175-180.

Yelon, S.L., and Schmidt, W.H. The Effect of Objectives and Instructions on the Learning of a Complex Cognitive Task. Paper presented at the annual meeting of the American Educational Research Association, New York, 1971.

Transition to Chapter 4

In Chapter 1, you read what this book is all about.

In Chapter 2, you read how needs and goals may be derived by comparing an existing course (or curriculum) with a desired ideal course or curriculum—the difference between the two (existing and ideal) defines a need. Needs are then expressed as goals, or general desired outcomes of the new or improved instruction.

The goals, in turn, are converted to the more specific form of performance objectives (behavioral objectives); you were shown how to write such objectives in Chapter 3. We wanted you to learn how to write such objectives before going on to how to organize your new course (or to reorganize an old course).

In Chapter 4, you will read about how to organize your course "from the top"; that is, how to generate increasingly specific objectives from more general objectives. We suggest six possible layers of such objectives—but you may need only two or three layers for your course. Read Chapter 4 with this in mind.

There is little research on how to organize instruction in regard to its overall structure. Therefore, several examples of course organization are presented in Chapter 4; other examples make up a part of Chapters 16 and 17. There is, however, some research on organization and sequencing of the smaller units within a course. This research is discussed in Chapters 5, 6, and 7.

Chapter 4

Organizing the Course

Leslie J. Briggs
Florida State University

In this Chapter the word "course" is used in a generic sense. The word is intended to refer to the total instruction being planned, whether it may be a brief workshop or job-training effort or a one-semester educational course.

Previous Chapters have illustrated the principle that instruction should be planned "from the top, down." That is to say, general needs and goals should be defined before the more specific objectives are selected.

However, there is no agreed-upon standard number of levels, from general to specific objectives, to serve as a guideline for the designer. For a brief workshop of, say, two days, there might be one general goal and perhaps 10 specific objectives to be accomplished by the participants. For a course of instruction taking 12 weeks, there might be three general goals and 30 specific performance objectives. For an entire K-12 school curriculum, there could be dozens of goals and hundreds (or thousands) of objectives, arranged either in a year-by-year "scope and sequence," or, in some skill areas, into complex skill hierarchies for each year of the curriculum.

It is common to express national goals for education in very broad, non-behavioral terms, such as: "education for citizenship," or for "vocational competence," or for "personal development," or for "quality of life." These broad statements have traditionally been considered acceptable for the purpose, even though they do not describe what a learner would be doing to demonstrate that he has reached these goals. Notice also that some or all of these goals

99

may not be demonstrated fully by the students until after they graduate from the twelfth grade. Therefore, a determination as to whether the goals are being reached would usually require gathering of data both during the learners' school years and in later years after they have entered their full adult roles in life.

In addition to such national goals, many states in the U.S.A. also have published goals for the public schools in the state. Individual public and private schools may also list their own goals. Within each school, a curriculum scope and sequence statement relates or translates school goals into year-by-year goals, which in turn may be translated into lists of objectives for each subject or skill area in the curriculum of the school. Within each such subject or skill area, the planned accomplishments for the year could be arranged in any number of "layers of objectives."

Again, there is no standard number of such layers of objectives representing a year of schooling. There might be three layers in social studies, or 20 layers in mathematics. Even two schools using the same curriculum might express objectives in different numbers of layers, representing differing amounts of specificity or detail. Some schools may simply list in serial order the specific objectives to be reached during the year. Finally, of course, some schools may list goals but not specific objectives. This practice might be found in the British "infant school" or in a school with a "humanistic" orientation, in which each child is free to learn whatever he or she wants to learn. Still another possibility is to arrange objectives in the sequence most compatible with the child's mental development, as proposed by Piaget (1970).

Due to the lack of a standard way to organize the objectives for either an entire school curriculum or for a one-year "course" in a given subject or skill area, *one* way of doing this is described and illustrated next. This method is essentially a combination of two methods the author has used and taught to students in the past (Briggs, 1970, 1975). The 1975 text, just cited, was used in an introductory course in the design of instruction, and the 1970 text cited was used in an advanced course. A student design product from each of these courses is reproduced as Chapters 16 and 17. These illustrate how the information in this book may be applied. (Chapter 17 was developed by Ms. Medsker in the fall of 1975 while she was enrolled as a student in the introductory course. Chapter 16 was developed by Miss Ackerman while she was enrolled in the advanced course in the summer of 1976.)

A Suggested Six-Level Method

1. Needs Analysis

As shown in Chapter 2, a need is often expressed as the difference between goals a school would like to achieve and goals it is currently achieving. Another way of stating a need, however, is in terms of something one wishes to teach but which is not currently being taught at all. Still another way of identifying needs is to ask the learners or the prospective students what they think they need to learn. Finally, another method could involve consensus techniques to determine what a group of "experts" believe that citizens of the future will need to know how to do. Notice that none of these methods of needs analysis depends entirely upon traditions reflected in earlier school curricula. Nor is a single kind of needs analysis utilized when new or revised curricula are being developed. Quite often a new curriculum is designed on the basis of the way a particular group of persons believe that science (for example) should be taught. But another group might disagree about what should be taught and how it should be taught. It appears only reasonable to ask that curricula should be capable of being defended on the basis of statements of reasons why the intended learners need that particular content and method of instruction.

See Chapter 17 for an example of one form of needs analysis that requires no special technology, and hence is within the scope of an introductory course.

2. Goal Definition

The goals for the instruction should, of course, be consistent with the desired goals associated with the needs analysis, at least in this particular method for organizing a course of instruction.

Since goals are broader than objectives, goals often are not stated in behavioral terms, because no one test or other assessment instrument would be adequate to evaluate the attainment of the goals. Even so, goals *could be* stated in behavioral terms, followed by an indication of the variety of assessments that would be needed to verify attainment of each goal. As an alternative procedure, an independent ("outside") evaluator may be invited to design an evaluation program, either to determine whether the goals were met, or to determine the value of the goals, or both. Such an evaluation may also address the question "Were the goals worth what it cost to achieve them?" Scriven (in Talmage, 1975) has even suggested that the evaluator should not even know what the goals were; he should, instead, determine the value of the outcomes, whether planned or unexpected.

There are, then, clearly three choices: (a) to state the goals in behavioral terms so that assessment can be addressed directly to the goals, or (b) to state the goals in non-behavioral terms, leaving it to the evaluator to decide how to assess goal attainment, or (c) leave the goals unassessed, and stated in non-behavioral terms, with the plan that achievement will be assessed either at the level of unit objectives or specific objectives.

Referring again to Chapter 17, the goals written by Ms. Medsker were stated in behavioral terms, but not in the detail she included in the five-component method of defining the specific behavioral objectives, as described in Chapter 3.

3. Life-Long Objectives

Since some courses are designed to be the sole source of instruction in the subject or skill area, while other courses are only parts of a total program of instruction, it is desirable to make the intent explicit. For example, if a single course in typing is to be sufficient for the learners to obtain positions as typists or to type their own school work adequately, this can be stated in relation to those later activities. On the other hand, if a course in algebra is the first course in a degree program in mathematics, that intent should also be made clear. Such statement of the long-term purpose of the course in the life of the learners can help in a review of the more detailed objectives for relevance, suitability, and adequacy. The content of the course, in turn, could then be more appropriately selected or developed.

In adult education of the non-degree, non-credit type, it is often the case that a single course meets a need perceived by the learner. Thus, one may learn to sew well enough to make one's own clothing without further training or experience beyond the sewing course. Or one may learn enough about music to enjoy listening to it and discussing it with others for the remainder of one's life. Presumably, if one wished to be an employable *designer* of clothing or a music *teacher*, the same courses would be inadequate as the sole source of instruction.

Even in the case of a course being adequate as the sole formal instructional course, it is sometimes necessary to specify the subsequent *learning* experiences that need to take place to meet the long-term need. Adult learners thus take the responsibility to pursue those subsequent experiences, but they may need to be informed, during the course, of the nature of those experiences, where they may be accomplished, etc. Thus, a statement of a life-long objective as an outcome of the course can assist the learners to understand what is taught during the course, as distinct from the learning that must take place in subsequent courses, in on-the-job training situations, or in self-managed learning experiences. Such a statement can also help the enrollees to avoid making inappropriate assumptions about the level of expertise that can be expected to result from the course alone. It is a designer's ethical responsibility to assist the learners in such matters as well as to avoid deliberate misrepresentation of the value of the course. This responsibility appears equally clear whether adults are paying fees for courses or whether taxpayers are supporting the education for children. In the latter case, the responsibility is not only to the learners, but also to their parents and to the community. It may be not only ethical but also motivating to the learners to present clear-cut statements as to the relevance of the course for meeting long-term needs; attempting to do so is a good experience for designers, since it reminds them of the constant need to review the planned instruction in light of the total purposes and context of the course.

In the elementary design course taken by Ms. Medsker, Chapter 17, no life-long objectives were required. But the reader may wish to pause here to read the first portions of Chapter 16, to note the difference between the life-long objectives and the end-of-course objectives, as stated in Miss Ackerman's design plan.

4. End-of-Course Objectives
One or more end-of-course objectives serve not only to guide

the development of unit objectives and specific objectives, but also to distinguish those performances which are expected by the end of the course from those additional experiences which may be required to reach life-long objectives, as we have just seen.

Again, such objectives may or may not be stated in behavioral terms, depending upon the levels at which performance is to be assessed. That is, if a final examination is planned, behavioral course objectives are needed as a cross-check upon the *validity* of that assessment of learner performance. The details of this relationship between objectives and tests are given in Chapter 6.

It is a good experience for you to state, in behavioral terms, *all* objectives, at every level described in this Chapter. You might begin by outlining the course into topics, but sooner or later you need to switch to behavioral terms in order to avoid ambiguity.

An example by Gagné and Briggs (1974, pp. 76-77) distinguishes between life-long and end-of-course objectives, and at the same time shows the need to avoid ambiguity. Suppose, for example, we identify a course objective first as merely a topic, "the environment." Sub-topics under this, which might become course units, could be "air," "water," and "animals." So far, so good. But exactly what is the student to learn about each of these topics?

In an attempt to answer this question, we might next say, for example, that under the unit on "animals," the learner must "acquire a life-long respect for the importance of conserving natural wildlife." There are two problems with this statement. First, one could not expect that a "life-long respect" is established by a single unit of instruction. This might be a good life-long objective, as long as one realizes that other experiences, beyond this course, are needed for its achievement. Second, the statement does not imply what *could* be expected at the end of the unit of instruction. Perhaps a reasonable objective under the unit on "animals" would be:

> "Students will be able to identify instances in which a lack of wildlife conservation has produced undesirable consequences."

Some principles emerge, then, relating to life-long and end-of-course objectives.

1. *Life-long* objectives are worth the trouble because they:

a. Remind the designer to inform the learner whether the instruction being offered is adequate as the sole learning experience, or whether later experiences are also required.

b. Remind the designer to keep in mind the future life of the learner when end-of-course objectives are being selected.

c. Help the designer decide whether it is feasible to assess the learner's performance in reference to a future outcome (obtaining a job based on ability to type 60 words per minute), or whether only end-of-course objectives are to be assessed.

2. *End-of-course* objectives are worth the trouble because:

a. They help the designer decide upon the type of end-of-course assessment of learner performance that is appropriate.

b. They provide a baseline against which to justify the need for each unit objective; unit objectives, in turn, are the baseline for defending the need for the specific objectives.

c. The objectives are the baseline against which assessments can be judged to be valid.

d. "Dead wood" that creeps into the course planning can be detected by asking: "Is this specific or unit objective really needed to reach the course objective(s)?"

Final examinations. Whether final examinations are needed at the end of the course depends upon the nature of the course objectives. It is useful to contrast the nature of memorized material (information objectives) and skill objectives. (Finer distinctions among types of objectives are introduced in Chapter 5.)

If a final examination is to be administered, rather than requiring a course product from the student, as represented in Chapters 16 and 17, the learners will need to know whether the examination will require them to generate solutions to problems which are new and more complex than those solved earlier, or whether the final examination is simply a retention test composed of sample questions from all previous tests. In the first instance, an intellectual skill is implied, in which the learner recalls, transfers, and uses in more complex combinations the rules learned earlier in the course. In the second instance, information objectives are implied. To prepare for the final examination, the learners would, in the first instance, review rules and earlier problem-solving experiences; while, for the second instance, they would review facts, names, labels, and organized information.

It is the bias of this writer that even information objectives should be specified clearly in order that the learner know *what* information to learn and to review for the test. Otherwise, the student attempts to recall *everything*, knowing that the test might consist of a random sample of all information presented in books and lectures. This appears to represent an unreasonable memory demand. It would appear better to specify which information is important enough to justify sufficient overlearning and review as to result in long-term recall, and which needs only to be understood in context to grasp a concept or an idea. While it is often justifiable to expect memorization of such things as chemical symbols, important formulae, and critical definitions, the designer should be sure that these demands are sufficiently modest to allow the student time to demonstrate higher levels of skill and understanding.

It appears fair to say that schooling and examinations in years gone by have required too much memorizing at the expense of problem-solving, but it also appears that schooling has improved in this respect in recent years. Even now, however, teachers and designers often fail to achieve ideal balance between information objectives and skill objectives.

It is a good practice after the end-of-course objectives have been stated to next prepare the final examination. Then, an inspection of the two allows the designer to ask: "Are these the objectives I really want for the course? Is this the way to assess learners' performance in the course?" The reader will understand the many implications of this last question after seeing Chapters 5 and 6.

Substitutes for Examinations. The nature of the "culminating activity" for a course might take many forms: a written test; performance of a demonstration or a simulated or "real-life" activity; or producing a product, such as a work of art or a composition, or the student products in Chapters 16 and 17. The product, if a speech, might be evaluated as it is being delivered, or it may be recorded for later evaluation. In the case of the speech, one is essentially evaluating a "process," to be heard as it is executed. In the case of a work of art, the evaluation may be done either as the student performs (process), or, the art work (product) may be evaluated later. In either case, informing the students in advance of the criteria for the evaluation is a good practice. This is often done by providing a "criterion sheet" listing the features of an acceptable product or process, along with "points" or "weights" to be used in scoring. One may also provide a basis for converting scores to grades. Examples of such criterion sheets are found in the "Transition to Chapter 16."

5. Unit Objectives

Unit objectives also may be stated in either behavioral or non-behavioral terms, depending upon the level at which assessments of learner performance are to be made. Some courses may not utilize unit objectives because the structure of the course may be adequately represented by using only end-of-course objectives and a series of specific behavioral objectives.

The use or non-use of unit objectives may also depend upon how large a "chunk" of instruction is being planned. Planning of the instruction for an entire year might be facilitated by using unit objectives, whereas planning for a four-week session may not be facilitated by use of unit objectives.

Often it is convenient to list unit objectives because they imply the importance of the sequencing of the units: unit 1 may be an information unit, while subsequent units may require intellectual skills and cognitive strategies. There would thus be transfer of learning from one unit to another.

In the case of a course composed entirely of information objectives, the purpose served by unit objectives is simply to provide an outline of the total set of information objectives. For example:

Course Objective: Asian Cultures

Unit 1:	Unit 2:	Unit 3:
Japan	Korea	China

In such a course, the specific objectives under each unit could require the learner to state specified information about different aspects of the culture of each of the three countries, such as: education, religion, government.

Note in the above example that the course and unit

objectives are in the form of "topics" (non-behavioral form), while the specific objectives employ the verb "state," which is a specified behavior in which the verb itself implies information objectives rather than intellectual skill objectives.

It is also apparent that the course in Asian Culture could have been organized in other ways, having unit objectives in education, religion, and government, under which specific objectives would then relate to the three countries. The basis for a decision between the two ways of organizing the course would appear to hinge upon the preference of the designer as to whether *countries* or *institutions* are to be the focal points for the instruction. In either way of organizing the course, *sequence* is not psychologically a crucial question, since one sequence will probably involve no more transfer or facilitation from objective to objective or unit to unit than would another sequence. The designer might have *logical* reasons for preferring one sequence over the other, but there appear to be no psychological reasons for such preferences.

Another issue that often arises is whether the units of instruction should be arranged in the same sequence in which a real-life activity is performed. For example, in driver education one might teach traffic laws before teaching the operation of the vehicle, while in the actual performance of driving, one first unlocks the door, then takes the driver's seat, then inserts the key into the ignition switch, and then drives according to traffic laws. In another example, one might teach addition and subtraction before teaching how to balance a bank account. In both examples, there are sets of information and skills (both intellectual and motor) to be learned before the learner performs the operation in the sequence used by already skilled persons in real life.

In the opposite case, one might teach ice skating roughly in the order that the skill is performed (putting on the skates, getting into motion, etc.), with the exception of teaching safety precautions first.

As a skill progresses, of course, the level of attention to details changes drastically. A skill that seems to be a simple motor chain when performed by the experienced expert (threading film in a motion picture projector, for example), requires, for *learning*, the prior mastery of discriminations, concepts, and very likely verbal chains to support the motor chain. While learning to thread a projector may seem to be a motor skill because the expert does it faster than does the beginning journeyman, actually the initial learning does not consist of moving the hands faster and with more precision, but rather in *knowing what to do* with the hands.

A final consideration in deciding how to state unit objectives hinges upon communicating with team members. When a designer is to develop and teach a course alone as a one-person effort, it may be convenient to simply state unit objectives as "topics," as in the example of the Asian Culture course. But if a number of people are to operate as a team, the behavioral form of statement is more specific and less subject to differing interpretations as to the intent. The unambiguous nature of behavioral statements can avoid lost motion both in designing the instruction and in design of measures for assessment of achievement by the learners.

A general rule thus emerges: if learner performance is to be measured at the level of unit objectives, or if a team design effort is involved, or if the course structure is complex, then the great care needed to state behavioral unit objectives is probably worthwhile. In the opposite circumstances, using topics rather than behavioral statements may be sufficient to suggest the nature of the unit objectives, and to imply the relationship among the units.

6. Specific Behavioral Objectives

The five-component method of writing behavioral objectives (Chapter 3) may be applied for any or all of the six levels discussed here. Once one has acquired the skill of writing objectives in this form, little difficulty should be encountered in applying the skill to all six levels, when needed. Whether objectives are written in behavioral or other terms at various levels, one should be able to justify the more detailed objectives on the grounds that they support, or are a necessary part of, objectives at a higher (more general) level. For this reason, the designer must have the ability to *order* objectives from general to specific, with no "reversals" of this relationship among the various levels of objectives.

Because of the above, the author, in stating course requirements for a design course, includes this criterion for evaluating students' work: "Is there an orderly progression in complexity

from specific, to unit, to course objectives?" A second requirement, consistent with this Chapter, is: "Are objectives stated in
the five-component form for at least the level(s) at which
performance is to be assessed?" Some students find that it clarifies
their own thinking about the course to state all six levels in
behavioral form. Others describe unit objectives as topics, and
specific objectives in behavioral form. Still others, planning to
assess performance at the unit-objective level, nevertheless state
specific objectives also in behavioral form, especially for intellectual skills.

Drawing Instructional Maps

As one way to demonstrate how objectives in various
domains of learning interact with each other in reaching the final
outcomes of the course, a format called "instructional maps" has
been developed by various authors. Such a map shows the teaching
sequence and the interactions for specific behavioral objectives in
the domains of information, intellectual skills, attitudes, cognitive
strategies, and motor skills. Such maps may stop at *level 6*,
showing relations among specific behavioral objectives, or they
may include "enabling objectives" within a single objective, as
discussed in Chapter 5.

Examples of instructional maps are presented in Figures 2
and 3 in Chapter 13. Figure 2 shows how a course objective is
broken down into unit objectives, and Figure 3 shows how a unit
objective is broken down into specific behavioral objectives.
Figure 4 of Chapter 13 is a "first approximation" of the next step
in analysis, analyzing each objective into its component parts,
which is discussed more thoroughly in Chapter 5.

Research in Organization of Courses

This Chapter does not include a summary of research related
to the topic, as is the case for some Chapters of this book. The six
levels of stating goals and objectives, as outlined in this Chapter,
are based mostly upon the author's experience in designing courses

and in helping students with their designs.

Many of the issues discussed in this Chapter have to do with the sequencing of the instruction for units and for specific objectives. Unfortunately, most of the research on sequencing of instruction has dealt with sequencing at a smaller "size of chunk," such as frames within a programmed instruction unit requiring only a few minutes or hours of instruction rather than days or months. However, the research that was known to the author was presented in an earlier monograph (Briggs, 1968).

The reader may find sources in the area of curriculum development, but again, due to the magnitude of the task, curriculum builders must depend more on experience and judgment of experts than upon highly controlled research designs.

The reader may find other examples of course organization in Briggs (1972), in addition to the examples in this book in Chapters 16 and 17.

Summary

In this Chapter, the organization of a course is treated as a matter of identifying increasingly smaller objectives to support the needs and goals previously stated for a new course design. A "six-layer" method of organizing an entire course is outlined, with the suggestion that briefer courses would require fewer layers of objectives.

It was recommended, as a minimum, that objectives be stated in behavioral terms for those levels of objectives at which assessments of learner performance are to be made.

While designers often first outline a course in terms of topics, representing the "structure of the discipline" as seen by experts, ultimately the course should be organized as the *learner* will encounter it. The advantage of behavioral objectives, at all levels, is the focus on *learner performance*, not teacher performance.

Instructional maps were presented as one format for showing the organization of the objectives, once they are decided upon.

Little research could be cited to aid the designer, so experience in course design was the primary basis for this Chapter.

References

Briggs, L.J. *Sequencing of Instruction in Relation to Hierarchies of Competence*. Pittsburgh: American Institutes for Research, 1968.

Briggs, L.J. *Handbook of Procedures for the Design of Instruction*. Pittsburgh: American Institutes for Research, 1970.

Briggs, L.J. *Student's Guide to Handbook of Procedures for the Design of Instruction*. Pittsburgh: American Institutes for Research, 1972.

Briggs, L.J. *An Overview of Instructional Systems Design*. Tallahassee: Florida State University, 1975 (mimeo).

Gagné, R.M., and Briggs, L.J. *Principles of Instructional Design*. New York: Holt, Rinehart, and Winston, 1974.

Piaget, J. *Piaget's Theory*. In P.H. Hussen (Ed.), *Carmichael's Manual of Child Psychology*, Vol. 1. New York: John Wiley, 1970.

Scriven, M. In Talmage, H. (Ed.), *Systems of Individualized Education*. Berkeley: McCutchan Publishing Corp., 1975.

Transition to Chapter 5

At the conclusion of the work described in Chapter 4, you have stated general goals for your course and used those to derive objectives which are arranged (usually) into groups, each group supporting a course or unit objective.

Just as you justify the need for each specific objective in terms of facilitating the accomplishment of a larger unit objective, you will later on justify the content of instructional materials as needed to enable the learner to master the objective (Chapter 8 and 9). By this means, "pet" content and objectives are denied admission to the course unless these supporting relationships can be demonstrated. This prevents "dead wood" (irrelevant and unnecessary material or objectives) from creeping into the course.

But there is another step between the objective and the design of supporting instructional material and learner activity. That step is the analysis of each objective into its component parts, as described in Chapter 5.

Chapter 5

Analysis of Objectives

Robert M. Gagné
Florida State University

Once the objectives of a unit or course of study have been defined (Chapters 3 and 4), the design of a plan for instruction is on firm ground. The aims of the instruction (the "what" to teach), however large or small, are at that point unambiguously determined. In proceeding with systematic instructional design, the next major stage to be completed is to determine the *means* of instruction, the "how" to teach. In order to do this properly, however, some further analysis must be accomplished.

As applied to the activities of instructional design, the analysis of objectives is sometimes called *task analysis*. It has three separate components. These are:

1. *Information processing analysis* of the human performance, to reveal its sequence of mental operations;

2. *Task classification*, categorizing the type of learning outcome represented by the task (or a collection of tasks), as a means of identifying necessary conditions for learning; and

3. *Learning task analysis* of the performance and of its mental operations, to reveal the prerequisities of learning and desirable sequencing of learning events.

The first kind of analysis, information-processing analysis, is not always conducted, because it is not always necessary. However, when it is done, it constitutes a prior step to the accomplishment of the third type, learning task analysis. The second and third component activities of analysis yield information of specific usefulness in instructional design. Task classification, for example, results in identification of the external and internal conditions of the learner which are to be taken into account in designing instruction. Learning task analysis yields more specific information about the internal states of the learner's memory, resulting from prior learning, which contribute to the learning of the new capability reflected in the desired performance.

These three primary procedures of analysis will be described in the order previously listed. It is important for the reader to bear in mind, however, that they all fit together to provide the needed conceptualization for instructional design. These activities are not alternative approaches to task analysis; rather, they are simply parts of a total procedure. Although they are described separately in the following sections, later portions of the Chapter will attempt to show how they relate to each other.

Information-Processing Analysis

Assuming that an accurate description of the expected human performance in the form of an instructional objective is at hand, it may be found desirable to make an analysis of this performance for the purpose of revealing the *mental operations* involved. Such an analysis is not always necessary, but may be particularly useful in identifying the "hidden steps" required for a complex performance. For example, the performance of reading aloud a printed word may be described by the objective: "Given a printed word familiar in the oral vocabulary, the student identifies the word by saying it aloud." However, it may readily be realized that this performance, as a whole, involves the following steps:

(1) Registers the
      printed word

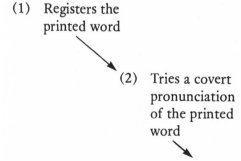

        (2) Tries a covert
              pronunciation
              of the printed
              word

(3) Matches sound
of printed word
with word
available in oral
vocabulary

(4) Overtly
pronounces
printed word

The importance of this kind of analysis is shown by the fact that steps (2) and (3) represent capabilities that must have been previously learned, and therefore must be subject to further analysis of the "learning task analysis" variety. For example, step (2) implies that the human performer in this case already has available to him the skills required for "trying a covert pronunciation of the word." Also, step (3) implies that the performer already "knows" the particular word, or has it in his listening vocabulary. The statement of the objective itself does not convey these mental operations.

The need for an information-processing type of analysis may be equally demanding when the performance consists of *overt* actions rather than covert mental operations. For example, consider the following objective: "Given two-place numbers, vertically arranged, and the oral direction to subtract, applies rules to obtain the difference." One of the commonly used algorithms for subtraction requires the following steps, which may be overtly carried out:

(1) Identifies top
number in
ones column
as smaller
than bottom
number

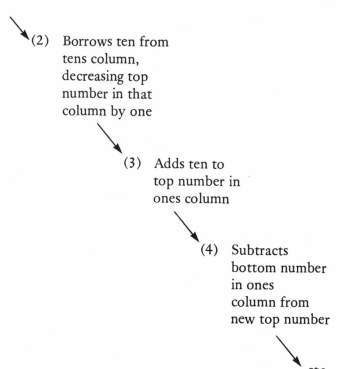

(2) Borrows ten from
     tens column,
     decreasing top
     number in that
     column by one

(3) Adds ten to
     top number in
     ones column

(4) Subtracts
     bottom number
     in ones
     column from
     new top number

                                                        etc.

Here again, whether each of these steps is carried out overtly or covertly, they represent unitary performances requiring previously learned capabilities (i.e., prerequisites). Each individual step implies something that the learner must have available in his memory as a result of prior learning, if he is to learn to subtract two-place numbers. Thus, each overt step indicates the need for the further analysis, to be described as "learning task analysis."

When single instructional objectives are analyzed in this way, it is in recognition of their characteristics as *procedures*. That is to say, the nature of the learned capability that makes possible the desired performance is a *procedural rule* (Gagné, 1977). Many skills, both intellectual and motor, have this character, although not all do. The complex rule for long division, as analyzed by Gilbert (1962), is an interesting example. A number of examples of elementary mathematics tasks have been analyzed into procedural steps by Resnick, Wang, and Kaplan (1973). As for tasks with motor components, the part-skills involved in such performances as threading a needle, tying a shoelace, or parallel parking an automobile provide illustrations of components that may readily be revealed by an information-processing analysis.

How Is the Analysis Done?

It would appear that a particular mental set is necessary in order for a person to make an information-processing analysis. First, he must adopt the point of view that complex human performances can indeed be conceived as being composed of simpler parts. To analyze them in this way is not to imply that they are any less intricate as instances of human functioning. Such an analysis, when finished, will still fail to reveal the finely tuned structure of a complicated human act. Nevertheless, it is reasonable to think that these "parts" of the act are genuine components. Uncovering them has a distinct usefulness in revealing some of the principal requirements for learning.

When the steps of an information-processing analysis are overt ones, they may be identified by direct observation of other people's performances. Such is the case, for example, with procedures requiring motor performances like printing a letter or parking a car. It is usually helpful, too, to observe one's own performance in such instances—descriptions of other people's behavior are sometimes too crude to reveal all of the essential steps that make up a complex procedure.

Performances that partake of intellectual skills often include steps of which the individual is not conscious. Sometimes, these may be made conscious by attending to them, and this kind of examination of one's own behavior can reveal steps of information processing that otherwise would remain hidden. An example of such a step is *rehearsal* of verbal material that one is trying to remember. Rehearsal may often be done covertly, and without conscious attention; it may also be attended to and done deliberately. It is, then, a step of information processing which may be revealed by examining one's own behavior, and which is considered by some learning theories as an essential component of remembering (Atkinson and Shiffrin, 1968).

Some aspects of information processing, however, may be truly *unconscious*, in the sense that they cannot be revealed by attending to one's own behavior (Mandler, 1975). How can these be discovered? A commonly employed approach is to infer what kinds of *simple* processes would need to be used to perform the act, as though it were being done by a computer. This is the method often employed by learning theorists who attempt to represent the processes of learning and memory (cf. Anderson and Bower, 1973; Tulving and Donaldson, 1972). When this method is used, the individual processing steps have the status of hypotheses, which are then often subjected to intensive empirical investigation. Or, the steps which have been inferred by means of a computer analogy may be compared with protocols of human performers who have been asked to "think out loud" while solving problems (Newell and Simon, 1972).

Inferential analysis of steps in information processing, how-ever, may be accomplished without intricate knowledge of computer processing. The primary reason why this kind of analogy works well is that computer operations are fundamentally simple ones. The best rule for information-processing analysis appears to be: Carry the analysis to the point at which you are convinced the operations are simple. Mental operations like identity matching (discrimination), matching with a category, separating, combining, moving right, left, up, and down, or doing something before or after, are all simple operations, and there are many others. Some examples in the following section illustrate the convincing clarification of complex performances which can result from their analysis into simple components.

Representation as Flowcharts

Analysis of the information-processing variety are often represented as flowcharts (Merrill, 1971). These are designed to display (1) *inputs* to the performance (such as objects or symbols), (2) *actions* or mental operations to be undertaken, and (3) *decisions* which lead to alternative actions or action sequences. The whole chart exhibits the *sequence* of such events, including the alternative sequences of actions. The final action in the sequence is usually considered the *output* or this may be indicated as a product of this final action. The different components of the flowchart are usually represented by different shapes of boxes, often as follows:

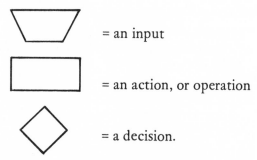

= an input

= an action, or operation

= a decision.

Thus, the performance of subtraction of two-place whole numbers may be represented in flowchart form as in Figure 1. The input, represented as a trapezoidal box, is the printed set of numbers arranged vertically with a minus sign. Decisions, represented by diamond-shaped boxes, reflect categorization of the numbers as larger and smaller, leading to alternative decisions. The remaining rectangular boxes display the operations of borrowing, simple subtracting, and recording in proper columns. Notice that the entries in the diamond boxes imply *simple* operations that the learner is expected to know how to do. Of course, as will be seen later, he may know how to do them because he has previously *learned* how.

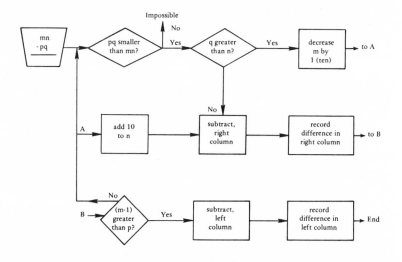

Figure 1. *An information-processing analysis of the subtraction of two-place numbers.*

An excellent example of an information-process analysis applicable to the decoding of reading material has been provided by Resnick and Beck (1976). This is reproduced in Figure 2.

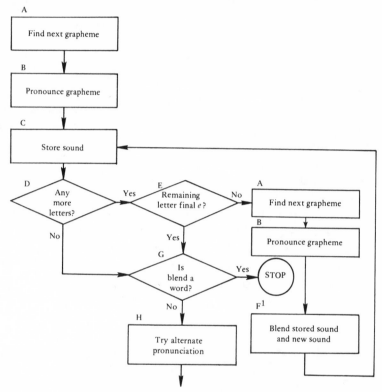

Figure 2.   *An information-processing analysis of a decoding skill.
(From Resnick, L.B., and Beck, I.L. Designing Instruction in Reading: Interaction of Theory and Practice. In
J.T. Guthrie (Ed.),* **Aspects of Reading Acquisition.**
*Baltimore: The Johns Hopkins University Press, 1976.
By permission of the copyright owner, The Johns
Hopkins University Press).*

It will be realized, then, that information-processing analysis of human tasks is often a valuable undertaking. By this means, complex human performances can be seen as being made up of separate steps connected in a sequence that has alternative sub-sequences within it. The individual steps revealed by such an analysis are sometimes overt actions, and sometimes covert mental operations. In either case, the aim of the analysis is to reduce a complex kind of behavior to components which are simple. These components, in turn, may be simple because they are inherently so (as in matching identities), or because they have been previously learned and perhaps practiced many times.

The usefulness of an information-processing analysis is seen in two kinds of outcomes. First, such an analysis reveals the simpler entities that must be learned if they are going to be put together to make up a more complex performance. These previous learnings need to be planned in an instructional design. Second, the sequence of activities (as revealed by the flowchart, for example) specifies the nature of the total complex performance which must be learned. If there are procedural steps in the performance, these must be accurately represented in the performance tested as the outcome of a designed program of instruction.

Task Classification

Beginning with well-defined instructional objectives, one may undertake to *classify* the tasks they describe, either before or after doing an information-processing analysis. The order in which these two parts of task analysis are done does not matter. They are quite different procedures. The outcomes of either or both serve as inputs to the kind of analysis called learning task analysis (to be described in the next section).

It is apparent that human performances can be classified in many different ways. For example, one dimension of task variation is obviously the *stimulus*—whether visual, auditory, tactile, kinesthetic, or some combination of these. Further, the stimulus is patterned in various ways—it may consist of single points of light, a sinusoidal sound wave of particular frequency, or the complex patterns provided by pictures, printed text, or spoken speech. To classify tasks on the basis of such an enormous variety of stimulus variations would be a very large undertaking, and one which would scarcely serve a useful purpose for the understanding of what must be learned. Similar considerations apply to *responses*. Here again, the human individual can respond in a great variety of ways—with his hands, his feet, his head, his voice box. Furthermore, many responses are *functionally equivalent* for human performances; if we expect a learner to identify a printed *e*, we accept as equivalent a response which points to the *e*, underlines the *e* with a pencil, or rubs out the *e* with an eraser. The responses are quite different, yet we think of "identifying an *e*" as a common description of the performance. That is, several action verbs may be suitable for inferring that the capability verb in an objective has been satisfied in the performance.

Stimuli and responses, then, are much too fine-grained dimensions of human tasks to be used for purposes of classifying "what is learned." We must look instead for more general kinds of entities. We find these by asking, regardless of what specific stimuli and responses are involved, *what different kinds of mental processing may be established by learning?* This question makes us seek a classification of human performances differing from each other in terms of the kind of *encoding* that takes place in learning, the kind of *memorial organization* that such performances must have (so far as we know this), and the kind of *retrieval process* that must be required to recall them so that they can be exhibited (or used). This type of learned entity is what is called a *capability* by Gagné and Briggs (1974). The retained memorial organization that results from learning provides the learner with a capability of performing in particular ways, and in ways whose generic characteristics can be distinguished.

A number of different ways of classifying human tasks as learned capabilities have been proposed. Two of the best known will be mentioned here.

The Taxonomy of Bloom and His Associates

Three general categories of learned capabilities have been proposed by Bloom and his co-workers (Bloom, *et al.*, 1956; Krathwohl, Bloom, and Masia, 1964; Bloom, Hastings, and Madaus, 1971). These are called the *cognitive domain*, the *affective domain*, and the *psychomotor domain*. As the phrase implies, the cognitive domain includes broadly the capabilities that comprise knowing; that is, they make possible appropriate performances to stimuli that are processed symbolically by the learner. Usually, this means that the stimuli themselves are symbols: words, sentences, numbers, and number statements. The affective domain encompasses the kinds of learned states that affect interests, attitudes, likes and dislikes, and commitment to courses of action. The word "affective" implies that some feeling or emotional tone is expressed by learner performances in this domain. Psychomotor behavior refers to the class of performances that are expressed as skilled muscular movements forming a pattern which has some purposeful outcome.

Since these are broad domains composed of many kinds of performances, it is reasonable that they should be divided into further sub-categories. Brief definitions of the subcategories of the cognitive and affective domains may be described as follows:

- *Cognitive Domain*

  Knowledge—recalling specifics and universals, methods, patterns, etc.

  Comprehension—knowing what is communicated by making use of the idea.

  Application—using abstractions in particular and concrete situations.

  Analysis—breaking down a communication into its parts so that the relations among them are made explicit.

  Synthesis—putting together elements and parts so as to form a whole.

  Evaluation—judgments about the value of material and methods for given purposes.

- *Affective Domain*

  Receiving—willingness to receive or attend to stimuli.

  Responding—responding to stimuli, going beyond mere reception.

  Valuing—responding in a way that indicates an object, phenomenon, or behavior has worth.

  Organization—responding which indicates values organized into a system, with establishment of dominant and pervasive values.

  Characterization by a value or value complex—behavior indicating an internally consistent value system, controlled by pervasive generalized tendencies, which may be integrated into a total philosophy.

Performances made possible by programs of instruction can be categorized into these subordinate categories with a fair degree of accuracy and consistency. For purposes of designing tests, the many additional subcategories of this taxonomic system (as described in the references) can be employed by test designers to characterize the kinds of responding intended. Many examples applicable to a variety of school subjects are described by Bloom, Hastings, and Madaus (1971).

The Taxonomy of Gagné

As described in several publications (Gagné, 1972; Gagné, 1976; Gagné and Briggs, 1974), the system of task classification proposed by Gagné comprises the five categories of *verbal information, intellectual skill, cognitive strategy, attitude,* and *motor skill.* The last two of these categories, attitude and motor skill, correspond to Bloom's affective and psychomotor domains. Gagné's proposal is that the "cognitive domain" requires the three major categories of verbal information, intellectual skill, and cognitive strategy. As a whole, the five categories of this classification system have been deliberately derived from a consideration of "what is learned," in the sense of different types of learned memorial organizations. The basic postulate of this system is that the mental processing required for learning and retention of verbal information is demonstrably different from the mental processing required for the learning and retention of intellectual skills; and that similar differences exist among all five categories of learned capabilities. It may be said that the comparable postulate of Bloom's system is that his categories differ in their measurement requirements, that is, in what is required to test the various human performances. Thus, these two systems have different bases for their derivation. While many parallels between them can be pointed out, there is at least an equal number of incompatibilities.

Brief definitions of Gagné's categories of human capabilities may be given as follows. In the case of intellectual skills, important subcategories are also defined.

- *Verbal Information*—stating propositions (names, facts, connected sentences) in terms of their meaning.
- *Intellectual Skill*—demonstrating the application of

regular symbolic relationships to specific instances.

Rule—demonstrating the application of a regular relation between classes of objects.

Defined concept—classifying instances in accordance with a definition (i.e., a definitional rule).

Concrete concept—identifying instances of a class of objects having common physical features.

Discrimination—distinguishing one object or object quality from another.

- *Cognitive Strategy*—controlling or modifying the learner's internal processes of learning and thinking.

- *Attitude*—choosing a course of personal action towards some object, person, or event.

- *Motor Skill*—executing muscular movements coordinated to the achievement of some goal or product, and characterized by smoothness and precise timing.

The tabulation of categories should be read somewhat as follows: We know that a learner has acquired the kind of capability called *verbal information* when he can "state the propositions he has been taught in terms of their meaning." We know that a learner has acquired an *attitude* when he "chooses a (designated) course of personal action towards some (designated) object, person, or event." Similar readings apply to each of the other categories.

In the remainder of this Chapter, we shall employ Gagné's categories in further exposition of task analysis procedures. Their advantages are at least these: (1) simplicity (fewer subcategories); (2) clear relation to objectives (see Gagné and Briggs, 1974, Chapter 5); and (3) direct relevance to the major categories of mental processing employed by contemporary learning theories and related learning research (see Gagné, 1976). Examples which illustrate the meaning of each category are contained in Table 1, reproduced from Gagné (1974). The reader may wish to try his hand at task classification of the following performances, which are stated deliberately in somewhat imprecise form:

1. Skating a figure eight
2. Ordering "i" and "e" in spelling the word "reprieve"

Table 1

Gagné's Categories of Learning Outcomes,
with Examples of Each*

Learning Outcome	Example of Human Performance Made Possible by the Capability
Verbal Information	Stating the provisions of the First Amendment to the U.S. Constitution
Intellectual Skill	Showing how to do the following:
Discrimination	Distinguishing printed b's from d's
Concrete Concept	Identifying the spatial relation "below"
Defined Concept	Classifying a "city" by using a definition
Rule	Demonstrating that water changes state at 100° C.
Higher-Order Rule	Generating a rule for predicting rainfall, given conditions of location and terrain
Cognitive Strategy	Originating a novel plan for disposing of fallen leaves
Attitude	Choosing swimming as a preferred exercise
Motor Skill	Executing the performance of planing the edge of a board

*From Table 3.1, Gagné, R.M., *Essentials of Learning for Instruction*. Hinsdale, Ill.: Dryden Press, 1974. Reprinted by permission of the copyright owner, Holt, Rinehart, and Winston.

3. Mental rehearsal of a list of words to be remembered
4. Knowing how to show a child what "longitude" is
5. Crossing the street to avoid meeting someone
6. Telling someone the height of Mt. McKinley.

The Results of Task Classification

The classification of tasks into the categories of verbal information, cognitive strategy, attitude, motor skill, and intellectual skill (with its subordinate categories, when appropriate) has the effect of introducing considerable clarification into the procedures of instructional design. First, it reduces the number of items with which one must deal. It is not uncommon for a single course, for example, to have as many as a hundred objectives. While instructional planning is possible for each single objective, great economy of thought is achieved by classifying a total set into five categories.

Each of the five categories of objectives represents a type of capability to be learned. Each capability, in turn, carries specific implications regarding what must be done to insure its efficient learning, as will be shown in subsequent chapters. Irrespective of the specific content of the objective (defined primarily by the "Situation" part of the objective statement), rules can be applied to each category which identify those external conditions that will best support the internal processes of learning (Gagné, 1976). One kind of supportive learning condition is itself an "internal" one. It consists of the already existing contents of memory, that have been established by prior learning. The consideration of this condition brings us to the third procedure of task analysis.

Learning Task Analysis

A learning task analysis is so called because it pertains both to the present conditions for learning and to the prior effects of learning. The present condition to be revealed by the analysis of any particular objective is *what must be recalled* (or made accessible to working memory). And what can be recalled must have been stored as a part of long-term memory, in other words, as a result of *previous learning*. The key word, then, to express the focus of learning task analysis is *prerequisites*.

The basic idea of prerequisites is simple enough. When a young student undertakes to learn how to write an expository sentence, he must be able to recall, as prerequisites, some words to place in the sentence. Another obvious prerequisite that must be possessed is a set of rules for placing differing types of words in a proper order, so that an "agent" word comes first, followed by an "action" word, and this in turn followed (as one alternative) by an "object" word. It is not difficult to realize, either, that this set of syntactic rules themselves have prerequisites—the identification of words as belonging to the classes "agent," "action," and "object." Other examples occur in mathematics: sums of single-place numbers are prerequisite to the adding of multiple-place numbers; multiplying numbers is prerequisite to long division.

Essential and Supportive Prerequisites

These familiar examples illustrate a type of prerequisite which is *essential* to the new capability being learned. That is to say, the performance of multiplying multi-place numbers requires the prerequisite of adding multi-place numbers because the latter is actually incorporated in it. It is not possible to possess the capability of "multiplying multi-place numbers" without at the same time possessing the more elementary capability of "adding multi-place numbers." (This statement, of course, assumes that typical procedures of manual computation make up the performance called "multiplying.") This is the meaning of an *essential prerequisite*, about which more will be said later.

It is possible, however, to encompass another meaning in the word prerequisite, by referring to a recalled entity which, while not essential, may aid the new learning by making it easier or faster (Gagné, 1977, Chapter 11). Such a prerequisite is *supportive* of learning. Again, simple examples may be used to illustrate this class of prerequisite. A positive *attitude* towards communicating precise meanings to others may aid the learning of sentence construction. A similar positive attitude towards "checking" arithmetic computations may aid the learning of computational procedures by helping the learner to avoid gross errors. If the learner is engaged in acquiring the informational content of a passage of printed text, a previously acquired *cognitive strategy* of connecting words with visual images may speed up the learning. This kind of prerequisite helps, or supports, the new learning. It is not *essential*, however, because it is not actually incorporated into the entity that is learned. (See the curriculum maps in Figures 2 and 3 of Chapter 13 for other examples.)

Both essential and supportive prerequisites may be identified for each category of learned capability. They are different, however, for each type; this is one of the principal reasons why task classification must precede a learning task analysis. In the following sections, our discussion of prerequisites for each type of learned capability begins with *essential* prerequisites, and goes on to mention other prerequisites which may be supportive of learning, although not essential.

Prerequisites for the learning of intellectual skills. Intellectual skills which are the objectives of a course of study or other program of instruction can usually be analyzed to reveal simpler skills which compose them, and which therefore may be classed as essential prerequisites. To illustrate how this is done, we choose the skill of *subtracting whole numbers.* Assume that subtraction is represented by vertically arranged sets of numbers like the following:

(a)	473	(b)	2132	(c)	953	(d)	7204
	-342		-1715		-676		-5168

Assume also that the rules to be learned in these computations involve "borrowing" (which is, of course, only one of several possible ways of doing subtraction). The four examples illustrate four *prerequisite rules* which must be learned if the total skill of subtracting whole numbers is to be acquired. Example (a) illustrates the skill "subtracting one-place numbers in successive columns, without borrowing," a relatively simple rule which is also involved in each of the other examples. Example (b) illustrates a skill which may be described as "subtracting when several borrowings are required, in non-adjacent columns." In this particular case, borrowing occurs twice in non-adjacent columns; obviously, it might occur additionally if larger numbers were to be subtracted. Example (c) illustrates the important sub-skill of "successive borrowing in adjacent columns." Here borrowing must be done in the first column on the right, so that 6 can be subtracted from 13, and again in the next column, so that 7 can be subtracted from 14. Example (d) shows still another subskill, subtracting when borrowing must be done across zero, or "double borrowing."

Each of these instances, then, indicates the kinds of rule-governed procedures that may have to be employed in any particular example of subtraction of whole numbers. By analyzing what operations are required, it has been possible to identify *four prerequisite skills*. These are essential prerequisites in the sense that they are actually incorporated into the total intellectual skill called *subtracting whole numbers*.

Hierarchies of Intellectual Skills

An interesting and important additional point to be made about learning task analysis is this: *The prerequisites of an intellectual skill also have prerequisites*. In other words, the immediately subordinate (and essential) skills of a given skill can themselves be further analyzed. In the case of whole-number subtraction, for instance, the three different skills reflected in examples (2), (3), and (4) obviously all require an even simpler skill, which may be described as "subtracting when a single borrowing is required, in any column." This, then, is a prerequisite to these other more complex subskills.

When the process of learning task analysis is carried out at successive levels of complexity, the result is what is called a *learning hierarchy*. Such a hierarchy for whole-number subtraction is represented in Figure 3. Notice that the process of analysis reveals increasingly simpler skills as it is continued from the top down. Each of these skills is represented in a box in which an abbreviated statement of an objective appears. As one continues to uncover successive prerequisites, it is evident that what is being represented is rules of diminished complexity (for example, rule VII vs. rule V), and subordinate skills which are actually concepts (VI, for example, might be stated as "identifying subtractable number pairs").

Learning task anlaysis is carried out by asking the question of any given intellectual skill: "What simpler skill(s) would a learner have to possess in order to learn skill X, the absence of which

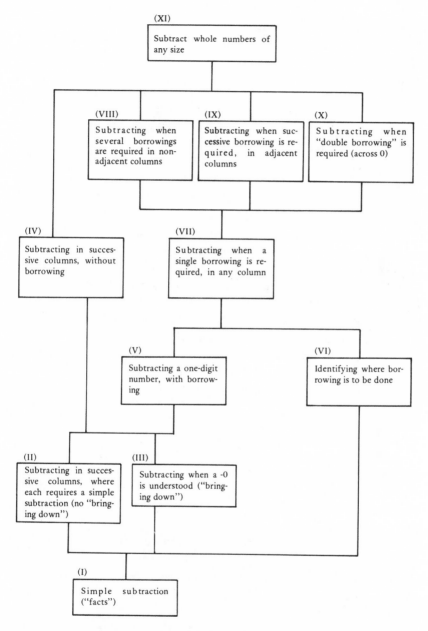

Figure 3. *A learning hierarchy for subtraction of whole numbers. (From Gagné, R.M., and Briggs, L.J. **Principles of Instructional Design**. New York: Holt, Rinehart, and Winston, 1974. By permission of the copyright owner, Holt, Rinehart, and Winston.)*

would make it impossible for him to learn skill X?" That is to say, in conducting such an analysis, one seeks to identify *essential* prerequisities, those subordinate skills which are actually incorporated into the skill to be learned (Gagné, 1977). How far is the process of learning task analysis continued—how simple must the skills be at the "bottom" of the hierarchy? Theoretically, the process of analysis might be continued to arrive at the simplest possible memorial entities. However, the practical limit is provided by the level of "entry skill" one either assumes or knows to be characteristic of the learners for whom instruction is being designed. In the hierarchy for subtraction, Figure 3, the analysis is carried to the point of "simple subtraction." In other words, for the instructional purpose intended, it is assumed that students already know how to subtract single-place numbers.

Another example of a learning hierarchy is shown in Figure 4. In this case, the target skill in the top box is one of the skills· involved in beginning reading; thus, it is itself a subordinate skill in a more elaborate learning hierarchy. Prerequisites for this target skill are indicated in the second row of the hierarchy, and those for one of these subordinate skills (the most interesting one) in a third row. The reader may imagine himself as a five-year-old, having to learn these subordinate skills. What is it that he already must know how to do, if he is going to learn them? Here is a hint pertaining to the analysis of subskill IV: Some syllables (like "ing") may be familiar because they occur frequently; others ("tent" is a possibility) may have to be "decoded" by the blending and combining of letters.

Supportive Prerequisites for Intellectual Skills

Besides the essential prerequisites which can be represented as learning hierarchies, other previously learned memorial entities may help the learning of an intellectual skill. It is not uncommon, for example, for some specific kinds of verbal information to be useful when one is learning a new intellectual skill. If one is learning concepts of wildflower types, the names of the flowers themselves, as well as the names of plant parts, may be helpful for learning (for example, when learning is done from a wildflower handbook). Or, if one is learning a rule of periodic motion, names

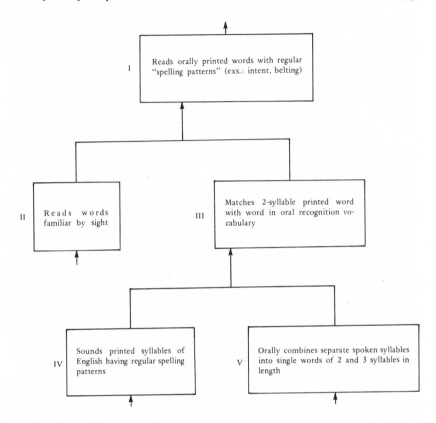

Figure 4. An uncompleted learning hierarchy for one of the skills of beginning reading.

of objects or object-qualities such as "pendulum" and "period" may be involved as common labels for the objects and relationships contained in an example. Furthermore, as has frequently been observed (Gagné, 1977), verbal statements of rules very often function as cues for the learning of rules, and thus may constitute supportive prerequisites to such learning. It is not at all unusual, then, to find that concept or rule learning is aided by prior learning of some relevant kinds of verbal information. But such an observation should by no means lead to the confusion of supportive prerequisites with essential prerequisites.

As in the case of other kinds of learning outcomes, intellectual skill learning may also be supported by cognitive strategies. The learner may have at his command strategies for attending to relevant features of the skill to be learned, strategies for encoding the concept or rule (including visual imagery), strategies for retrieving and applying the rule, among others. Such cognitive strategies, if they are good ones, may speed up the learning, make it more easily memorable, or improve its applicability to new situations. We shall have more to say about the nature of cognitive strategies in a later discussion of *their* prerequisites.

The helpful effect of attitudes in learning has already been mentioned. Of course, a positive attitude toward mathematics will be supportive of the learning of its rules. A strong interest in the classification of birds is likewise helpful in the learning of the necessary concepts of appearance, structure, and living habits.

It may be noted that learning hierarchies for intellectual skill objectives, defined in their strict meaning as in the previous section, include only essential prerequisites, and make no attempt to represent supportive prerequisites. However, as a later step in instructional design, these latter prerequisites may be represented in a kind of "expanded hierarchy," or "instructional map" (cf. Cook and Walbesser, 1973; Chapter 13).

Verbal Information—Prerequisites

The analysis of prerequisites for the learning of verbal information is founded upon a research base that has not yet yielded results as clear-cut as are those for intellectual skills. Nevertheless, some parts of the procedure can be fairly well described.

Essential prerequisites for verbal information. The essential prerequisites for learning verbal information give the impression of being rather far removed from the information itself. Actually, they are mainly some intellectual skills which may have been learned in early years. According to cognitive learning theory (for example, Anderson and Bower, 1973), verbal information is encoded into memorial organizations that represent *propositions*, which have identifiable components such as an agent, an action, an object, and a setting. In order for such encoding to take place, there must be available to the learner some rules of language, which are in effect *syntactic rules*. Thus, it is that the essential prerequisites for acquiring verbal information make up a set of intellectual skills that are usually learned early in life, and are therefore well-practiced skills of language usage.

It is possible, of course, that the simplest form of verbal information—labels, or names—does not get encoded in propositional form, but in some other way. Tulving (1972), for example, suggests that learning single words, or word pairs, may be stored as "episodic memories," in contrast to the "semantic memories" one would expect for propositions ("facts," "generalizations," etc.). If such simple memories are indeed stored as episodes, then syntactic rules would not be considered essential prerequisites.

Supportive prerequisites in information learning. The greatest amount of evidence about prerequisites for information learning pertains to supportive prerequisites. Evidence from a variety of sources indicates that single items of information are most readily learned and retained when they occur in a larger context of meaningful information. This context may be learned immediately before the new "fact" to be acquired, or it may have been learned a long time previously. Ausubel's (1968) theory of meaningful verbal learning proposes that any new idea is learned by being incorporated into a "cognitive structure." The latter is an organized network of meaningfully related concepts and propositions, previously learned and stored in the learner's memory. Contemporary cognitive theories of learning (e.g., Anderson and Bower, 1973; Rumelhart, Lindsay, and Norman, 1972) usually postulate that encoding and storage of new "facts" involves the embedding of the new information into "schemata" which have their origin in previous learning.

It seems fairly clear that the learning of any new piece of information (such as a "fact"), as well as its retention, is aided by the accessibility of related facts, or by an organized meaningful schema of information which has previously been learned. Thus, prior learning of meaningful information is itself supportive of the learning of new information.

Other kinds of supportive prerequisites affect information learning. Attitudes and cognitive strategies operate to support information learning and retention in much the same way as they do in the case of intellectual skill learning. As an example of the latter, "mental rehearsal" of a list of names to be remembered is usually an aid to their retention.

Cognitive Strategies—Prerequisites

Cognitive strategies are internally organized skills by means of which the learner exercises control over his own processes of attending, learning, remembering, and thinking. Because of this function, they are called "control processes" in modern learning theory (Atkinson and Shiffrin, 1968). Although they are considered important constructs of theory, and at least equally important outcomes of schooling (Bruner, 1971), knowledge of how they operate is limited. We shall therefore be able to record little here about their prerequisites.

The capabilities that constitute cognitive strategies are considered by some theorists to be maturationally determined, and to depend (in the "prerequisite" sense) upon progressive development of the human nervous system. This is the view of Piaget (1970), who considers that the development of cognitive strategies (describable as increasingly complex forms of logical thought) takes place in a number of stages extending over a period of eleven or more years from the time of birth. An opposing view, expressed by Gagné (1968, 1977), and perhaps implicitly held by many psychologists, is that the prerequisites of any particular cognitive strategy are a set of interrelated intellectual skills which generalize (that is, exhibit transfer of learning) to an increasingly broad variety of situations. This theory holds that the prerequisite learning of *specific rules* such as those involved in conservation of volume, conservation of weight, conservation of substance, etc., leads to the development of a generalized *strategy* which enables the learner to deal with novel conservation tasks of a variety of sorts.

It may be, then, that certain basic intellectual skills will turn out to be *essential* prerequisites for cognitive strategies. In any case, however, it would appear that intellectual skills involving the processing of symbols are likely at least to be *supportive* prerequisites for such strategies as encoding material to be learned, and for solving problems. For example, the intellectual skill of transposing terms in statements of equality like $a = \frac{pq^2}{2n}$ may well be of help in acquiring cognitive strategies useful in mathematical thinking. Similar considerations apply to verbal information of the organized, meaningful variety. As a supportive prerequisite, a rich store of verbalizable knowledge may be of aid to the learning and refinement of the kinds of cognitive strategies that influence the efficiency of problem-solving.

Attitudes—Prerequisites

Attitudes are mental states that predispose the individual towards some choice of personal action—action which in turn is directed towards some class of persons, things, or events. What memorial entities might be prerequisite to the establishment of such states?

It is possible to conceive of particular attitudes that require certain kinds of prerequisites. For example, if the learner is to acquire a positive attitude towards fairness in lending practices, he must probably have available some intellectual skills which enable him to choose suitable actions towards statements of interest rates. In other words, he needs to be able to compare interest rates when stated per month with those stated per year, or to compare rates compounded annually with those compounded daily. These essential prerequisites will make it possible for him to choose appropriate personal actions; lacking them, an attitude towards lending practices can be only of the most general sort (such as being suspicious of *all* interest rates). Perhaps the important thing to note here is that while intellectual skills may be prerequisites to attitude formation in some instances, they are not themselves the attitude, nor do they insure the learning of an attitude. A person can know all about interest rates, without that being a clue to his attitude towards fair lending practices.

A similar case can be made for information as prerequisite to attitude learning, again in some cases. Choosing a course of personal action may require knowledge about the situation in which such a choice is to be made, if the attitude is to be more than a very general "feeling."

Motor Skills—Prerequisites

A motor skill is a capability that enables the individual to execute some smoothly and precisely timed pattern of muscular movement, such as is seen in swimming, in planing the edge of a board, or in printing a letter. When more than one muscle group is involved, or when different movements are required of the same limbs of the body at different times, motor skills may be analyzed into part-skills. An example of the former sort is swimming the crawl, which has component part-skills pertaining to the movement of the legs, the movement of the arms, and the movement of the head in breathing. These skills may actually be practiced separately; for example, the swimmer in training may practice leg movements alone while floating on a board under the upper part of his trunk. An example of the second sort is provided by an industrial job of parts assembly requiring the operator to reach into four different bins with his right hand, and perform a different assembly movement with the part returned from each bin. These part-skills may also be practiced separately before being put together into a total skill.

When practiced separately, part-skills obviously become essential prerequisites for the total skill. Generally, the evidence is clear that these part-skills behave as one would expect in contributing to the learning of the total skill—that is, they show positive transfer of learning to the learning of the whole skill (Gagné and Foster, 1949). Interestingly enough, though, the evidence is not clear-cut on the question of whether practicing part-skills first before practicing the whole skill has an advantage in efficiency over practicing the total skill from the beginning. The question is more complex than it seems, and a general answer cannot be given at present. Presumably, some particular characteristics of the total skill will turn out to be differentially operative in determining the answer to this problem.

Another "part" of a motor skill may also be learned with the totality of the skill, or may instead be learned as an initial step, thus becoming in effect an essential prerequisite. This part is called the *executive subroutine* (Fitts and Posner, 1967). It is the intellectual skill which governs the sequence of movements in the skill; actually, a procedural rule. The printing of the letter E, for example, involves the steps of (1) drawing a vertical straight line, (2) drawing a horizontal line connecting at the top, (3) drawing a horizontal line connecting at the bottom, and (4) drawing a shorter horizontal line connecting the middle. This subroutine (or one equivalent in outcome) must be learned and followed regardless of how much "motor skill," in the sense of smoothness and timing, may be exhibited. The subroutine may be learned separately (and usually is) early in the practice of printing the letter E. When so learned, it can be conceived as an essential prerequisite for the total skill.

A Summary Table

The various kinds of learned capabilities have various kinds of prerequisites—previously learned entities which are available from the learner's memory at the time new learning begins. Some prerequisites are *essential*, that is, they are incorporated into the newly learned entity. Some are not essential, but nevertheless supportive, in the sense that they may aid the new learning—speed it up, or make it less effortful. Table 2 lists the kinds of prerequisites we have described in preceding sections.

Table 2

Essential and Supportive Prerequisites for
Five Kinds of Learning Outcomes

Type of Learning Outcome	Essential Prerequisites	Supportive Prerequisites
Intellectual Skill	Simpler Component Intellectual Skills (rules, concepts, discriminations)	Attitudes Cognitive Strategies Verbal Information
Verbal Information	Meaningfully Organized Sets of Information	Language Skills Cognitive Strategies Attitudes
Cognitive Strategies	Specific Intellectual Skills (?)	Intellectual Skills Verbal Information Attitudes
Attitudes	Intellectual Skills (sometimes) Verbal Information (sometimes)	Other Attitudes Verbal Information
Motor Skills	Part-skills (sometimes) Procedural Rules (sometimes)	Attitudes

Applications of Task Analysis

The results of "task analysis" are of use in virtually all of the further steps of instructional system design. Here is a summary of what is available when analysis has been completed:

- *Product A.* A list of instructional objectives. This product, of course, was available before analysis began.
- *Product B.* An information-processing diagram indicating the mental operations involved in milestone (target) objectives.
- *Product C.* Classification of each objective into classes of learning outcomes (intellectual skill, verbal information, cognitive strategy, attitude, motor skill).
- *Product D.* A notation of the type of prerequisite required for, or helpful to, the learning appropriate to each listed objective.

Application to assessment of learning outcomes. These products are of use in subsequent design of situations and instruments for assessing the outcomes of learning (Chapter 6). The classification of objectives (Product C) enables the test designer to identify the general type of test to be developed—that is, whether it is to measure the application of rules, the recall of knowledge, the execution of a motor skill, or whatever. The objectives themselves (Product A), of course, furnish the designer with the specific information needed to develop domains of items relevant to specific outcomes. Product B, when available, may be of particular help in the design of tests and testing situations which represent target objectives of a program of instruction.

Application to design of instruction. The results of task analysis are applied to instructional design in terms of plans for instructional materials, delivery procedures, and the selection of media (Chapters 7, 8, and 9). The basic descriptions of objectives (Product A) are essential to these procedures. Conditions established by instructional materials and delivery procedures should be designed to conform with the requirements of each type of learning outcome, as given by Product C. Final tasks, such as problem-solving situations for student practice, can be guided by the identification of mental processes available in Product B.

A particularly important role in instructional design is played by Product D, which identifies prerequisites for the learning of each objective. Further consideration of these prerequisites may lead to the identification of "enabling objectives"—knowledges or skills whose presence was not previously detected, but which may be essential for the attainment of the objectives listed in Product A. Once prerequisites are identified, decisions can also be made about desirable sequences for instruction, perhaps taking the form of "instructional maps" (Chapters 7 and 13).

Summary

1. *Information processing analysis* is carried out to reveal the mental operations involved in a human performance. This kind of analysis is not always undertaken, because the performance may be so relatively simple that no such analysis is necessary. When it is done, it reveals intellectual skills which need to be further analyzed by means of the procedures of "learning task analysis."

2. *Task classification* is undertaken to categorize large numbers of objectives into the classes of (a) intellectual skills, (b) verbal information, (c) cognitive strategies, (d) attitudes, and (e) motor skills. These categories enable the instructional designer to consider the instructional requirements for five categories of outcome, rather than having to deal with scores or even hundreds of individual objectives, and having to make independent decisions about each.

3. *Learning task analysis* is aided by previous findings of information-processing analysis (when this is done), and also by the classification of tasks. This kind of analysis is undertaken to reveal the prerequisites of what must be learned. That is, the results will provide a description of the accessible contents of the learner's memory which are either required or desirable at the time new learning occurs.

4. The results of these three kinds of task analysis have considerable importance for the design of instruction. Besides the instructional objectives with which analysis begins, they yield as products an information processing diagram of operations involved in the tasks to be learned, classification of the objectives, and an indication of essential and supportive prerequisites.

References

Anderson, J.R., and Bower, G.H. *Human Associative Memory*. Washington, D.C.: V.H. Winston & Sons, 1973.

Atkinson, R.C., and Shiffrin, R.M. Human Memory: A Proposed System and Its Control Processes. In K.W. Spence and J.T. Spence (Eds.), *The Psychology of Learning and Motivation*, Vol. 2. New York: Academic Press, 1968.

Ausubel, D.P. *Educational Psychology: A Cognitive View*. New York: Holt, Rinehart, and Winston, 1968.

Bloom, B.S. (Ed.). *Taxonomy of Educational Objectives. Handbook I: Cognitive Domain*. New York: David McKay, 1956.

Bloom, B.S., Hastings, J.T., and Madaus, G.F. *Handbook on Formative and Summative Evaluation of Student Learning*. New York: McGraw-Hill, 1971.

Bruner, J.S. *The Relevance of Education*. New York: Norton, 1971.

Cook, J.M., and Walbesser, H.H. *How to Meet Accountability with Behavioral Objectives and Learning Hierarchies*. College Park: University of Maryland, Bureau of Educational Research and Field Services, 1973.

Fitts, P.M., and Posner, M.J. *Human Performance*. Belmont, Ca: Brooks/Cole, 1967.

Gagné, R.M. Contributions of Learning to Human Development. *Psychological Review*, 1968, *75*, 177-191.

Gagné, R.M. Domains of Learning. *Interchange*, 1972, *3*, 1-8.

Gagné, R.M. *Essentials of Learning for Instruction*. Hinsdale, Ill.: Dryden Press, 1974.

Gagné, R.M. The Learning Basis of Teaching Methods. In N.L. Gage (Ed.), *The Psychology of Teaching Methods*. Seventy-fifth Yearbook, National Society for the Study of Education. Chicago: University of Chicago Press, 1976.

Gagné, R.M. *The Conditions of Learning*. 3rd Ed. New York: Holt, Rinehart, and Winston, 1977.

Gagné, R.M., and Briggs, L.J. *Principles of Instructional Design*. New York: Holt, Rinehart, and Winston, 1974.

Gagné, R.M., and Foster, H. Transfer of Training from Practice on Components in a Motor Skill. *Journal of Experimental Psychology*, 1949, *39*, 47-68.

Gilbert, T.F. Mathetics: The Technology of Education. *Journal of Mathetics*, 1962, *1*, 7-73. Reprinted in Merrill, M.D. *Instructional Design: Readings*. Englewood Cliffs, N.J.: Prentice-Hall, 1971.

Krathwohl, D.R., Bloom, B.S., and Masia, B.B. *Taxonomy of Educational Objectives. Handbook II: Affective Domain*. New York: David McKay, 1964.

Mandler, G. Consciousness: Respectable, Useful, and Probably Necessary. In R.L. Solso (Ed.), *Information Processing and Cognition. The Loyola Symposium*. Hillsdale, N.J.: Erlbaum Associates, 1975.

Merrill, P.F. *Task Analysis: An Information Processing Approach*. Tallahassee: Florida State University, CAI Center, 1971 (Tech. Memo No. 27).

Newell, A., and Simon, H.A. *Human Problem Solving*. Englewood Cliffs, N.J.: Prentice-Hall, 1972.

Piaget, J. *Piaget's Theory*. In P.H. Mussen (Ed.), *Carmichael's Manual of Child Psychology*, Vol. 1. New York: John Wiley, 1970.

Resnick, L.B., and Beck, I.L. Designing Instruction in Reading: Interaction of Theory and Practice. In J.T. Guthrie (Ed.), *Aspects of Reading Acquisition*. Baltimore: The Johns Hopkins University Press, 1976.

Resnick, L.B., Wang, M.C., and Kaplan, J. Task Analysis in Curriculum Design: A Hierarchically Sequenced Introductory Mathematics Curriculum. *Journal of Applied Behavior Analysis*, 1973, *6*, 679-710.

Rumelhart, D.E., Lindsay, P.H., and Norman, D.A. A Process Model for Long-Term Memory. In E. Tulving and W. Donaldson (Eds.), *Organization and Memory*. New York: Academic Press, 1972.

Tulving, E. Episodic and Semantic Memory. In E. Tulving and W. Donaldson (Eds.), *Organization and Memory*. New York: Academic Press, 1972.

Tulving, E., and Donaldson, W. *Organization and Memory*. New York: Academic Press, 1972.

Transition to Chapter 6

We now ask the reader to go into a temporary "holding pattern" in his thinking about the teaching aspect of instructional design, in order that we may now introduce the testing aspect of design.

Chapter 5 ended with how one breaks down objectives into their component parts, variously called: enabling objectives, subordinate competencies, essential prerequisites, and supporting prerequisites.

These component parts of each objective represent the lowest level (in terms of size of unit) at which one would normally prepare assessments of learners' performances. Assessments in increasingly larger units could include any or all of the following: specific objectives, unit objectives, and course objectives.

Chapter 6 shows when and why assessments at these various levels may be needed. It also shows how to design tests for objectives in all domains of learning outcomes. We placed Chapter 6 where we did because we want you to become accustomed to thinking of objectives and their assessments in close harmony. They need to be compatible with each other—to be congruent. The tests must be valid (appropriate) for the stated objectives.

Assessments for monitoring pupil progress, and for conducting diagnosis and remedial instruction, need to be pin-pointed to the objectives. Hence, we call them "objective-referenced tests." Such tests are also useful for formative evaluations conducted in order to improve the instruction itself.

Towards the close of the Chapter we introduce another kind

of test—the norm-referenced test, which is useful primarily in summative evaluation of the course.

If you are unable to accept our "holding pattern," go on to Chapter 7, which begins the teaching strategies to be planned. But we hope most readers will choose to accept our rationale for Chapter placement.

Chapter 6

Assessing Learner Performance

Leslie J. Briggs
Florida State University

Whether a unit or course of instruction is designed by a teacher (Chapter 8) or by a team of designers (Chapter 9), it is essential that some means be developed to determine whether the desired learning has taken place as a result of the instruction. The most common way to assess whether the desired learning has taken place is to administer assessment tests to the students at the conclusion of appropriate units of instruction.

Actually, a number of purposes are served by the design and administration of achievement tests. These various purposes are fulfilled by a careful decision as to what kinds of tests are needed and "how much territory" each test should cover. The "size of chunk" of instruction to be reflected in each test is closely related to the purpose it is to serve.

The word "test" is used in a broad sense, not restricted to written tests. We intend the word to include any appropriate observations and measurements of learner performance needed to determine whether the instructional objectives have been reached. Such measures could include observing the *process* of performance, as when a student makes a speech, or observing and assessing the *product* of performance, as in evaluating an essay or a work of art produced by the learner. Some observations need to be made "unobtrusively"—such as observing whether a pupil *chooses* to read a book during a "free activity" period, as a measure of an attitude objective in a reading program. Other measures, such as a test in adding fractions, need not be unobtrusive—it does no damage to the validity of the test for the learner to know he is being tested (for an intellectual skill objective in the mathematics program).

Some of the purposes for developing assessments of learner performances are next described.

Purposes of Achievement Tests

Each teacher or design team needs to decide when and how often various tests might be useful. Appropriate tests should then be prepared in advance, so that due care is taken in their construction. It is for this reason that this Chapter is placed where it is in this book. Once the entire course is blocked out by stating objectives at several levels, representing different "sizes of chunk" of instruction, the decision as to "how many levels to test for" can be made.

Referring back to Chapter 4, we see that it would be possible to construct assessments of the learners' achievements at more "levels" than would be practicable, so some decisions have to be made in order that "testing time" does not crowd out "learning time" in the schedule of instruction. Stated another way, it would be possible to consider assessing performance at each level of course organization listed in Chapter 4. Thus, we could have:

1. Assessments to see whether the *need* had been met.

2. Assessments to see whether the *goals* had been met.

3. Longitudinal studies to see whether the learner realized *life-long* objectives after completion of the instruction.

4. "Final examinations" to see whether the end-of-course objectives were met.

5. "Unit tests" to see whether the unit objectives were met.

6. Tests over each specific objective to see whether those objectives were met.

7. Tests over each "enabling objective" within each specific objective; this might be considered most seriously for the "essential prerequisites" of each objective (Chapter 5) represented by learning hierarchies for intellectual skill objectives.

In addition, if we consider the entering knowledge and skills that each learner possesses when he begins the course, we could consider the following:

8. Tests of basic skills helpful in undertaking the new instruction, such as reading and computational skills.

9. Tests of prerequisite skills essential for beginning the new course, such as tests over skills presumed to have been learned in Algebra I before enrolling for Algebra II. If a student failed to pass such a test, he would be assigned "remedial" or "catch-up" work to be completed before he could be expected to begin study of objectives in the new course of instruction.

10. Tests over the objectives of the new course itself to determine whether some students could skip study of some or all of the objectives in the new course.

Beyond the above types of achievement tests, one could consider a survey of the learner's interests, hobbies, and preferences, as well as a study of his entire family background and prior educational history.

Obviously, it is not practical, under normal circumstances, to do all of the above kinds of testing and data-gathering. Some of these tests would be more relevant for a course like Algebra II than for social studies, because it is assumed that there are different ratios of intellectual skill objectives to information objectives in the two subject areas. Thus, recall and transfer of skills learned earlier would possibly be more important for Algebra II, while ability to learn new information may loom larger in social studies. (This is not to say, however, that both kinds of outcome are not important in learning both subjects.)

Another factor in selecting the "levels" at which assessments might be made is related to the type of delivery system anticipated (see Chapter 9). If an "individualized instruction" delivery system is to be developed, such as the delivery systems described by Weisgerber (1972) and Talmage (1975), then it is essential to develop tests of the entering capabilities of each learner and tests over each component of each objective. (These are items 6-10 in the above listing of types and levels of tests.) Such tests are needed to determine the "entry point" in the new course that is appropriate for each learner, and to monitor each learner's progress, in small increments, to prevent failures and to minimize remedial instruction on the objectives of the new course.

So far, we have discussed those purposes of assessment that refer to the progress of each learner in the new course. But another purpose for some of these assessments is to improve the course itself (formative evaluation; see Chapter 10). By giving tests at the levels of enabling objectives, specific objectives, unit objectives, and course objectives, we gather the data base upon which to design improvements into the course before it is used for the next group of learners.

Make no mistake about it—under present teacher-pupil ratios in education, the teacher cannot be expected to offer true individualized instruction to each pupil in the class unless an individualized delivery system has been designed for this purpose. Even when school districts have adopted such delivery systems, experience suggests that it takes at least a year for teachers to employ them to their maximum advantage (Briggs and Aronson, 1975). Such delivery systems include the types of tests essential to determining each learner's entry point and to monitor progress of each learner. Other features of such delivery systems consist of (a) methods of indexing material in accordance with the objectives; (b) alternate media and materials for students with varying entry skills, so that more than one approach to mastery of each objective is offered; and (c) teachers' guides to assist both teachers and pupils in operating the system.

Short of such delivery systems as those just described, a teacher does not need and could not use effectively all the types of tests listed earlier in this Chapter. Nevertheless, for the purpose of this book, it is fortunate that the *principles* of designing assessments of learner performance are the same, whatever the "size of chunk" of instruction that is to be measured by the tests.

Principles of Design of Assessments

In the context of this Chapter, we are concerned primarily with a type of assessment that has recently been termed "objective-referenced" testing (Gagné and Briggs, 1974, Chapter 9). The word "objective" refers directly to the objectives of the instruction to be designed, whether these objectives refer to enabling objectives, specific objectives, unit objectives, or course objectives. So, regardless of the "size of chunk" of instruction to be assessed in terms of learner performance, the principles of constructing such tests are the same. (Note that this use of the term "objective-referenced" tests is entirely independent from the term "objective tests," as distinct from "essay-type tests." Each of these latter two types of tests may or may not be relevant for some of the objectives in a course.)

Our present use of the term "objective-referenced tests" is a more satisfactory term, for our purposes, than an earlier term, "criterion-referenced tests." This latter term means that a teacher or designer states in advance the score (level of performance) that a student must earn on the test to be deemed to have achieved the objective to which the test refers. As will be seen very soon, "objective-referenced tests" *are* interpreted as intended by the phrase "criterion-referenced," but this is only one of several concerns about the nature of such tests.

Refer back now to Chapter 3. It was seen there that instructional *objectives* may contain five components:

(1)   the situation;
(2)   the learned capability;
(3)   the object;
(4)   the action; and
(5)   the tools and other constraints.

If we had chosen to do so, we could have listed, in Chapter 3, a sixth component, which we actually chose, however, to reserve for introduction in this Chapter:

(6)   the criterion of performance.

The five components of an objective (listed above) describe not only the objective as it is used by the designer to design the instruction, and by the student to guide his learning and study efforts, but they also tell us *how to construct a test* to measure learner performance on that objective. Then, the sixth item, added above, tells us to decide how well a learner must perform on the test to be considered "satisfactory" or "A," or any other desired way to separate acceptable performance from unacceptable performance. "Acceptable" performance for an attitude objective or a cognitive strategy objective may often be set as "any improvement in the desired direction," while an "acceptable performance" (criterion) for adding fractions may be "8 out of 10 correct," or even 100 percent. In this latter case we say that "mastery is the criterion," while in the former case we may say "any improvement is the criterion." There may be instances in which 70 percent is the criterion, such as in comparing a student's written "criticism" of an art object with the "art criticism" summary written by a professional.

Regardless of the domain of learning outcome represented by the objective, and regardless of the performance criterion set for "mastery" or "satisfactory," the test over an objective should have three characteristics (Gagné and Briggs, 1974), described next.

Validity

In an objective-referenced test, validity can be determined by comparing the test with the objective it is designed to measure. The test itself, and the directions given to the student, as well as the total test situation, must conform to the five-component objective.

Of special importance are the two verbs in the objective: the capability verb and the action verb. If the capability verb in the objective is "generate" (a solution to a problem), a test would not be valid if it requires only the recognition of a solution prepared by someone else. If the action verb was "in writing," an oral report is ruled out.

The *capability* verb may be taken as the *intent* of the objective, and it is important that the intent be preserved in the test that is designed. Otherwise, one could design a test for a *different domain of learning outcome* than was intended, resulting in an invalid test.

The *action* verb is the key to the exact form of behavior on the part of the learner that is taken as an *indication* that the intent of the objective has been satisfied by the type of test presented to the student. There may be several suitable action verbs for a given capability verb. For example, if the objective intends that the learner can *discriminate* rectangles from circles (without necessarily knowing their names), the action verb could be *by pointing to* all the circles, or by *drawing a line* under each circle, given a sample circle and the direction: "*underline* (or point to) all the shapes that are like this one." The choice between *pointing to* and *drawing a line under* is a purely arbitrary one, since the purpose of the objective and the test is not to teach and measure ability to draw a line, but the ability to *discriminate* the two shapes. As long as the distinction between the *intent* (*capability* verb associated with a domain of learning outcome) and the *indicator* (action verb) is well understood, it matters little which action verb is chosen, as long as it represents a *capability the learner is known to already possess*. One could then choose an action verb that is convenient: *underlining on paper* if the tests are to be scored at home by the teacher, or *pointing* if the tests are to be administered individually to each learner.

While the capability verb (intent) is thus the key to validity of the test, the designer must not specify an action verb that is not presently in the capabilities of all the learners. (Variations in the example of the circle would be to have a blind child perform by touch instead of by viewing shapes of various objects.)

While the two verbs loom large in importance with respect to test validity, the other elements must also be attended to. For example, if the situation is changed (as in changing computing "problems" from the form of numbers to verbal form), the test would be invalid. If the shapes were changed from "circles" to "trapezoids" in a discrimination objective, another invalid test would result. Finally, if the "tools" were changed from "slide rule" to "computer," in a computational objective, another source of invalidity would result.

The entire point of objective-referenced tests, then, is that they must measure what the objectives describe, not something else. In our view, it is wrong, both "technically" and ethically, to present objectives that lead students to learn one capability but to give them a test that measures a different capability. However, when learners are permitted to choose some or all the objectives they will attempt to reach, the assessment for each learner would be adjusted accordingly.

It follows from the above that one must be careful before condemning the practice of "teaching to the test." This phrase has a different significance for the different domains of learning outcomes. If one has an objective of requiring the memorizing of a poem, one surely must teach the poem to be memorized, and test for that poem, not some other poem. The learner thus knows at the outset *the exact words he must say* when reciting that poem as a *test*. On the other hand, if one has the objective of "solving linear equations," a variety of examples are used for teaching to be sure that variations in complexity and other features of such equations are encountered during learning. Then, of course, one selects *another sample* of such equations when designing the test, to be sure that true rule-using is demonstrated, not the memorization of answers to specific equations.

The most "sticky" question, perhaps, is how to make tests for information objectives. The conventional practice has been to design a test which samples, more or less at random, all the information presented in books and lectures. This approach has a large element of "luck" built in. Two students who actually have equal amounts of knowledge of the entire content may make quite different scores on the test because one reviewed more of the items that happened to be on the test than did the other. This problem is discussed in other Chapters of this book, so we here simply recommend that: (a) objectives be reviewed to see if there are too many information objectives, and too few of a higher order, such as rule-using and problem-solving; (b) only important information objectives are stated to the learners; and (c) the test cover only the information objectives given in advance to the students, not other objectives. If this is "teaching to the test," so be it.

The above recommendation is consistent with the use of objective-referenced tests as an aid in monitoring learner progress on the stated objectives, and as a way to detect the need for remedial study. For other purposes, such as awarding prizes for those who "know the most about the subject," one can employ another type of test, called the "norm-referenced test," discussed later in this Chapter.

Also, later in this Chapter (and the reader may wish to refer to them now), we present examples of objectives and their associated tests. But now we go on to other features of acceptable objective-referenced tests.

Reliability

For present purposes, a test is reliable if it is an *adequate* measure of the capability being assessed. There are several facets of an adequate objective-referenced test.

The *length* of the test is often taken to reflect whether a large enough sample of the performance required by the objective was observed to make a dependable estimate of the performance. However, one cannot judge this aspect of adequacy simply by noting the number of "items" or "problems" required by the test. In general, however, reliability is related to the question: "Did the learner perform the *action* verb in the objective long enough (or enough times) to enable you to make a dependable inference that the *intended capability* has been demonstrated on the test?" An affirmative answer to this question, would, in effect, imply that the learner couldn't have performed that well by chance or by a lucky guess; it might also imply that he could repeat the performance again if called upon to do so.

Note next that one "item" may be sufficient for a test over one objective, but several items may be needed for other objectives. If an objective requires the learner to "write a 300-word theme on a topic of his choice, in class, during a one-hour period, with no references and no grammatical errors," it would appear that writing one such theme would be an adequate measure of the attainment of the objective. On the other hand, for an objective in algebra, the conventional practice has been to present 10 or 20 "problems," depending on the complexity of the skill being assessed. Whether one would need fewer items for an enabling objective, such as "collecting terms," than for a terminal objective, such as "solving linear equations," is not known to this writer.

One reason for requiring several items for some tests is to avoid "distortion." For example, if one presented only one item for an algebra test, there would be some possibility that a learner had encountered that specific equation before, and hence could give the answer from memory; furthermore, he may have memorized the steps in the solution. Teachers have conventionally required students to "show their work" on such tests; this usually would have diagnostic value and it would be a way of detecting memorized answers. But the possibility that a particular equation is *not* new to the student, even when the teacher did not use it during instruction, may be one reason why we seldom see a "one-item algebra test."

Other aspects of reliability which are relevant to norm-referenced tests, but not to objective-referenced tests, will merely be listed here. Their significance can be understood by consulting standard texts in tests and measurement.

Objective-referenced tests *need not*:

1. Result in a "normal curve," where the scores for a group are plotted by the number of students who earn each score.

2. Have any pre-determined level of difficulty.

3. Discriminate with equal precision among all levels of performance, as long as they afford reliable "yes-no" decisions as to whether each learner did or did not perform according to the standard (criterion) set for "satisfactory."

It follows from the above that you do not need to revise your test in order to obtain a normal curve, or to make it more or less difficult, or to enable you to rank-order pupils in an accurate fashion. You need only to check to see that the wording of the test is not confusing, and that the actions performed by the student enable you to say whether he is ready to go on to the next objective; that is, you need a "cutting score" that differentiates acceptable from unacceptable performances. Ways to improve your tests are found in Chapter 10.

Examples of Valid Tests

Two sets of examples of valid objective-referenced tests are found in Chapters 16 and 17, relating to the course designs produced by two students of instructional design. Chapter 17 was written by a student in her first (introductory) course in design; Chapter 16 was written by a student in her second (advanced) design course.

Experience in teaching the two courses mentioned above suggests that, for most students, a Chapter like the present one, including a few examples, is sufficient for learning to make valid tests. For a more complete discussion (and more examples), see Gagné and Briggs (1974, Chapter 9).

Cognitive Strategy Objective

The writer has come to suggest that there are several "sub-domains" of cognitive strategies, which differ in the following respects: (a) how *general* they are; (b) whether or not they relate to a single subject; and (c) whether or not they are accomplishments in themselves, or tools for solving problems.

Let us list a few examples. Some of these may be difficult to distinguish from "higher-order rules" (problem-solving), and some may be recognized as so rare as to surely deserve a separate class of performance in the taxonomy.

1. A student has missed the instruction on "collecting terms" in an algebra unit, but he later passes a test on "solving linear equations," which requires the collection of terms. He "discovered" both the need and the rules for collecting terms. This feat seems beyond the "problem-solving" exhibited by other students, who were "taught" each step in solving equations. He must have invented a method for collecting terms. Whether or not he is capable of equal feats in other subjects would be interesting to discover. Our (hypothetical) data tell us only that he can do such things for algebra.

2. Another example would be the ability to make inferences that other students cannot make, given the same relevant prerequisites. For example, suppose a group of students have been taught to find the areas of rectangles and circles, but not the areas of any other shapes. (This is not the usual curriculum sequence, but it will serve our illustrative purpose.) Suppose, next, the teacher, as a challenge (not as a measure of prior learning), says, "Can you find the area of this shape?":

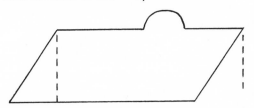

All relevant dimensions of the shape could be put on the board along with the shape. The values of both dotted lines and solid lines would be given, as well as the diameter of the half-circle. Suppose only one student in the group solves the problem. Suppose the following have not been taught, but were inferred by the one student:

(a)   The parallelogram can be viewed as a rectangle; therefore the values for the dotted lines, not the sloping lines, can be multiplied by the value of the horizontal lines.

(b)   The area of a full circle can be computed by noting that diameter = 2 times the radius; then, half that result is used in computing the total area of the shape.

Our student thus invented strategies specific to this particular problem, just as our algebra student did. It is clear that both students "went beyond what they were taught." This is different from finding areas for shapes that were directly taught (rule-using).

3. Another form of strategy would be the use of skills from one area of knowledge to solve problems in other areas, such as using natural science theories and equations to solve problems in social studies.

4. Another kind of strategy seems more general, such as listing a large number of uses for any object named, or for being the first in any classroom subject to come up with novel solutions to problems.

5. Finally, there are the inventors who discover both the "problem" and the "solutions." They do not necessarily respond to problems others present to them; they see new relations among items of knowledge that nobody else sees.

It is not clear whether these five examples are more alike or more different, nor is it clear whether or not they are listed in an ascending order of complexity or novelty. All five of these may be different from a personal style that is very general. That is, one person, when confronted with *any* problem, may first list all the alternate solutions he can think of (the divergent thinker). Another person may first break up the problem into smaller problems (the analytical or convergent thinker).

It would appear that eventually one might expect several sub-classes of cognitive strategies to emerge, but the present literature on creativity is beyond the scope of this book.

Having said all of this, let us formally state an objective for example 2, above: "Given only instruction on using formulae to find the areas of rectangles and circles, and no other shapes, the learner can originate an area solution for combined and modified shapes by 'restructuring' the shapes so as to be solvable by the two formulae taught, and orally present and explain his solution, with no references or other aids." (Yes, the five-component objectives often result in inelegant language.)

The test for this objective is clearly: "Can you find the area of this shape and explain orally how you arrived at the solution?" The shape and its dimensions are then presented.

There seems little doubt that the performance does require the capability verb, *originate*, rather than *generate*, which would be the case of a complex problem for which all the rules are applied without having to "restructure" the problem. The remaining question, then, is *how many* such problems are needed to be able to infer the capability to *originate*? In this example, one problem might be convincing. Also, bear in mind that this objective may be beyond the reach of many students, and hence probably should not be a "required" objective, unless the teacher has a program for helping students develop strategies. Solving one such problem in a year might be a feat for one student, while another may be able to repeat such accomplishments almost daily.

Cognitive strategies presumably underlie such measurements of productive thinking as have been designed by Johnson and Kidder (1972) in psychology classes. Students were asked to produce theories and answers to problems posed. Creativity as a general trait not associated with a specific school subject has been investigated by Guilford (1967).

Problem-Solving Objective

Here, again, we often face some fine distinctions between cognitive strategies and higher-order rules (problem-solving). There seem to be three rather separate criteria for classifying an objective as problem-solving.

1. If one has to decide for himself *which* rules, among many taught, should be selected and used for a particular problem that is faced, this clearly is of a higher order than the simple demonstration of each rule, separately.

2. If one has to "see for himself" a higher-order rule, having been taught only separate, subordinate rules, this seems to require generation of a new rule.

3. If one has to synthesize several selected, applicable rules, into a new product or application, this appears to partake of problem-solving.

We will adopt example 3 above, restating an objective listed in briefer form in Gagné and Briggs (1974, p. 85).

"Given only instruction in rules of grammar and composition, the learner will *generate*, in writing, a paragraph describing a person's actions in a situation of fear, by synthesizing applicable rules."

The directions for a test over this objective might read: "Within 30 minutes, please write a paragraph describing how a person acts when he is afraid; use the rules you have been taught in grammar and composition; no references may be used."

Perhaps a *fourth* element appears in this example: the need to generate the content of the test performance, in contrast to the area problem, just discussed. The learner is not given unpunctuated sentences to put together by re-arrangement. He is asked to *compose the paragraph* in such a manner as to synthesize the separate rules learned previously.

Note that no criterion for acceptable performance was stated either in the objective or in the test as given to the student. The teacher could then choose to say "without any error in grammar or punctuation," or the teacher could define an adequate description of fear (criteria for evaluation). An alternate procedure would be to explain that after the paragraphs are evaluated, students will have a second chance, using feedback about errors made on the first paragraph, to be provided by the teacher. This procedure is often referred to as "competency-based instruction"—the students keep working until they are successful, using corrective feedback from the teacher. If a student requires an unusual amount of prompting by the teacher to write the first acceptable paragraph, it would be well to ask the learner to write a paragraph on a different topic to be sure that the intended capability was acquired. Sometimes, in order to keep this "mastery based" (competency-based) method from becoming too tedious, the learner may go on to another objective (for which the first is not an essential prerequisite), and come back later to resume work on the first objective.

Rule-Using Objective

Learning to use rules is a central thrust of much of school learning. For example, to use the rule A = xy to find the area of rectangles, the learner must have previously learned that "A" means area, and that x and y are the two dimensions to be multiplied. The learner would have also learned to describe what area means in his own words, and perhaps to associate the results in terms of "square inches" to the counting of squares drawn within the rectangle.

Rules are used in science to compute force, volume, velocity, and many other such measurements. Again, the student needs not only to apply the formulae in computations, but to explain how the component concepts are associated and perhaps to "prove" the rule, or explain why the rule is correct.

Rules in social studies include skills such as interpreting data in graphical form, and learning to use the separate components of an analysis of a position on a controversial issue—the warrant, the premise, the backing, the conclusion, etc. Inquiry methods in social studies are thus often as systematic as methods in physical science, with the exception that the students' final "answers" to social issues leave room for personal values to have impact. This is not to say that there are not values and ethical problems in science—the informed citizen knows that.

There are rules in games, as taught in physical education. Some of these take the form of defined concepts: "A strike is a penalty against the batter; a ball is a penalty against the pitcher." Another rule is "three strikes and you are out" (exception: not if the third strike is a foul ball).

There are rules in music, art, and languages. Often the rules in social science are called "generalizations," but many of them have the features of rules as used in this book. While history is often taught as though only information objectives were involved, another Chapter (Chapter 8) has suggested problem-solving objectives for history, although the writer is not sufficiently knowledgeable in that area to show how such instruction would be planned.

For our example of a rule, we will follow on with the composition topic used for the problem-solving example, above.

Objective: "Given a mixture of correctly and incorrectly-punctuated compound sentences on a sheet of paper, the learner will *demonstrate* the appropriate punctuation rule by placing a check-mark opposite correct examples, and correcting in writing the other examples; no references may be used."

The test: "The following sentences are all intended to be compound sentences. If a sentence is punctuated correctly, write a checkmark in the space. If it is not punctuated correctly, correct it in pencil. No references may be used."

...... 1. John went to the store and he bought a loaf of bread.
...... 2. I like to eat apples, and I like to eat oranges.
...... 3. There are good days and there are bad days.
...... 4. Some times are good, and some times are bad.

It may be noted that the learner is assumed to have passed a previous test requiring him to demonstrate that he recognizes a compound sentence when he sees one, perhaps by distinguishing it from other sentence forms. There would appear to be an option in sequence—to teach students to recognize all forms and then to punctuate them, or teach both at once for a single form, and then repeat the spiral for other forms. A general rule is "Get to the higher forms of learning quickly for a small unit, then repeat for another unit." Thus, rather than teaching 100 concepts to be related later to 20 rules, teach five concepts belonging to one rule, then teach use of the rule, then teach a few more concepts, etc. This avoids the boredom of encountering too many discriminations and concepts before "putting it all together" to learn to use a rule, or to solve a problem.

Defined Concept Objective

This kind of objective requires the learner to use a definition in order to *classify* a concept. Note the difference between *use a definition* and *memorize a definition*; the latter is a form of *information* learning often called "memorizing." One may memorize a definition first, but then he must *interpret* that definition by encountering examples and non-examples of the concept.

Suppose we arbitrarily define a "family" as "a man and a woman, living together with their own children." (Or, "husband and wife" could be substituted in the definition.) We could place other limits, such as the man and woman are not blood relatives, or there may also be aunts, uncles, and grandparents of the children. We will use our original definition for our example.

Objective: "Given lists of persons living together, with any blood relationships noted, the learner will orally classify each group as a family by using the definition."

Test: "Please say "family" or "not a family" for each group, using the definition given. Each group is living together.

...... 1. Two brothers and their father.

...... 2. A man, a woman, and their two children.

...... 3. A grandfather and his grandson.

...... 4. A man and his mother and father.

Presumably, the learner could also use the definition to explain why he classified each group as he did, thus reducing the probability of chance success.

The objective and the test could, of course, be handled differently. One could ask the learner to name his own examples of family groups, and to name some non-family groups. There are often several options for expressing the intent of the objective, and for devising the test.

Note that the form of the test does not automatically identify the capability being measured. A multiple-choice test can be used for concepts as well as for information learning, and an essay test can measure either problem-solving or information.

Concrete Concept Objective

It appears easier to classify with confidence objectives in the categories of discriminations and concrete concepts than is the case for the often blurred line between problem-solving and cognitive strategies.

Sometimes discriminations and concrete concepts seem to be learned almost simultaneously.

Take the example of discriminating a square from a triangle. One can use a matching technique for teaching and testing.

A teacher, using a chalkboard, could make statements such as these:

1. "These two are the same shape": □ □

2. "These two are not the same shape": △ □

3. "John, do you want to point to all the shapes that are like this one?": □

4. "Mary, can you point to all the shapes that are like this one?": △

Obviously, an alternative is to introduce the *names* of the two shapes at the same time that discrimination is taught. Then the sequence could be like this:

1. "This shape is a square."   □
2. "This is also a square."   □
3. "How are the two different?"
4. "This is a triangle."   △
5. "This is also a triangle."   △
6. "How are the two different?"

(At this point the procedure may be repeated with various colors of chalk, with shapes differing in size, so that *size* and *color* are recognized as not important in recognizing the two shapes. Objects, such as cardboard cutouts, could also be introduced—or pieces of rope, or children standing on the floor to form the shapes.)

For the sake of illustration we will assume that the children have learned to discriminate the shapes by pointing to matched pairs, but that they do not yet know the names of the shapes.

Objective: "Given prior discrimination training for squares and triangles, the learner can *identify* squares and triangles when asked to 'point to all the squares' (or triangles), without assistance."

(There seems no need to specify *how many* examples, as some writers of objectives do. The *intent* and the *action* are clear. Other actions could be "group the squares together" or "underline all the squares.")

The point is that the *name* of the shape is the matching cue, while in the next example, *discrimination*, the name is not used—just the shape itself.

The test: "Here are eight shapes. John, will you come to the board and point to all the triangles? (Pause) Now, will you point to all the squares?" Some teachers might then add (pointing): "What is the name of this shape?"; etc.

In teaching such an objective, one uses a *variety of examples* (one of the "conditions of learning" for concrete concepts, when "presenting the stimuli").

Also, when testing, one uses another set of examples, varying both within the set and different from the set used for teaching (such as drawing *huge* squares, or very small ones).

Discrimination Example
Following on with the previous example of concrete concept,

the discrimination objective is easy to state.

Objective: "Given a number of squares and triangles drawn on the chalkboard or on a piece of paper, the learner will *discriminate* them by pointing to the shapes matching the one the teacher points to, without assistance."

Test:

1. "Point to all the shapes that are like this one.":   □

2. "Point to all the shapes that are like this one.":   △

Information Examples

Recall that three sub-categories of information objectives have been identified:

1. Names and labels: telephone numbers, names of people, symbols for chemical ingredients.

2. Facts: "The Declaration of Independence was signed on July 4, 1776." "The store is located south of the church."

3. Substance learning: ability to summarize the essential content of a lecture or a chapter in a book.

We will choose substance learning for our example, since objectives and tests for the other two can be very simple, such as: "here are the facts and names I want you to remember."

Objective: "Having read the Bill of Rights, the learner will state in writing, in a 20-minute period, the principal protections to individual liberties provided there, with no use of references."

Test: "Please list on paper in your own words the major areas of protection to individual liberties that are mentioned in the Bill of Rights. Do not use any notes or references: there is a 20-minute time limit. Begin."

On all such tests, the teacher may notify the students, in advance of the test, of the criteria of performance desired. In this case the teacher could add: "Be sure (or try to) list at least eight different areas."

Perhaps to most teachers, discussion of how well the goals of the Bill of Rights are being achieved would be a more worthwhile objective than the one given here for the purpose of illustrating *substance learning*. But it is equally sensible to be sure the students know what the Bill of Rights *says* before they can intelligently discuss *how* or *how well* it has been implemented, or how it could be implemented *better*. Here is an example of an information objective that probably *is* worthwhile, not so much in itself, but as prerequisite for a problem-solving objective to follow. Perhaps a discussion would also be in order to be sure the concepts and rules in the Bill are understood. Surely, it would be of doubtful value to have many such information objectives that do not lead to more advanced exercises.

How long such objectives should be recalled fully is uncertain. Of course, the student of government will continue to make more use of such an objective than do others. Even if you or I cannot recall as many as eight personal liberties so "guaranteed," it is presumed that some earlier discussion of the Bill of Rights has had a permanent effect on us as citizens. Gagné and Paradise (1961) have shown that ability to solve a problem is often retained well even if recall of some of the enabling objectives, useful originally to be able to learn, are forgotten. This appears to apply also to motor skills, such as swimming, in which the early separate instructions on kicking or breathing are forgotten after years of swimming, although the whole act of swimming is still done "correctly."

Designers need to consider the *purpose* of stating information objectives. If some of them have no purpose beyond recalling them on a final examination in a course, their value may be questioned. While it is true that competent adults have a vast store of information, it is not the information alone that makes them competent, but rather the *skills* that grew out of other objectives in the curriculum.

For the above reason, this writer has ceased to give tests over information objectives in his own courses, but the students are sophisticated learners, and the course objectives require problem-solving (see the "assignment sheets" at the close of the "Transition to Chapter 16"). The students know that they must acquire the information before they can attempt to do the assignments. While this writer *likes* courses with problem-solving objectives, he does not deny the need for some "information courses." Even so, *some* experience in applying the information is often a concern in courses that are heavily oriented toward acquiring information.

Motor Skill Example
Chapter 7 discusses the fact that "motor skills" are often

incorrectly so classified. Thus, the cautions given there will not be repeated here. We therefore borrow another example (modified) from Gagné and Briggs (1974, p. 85).

Objective: "Upon request, the learner can execute the performance of backing a car into a driveway by manipulating all controls properly, upon the first attempt."

Test: (Conducted after other tests in a protected, simulated environment.) "Please prepare to back the car into that next driveway you see on your right."

It is often of value to practice a skill in a safe or protected environment. Some aspects of driving a car are first practiced in simulators rather than in a real car. Later, the student may be taken to "driveways" or "parallel parking spaces" marked out on an open field, not accessible to regular traffic. Such exercises are sensible precautions. They permit learning and confidence development before facing the hazards of a city street, and they can prevent injury and property damage.

Note that simulators are deliberately designed to omit some "real-life" features of the skilled act as practiced later. A pilot-training simulator cannot be crashed onto the runway. A missile-firing simulator does not fire a real missile with a live warhead.

The phrase "protected environment" is even used in training of instructional designers. As a student you can submit your designs to critique by an instructor before you try them out in a classroom.

Simulators used to train electronic technicians will not give the unwary student a severe electrical shock. Teachers in training often first present a "lesson" to their peers, with videotape recordings, which can be played back immediately for learning purposes.

Attitude Example

In Chapter 7 we distinguish between those attitudes toward specific ideas or concepts that might be established or changed in an hour of instruction, and those attitudes which take much longer to develop, modify, or reverse.

We also note that some teachers do not believe that they should determine the direction in which students might change their attitudes. They may believe in presenting both sides and letting each student choose his or her attitude or position.

It appears, then, that a taxonomy of attitudes may later emerge, because the *methods* for influencing attitudes may vary along such dimensions as these:

1. Whether or not a present attitude exists—whether a *new choice* is confronted by the learner, or an opportunity to modify a previous attitude.

2. The age of the learner.

3. The importance of the matter about which an attitude is considered.

4. The length of time over which information or experiences related to the attitude have influenced the learner.

5. The intensity of prior attitudes about the matter under consideration.

6. The amount of knowledge gained before the attitude is formed.

Our example is intended to be a non-controversial one, as follows.

Objective: "Between September and June in the school year, the learners will increase the frequency of choosing to display concern for the welfare of other children, through words and deeds observable to the teacher."

Test: (An unobtrusive one). The teacher simply keeps anecdotal records of acts of kindness and concern for others displayed by each child. The number of such acts may be plotted month by month or they may be recorded only in September and June (or any other comparable time periods).

Whether the teacher informs the children that such records are being kept is a decision for the teacher to make. Some teachers will choose to reinforce some such instances observed. If a child is popular with the group (is a respected model in their estimation), openly rewarding of his kind acts may be undertaken. Some teachers will also choose to discuss such acts, to supplement and make more concrete such "rules" as "we should be kind to each other."

In general, seeing a respected model rewarded seems to have more influence than admonitions and slogans, but some children are often strongly influenced by both techniques.

Course Design Objective

This concludes our discussion of how objectives and tests should be inspected for congruence with each other, when objective-referenced tests, with defined levels of desirable criterion performance, are employed to determine whether each learner has met each objective.

Some designers set a "course design objective," such as, "This course will be considered to have met *our* objective when 80 percent of the learners reach criterion on 80 percent of the tests over the objectives." Some use 90/90, or other such criteria. As mentioned in other Chapters, ideally *all* learners would master *all* objectives at a high criterion level, at least for intellectual skills commonly agreed to be needed. Then, lower expectations could be entertained for other types of outcomes of the instruction.

When delivery systems built around individualized instruction and the "mastery" concept are employed, a major variance among learners is the *time* it takes to master each objective. Thus, there may be a "normal curve" representing *time to mastery* for the class, but a highly skewed distribution of scores on objective-referenced tests, since most students are successful. In short, a normal curve for scores on objective-referenced tests is *not desired*. As will be seen next, this situation is different for "norm-referenced tests."

Other implications of the mastery concept are drawn by Bloom, Hastings, and Madaus (1971).

Norm-Referenced Tests

It has been shown that *objective-referenced tests* have the following advantages:

1. They refer back to the planned outcomes (goals and objectives) of the instruction.

2. They are useful for monitoring pupil progress; the results show when a learner needs more study, and when he is ready to go on to a new objective.

3. When tests over essential prerequisites within an objective are employed, they have diagnostic value—they show where

remedial study should be focused.

4. They help make a "yes" or "no" decision as to whether the desired criterion level of performance has been reached on an objective. They are thus useful for the mastery level desired for key skills in that they clearly show that either a capability has been mastered or that it has not. They are also useful where lesser degrees of accomplishment are acceptable.

Norm-referenced tests, on the other hand, usually do not serve any of the above purposes. Since they typically cover larger units of instruction than do objective-referenced tests, they are more useful at the end of a term or year of instruction. Such tests usually measure a *mixture* of objectives such as may be found in tests of "reading comprehension" or "science knowledge." Such tests are often useful for *summative* evaluations but not so much for *formative* evaluations (see Chapters 10 and 11). They usually would not enable a designer to pinpoint exactly where the instruction needs to be improved, nor would they often be of much diagnostic value for a single pupil. They *are* often used to compare one group with another (or with several other groups for which "norms" are available).

For global measures, such tests are useful, but even here there is danger that a norm-referenced test may be more closely related to the objective of school A than school B, thus opening the door to faulty interpretation, unless it is generally agreed that *both* schools should be teaching the skills or information measured by the test.

Due to the way that norm-referenced tests are constructed to cover a global area of skill or information, and due to the fact that they are designed to give reliable discriminations among pupils from high to low in achievement, they are useful for comparing or ranking purposes (provided that they are reasonably valid for the intended outcomes of the school).

Norm-referenced tests may be designed by teachers or by teams of measurement specialists. Thus, the term *teacher-made tests* refer to the former case. The term *standardized test* is used when a test has been designed to discriminate well among students, and when the tests have been given to large numbers of pupils in a particular age range. These scores become the "standard" against which to compare the performance of individual pupils or groups. Scores may then be interpreted by use of norms expressed either as grade-equivalent scores or percentiles.

The process by which a test is made to *discriminate* well among pupils involves deleting some old items and inserting new ones. The end result often is that the tests measure intelligence as much as what was taught to the pupils. At least such test results are usually correlated with intelligence test scores. This may be a legitimate state of affairs for assessing global performance, but it may not be a valid assessment of the attainment of the objectives which the course was designed to promote.

Particularly when individualized programs of study are designed for the mastery concept, and when achievement is measured by *objective-referenced tests*, the correlation between intelligence and success on the tests may be near zero (due in part, perhaps, to the restricted range of achievement scores). It is possible that, at the same time, the correlation between intelligence and *learning time* might be a relatively high negative figure.

To put the matter succinctly, if one has designed an objective-based instructional system, and if those objectives are valued highly, there seems no need for norm-referenced tests until it is time for a summative evaluation. Even then one must decide whether the outcomes reflected in *objective-referenced tests* are more or less valued than the outcomes measured by the norm-referenced test.

Due to the increasing interest in competency-based instruction, the future may see the development of a new area in standardized tests—*standardized objective-referenced tests*. However, at the present one must say that "standardized" tests are closely linked to "norm-referenced," and "project-designed" (objective-referenced) tests are closely linked to "criterion-referenced."

There could be a use of the present kind of standardized test which is "criterion-referenced" (a cutting score for "satisfactory" is set), but it is not clear what use one would make of such information, since it would not have diagnostic value in reference to the objectives of the course.

Those interested in the techniques for development of standardized tests may consult other books, such as Cronbach (1970) and Thorndike and Hagen (1969).

Summary

The purposes of designing assessments of learner performance were stated. These purposes were linked with the "size of chunk" of instruction for which assessments are useful: entry tests, prerequisite tests, and tests over specific objectives, unit objectives, and entire courses.

The principles of designing *objective-referenced tests* were discussed. The manner in which *validity* and *reliability* of such tests are examined is quite different from the way in which *norm-referenced* tests are examined.

The concepts of competency-based instruction, mastery, and individualized instruction were viewed as compatible with objective-referenced teaching and testing.

Pairs of examples of objectives and their associated tests were presented for each domain of learning outcome, along with comments on how the instruction may be designed.

Finally, objective-referenced tests were contrasted to norm-referenced tests, touching on differences in how they may be designed, used, and interpreted.

Objective-referenced tests were viewed as suitable for many purposes up through the conducting of formative evaluations of the instruction. Norm-referenced tests were viewed as useful for summative evaluation, provided that attention is given to both the objectives of the course and the mixture of objectives measured by the norm-referenced tests.

Objective-referenced tests were seen as useful for diagnostic purposes and for monitoring of pupil progress. Norm-referenced tests were seen as useful for comparing programs or groups.

References

Bloom, B.S., Hastings, J.T., and Madaus, G.F. *Handbook on Formative and Summative Evaluation of Student Learning.* New York: McGraw-Hill, 1971.

Briggs, L.J., and Aronson, D. An Interpretive Study of Individualized Instruction in the Schools: Procedures, Problems, and Prospects. (Final Report, National Institute of Education,

Grant No. NIE-G-740065.) Tallahassee: Florida State University, 1975.

Cronbach, L.J. *Essentials of Psychological Testing.* 3rd Ed. New York: Harper and Row, 1970.

Gagné, R.M., and Briggs, L.J. *Principles of Instructional Design.* New York: Holt, Rinehart, and Winston, 1974.

Gagné, R.M., and Paradise, N.E. Abilities and Learning Sets in Knowledge Acquisition. *Psychological Monographs: General and Applied*, 1961, 75 (whole No. 518).

Guilford, J.P. *The Nature of Human Intelligence.* New York: McGraw-Hill, 1967.

Johnson, D.M., and Kidder, R.C. Productive Thinking in Psychology Classes. *American Psychologist*, 1972, 27, 672-674.

Talmage, H. (Ed.), *Systems of Individualized Education.* Berkeley: McCutchan Publishing Corp., 1975.

Thorndike, R.L., and Hagen, E. *Measurement and Evaluation in Psychology and Education.* New York: John Wiley, 1969.

Weisgerber, R.A. *Perspectives in Individualized Learning.* Itasca, Ill.: F.E. Peacock Publishers, Inc., 1972.

Transition to Chapter 7

Chapter 7 begins where Chapter 5 left off in so far as the planning for teaching, as distinct from assessment, is concerned.

Armed with the overall structure of the course from Chapter 4, stated as unit and specific objectives, and with the analysis of each objective from Chapter 5, one can next design individual lessons. The first two steps for such brief segments of instruction are (1) to determine the sequence of the enabling objectives for each objective, and (2) to choose how to implement the desired instructional events (teaching steps) for each enabling objective.

These two steps are called the "strategy of instruction," knowledge of which is needed both by teachers as designers and by design teams. After Chapter 7, the "tactics" of instruction are treated separately for the teacher-as-designer (Chapter 8) and for teams-as-designers (Chapter 9).

Chapter 7

Designing the Strategy of Instruction

Leslie J. Briggs
Florida State University

At this point in our overall account of how instruction may be designed, it is necessary to acknowledge two distinctly different mechanisms by which instruction is designed and delivered. These two mechanisms will be referred to as: (1) the teacher (or instructor) as designer, and (2) the design team as designer. These two mechanisms will be briefly described, and then it will be shown how the two mechanisms influenced the organization of this book.

When a teacher, working alone, is both the designer and the deliverer of the instruction, the teacher usually *selects* rather than *develops* the instructional materials to be used by the learners. This is because the teacher has neither the time nor the training needed to design effective materials. But, by carefully selecting from among available materials, the teacher can choose those materials that appear suitable for the objectives of the instruction. Then, by considering how the materials may be sequenced and used by the learners, and by identifying which "instructional events" (teaching steps) those materials can accomplish, the teacher can plan to supply any such events for which the materials and pupil activities are not sufficient.

The teacher, then, is not only the designer and manager of the instruction; the teacher is also a professional "gap filler"—a supplier of instructional events not supplied otherwise. Thus, the teacher seeks materials having both appropriate "content" and appropriate "instructional features," such as self-tests, exercises, pauses for pupils' responding with subsequent feedback, etc. Some textbooks may have the objectives specified for the learner; other materials, such as programmed instruction, require frequent responding by the learner so that feedback can be supplied more frequently. Under this (conventional) arrangement, then, the teacher is both the designer and the deliverer (manager) of the instruction. Chapter 8 shows how a teacher can design lesson plans, using existing materials.

The alternate mechanism involves a team of persons who design the curriculum and the materials. Such teams typically have teachers and administrators as members to help insure that the materials designed will be suitable for teachers and their pupils, and will be usable within the school environment. Such teams develop and test instructional materials, write teachers' guides, conduct assistance programs for teachers, and help evaluate the outcomes of the program as conducted by teachers. Chapter 9 describes how such teams operate.

In military and industrial training, the two mechanisms also apply. Some instructors design and deliver instruction as individuals working alone, just as teachers in school systems do this. More frequently, a design *team* works as described above for school systems (see Chapters 12 to 15).

Regardless of the type of institution in which instruction is to be conducted, the same general design procedures apply. There are, of course, differences among institutions in types of goals and objectives, and there are differences in age of the learners. But the basic principles of learning and teaching, as well as the design processes to enhance instruction, are generally applicable. Apart from management differences, "instruction is instruction," although it may be called "education" in the schools and "training" in industrial and military settings. Of greater significance is the fact that the objectives of instruction for all these institutions can be classified into the same taxonomy of domains of outcomes, as described in Chapter 5. When that step has been accomplished, the design of both instruction and assessments of learner performance can then be undertaken.

Figure 1 presents an outline of these two different mechanisms for the design of instruction. It may be seen in Figure 1 that the first seven steps in the design process are the same for both mechanisms for design. Then, there is a "fork in the road," as

The Overall Design Sequence

1. Determining needs and goals.
2. Organizing the course and the units of instruction.
3. Writing and objectives and determining their sequence.
4. Analyzing the objectives.
5. Preparing assessments of learner performance.
6. Sequencing the instruction within each objective.
7. Listing instructional events for each enabling objective.

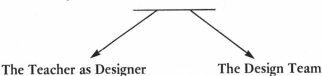

The Teacher as Designer   **The Design Team**

Lesson Planning:
8a. Selecting materials.
9a. Designing activities.
10a. Managing the instruction.
11a. Evaluation.

8b. Selecting type of stimulus.
9b. Selecting media.
10b. Selecting conditions of learning.
11b. Writing prescriptions.
12b. Developing materials.
13b. Formative evaluations.
14b. Assisting the teacher.

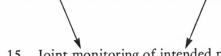

15. Joint monitoring of intended process.
16. Field tests and revisions (formative evaluation; Chapter 10).
17. Summative evaluation (Chapter 11).

Figure 1:   *The design process for teachers and for design teams.*

shown by the first pair of arrows pointing to "The Teacher as Designer," on one hand, and "The Design Team," on the other hand. After this pair of arrows, steps 8 to 11 are shown for the teacher who *selects* materials (Chapter 8), and steps 8 to 14 are shown for the design team which *develops* materials (Chapter 9). After that, a second pair of arrows indicates that the remainder of the entire process (steps 15 to 17) can be a joint effort of the teacher and the design team.

The 17 design steps shown in Figure 1 correspond roughly to the organization of Part I of this book. However, some further comment is needed both to relate earlier Chapters to the present Chapter and also to explain why there is a slightly different *sequence* in the placement of Chapters 2 to 6 as compared to the first five steps in Figure 1.

The Early Stages of Design

Chapter 2 dealt with determination of needs and goals; this is Step 1 in Figure 1. In a school, this step may have been taken before the teacher or design team begins work. The school may have conducted a review of its curriculum as related to perceived needs and goals. On the other hand, the school may present a general problem to a design team, such as "high drop-out rate," with the request that the team solve this problem, whether it means a change in curriculum content, in teaching methods, or administrative changes.

Note next that Chapters 3 and 4, "Writing Objectives" and "Organizing the Course," are reversed in sequence as compared to Figure 1. This is entirely intentional, and it was done for the following reason. The *Chapter* sequence is the *learning* sequence for the novice instructional designer, for whom this book is intended. We wanted you to first learn how to write objectives, without being concerned with what objectives should be chosen for description. The sequence in Figure 1, on the other hand, is the order in which the *experienced designer* would actually work. So, the Chapter sequence is the *learning* sequence, and the Figure 1 sequence is the *job performance* sequence. (There are many other instances in which the learning sequence is, and should be, different from the performance sequence.)

You might ask at this point: "But isn't there something left out between Steps 1 and 2 in Figure 1?" Yes, if you are familiar with "curriculum scope and sequence" statements. Such statements often take the goals of the school as given, and then block out, year-by-year (and perhaps subject-by-subject) the instruction to be accomplished. The results of that action serve as blueprints for the year's work for each teacher. Such statements may list the actual specific objectives for the year, but if not, the teacher or design team bridges the gap between the scope and sequence statement and the objectives for the year. In Chapter 4 and in Figure 1 we have used the word "course" to refer to each year of instruction in schools. Often, to be sure, a term, or semester, or quarter is associated with a "course," and in industrial and military training a course may be of any duration. Suppose, then, that the objectives are now known, regardless of what "course" means.

Chapter 5 dealt with "analysis of objectives" into their component parts. These component parts are often called "subordinate competencies" or "enabling objectives." In Chapter 5 they were called "essential prerequisites" and "supporting prerequisites." Whatever these parts of objectives are called, they usually have importance for determining the *sequencing of instruction within the objective*. (The sequencing of instruction *among* objectives was accomplished earlier when "organizing the course." See Chapters 4 and 13.) It is at this point of deciding the sequencing *within* an objective that the thread of thought from Chapter 5 about the design process is picked up at the next heading in this Chapter.

But, just before doing so, a comment is needed on why Chapter 6, "Assessing Learner Performance," is placed where it is. Why not later, since one teaches before assessing the learner's achievement? Again, the explanation lies in the distinction between the *learning* of instructional design and the *practice* of it. We wanted you to learn to match your assessment procedures with your instructional objectives, so we put the two Chapters adjacent to each other in the sequence. But even after you are an "old hand" at design, we still encourage you to keep to this sequence—that is, to *design* your assessments at this point in the sequence, even though you will not *use them* to evaluate learners' performance until much later. Why? Because after you have gone into the great detail needed to select or design your instructional materials, you might become "content oriented" when making your tests, if you put them off to a later time. It would be very easy to make the mistake of preparing "information" tests over the content of the instructional materials you just finished designing, whereas the objective that led you to develop that content might have required rule-using or problem-solving on the part of the learner. Even after many years of experience it is desirable to keep this distinction between these two sequences:

The Design Sequence	*The Classroom Sequence*
1. Objectives (for your use)	1. Objectives (to the students)
2. Assessment Instruments	2. Instruction
3. Instructional Materials	3. Assessment

We now pick up the design sequence with Step 6 in Figure 1, sequencing of instruction *within* objectives. It is the determination of the sequencing of enabling objectives (within each objective) and the selection of the desired teaching steps for each enabler that we refer to as the "strategy of instruction."

Sequencing of Instruction

Many important ideas bearing upon the matter of sequencing of instruction *within* an objective itself are found in Chapter 5. Stated differently, the task is to identify the enabling objectives for each objective and to decide in what order they should be taught. Teaching experience can be helpful at this point, but there also exists the possibility that in the past one has overlooked some enabling objectives, thus making the learning either slower or less effective than it could be. One needs to use experience with objectives for which past teaching was effective, but one also needs to be alert for ways to improve instruction by careful identification and sequencing of the enabling objectives. (It is assumed that the sequence of instruction *among* objectives has already been determined, as described in Chapter 4.)

Sequences for Intellectual Skills

The reader should refer back, at this point, to Figure 3 of Chapter 5, which presents the enabling objectives for the task (objective), "Subtract whole numbers of any size." It is seen there that there are eight enabling objectives for this task. In Chapter 5 these enabling objectives are called "essential prerequisites." The eight enabling objectives in that Figure 3 are numbered, by Roman Numerals, to suggest the teaching sequence. Notice in Chapter 5 that these enabling objectives make up a "learning hierarchy," in that simpler skills appear near the bottom of this hierarchy, and more complex skills are found near the top. Other examples of learning hierarchies for objectives in the domain of intellectual skills are found elsewhere (Gagné and Briggs, 1974; Chapters 16 and 17 of this book).

Note also that when such a hierarchy has been accurately drawn up, if one identifies the sub-domain for each enabling objective, the sequence also goes from simpler sub-domains to more complex ones in Gagné's taxonomy (see Table 1 of Chapter 5). Thus, if *discriminations* are needed, they would be taught before any necessary *concepts*, which in turn would come before *rules* or *higher-order rules* (problem-solving). Examples of hierarchies, covering several such sub-domains of learning, and noting the type of learning for each prerequisite skill, are found elsewhere (Briggs, 1972). It is not that one deliberately constructs the hierarchy to bring about this ascending order among the sub-domains for an intellectual skill task; rather, this is an outcome of a thorough task analysis. The hierarchy shown in Table 1 of Chapter 5 represents a task in which the prerequisite skills are all simple *rules* needed to master a more complex rule. In some advanced courses, such as Calculus II, some hierarchies might consist of entire sets of problem-solving acts arranged in ascending order of complexity. At the other end of the scale, it is possible to imagine a hierarchy of subordinate *concepts*, all of which need to be learned before a more complex concept is learned.

It should be noted that the word "hierarchy," in its pure form, refers only to objectives in the *intellectual skill* domain. But if one also draws an "instructional map" (Chapter 13) to show not only the *essential* enabling objectives but also the "supporting prerequisites" (Chapter 5) one might interrupt the teaching sequence suggested by the hierarchy alone in order to insert supporting prerequisites at appropriate points in the sequence. Alternatively, one might teach the "supporting" elements first, then begin the sequence suggested by the hierarchy. (See the instructional maps presented as Figures 2-4 in Chapter 13.)

While considerable research has verified the usefulness of learning hierarchies when planning the teaching sequence for intellectual skills (Gagné, 1977; Briggs, 1968), it is not claimed that any departure from the suggested sequence makes learning impossible. Due to the wide range of entering competencies of learners, and due to the variety of strategies they may employ in their own learning activities, the most that can be claimed is that for the *majority* of learners, a sequence based on the hierarchy should be more effective than any other basis for sequencing the enabling objectives. What would happen, then, if some pupils had not been present when some of the enabling objectives were taught? One such absent pupil might fail to pass a test over the objective, while another pupil might discover for himself some of the rules which were taught to others who were present, and hence pass a test over the objective. But, on the average, it should be apparent that "catch up" instruction for absentees would be needed when intellectual skill objectives are being taught. Otherwise, learners might not only fail to learn one objective, but also fail on others for which the first objective is an essential prerequisite. The "absentee" situation would be easily managed in a self-paced, individualized program; the pupil merely picks up where he left off before the absence.

A learning hierarchy appears deceptively simple once it is presented to the reader. But it takes careful work to derive an adequate hierarchy. Therefore, a designer would do well to consult with others when this task is undertaken. Many diagrams labeled as hierarchies are nothing more than verbal or motor chains indicating the sequence in which information is to be summarized by the learner or the order in which a manual procedure is to be carried out.

Sequences for Verbal Information

The matter of sequencing the instruction for verbal information objectives is quite different from that for intellectual skills, because there may be little or no transfer from learning of one item of verbal information to another. For example, if two telephone numbers are to be memorized, it matters little which one is memorized first. Both numbers are arbitrarily determined insofar as the learner is concerned. There is no logical way for the learner to "figure out" why the two persons have those particular numbers assigned to them by the telephone company. Such "arbitrary" items of information may as well be arranged in a random sequence as in any other, for learning purposes. *How each* number is learned is another matter, to be considered later.

On the other hand, *meaningful* items of verbal information may be arranged in a learning sequence based on logical relationships among the items. If one were to learn to list the major events leading up to the writing of the Declaration of Independence, it would be reasonable to present those events in their historical sequence, rather than in a random sequence, during learning. Such a meaningful sequence, as well as the entire meaningful context in which the events occurred, are useful "conditions of learning" for meaningful information objectives. (The meaning of "conditions of learning" is further discussed in Chapter 9, but briefly, it means "how the instructional events [teaching steps] are to be accomplished.")

Another example of meaningful information could be the task of learning to recite a poem, such as "Old Ironsides." The words of the poem are not arbitrary or meaningless to the learner in the sense that telephone numbers are arbitrary and meaningless. But, in reciting the poem, the learner is not permitted to substitute his own words for those of the poet, even if the meaning is the same. Such substitutions, by definition, are "errors" due to the intended outcome conveyed by the word "recite" in the objective. The idea that one should "practice" the poem in the order in which the words are printed is too self-evident to require discussion (with the exception of "backward chaining," discussed later), but whether to practice in whole or in part is another matter.

The situation regarding "errors" in performance is much different in a form of verbal information learning which has been called, in the past, "substance learning" (Briggs and Reed, 1943). This form of learning is that which has been dealt with extensively by Ausubel (1968). In this form of learning, the objective is *not* for the learner to give back, verbatim, the words he received, as was the case in reciting the poem. The intent, rather, is that the learner summarize, in his own words, the main ideas received. Teachers are accustomed to asking pupils to explain an important idea or concept "in your own words" in order to be certain that the pupil "really understands" the matter rather than producing, say, a definition memorized from a book or a lecture.

The importance of sequencing, for the form of verbal learning represented by substance learning or "organized information," is not only to present the information in a logical order and in a meaningful context, as in learning the events leading to the Declaration of Independence, but also to implement such "conditions of learning" as giving at the outset an "advance organizer," in the words of Ausubel (1968). This organizer is a brief, general statement relating to the details that are to follow, stated in an highly abstract form. Then, the message is presented with the intent that the learner will not merely listen (or read) passively, but will organize the material in his own way by utilizing his existing cognitive structure. This structure refers partly to the prior information the learner may be able to relate to the new information, but perhaps more significantly, to the personal organization the learner imposes upon the new material to enhance its meaningfulness, thus aiding in recall of the substance of the information.

Sequences for Cognitive Strategies

It is not entirely clear that efforts to help the learner achieve cognitive strategy objectives should be called "instruction" in the same sense that intellectual skills and information outcomes result from "instruction." Perhaps it would be more accurate to say that the teacher provides an environment intended to foster self-initiated learning. Certainly, the sequencing of learner activities for such objectives is usually more learner-controlled than teacher-controlled. Sometimes the teacher poses a specific problem to be solved, asking the learner to originate both the approach and the actual solution. The example given in Chapter 5 for such an objective is: "Originating a novel plan for disposing of fallen leaves."

For such an objective one teacher might employ "guided discovery," by presenting a sequence of questions designed to stimulate thinking about the problem by the learner. Presumably, the teacher would not present much information, as in teaching intellectual skill or information objectives. Another teacher might present only the objective, thus leaving the student to learn without further guidance to his thinking. In either case, the learner may recall and use many intellectual skills and sets of information, but the sequence of recall may be determined by the learner rather than by the teacher or instructional materials.

While curricula have been planned to foster cognitive strategies on the part of the learner, they usually do not provide rigid sequences of materials or activities. Rather, they provide stimulating questions and a rich array of resource material. Sometimes the objectives are not stated for the learner; it is up to the learner to provide both self-direction and self-evaluation of progress. In the "open school environment," the teacher may refrain from giving either positive or negative feedback. The teacher may respond to requests for information, thus serving as a resource person, but not as an evaluator. Under this approach, there are no "right" or "wrong" answers. As in science, the teacher may leave it to the learner to discover how to confirm or disconfirm his hypotheses or solutions to problems by designing his own "check" procedures; the confirmation is not achieved by asking someone else whether the answer is "correct."

It should be evident that while no rigid teaching sequences may be appropriate for this kind of educational objective, the learner almost certainly will not make much progress unless he enters the experience with a sizable repertoire of knowledge and skills, which themselves might have previously been taught by careful sequencing of instruction. It is also evident that an attitude is needed which enables the learner to profit by such an "open" method. If the subject is science, certain motor skills will be needed to conduct experiments—skills which were learned by highly prescribed sequences of practice exercises.

It is clear that if all the domains of outcomes listed in Gagné's taxonomy (Chapter 5) have their place in education, and surely few would doubt this, then it follows that no one method of instruction (including a method of sequencing) will result in this variety of outcomes. Therefore, it appears useless to try to decide whether or not *all* instruction should be highly structured and carefully sequenced; it *does* appear reasonable to decide this for each domain of desired outcomes. It is equally futile, then, to debate the merits of an "open school" vs. a "structured curriculum"—it is *useful* to choose between these alternatives for *specified domains of learning outcomes.*

Sequences for Attitude Objectives

In order to consider sequences for instruction designed for attitude objectives, it is first necessary to make several distinctions.

First, an attitude is related to, but is not synonymous with, the affective domain (see Chapter 5). Attitudes deal only with choices of decision and action, toward or away from a person, object, idea, or activity. As used here, the word attitude does not refer to feelings and emotions, nor is it the same as investigations through use of inquiry skills concerning controversial issues which in the long run may make up personal value systems.

Second, an attitude toward a specific topic in the curriculum may be stated as an objective to be achieved by a single lesson. In contrast, an attitude toward the "course" or "subject" or indeed toward the entire school and its curriculum may take much longer in its formation.

Third, *establishing* an attitude may require different instruction than would be needed to *change* an existing attitude.

Fourth, the effective methods for establishing or changing attitudes appear to differ somewhat according to the age of the learner (and no doubt also according to his total prior life experiences).

The following discussion of possible sequences of instruction needs to be considered in light of the above distinctions.

In general, the sequences for attitude instruction and the "content" conveyed in those sequences probably need to be tailored to the specific combination of the above situations concerning attitudes.

For example, if one wishes to establish a positive attitude toward a concept which is new to the learner, say, the Libertarian Party, it is possible that this objective could be achieved by a single lesson consisting of a persuasive communication. Research has often shown that a single film, for example, can significantly influence attitudes, particularly if no conflicting attitude already exists in strength. It is clear that only learners above a certain age would even understand such a communication, much less be influenced as desired, unless the abstract principles of the Libertarian Party were vividly dramatized in concrete forms which young children could understand. But if the learners had already formed strong attitudes *against* that party, it is unlikely that one "persuasive communication" would, in fact, be persuasive.

In general, observing a respected human model displaying the desired attitude and being rewarded for it is more likely to have the desired effect than a more direct persuasion effort.

While for information objectives or intellectual skills, children learn best by "direct purposeful experience" (Dale, 1969), such as encountering physical objects, persons, or animals in the "real" world, their attitudes may be molded by the parent who simply says "Don't touch the stove; it is hot; it will burn you and hurt you." Adults, on the other hand, can learn information and many intellectual skills by reading, while their entrenched attitudes are changed more by direct experiences in the real (or a simulated) situation (Wager, 1975).

Sequences for Motor Skill Objectives

Many errors are made in the analysis of motor skills—and even in *classifying* learned activities as motor skills. Many such errors may arise through failure to distinguish between how the learner knows what to do with his hands and the actual manual performance. For example, most people do not repair their own TV sets; they hire a technician to do it. This is not primarily because the technician has more skilled use of his hands than do his customers; it is because the technician knows how to decide what to do with his hands. Some customers, in fact, may be more skilled in using hand tools than is the TV repairman. It takes only normal manual dexterity to correctly perform a TV repair, although with practice, the technician might perform an operation more quickly.

Learning to skate or to hit a baseball, on the other hand, are true examples of learned motor skill. An adult who has normal physical dexterity but who has never been on skates will make a much poorer showing on his first attempt to use them than on his first attempt to replace a vacuum tube in a TV set, given that he is told which tube should be replaced.

A second kind of deceptive task is performing a procedure that is best done in a fixed sequence, such as starting the engine of an automobile. One first unlocks the door, then seats himself, then places the left foot on the brake, then inserts the key in the ignition, etc. To be sure, when a young child, the person had to *learn* to use keys, *learn* to seat himself, etc. But later, when learning to drive the car, the person needs to *learn what to do in what order* more than he needs to learn *how* to do each of these separate acts.

In the learning of all the examples mentioned above, verbal instructions can aid the learner. In the case of true motor learning, statements such as "keep your feet closer together" (skating) or "step up closer to the plate" (baseball), can make more effective the practice efforts needed to develop a smoothly flowing motor action.

In the example of replacing a vacuum tube, directions such as "don't pull on the glass part" are useful for safety, but not directly contributive to the manual action. In the case of starting the automobile engine, a memorized verbal list could be learned thoroughly before the first "practice" session. Alternatively, the learner could observe repeated demonstrations, which he could internalize for himself as either visual images or verbalizations of the actions observed, or both. After years of driving, of course, the person may perform the act without being aware of the verbal sequence which initially helped him to learn; but, if called upon to do so, he could describe the procedure in his own words.

In summary, much "motor" learning is really either information learning (verbalized steps in starting the car), or is highly dependent upon use of intellectual skills (determining the cause of the malfunction in a TV set). This is not to deny the importance of practice (as in hitting baseballs). Note that in a skill such as baseball or golf, the verbal information or directions supplied by a coach may be interspersed with practice over long time periods. Unlike an intellectual skill, such as "adding fractions," the "teaching" of motor skills goes on for years, because the "mastery concept" which applies to intellectual skills does not apply to motor skills, nor indeed to cognitive strategies or attitudes. Once a child "really learns" to add fractions, he never needs to be taught that skill again, provided that he uses the skill reasonably often. On the other hand, a professional baseball player continues to receive instruction (coaching) for many years, because no matter how much experience he has, he will not hit a home run every time at bat.

Much research has been conducted on how best to intersperse observation of demonstrations with practice sessions for such skills as assembling a carburetor (Lumsdaine, 1961), in which one must learn to discriminate parts and shapes, to visualize how they fit together, and to actually fit them together in proper sequence, supported both by verbal instructions and repeated practice. In general, the results of such research are comparable to the question of whether to memorize a poem by practicing it in its entirety or by practicing it one stanza at a time. If the procedure or poem is brief, practicing the entire task is recommended after observing (or reading) the entire task. For longer sequences, whether assembly tasks or memorizing poems, demonstration and practice in small parts of the task are recommended, followed by practice of the entire task.

Planning the Instructional Events

Referring back to Figure 1 in this Chapter, Step 7 is the last of the steps which needs to be taken by all designers, regardless of whether a teacher is working alone as the designer or whether a design team is doing the job. That is, the "events of instruction" (teaching steps) require the designer's attention in order that the instruction achieve its purpose, whether the instructional materials are to be selected "off-the-shelf" or new materials are being designed.

The events of instruction are designed to take the learner from his state of partial or complete lack of capability to perform an objective in the curriculum to the ability to perform it at an acceptable level of competence. For key intellectual skills, such as "adding fractions," a "mastery" level of competence may be required, so that instruction and practice will continue until the learner can correctly add any set of fractions. In the information domain, one might accept 80 percent correct performance on an appropriate test, while for attitudes and cognitive strategies, "any change in the desired direction" may be welcomed as an outcome.

Whatever the degree of competence selected as reasonable for the objective, accomplishment of it usually results from the combined effort of the learner, the teacher, and the designer of the instructional materials. In some instances fellow students or parents assist in the instructional process.

Said differently, some of the "events" of instruction may be "built into the instructional materials"; others are supplied by the teacher or by the learner himself, or by individual or group activities planned by the teacher.

What, then, are these events of instruction, or teaching steps? As listed by Gagné and utilized in subsequent works (Gagné, 1977); Gagné and Briggs, 1974), these events are:
1.   Gaining attention.
2.   Informing the learner of the objective.
3.   Stimulating recall of prerequisite learnings.
4.   Presenting the stimulus material.
5.   Providing "learning guidance."
6.   Eliciting the performance.
7.   Providing feedback about performance correctness.
8.   Assessing the performance.
9.   Enhancing retention and transfer..

Are the above events merely the whim of theorists, or are they found in the real world? This writer has had occasion to ask groups of teachers to view a brief film of a teacher leading a lesson in a classroom, and to mark off on a checklist which of the above events were observed. There was a high degree of agreement among the teachers as to which events took place, even though the teachers had never seen this list of events before. While the exact wording of these events may be new to many experienced teachers, they apparently recognize these "teaching steps" as commonly occurring in most classrooms.

The more sophisticated the learner, the more of these events he may somehow ferret out for himself, without being aware that these are distinct aspects of his study effort. The learner may range about in a Chapter in a book, asking himself "What am I supposed to be able to do with this material? Which parts do I need to remember? Which parts must I be able to use to solve some kind of problem?" Here the learner is seeking to determine the objectives of the Chapter, when neither the teacher nor the book has specified the objectives. Sometimes this ambiguity may be profitable, but in many other instances a list of objectives or sample self-test questions could save the learner much time, so that his study could be more clearly directed towards the desired objectives. Also, when tests are to be taken over the materials, having the objectives provided could save the learner unnecessary anxiety as to the type of performance (in regard to the material) which is expected of him. Under the "open school" philosophy, the learner sets his own objectives and evaluates himself. But under other, more conventional modes of schooling, if the teacher is to evaluate the learning, why should not the teacher supply the objectives? In order not to fall into a procedure for "tricking" the student, and to promote trust and honesty in the teacher-learner relationship, the teacher can use objectives to promote both learning and trust, as well as to promote self-confidence on the part of the learner.

For adult learners, such as graduate students, it may only be necessary to agree upon the objectives; then the student "teaches himself," after which his performance is evaluated. It is not a "cut and dried" matter—the teacher (or other designer) needs to decide which events to supply for the learners, and which they may be expected to supply for themselves. Beyond this, a pretest may be given to decide which objectives have previously been learned by the student, so that each student can "by-pass" unneeded instruction. Systems of individualized instruction usually supply both the means for such "by-passing" and the means to enable the learner to progress with a minimum of direct help from the teacher.

With the understanding, then, that not all nine of the above events invariably must be designed into the materials or performed by the teacher, we turn to a brief discussion of some ways to accomplish each event. Chapter 9, which deals with "conditions of learning," contains more detailed guidelines on how to plan to achieve each event, for each type of learning outcome.

Gaining Attention

Techniques for gaining attention clearly need to vary with the age of the learner. With young children, one must often employ novel stimuli, such as a colorful object, an unusual sound, or a startling question, to catch attention. When most of the learners in a group have "come to order" as a result of such stimuli, teachers often cajole the others to order by direct requests for silence or by questions such as "Who is still talking?," or a statement such as "See how quietly Mary and Jim are sitting." One teacher, in a motion picture film demonstrating a combination of "contingency management" techniques for gaining attention and a method consisting of programmed texts and small-group work for first grade reading, said "Fold your hands and sit quietly" at the opening of each class session. She then simply waited until all children were quiet; she never praised those who were attentive early nor reprimanded those who were the last to be attentive. Each teacher of young children develops techniques similar to these.

In many activities for individualized instruction programs, such as in reading for elementary schools, it is less frequently necessary to gain the attention of the entire group. Since each learner starts each new activity when he or she is ready for it, pupils soon learn to turn their individual attention to the new material, often arranged in the form of "modules" having many self-instructional features (see Gagné and Briggs, 1974, Chapter 10; and Briggs and Aronson, 1975).

For learners at all ages, one aspect of gaining attention is to introduce a new lesson by appealing to some interest the learners are known to have. Introducing a computational skill might involve questions such as "How would you like to learn to find batting averages in baseball?" or "How could you change a recipe for a dish for three persons to serve nine persons at a party?"

At the university level, attention tends to be gained when the bell rings or the professor opens his notebook. Simply quietly waiting for attention often works well. At other times humor may be employed, such as "With the present high tuition fees, do you want to keep chattering or get down to work?" In a small seminar, the professor may simply say "I believe Mr. Jones reports today; is everybody ready?"

In adult education, for those who had little education as children, a teacher might well gain attention by saying "Which of you want to learn how to open a bank account and which want to learn how to apply for a job?"

Maintaining attention may require still other techniques. During a lengthy group session, brief break periods or changing the media or nature of activity are helpful. In working with individuals it may be useful to refer to a longer-term goal that is being sought through study of a series of objectives. In a lecture or text, frequent referral to an outline may be useful, such as the references to Figure 1 in this Chapter. This helps keep the learner from feeling "bogged down" due to "losing his place" in the overall outline. "Place-keeping cues" thus may maintain attention and result in improved learning.

Just as teachers use techniques to gain and to maintain attention, so also do designers of instructional materials. Writers of books often use rhetorical questions to gain attention. Pictures or graphs may be used for variety or to arrange data more conveniently. Some writers of "branching programmed texts" humorously chide the learner when he fails to follow directions— "Nowhere in this text are you told to turn to this page. Were you just curious, or didn't you understand the directions? Did your attention wander? Now go back to page 38." When the programmer presents a multiple-choice, self-test question, including among the alternatives one ridiculous answer, and refers the reader to different pages depending on the answer chosen, the feedback page for the ridiculous answer might read "Oh, come on, now. *Nobody* is *that* stupid. Were you just curious or inattentive? O.K., have your fun if you want to, but go back to page 50 now." It is not known how these techniques influence learning. They may help redirect attention if the learner had actually chosen such a page because of inattention. Some learners may enjoy or be spurred on by the humor; others may be annoyed that their time was "wasted." Whether texts containing such techniques are popular because of the humor or because of the clarity of presentation of the serious content is not known.

Film-makers apply a variety of techniques to *gain, focus,* and *maintain* attention. These include humorous cartoon-like characters, unusual voices (Donald Duck), and exaggerated actions or sounds. Films can employ slow motion and fast motion, as well as normal motion, and by animation techniques they can show theoretical processes, such as movement of electrons in a circuit. Pop-in arrows or labels call attention to specific parts of a visual diplay, and sound narration is used to focus on the meaning of the picture being shown. Labels, superimposed upon the picture, are often used to aid in identifying objects such as in assembling a piece of machinery. A review of film research has resulted in detailed guidelines for film-makers for several events of instruction (Aronson, 1977).

Sudden changes of plans. The event, gaining attention, can be predesigned by the teacher when planning a lesson, or by the designer of instructional materials.´ The event may also be performed spontaneously, "on the spur of the moment." While it is good practice to design all instructional events in advance, it is equally good practice to seize upon an unexpected happening to change how an event, or even an entire lesson, is managed.

Suppose, for example, a teacher had prepared several lessons on the topic of "climate." One lesson might be about how deserts are formed, and another might be concerned with how rainfall is brought about. On a given day, suppose that the teacher had planned to conduct the lesson about deserts. But just as the teacher was about to begin, suddenly it starts to rain. The teacher might suddenly change plans, and gain attention by saying "Look at it rain! How do you suppose rain is brought about?" Then the lesson on rainfall is launched.

Often an unexpected remark by a student leads a teacher to make such on-the-spot changes in plans. An obvious point is that the teacher should not only plan several lessons in advance, but also be ready to change plans for the day.

It should also be acknowledged, as a practical matter, that how the teacher "feels" at a given moment leads to sudden changes in plans. Sometimes a chance remark or happening interacts with the teacher's feeling tone of the moment, with a resulting "peak experience" for both teacher and pupils. Many teachers often wish that a tape recording or a videotape recording had been made of the session because of the feeling that "this will never happen again in exactly this same way."

Even apparently unfortunate happenings can often be turned into an advantage. For example, three days before writing this section of this Chapter, the writer was called by a student in a seminar conducted by the writer; the student said that he was not prepared to give an oral report scheduled for the next day. The student volunteered to contact the other members of the class if the instructor wished to simply cancel the meeting. The instructor replied that the class would meet, as he believed there was something else that could be done. Before the class met the next day, the instructor reviewed the situation, which was as follows.

Each seminar student had completed an oral report to the class, summarizing and analyzing different "models of teaching," some of which are described in a book by Joyce and Weil (1972). The students were then to give a second report, showing how each model of teaching could be used to develop a curriculum scope and sequence. The student who had called the instructor was to give the first one of this second round of reports.

The instructor decided to use the available hour to first state his own conclusions about the nine models of teaching which had been presented in class, then to ask the class for their conclusions. He planned next to focus the discussion on how these conclusions might help the students prepare their second report. The unexpected requirement upon the instructor for that class hour led him to feel challenged to make the most insightful conclusions he could. This led him to feel "up" to something he had not previously planned to do. Suspecting that the students also would be stimulated by the unexpected change of plans, the instructor recorded the entire session. The instructor stated that the recorder was brought in because this would be a "key session" or "turning point" in the course. The reaction was immediate attention; no student objected to having the discussion recorded. The tape recording now contains content never brought up in earlier offerings of the seminar. And the students not only responded well in making their own contributions, but several said: "This is just what I needed today. Now I'm ready for my second report."

This unexpected happening not only helped the present class, but such a session will be worked into the schedule for future offerings of the course (an example of formative evaluation in the context of a seminar). Perhaps another moral of this story is that even an "old hand" at design is never finished with redesigning his course. This kind of experience is believed to be quite common, whether conducting "live instruction" or writing a book or other instructional materials. The rule which might be generated from such experiences appears to be: "Pre-plan as well as you can, but be ready to change on short notice." The writer has made a note to himself to send a copy of this book to the student who called that day in appreciation for his part in this unexpected event.

Informing the Learner of the Objective

As seen in the previous section, objectives are often alluded to in the process of gaining or maintaining attention. Since a teacher wishes to gain attention in order to direct the learners' activity toward a given objective, often it is natural to gain attention and announce the objective in a single statement.

With young children, the objective is announced more informally and less abruptly. Probably no experienced teacher of young children would open a session by saying "The objective for today is . . .," although such a statement would be very reasonable for older learners. The teachers of young children "lead up to" the objective, usually in an inductive series of questions, often related to real objects in the classroom. The child's understanding of *what* he is to try to learn is enhanced by using small steps and simple language. If the child wants to know *why* he should learn something the teacher has asked him to learn, the teacher may need to relate the objective to something else the learner is known to want to learn to do or something the learner simply enjoys doing.

Often, inducements are offered, such as, "When you finish writing these sentences, you may go to the clay-modeling table." At a very young age, children will often accept the learning of an objective simply to please the teacher. Many teachers might wish that this behavior lasted longer, but for good or ill, the time soon comes when the learner must be shown the value of the desired learning. When a teacher fails to convince the learner of such values, various forms of coercion may creep into the picture. Even though teachers might prefer persuasion over coercion, they might resort to the latter either as a matter of conscience or because they also feel coerced to produce results.

It is a controversial matter as to how hard teachers should "push" reluctant learners, but several techniques to promote learning are used. These include making the activity so interesting that the learner is easily persuaded, or use of "contingency management" in which a preferred activity is offered as an inducement for taking part in a less preferred activity, as in the illustration cited above concerning writing sentences and clay-modeling. Another approach is to design interesting small-group activities, so that a child wishes to participate equally, even if it means learning to do something that otherwise does not hold much interest for him. And, again, under the "open school" philosophy, a child is neither persuaded, induced, nor coerced; he is left to choose his own objectives and to evaluate his own progress. Under that approach, coercion by use of "grades" is eliminated. Some teachers like this approach; others feel that they would be avoiding their responsibilities under the approach.

A common argument against the "open school" is that children do not *know* what they need to learn. The counter-argument is that traditional schooling is by nature coercive, and hence it stifles the learners' natural curiosity—that if left alone, children will learn what they need to learn without the undesirable effects of withdrawal, rebelling, or dropping out. This matter deserves serious investigation, and no data-based conclusion will be offered here. This writer's view is that adults are responsible for children's education, and that there should exist in the curriculum both "core objectives" needed by all children, and "enrichment objectives" which are selected by the learner. The writer believes that making core objectives clear to the learner is a humane act, if teachers are to evaluate pupil progress, because it gives the learner an honest account of how his performance will be evaluated.

There are many ways to make objectives clear to the learner. Several techniques are suggested:

1. Be sure the objective is phrased in language that the

student to be instructed can understand.

2. Demonstrate how to perform the objective.

3. Give practice tests which are parallel forms of the evaluation test; both tests should be valid for the objective.

4. Show the components of the objective; that is, show the enabling objectives and how they contribute to the total objective.

5. Make it as simple as possible. Some objectives are rather obvious, like "practice your throw to home plate"; but if a learner is to read the Bill of Rights, explain what he is expected to do after reading.

6. Never "hide the objective" or keep the learners "guessing what will be on the test." (This is *not* "teaching the test"—it is just plain fair play, as you would like to receive from *your* teachers.)

7. Say or write the objective, and illustrate it in a variety of ways if the learners appear not to understand it as first presented.

8. Show the learners samples of acceptable work done by other learners or by the teacher, and show the value of the objective for later goals the pupils wish to achieve.

Many arguments have been presented against informing the learner of the objective. One argument is that the student will learn only the stated objectives, thus missing important objectives that were not stated. A wise teacher stays alert to unexpected but desirable outcomes of the instruction, and reinforces them when they occur. The teacher then simply adds those to the list of objectives for the next group of learners.

Even if research studies revealed no difference in achievement between informing the learner of the objective and not doing so (see Chapter 3), this writer would still argue for informing the learner of the objective, on the humane grounds of avoiding unnecessary anxiety and promotion of a relationship of honesty and trust between teacher and learner.

In his own teaching, this writer employs objectives in two distinct ways, based on the purpose of the course and the entering competencies of the student.

For an advanced graduate course intended to teach *instructional design skills*, such as those described in this book, the writer gives the students, on the first day of class, four "assignment sheets." Each of these four sheets contains three distinct elements: (a) an objective, written in the five-component form first suggested by Gagné and Briggs (1974), as discussed in Chapter 3 of this book; (b) a list of the components of the assignment to be found in a correctly completed student product; and (c) a list of criteria on the basis of which the product will be evaluated. Thus, *all* the objectives of the course are given to these advanced students at the time of the first class meeting. Students report that this practice is very helpful, in that they can scan the entire course requirement before starting work on the first assignment. These four assignment sheets are reproduced at the close of the "Transition" to Chapter 16.

In the seminar mentioned in the preceding section of this Chapter, the students have previously completed the advanced course just described, as well as other courses in learning theory, statistics, research methods, and other instructional design courses. Many of the students are in their final year or quarter of course work in a doctoral program. For this course, the instructor announces only the purposes of the course and the nature of the required two oral reports, described earlier. Each student chooses one or more models to study and report to the class. How students prepare the reports is entirely up to them; the basic text, mentioned earlier (Joyce and Weil, 1972), and another, by Snelbecker (1974), give information as well as references to original sources in which each author of the models gives his own account. Each student states his own "descriptive dimensions" as a basis for analysis of the model, and in the second report, each student derives his own application of the model. The previous account of an unexpected event of this course, given earlier in this Chapter, revealed one additional source of assistance that the instructor should supply or stimulate; but, even so, the instructor does not plan to present very detailed objectives like those given to the students in courses earlier in their doctoral program.

The culminating experience of a doctoral student is the dissertation. The candidate ideally identifies his own research topic, and seeks out a professor to direct the dissertation work. Several other faculty members serve on the student's advisory committee. The student is expected to design adequate procedures for meeting his own objective, aided by consultation with the committee members. Here, no objectives are given to the student, who is expected to have previously learned how to investigate problems such as the one he has chosen for his dissertation. The committee evaluates the plan as presented in a prospectus, and it evaluates the execution of the plan as described in the dissertation. Adequate standards of writing are expected, along with a format and style conforming with usage in a selected style guide.

In conclusion, the detail in which objectives need to be given to the learner depends upon the learner's sophistication. Less sophisticated learners attempting to learn intellectual skills deserve rather detailed objectives. More advanced students may need only a goal rather than specific objectives. For the dissertation, the student is expected to choose his own objective and to reach it with a minimum of guidance.

Objectives for an information course need to specify which information is to be retained in long-term memory, as nobody can retain all the information he encounters in school.

As with other instructional events, then, the degree to which objectives are provided by the teacher or by the learner depends both on the nature of the objective and the sophistication of the learner.

Stimulating Recall of
Prerequisite Learning

For intellectual skill objectives, the fact that the enabling components are taught in the order suggested by the learning hierarchy tends, in itself, to promote transfer from one part to the next. Especially if the learner is informed that each new learning requires use of some prior learning, he may acquire a "mental set" to ask himself "I wonder what I learned recently that would help me see how to take this step?" The consistent use of such a set could enable the learner to develop his own strategies of learning, thus making it seldom necessary to receive a prompt from the teacher. In the sample hierarchy presented in Figure 3 of Chapter 5, for example, if a learner were working on a subtraction problem requiring "double borrowing," he might help himself by asking "How can I use what I learned about single borrowing to help me with this problem?" If the student is "stuck" on the problem, the teacher would ask a similar question of the learner to stimulate recall and use of the prior learning as an aid for the new learning.

Suppose a learner was asked to develop an explanation of

how a heating system for a house operates to raise the temperature. The learner might make use of a number of rules such as "warm air rises" and the rules that govern the operation of the thermostat. If the learner were part way through this explanation but could not see how to explain how the furnace turns off at the proper time, the teacher might say "Do you remember how a thermostat works?" Presumably, if that question failed to help, the teacher might then follow with a more direct question or a suggestion to apply a specific rule.

It appears probable that a difference between a fast and a slow learner in a given school subject might hinge around the matters of how well earlier learning is recalled and how well the learner can decide which of the recalled learning is applicable for the need of the moment. Many "inventive" persons appear to relate elements of prior learning in a novel fashion which goes beyond directly taught relationships, such as "expand the binomial before collecting terms" in relation to a new type of algebra problem; here, the learner is directly told which prior skills to apply and in which order.

While the importance of recall of prior learning seems most clear for intellectual skills in which complex skills must be built upon simpler skills, it was also shown, in Chapters 4 and 5, that recall of learning in *another domain* may facilitate new learning. A teacher may need to suggest recall of information in order for the learner to take the next step in learning an intellectual skill, or the teacher may pause to help the learner invent a strategy for solving a problem. During lengthy periods, certain acquired attitudes and habits keep the learner at his new task.

Presenting the Stimulus Material

For learning of information, the matter of presenting appropriate stimuli is fairly obvious. If a poem is to be learned, the poem itself is presented in written or oral form before the learner can attempt to recite it. However, other questions involve whether the entire poem or only a part of it is presented before rehearsal begins. Older learners may be given the entire poem, and each learner may decide whether to read and rehearse in parts or in whole. If one memorizes many poems over a period of time, he also develops his own strategies as to how long to try to recall a line before he "peeks" at the poem to prompt himself. In a teacher-controlled mode of practice, the teacher might orally supply the needed prompt.

Learning of lists of "paired associates," such as pairing chemical symbols with chemical names, or learning the equivalent French words for English words, is most likely to require learning of small numbers of pairs at a time. This is partly because there is less meaningfulness to the whole task, as compared to learning a poem. Again, the teacher may present only a few pairs at a time, or the teacher may present a lengthy list of pairs, leaving it to the learner to decide how many to practice at a time. Research findings generally suggest that as the number of pairs increases, the time to learn increases disproportionately. Practice of a relatively small number, such as five to ten pairs, is more economical than practicing 100 at a time. This is not to say that learning a foreign language cannot be handled more effectively, such as learning short sentences in French rather than focusing upon vocabulary separately from meaningful sentences.

Learning to *pronounce* foreign words often requires very careful cycles of stimulus presentation, student response, and feedback. The teacher or an audiotape may pronounce a single sound or a word, after which the learner attempts to reproduce the sound. Then, the learner compares his sound with the "correct" sound, and tries again. Many repetitions are needed for sounds not heard in the learner's native language, while other foreign words will be easily pronounced with little repetition necessary.

In learning of organized information, the information must be presented to the learner in some form—by lecture, book, motion picture, etc. The information can be preceded by an outline or an "advance organizer" to help the student organize the information in a meaningful way, thus aiding both learning and recall. While too lengthy a stimulus presentation may make learning difficult for many students, sophisticated learners can learn by responding to and organizing the information while listening over relatively long periods, such as an hour or two hours. As most readers could testify, it takes a distinct effort to "listen well" during the second hour, as compared to the first.

Learners can listen effectively "faster than the teacher can talk," when relatively easy organized information is presented by the techniques of "speeded (compressed) speech." Recent techniques in recording enable a speaker's presentation to be speeded up to two or three times the speaker's rate without producing the sound distortions heard when a regular recorder is speeded up. With material such as a novel, where only the overall meaning and sequence of the story are to be retained, learners can listen at 1.5 to 2.0 times faster than the normal speaking rate without much retention loss, as compared to listening at the normal rate. In a few instances recall is even better at 1.5 than at 1.0 (the normal rate), and recall improves rapidly with practice, within reasonable rate limits (Domanski, 1975).

Even in lengthy presentations, however, learning can be further facilitated if the presentations include periodic review or summary statements, and pauses for posing questions for the student to respond to either overtly or covertly, followed by feedback as to the correct response. This technique can be implemented in lectures, books, TV programs—in fact, in every medium. Providing for student responding may be the best single "condition of learning" for organized information that is more "technical" than a novel, unless a more powerful condition may be an advance organizer or a meaningful organization of the presentation. Perhaps the more "difficult" the message, the more important the student responding and feedback. It is the failure to provide these features which may make lectures and books seem "boring," as compared to discussions and other more participative activities on the part of the learner.

In learning of verbal "chains," such as learning the alphabet or learning to recite the names of U.S. Presidents in the order of their incumbency, Gilbert (1971) has advocated learning the chain in a *backward* sequence (although the *recitation* is always in the forward sequence). Thus, a learner would recite YZ, then XYZ, then WXYZ, etc., until the entire alphabet is recited. Gilbert's rationale is that the terminal letters are thus more often reinforced, and it is normally the terminal letters that are difficult to learn. However, more research is needed to describe conditions under which the two practice sequences may be best.

In presenting stimuli to be *discriminated* by the learner, such as seeing the difference between a rectangle and a square, or a "d" and a "b," it is necessary to present those stimuli. But in helping the learner make the distinction between items in each pair, the teacher or the material needs to point out the *distinctive features* of each. The learner is taught to respond correctly to a large number of "d's" and "b's," perhaps first with block lettering on a chalkboard or in a book. When the learner can consistently point to the correct one of the two letters to match a sample letter the teacher presents, the discrimination (for *block letters*) may be assumed to have been learned. The teacher may next teach the *concepts* "b" and "d," by having the learner name the letters to which she or he points. Eventually, of course, when the concepts are thoroughly learned, the child can name the correct letter whether it is presented in block or lower case form, or in handwriting, whether the writing or printing be large or small, or regardless of the color used to present the letters.

Thus, a *variety of examples* is needed for both the discrimination and the concept learning stages of mastery of the letters of the alphabet. The condition of variety is also needed in rule learning such as to "collect terms" or "solve linear equations." These tasks are complex rules, each drawing upon the prior learning of simpler rules. The student must be able to *apply* these rules to any example given; he must not merely recite the rules in verbal form or memorize the answers for a few instances.

For young children, one would clearly present a number of examples of circles, not a formal definition of a circle, for both discrimination and concept learning. Concrete concepts, such as circles, are easier to teach to children than are abstract or defined concepts, because children learn well by simple questions and answers about objects they can see, but they often do not learn so readily those defined concepts such as "relativity" or "honesty." In dealing with such abstract concepts, when a child asks about them, one often gives examples of the concept, even though this is not adequate for adult learning. For example, if a child asks "What is honesty?," one might give several examples rather than a definition: "It is when you tell the truth" or "It is when you give back money you saw someone drop." But for older learners one might first give a definition: "A *root* is the part of a plant below the ground."

Providing Learning Guidance

Teachers and designers vary in their tendencies to give direct or indirect guidance to learning. The "didactic" teacher tends to use deductive sequences, such as giving a rule or definition, then some examples, after which the learner is asked first to *identify* examples and nonexamples from instances supplied by the teacher; then the learner is asked to *make up* his own examples. An "inductive" sequence would present a number of instances of two unlike items, such as odd numbers and even numbers; then by a series of questions the teacher would try to lead the learners to discover the difference between odd and even numbers. No general conclusion can be stated as to whether inductive or deductive forms of guidance are best. However, there is evidence that some individuals learn better by inductive sequences and some by deductive ones. Furthermore, the nature of the task needs to be considered.

When teaching simple rules that the learner can discover with some inductive guidance, it may be well to do so to give the learner an opportunity to experience the joy of discovery. But for more complex rules, it may save both time and frustration for the learner to be given the rule in a deductive teaching sequence, and to permit the child to be reinforced by successful *applications* of the rule.

Another aspect of guidance is in the "degree of prompting" given to the learner. In reciting a poem (information learning) it is just as well to supply the word or line the learner needs when he pauses in his recitation; if the needed word is "river," it seems pointless to say "You want a word for a body of water." On the other hand, in a problem-solving activity, an indirect prompt might be "How many mechanisms can you think of for applying force to an object?" This indirect prompt, if sufficient, may not only give the learner the pleasure of finding his own specific solution to the problem, but the learning *might be* retained and generalized better because the solution was largely "discovered" by the learner.

Obviously, it would be foolish to require the learner to discover everything for himself. He would end up frustrated and untutored. On the other hand, if no discovery is encouraged, the learner later may only be able to solve problems he has been taught to solve, not new problems he will face later. Schools cannot teach people everything they need to know in a lifetime, but schools can teach core skills which enable people to become problem-solvers.

In summary, for learning arbitrary material, like names of objects, direct prompting is sensible. For higher forms of learning, a good rule is to supply only a hint or indirect prompt at first, but to gradually increase the directness of later prompts until the learner succeeds with the problem. Figure 2 summarizes specific forms of providing learning guidance for various types of learning outcomes.

Eliciting the Performance

At some point, after the learner has interacted with materials used for instruction, it will be necessary for the learner to demonstrate whether he has learned. For information objectives, this demonstration may relate to the entire objective. But for the subtraction objective shown in Figure 3 of Chapter 5, a learner needs to demonstrate mastery of each essential prerequisite shown in the hierarchy. The learner might first demonstrate "simple borrowing" by showing that he can correctly subtract for the same examples used for the instruction; but this would be followed by demonstration of the same skill for other examples that are "new" to the learner, to be sure he has mastered the rule, not merely memorized \answers for a few examples. Later on, he would demonstrate "double borrowing," and so on.

Note that the performance elicited here is to determine whether the learner is ready to go on to the next competency in the hierarchy rather than to "grade" the performance. The test given later for grading purposes might cover *all* skills in the hierarchy to be sure the learner can subtract numbers of *any size* requiring both single and multiple borrowing.

Elicitation of such performances is needed frequently to "monitor progress" within a hierarchy of skills so that remedial instruction can be given when needed. More comprehensive tests help monitor progress from one entire objective to another. For objectives other than intellectual skills, more latitude might exist for determining how frequently the learner should perform in these informal "test-like" situations. Parts of motor skills could be

Type of Learning Outcome	Form of Guidance to Learning
Discrimination	Point to distinctive features of objects to be discriminated
Concrete Concepts	Give cues to identifying attributes
Defined Concepts	Present component concepts in proper sequence
Rules	Show how component concepts make up the rule
Problem-Solving	Provide minimum cues needed to lead learner to select and apply applicable rules
Motor Skills	Stimulate recall of sequence of acts; provide practice with feedback
Cognitive Strategies	Provide only indirect cues
Attitudes	Establish respect for human model; show his behavior and how he is reinforced
Names and Labels	Provide codes or memory bridges
Facts	Provide meaningful context
Organized Knowledge	Provide prompting in context of the organizational framework

Figure 2: Conditions for providing learning guidance.

so demonstrated before the entire skill is assessed by a "test." But, regardless of the domain of learning, the purpose of eliciting the performance is so that both learner and teacher are assured that learning has taken place; otherwise, additional instruction is required for the competency at hand.

Providing Feedback

After each performance has been elicited, as described above, the learner needs to know whether the performance was successful. Sometimes this is evident to the learner, because he can compare his answer to an "answer key," or he can see that he is correct, such as in "proving his answer" to a division problem by multiplying. If a motor skill is involved, he knows whether or not he has hit the baseball or whether he has ridden a bicycle to a destination point without any problem. For other examples, such as explaining the purpose of the Bill of Rights, the teacher may need to inform him of his success, or to indicate a missing or incorrect element in the response. When a performance is only partly adequate, the teacher's feedback has diagnostic value for defining the additional study needed. For some tasks only a nod or smile will convey the necessary feedback information to the learner.

Assessing Performance

This event may appear the same as "eliciting the performance" followed by "feedback," two instructional events just described.

It has already been suggested that "eliciting the performance" may be necessary for smaller units of instruction than are involved in tests for "grading" purposes. One distinction is that "eliciting" may be done several times in the sequence of learning within a single objective, while "assessing" is done after the learning and instruction have been completed for the entire objective.

There is a second distinction between "eliciting the performance" and "assessing performance," as the terms are used here. This distinction relates to the *adequacy* of assessment. During the often hurly-burly process of teaching, one cannot spend more time testing than teaching. Thus, a teacher accepts a response or two during the "eliciting" event. But, for an adequate measure of a performance on an objective, some assurance is needed that the assessment is *reliable, valid*, and *free from distortion*. These concepts were discussed in more detail in Chapter 6, so only brief comment is made here.

An assessment, to be *reliable*, usually requires response to more than one instance to be sure the answer was not attained by chance or by guessing. A teacher often quizzes a pupil either orally or in writing to be assured that a sufficient sample of all possible instances was observed, so as to rule out chance success.

A *valid* assessment is one which measures the performance described in the objective, not some other performance. This requires a *comparison* of the objective and the nature of the performance requested by the teacher. It is also necessary that the assessment be *free of distortion*. For example, if the teacher intended the learner to find areas of several rectangles by *multiplying* the two dimensions, there has to be a way to be sure the learner multiplied rather than having counted the squares he drew to represent the dimensions. It must also be certain that the learner could not have memorized the answers to the "test problems."

Enhancing Retention and Transfer

As the reader might expect, isolated "facts," such as names or dates in history, are usually not retained as well as "skills," such as adding fractions or skating. This suggests that only important facts should be tested for. Even "organized information" of the "substance learning" sort is more likely to be forgotten than are most skills. Judicious expectations should be employed as to how much information needs to be learned and retained for some future useful purpose.

But assuming that the objectives of a course reflect a reasonable balance of information *vs.* skills, so that the learner is not expected to be a "walking encyclopaedia," retention may be enhanced by *spaced reviews*. The readers are undoubtedly aware that for information objectives, a "review" every few weeks not only can reduce the need for "cramming" for an examination, but it can result in more long-term retention of the information. Skills such as computations also are well-resistant to forgetting if used reasonably often. And, as is well known, a skill such as swimming is often retained intact after years of no practice.

While isolated facts, such as "July 4, 1776," may be well recalled because of the rich meaningful associations and frequent "reviews" that occur, such facts are not "generalizable." On the other hand, once one has mastered the task of solving linear equations, he has the generalized capability of solving *thousands* of them. Such instances as "facts" have been called "reproductive learning" and such instances as solving linear equations have been termed "productive learning" by Gagné (1970). This means that there is "not much one can do with a fact," but there is often much of great importance that can be done with productive learning.

While retention of some facts and organized information can be important for some later purpose, they can also be "looked up" at a later time, if forgotten. In contrast, the skill of computation cannot be "looked up"—it would have to be "relearned" if needed later but forgotten in the meantime.

In addition to retaining skills, one needs to learn to generalize them soon after initial learning, if they are to be of greatest value in the future. How can a teacher or designer help the learner to generalize?

One answer to this question is to deliberately design "generalizing experiences" after the skill has been learned and demonstrated.

Suppose a teacher had taught and tested for *composing* correct compound sentences. How could a generalizing experience be conducted? One way is to change the context. The next day, the teacher asks the learners to write a 300-word composition on "The most exciting experience in my life." After giving appropriate feedback as to the creative writing the pupils accomplished to convey their sense of excitement, and rewarding those who reached the *new objective* (no doubt about describing experiences vividly to convey the recalled excitement), the teacher also marks on their papers *all incorrectly written compound sentences*. The purpose, of course, is to emphasize the need to keep using what was previously learned. · *

Take another example. Suppose a topic on "nutrition" has been completed and an appropriate assessment conducted. The next day after lunch, the teacher asks each child to write down what he selected for lunch at the cafeteria. The ensuing discussion is, of course, designed to promote *transfer* of the knowledge (demonstrated previously by a written test) to the real-life situation (and to attempt to induce an *attitude* about nutrition).

A final example. Suppose children have been taught to use rulers, yard sticks, and meter sticks to measure dimensions of objects like books, pencils, and desk tops. Use of these measuring instruments and conversion from English to metric units may have been mastered. The teacher might then ask pupils to measure dimensions of the room, and to discuss how a kilometer might be measured.

Teachers in elementary schools often display considerable ingenuity in devising generalizing experiences to help the learners apply what they have learned to a range of practical situations. In many cases, they may turn the sequence around, e.g., pose a practical problem, and teach rules and techniques as though they are merely incidental to finding the solution to the problem. In this way, some progress in devising cognitive strategies and problem-solving skills may result in the process of teaching a few rules.

Unfortunately, teachers of older students often present the discipline as they themselves (as experts) perceive it. The college teacher may assume too much about the students' ability to generalize. It might be useful if both high school and college teachers occasionally visited the elementary school to see how discovery and generalization are handled by the teachers there.

Summary

In this Chapter, we picked up the design process where Chapter 5 left off. Chapter 5 showed the importance of identifying both essential and supporting prerequisites which need to be included in the teaching of each objective.

This Chapter opened by reviewing the early stages in design—analysis of needs and goals; organizing the course; and defining objectives and preparing assessments of learner performance.

In this Chapter we defined "instructional strategy" as (a) determining the sequencing of instruction for each objective, and (b) designing the instructional events (teaching steps) to be employed. In showing *how* each instructional event may be planned and how such plans differ among types of learning outcomes, we have actually begun discussion of a matter to be pursued more systematically in Chapter 9—the matter of "conditions of learning." In this Chapter, when we contrasted, for example, how to provide learning guidance for various types of learning outcomes (Figure 2), we were depending upon the different conditions of learning that apply to various domains of outcomes. In short, the "conditions of learning" define *how to implement an instructional event* for a particular kind of outcome.

We chose to defer the systematic discussion of conditions of learning until Chapter 9, because this Chapter 7 is where the book "branches," as shown in Figure 1. *All* readers need the information through this Chapter 7, since the steps in design covered up to this point are needed by both teachers and design teams.

Readers intending to work alone as teacher-designers may wish to read Chapter 8 next. Readers intending to work as members of design teams may wish to skip Chapter 8 and go directly to Chapter 9. Since teachers have less planning time than do design teams, we deferred many details of design, including conditions of learning, for discussion in Chapter 9. But in this Chapter we "wove in" some of the "conditions of learning" most important for the teacher.

Since this Chapter concerns "instructional strategy" (planning of sequences and instructional events), Chapters 8 and 9 may be considered to cover "instructional tactics"—the finer details of the overall design.

This Chapter has not devoted a section to "research," as have some Chapters. One reason for this is that the whole field of "the psychology of learning" devotes itself to such issues as those discussed in this Chapter. Many single issues or recommendations covered in a sentence or two in this Chapter would require many research citations if full documentation were to be given. We have therefore cited some texts that the reader may refer to for further information.

To cite only two such works; the reader wishing more

information on sequencing of instruction could begin with Briggs (1968); for more detail on instructional events, see Gagné (1977).

References

Aronson, D.T. *Formulation and Trial Use of Guidelines for Designing and Developing Instructional Motion Pictures.* Unpublished doctoral dissertation, Florida State University, 1977.

Ausubel, D.P. *Educational Psychology: A Cognitive View.* New York: Holt, Rinehart, and Winston, 1968.

Briggs, L.J. *Sequencing of Instruction in Relation to Hierarchies of Competence.* Pittsburgh: American Institutes for Research, 1968.

Briggs, L.J. *Student's Guide to Handbook of Procedures for the Design of Instruction.* Pittsburgh: American Institutes for Research, 1972.

Briggs, L.J., and Aronson, D.T. *An Interpretive Study of Individualized Instruction in the Schools: Procedures, Problems, and Prospects.* (Final Report, National Institute of Education, Grant No. NIE-G-740065.) Tallahassee: Florida State University, 1975.

Briggs, L.J., and Reed, H.B. The Curve of Retention for Substance Learning. *Journal of Experimental Psychology,* 1943, *32* (6), 513-517.

Dale, E.A. *Audiovisual Methods in Teaching,* 3rd. Edition. New York: Holt, Rinehart, and Winston, 1969.

Domanski, M.A. *The Effect of Different Levels of Audio and Video Compression Upon a Televised Demonstration in Microbiology.* Unpublished doctoral dissertation, Florida State University, 1975.

Gagné, R.M. *The Conditions of Learning,* 2nd Edition. New York: Holt, Rinehart, and Winston, 1970.

Gagné, R.M. *The Conditions of Learning,* 3rd Edition. New York: Holt, Rinehart, and Winston, 1977.

Gagné, R.M., and Briggs, L.J. *Principles of Instructional Design.* New York: Holt, Rinehart, and Winston, 1974.

Gilbert, T.F. Mathetics: The Technology of Education. In M.D. Merrill (Ed.), *Instructional Design: Readings.* Englewood

Cliffs, N.J.: Prentice-Hall, 1971.

Joyce, B., and Weil, M. *Models of Teaching.* Englewood Cliffs, N.J.: Prentice-Hall, 1972.

Lumsdaine, A.A. (Ed.), *Student Response in Programmed Instruction.* Sponsored by Headquarters Air Research and Development Command USAF. Publication No. 943, National Academy of Sciences—National Research Council, Washington, D.C., 1961.

Snelbecker, G.E. *Learning Theory, Instructional Theory, and Psychoeducational Design.* New York: McGraw-Hill, 1974.

Wager, W. Media Selection in the Affective Domain: A Further Interpretation of Dale's Cone of Experience for Cognitive and Affective Learning. *Educational Technology,* July, 1975, *15* (7), 9-13.

Transition to Chapter 8

Chapter 8 goes from design strategy to design tactics for the teacher. It suggests a method of lesson planning that is consistent with the teacher's role as a *selector* rather than a *developer* of instructional materials.

The teacher *selects* instructional materials and *designs* learning activities to meet the objective of the lesson. Chapter 8 suggests some formats and procedures for lesson planning, and it deals with how to design various teaching steps. These teaching steps are the same for all domains of learning outcomes, but *how the steps are taken* differs among domains. It is this "how the steps are taken" that is discussed in further detail in Chapter 9 as "the conditions of learning."

For the reader who plans to work as a teacher-designer, Chapter 8 should give the overall picture. Then, if you wish to read the first half of Chapter 9, up to where team operations begin to be discussed, this will provide more information on the conditions of learning.

For the reader who wishes to be a team member, *developing* materials rather than *selecting* them, it may be most convenient to go on directly to Chapter 9 at this point.

Chapter 8

The Teacher as Designer

Leslie J. Briggs
Florida State University

While the several Chapters in Part I of this book may make it appear that the design of instruction is a complicated process, and it *is*, everything discussed in this book is intended to help you answer only three questions, as posed by Mager (1968):

1. "Where am I going?"
2. "How will I get there?"
3. "How will I know when I've arrived?"

When a teacher working as the designer tends to "get lost in the details" of planning, it may be useful to identify which of these three questions is being addressed.

In terms of the organization of Part I of this book, the Chapters can be classified as indicated in Table 1.

Probably, most of the Chapter classifications in Table 1 are clear to the reader, who may note, however, that Chapter 5 appears in both of the first two columns. This is because the analysis of objectives into their component parts serves two distinct functions: The first is to more explicitly show what must be taught ("Where am I going?"), and the second is to show how the instruction needs to be sequenced, one aspect of "How will I get there?" This Chapter discusses the three major questions, in turn.

"Where Am I Going?"

It will be assumed, at this point, that a teacher is to design a year's work for a group of students. It is further assumed that all

Table 1

Classification of Chapters

"Where am I going?"	"How will I get there?"	"How will I know when I've arrived?"
Chapter 2: Needs and Goals	Chapter 5: Analysis of Objectives	Chapter 6: Designing Assessments of Learner Performance
Chapter 3: Objectives	Chapter 7: Instructional Strategies	
Chapter 4: Organizing the Course	Chapter 8: The Teacher as Designer	Chapter 10: Formative Evaluation
Chapter 5: Analysis of Objectives	Chapter 9: Teams as Designers	Chapter 11: Summative Evaluation

the steps in Chapters 2-7 have been taken, either by the teacher or by others, such as curriculum personnel. The teacher, therefore, knows at this point *what* is to be taught. The "Where am I going?" question has been answered in several levels of detail, from statements of broad goals (Chapter 2) to enabling objectives (Chapters 5 and 7). The teacher is now ready to design each lesson for the day-to-day details of instruction. Each lesson focuses on either an objective or an enabling objective, and each teaching step is planned.

In so doing, the teacher is aware of the distinction between objectives which can be taught fully in a short time (such as "recognizing vowels"), and objectives which take a long time (such as "reading comprehension"). The former are often called "discrete" objectives because they stand alone as a small unit of instruction; the latter are often called "cumulative objectives" because it takes a long time to achieve them. The cumulative objectives, in turn, break down into two types: (1) those for which there are many enabling objectives, thus explaining the length of learning time, as for many intellectual skills, and (2) those which require long exposure to an entire class of stimuli, such as "enjoying classical music" (which also represents a different domain of learning).

It goes without saying that a teacher needs to have an objective (or an enabling objective) as the basis for each lesson, whether the lesson is a group exercise led by the teacher or an individualized instruction unit designed as a self-instructional "module." It is further clear, from Chapters 5 and 7, that a teacher needs to plan whole *series* of lessons in order to have the desired sequence of *both essential and supporting prerequisites.* Then, it is necessary to select materials and activities which will provide the *instructional events* (or *teaching steps*) for each lesson.

"How Will I Get There?"

This question might be rephrased as follows: "Considering the age of my students and the nature of the objective for this lesson, *which* instructional events do I need to supply for the students, and *how* shall I supply each?" Under the approach espoused by this book, *lesson planning* is a matter of *choosing and implementing instructional events.*

Recall from Chapter 7 that not all nine events listed there must be invariably supplied by the teacher. Some times, a lesson may require only three or four events; other times, a lesson may require *repeated application* of most of the events. There is no set series of events for all lessons, and some lessons involve *cycles* of events.

Recall also that instructional events may be supplied by materials, by activities, by teachers, or by the learners themselves. The teacher needs to decide, first, what events to supply; and, second, whether the event is supplied in the materials or by the teacher, etc. The teacher who is accustomed to this approach to lesson planning might even *suggest to the learners which events they should supply!* This might assist the learners to become better self-learners. It also might open up the teaching process to joint examination by teachers and learners, the outcome of which, it is predicted, would be that both teacher and pupils learn more and trust each other more.

A potentially important implication of the above is that *joint planning* of some lessons by teachers and pupils could improve study habits and morale, and it also could help the teacher assess the degree of independence in learning that the pupils can handle. Such joint efforts also tend to establish a "helping" rather than an "adversary" relationship between teacher and pupils, resulting in improved self-esteem for the pupils. An additional advantage for the teacher would be the ability to conduct lessons with minimal prompts, leaving a "discovery" opportunity available to the learners. Then, if the learners fail to "discover," they can be more directly prompted, thus allowing the pupils whatever degree of discovery opportunity they can use well at the time.

The Sources of Instructional Events

It has already been stated that the instructional events needed for a particular lesson might be supplied by the teacher, by the materials, by class activities, or by the learner. We present next a hypothetical "growth curve" to suggest the hypothesis that the *source* of the events can change with the age and sophistication of the learner. See Figure 1.

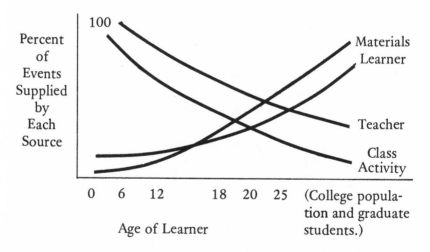

*Figure 1: Sources of instructional events. ***

*This is not a "scale"; the lines would exceed 100 percent if summed for an age level: only *relative* influences are intended.

The assumption underlying Figure 1 is, of course, that learners become capable of more independent learning as they grow older. Under present school conditions, at least, this appears confirmed by simple observation of where and how people learn. But there are those who would argue that Figure 1 is an artifact of conventional teaching methods, and that children would be both more independent and more creative learners if they were given complete control of their own learning at the outset. This writer, while favoring much self-determination by the learner, would predict that some key intellectual skills might be lost under complete self-determination, and that this would hamper later learning. This remains a legitimate issue requiring much more research.

Some sources of learning, of course, have been omitted from Figure 1. These sources actually include parents and peers. Parents would be a heavy influence at younger ages, and peer influence (for academic learning) would probably increase with age. Recently, however, teachers have made greater use of "peer teaching." Several teachers and educators have suggested that peer teaching is helpful for both the "teacher" and the "learner," not only academically, but also socially and emotionally. Evidence has also been advanced to show that older children in a family benefit from the "teacher role" they assume with their younger brothers and sisters.

Media as Sources of Instructional Events

The word "materials" as used in earlier portions of this Chapter is often taken to mean "printed materials," perhaps because of the earlier scarcity of non-print materials in the schools. But schools today often utilize many forms of both print and non-print materials. Print forms include books, programmed instruction, workbooks, and self-tests. Non-print materials include sound recordings, videotapes, slide-tapes, still and motion pictures, real objects for manipulation, and television.

How can a teacher use the concept of "lesson planning by use of instructional events" and also utilize the available variety of print and non-print materials? It is often difficult to identify or design events compatible with available materials. But the point of view in this book is that *materials can be selected and used to implement* the desired instructional events. In the next section of the Chapter we will present some illustrations of this. The general point is to select materials having appropriate content (stimuli) and to list the events the materials convey so that the teacher can supply the others.

But before we get to those illustrations, let us consider first a more general question: Suppose suitable materials are available in *several media*. How does one decide *which media* to employ? This *media selection* issue is equally important for the teacher as designer and for design teams which actually develop materials in various media.

Dale (1969) has listed educational media roughly in the order that they are effective for learners as they grow older. In his 12 categories of media, listed below, the lower numbers are generally recommended for younger learners, and the higher numbers for older learners. His 12 categories are:

  12. Verbal symbols
  11. Visual symbols
  10. Radio and recordings
   9. Still pictures
   8. Motion pictures
   7. Educational television
   6. Exhibits
   5. Study trips
   4. Demonstrations
   3. Dramatized experience—plays, puppets, role-playing
   2. Contrived experience—models, mock-ups, simulation
   1. Direct purposeful experiences

When one is dealing with "cognitive" objectives—information, intellectual skills, and cognitive strategies—a rule of thumb previously suggested by this author (Briggs, 1972), is: "Go as low on the scale as you need to in order to insure learning for your group, but go as high on the scale as you can for the most efficient learning." This "rule of thumb" should enable a teacher to first select an "ideal" medium, then to search for a suitable item in material catalogs, and then to analyze the material as to the events it can provide.

For attitude objectives, Wager (1975) has suggested that this age/media relationship "inverts" itself. Thus, a young child learns well by direct experience with objects when information or an intellectual skill is to be acquired, but he may acquire an attitude objective by verbal statements by people he respects, such as a teacher, a parent, or a prominent expert in a field of endeavor. Further discussion of media selection is found in Chapter 9.

Steps in Lesson Planning

Building on the foregoing discussion, we arrive at the following series of steps for planning a lesson:

1. Identify the objective (or enabling objective) for the lesson.
2. List the desired instructional events.
3. Select the ideal media.
4. Select materials and activities.
5. Analyze the material for events they supply.
6. Plan other means for the remaining events.

Each of the above steps will be discussed in turn, after which an example of a lesson plan will be presented. But first let us begin with an even simpler method of lesson planning.

Perhaps the briefest possible way to summarize the steps in lesson planning, consistent with the stance of this book, would be to simply reiterate the three questions raised at the opening of the Chapter (yes, we keep mentioning this; we consider these the "anchor points" in design, so to haul anchor again . . .).

Step 1: "Where am I going?" This question is answered when the objective of the lesson is specified.

Step 2: "How will I get there?" This question is answered when the teacher has chosen the instructional materials, media, and activities to be employed.

Step 3: "How will I know when I've arrived?" This question will be answered when the teacher has employed appropriate evaluation measures, which could consist of a combination of informal observations of pupil performance and administration of actual tests of performance. If a sufficient number of pupils perform at the desired level, the instruction may be said to have "arrived" at its destination. If a few pupils fail to demonstrate the desired level of performance, remedial instruction could be prescribed (Chapter 6 has elaborated on this).

Consistent with the above overall orientation as to the three major components or "anchor points" of lesson planning, we now turn to a discussion of more detailed steps.

Step 1: The objective. In Chapter 7 it was shown that teachers usually need to plan entire series of lessons. One reason for this is to take advantage of unexpected happenings. Another reason, in an individually paced program, is to permit pupils to progress at their own rates. Still another reason is simply to always be prepared, so that planning is accomplished well enough in advance to help adjust to unexpected demands on the teacher's time—time that otherwise would have been planning time. Finally, in the event of illness of the teacher, a substitute can work better on the basis of well-developed plans made in advance by the teacher.

Since planning time is becoming more scarce in many schools, if the teacher blocks out well in advance only the most salient features of each lesson plan in a series, the teacher can then use small bits of time to fill in the details, and a substitute teacher can be given whatever details are available when emergencies arise.

Thus, a teacher might first list the objectives for an entire series of lessons; then, as time permits, other details are filled in. When all details for one series are filled in, a second series can be begun. This procedure can help a teacher feel less under pressure—to feel that he or she is "ahead of schedule" in the planning effort. This enables a teacher to then "take a break" once in a while from the planning periods that are set aside for this purpose. A few such recreational "breaks" can lead to a more relaxed feeling as well as to better performance both in the classroom and in subsequent planning periods. Such an arrangement can contribute to the physical and mental health of the teacher, with consequent benefits also for the learners. A final benefit to this method of scheduling the planning time can be improved learning. Teachers, like others, cannot always be "creative" on a fixed schedule. By working well in advance of the class schedule, the planning can be done when the teacher feels "up" rather than "down."

The objectives are thus best identified and *written down* for an entire series of lessons. This enables the teacher, first of all, to consider whether a better *sequence* of objectives might be found.

Then, realizing that equipment failure, broken film, or a burned out bulb may interfere with the planned lesson, the teacher can be armed with some alternative lessons. A review to adjust to variable progress levels of pupils would represent a good use of time in such emergencies.

When the teacher has written down the objective of a lesson, consideration might next be given to how the objective should be communicated *to the learners*. A teacher may or may not wish to first record the objectives in the formal, five-step method presented in Chapter 3. While there are advantages to that method, even when a teacher is the sole designer and deliverer of the instruction, time pressure may often lead the teacher to record the objectives in a simpler fashion. Thus, a teacher may simply record "adding fractions" or "collecting terms" for mathematics lessons rather than using the complete, formal, five-step method which is so helpful in avoiding misunderstandings when an entire team is doing the planning.

In some manner, then, the teacher needs to record the objectives for his or her own use as well as to express these objectives to the students in language which they can understand.

In the case of intellectual skill objectives, the purpose of communicating them to the learners is: (a) to enable them to see the kind of performance that they will acquire and exhibit on a test as a result of the lesson; (b) to motivate them to see the value of the performance to be learned; (c) to help them realize that each learning activity requested of them is directed to a worthwhile outcome, and therefore the study effort asked of them is meaningful; and (b) to help them focus on the most essential parts of the materials.

In the case of information objectives, the communication of the objective to the learner helps the learner sort out *essential* information from *supplementary* information. For example, instead of asking pupils to read a chapter in a history book in preparation for answering just any questions which the teacher may ask, the teacher, by providing specific objectives, is helping the learners to identify which parts of the chapter they need only to "understand" in context of the entire chapter, and which parts they need to rehearse repeatedly to aid in later recall.

In order to avoid over-use of information objectives, the

teacher may consider a range of objectives on a chapter such as the "American Revolution":

1. List the major events leading to war.
2. State the role played by specified persons.
3. Show how economic factors led to conflict.
4. Explain how the expression "He is a Benedict Arnold" arose, and explain its meaning.
5. Identify the six dates you consider important and explain why.
6. Prepare a play reenacting the Boston Tea Party.
7. Prepare a skit involving a rebel, a Tory, and a Quaker.
8. Write a theme showing two strategies by which the War could have been avoided, and describe how life in America today might have differed had war been avoided.

The reader may have already noticed that only some of the above objectives are actually "information" objectives. Others require intellectual skills and cognitive strategies to be applied. Some require development of concepts and the use of concepts to relate ideas to reach a conclusion. It is thus clear that "American History" need not be restricted to learning or memorizing of information that is in the text book.

It also should be clear that the students' reading and study of the assigned chapter in the history book should take on a very different character for each of the objectives listed above. No doubt, teachers of history could devise even more worthwhile objectives. The main point is that the learner is left without guidance to his study effort if the objectives are not stated; and, in such a case, the students' performance on any test the teacher might administer following the study of the chapter would measure "luck" and "ability to guess what will be on the test" rather than mastery of any identifiable competence in history.

Opinions vary as to whether teachers should state attitudinal objectives to the learners. While most teachers would agree that they want to induce the students to have a positive attitude towards the course that is being taught, they do not agree on more specific matters, such as "Should I try to influence them toward capitalism and away from socialism?" Many social studies teachers (perhaps the majority) would favor an objective presentation of how the two economic systems operate, leaving the students free to arrive at their own conclusions. Many teachers would also stress "inquiry" processes as a way of studying economic or political systems. This approach emphasizes the intellectual skills in the analysis of controversial issues, rather than any specific set of attitudes and values to be sought as the outcome of instruction.

Apart from controversial social and political issues in educational curricula, teachers differ on whether or how they should try to influence or change attitudes of learners. Few teachers would disagree that "intellectual honesty" is a desirable outcome of education. Some would perhaps seek directly by *persuasive* techniques to show the learners why this is a valuable objective, while others would choose by *modeling* honesty in their own behavior to set an example which the learners may or may not choose to follow. Some, perhaps, would use a combination of the two techniques.

Some teachers feel that any attempt to influence attitudes of learners in a specific direction is a form of a coercion, and hence is to be avoided. Others, on the contrary, would feel a moral obligation to help establish those attitudes on which society is most in agreement, feeling that a part of their obligation for accountability to the citizens who support the school system is in this way discharged.

Because of the diversity of opinions just cited, this writer does not see it appropriate here to take a position on whether teachers should state attitudinal objectives either for their own planning purposes or for communication to the learners. But if a teacher does choose to attempt to influence attitudes of students, techniques relating to learning of attitudes are discussed in other Chapters of this book (Chapters 5, 7, and 9).

The next question to be addressed is "How much detail should be included in the objectives as they are communicated to the student?" In the case of intellectual skills, it might be helpful if the teacher presented a simplified wording of the learning hierarchy that was derived for the objective (see Chapter 5). Doing this would enable the learners to see why each lesson (for each essential prerequisite) needs to be mastered in order to perform the more complex skill represented as the "final task" in the objective itself. This might help convince the learners that it is essential to master each lesson in order to achieve mastery of the objectives, whose value, in turn, needs to be established for them by the teacher. Furthermore, the teacher can show how mastery of the specific objective relates to unit objectives, and hence to mastery of the course (see Chapter 4).

In the case of verbal information objectives, the teacher needs to inform the students as to *which items of information* need to be recalled later, which items need only to be understood in context, and which might be used to achieve a higher-order objective, such as the problem-solving history objectives listed earlier in this Chapter.

It is the domain of information learning that is most in need of careful statement of objectives by the teacher, in order to avoid invalid measurement of the learners' performance. Since it is obviously impossible for the students to learn and remember all of the information in an entire book, the students must be given a more limited set of information to be recalled on tests; or, information objectives should be reduced merely to whatever recall is needed to facilitate the learning of intellectual skill objectives. As emphasized repeatedly in this book, expecting students to answer any and every question that might be asked about the content of a text is not only an impossible expectation, but it is demoralizing for the learner. Information objectives, when used at all, should be reasonable in scope and should be clearly communicated to the student. The tests over such objectives should contain no "tricks" and no content beyond the stated objectives. Careful handling of the teaching of information objectives, and careful testing, can avoid "turning the students off" before they even get to the more problem-solving parts of the unit of instruction.

In conclusion, it is recommended that objectives be recorded for a whole series of lessons. Many reasons for this recommendation have already been given here. An additional reason is to make more efficient the search for materials, a later step in lesson planning.

Step 2: Listing instructional events. When a teacher has listed objectives for a whole series of lessons, it is possible to make better decisions as to how often to use the nine "instructional events" discussed in Chapter 7.

For young children, a teacher might decide to use all nine events for each of several lessons in a series, and the teacher might have to personally supply all these events. For example, in kindergarten, lessons would need to be brief because of the short attention span of the learner. The teacher would supply some events because the children cannot read, and they are not sophisticated in managing their own school learning. Events such as "gaining attention," "stimulating recall," and "providing learning guidance" may need to be provided for each short lesson. *How* the teacher provides each event was discussed in Chapter 7, but it may be said briefly here that such decisions are based on consideration of the learners' characteristics and the type of outcome represented by the objective to be learned.

In the case of kindergarten and first-grade children, concrete objects, the teacher's voice, and activities of the group tend to be the principal "media" of instruction. Therefore, for much instruction at this level, the lesson plan may be presented quite simply by a two-column format.

Figure 2 is a lesson plan for one objective in a series of objectives for a science curriculum (see Briggs *et al.*, 1966). Abbreviated objectives for a kindergarten unit on "measurement" were listed as follows:

Objective 1: Comparing lengths.
Objective 2: Linear measurement.

For objective 1, the formal statement of the objective (for the teacher) was approximately as follows: "Given pairs of *objects* of differing lengths, the child can *identify* them by pointing to 'the longer one' and the 'shorter one,' without prompting. (Standard: Learner gives correct response for objects differing by only ¼ inch.)"

In the above objective all five components discussed in Chapter 3 are present, as well as the sixth one—the standard of performance sought. This standard is included in this instance for convenience in establishing uniform testing procedures when teacher aides help with the testing.

While this objective itself requires the learning of concepts ("shorter one"; "longer one"), it is apparant that the child must *discriminate* before he can identify—that is, he must be able to "see the difference" in lengths of pairs of objects before he can

Instructional Event	Activity (Implementation)
1. Gain attention	Teacher holds up two dowels—one 4" and one 12" in length; asks questions such as "what are these?"
2. Stimulate recall	Teacher alternately holds up one dowel, then the other, evoking "large," "small," etc. Repeat with child holding objects.
3. Present stimulus	Teacher presents other pairs of dowels of increasingly similar length, evoking response.
4. Guide thinking	Teacher holds up pairs differing by only ¼ inch; first far apart, then close together, evoking such responses as "some left over," "same," "different," "longer," etc.
5. Elicit performance	Ask children to point to "longer one; shorter one."
6. Provide feedback	After each pupil response
7. Provide generalizing experiences	Use other objects such as boards or strips of paper
8. Assess performance	Individual performance tests by teacher

Figure 2: *A simple lesson plan for an elementary science objective.*

say which is longer or shorter. A teacher might attempt to establish the discrimination before the concepts, but for this example, the lesson plan assumes that both will be taught in one lesson. Also note that the learners are not "told" the objective at the outset; rather, the objective is inductively learned in the course of the lesson. This decision was made because the concrete objects (dowels, pencils, rulers, etc.) usually have more immediate appeal than do spoken words.

Notice in Figure 2 that a variety of examples is used in the lesson—pairs of dowels of widely differing lengths are used; the difference in length between pairs begins with large differences, then smaller ones; and a variety of types of objects is employed. The purpose of this latter variety, obviously, is to avoid associating "longer" and "shorter" only with pairs of dowels; the concept must be generalized to many types of objects differing in length. (In a classic example by William James, a pupil would say "vertical" only when a pencil was held in that position. Apparently, the teacher had not used a variety of examples of kinds of objects when that concept was being "taught.")

Note also in Figure 2 that "generalizing experiences" comes before "assessing the performance." Since more direct assistance from the teacher is reasonable for younger children, it also seems reasonable to do the "informal testing" during the lesson by eliciting performances and providing feedback, and to reserve formal testing for after the generalizing experiences, so that pupils will have feedback to responses to the generalizing objects used in the lesson.

For older learners, who are expected to be able to "generalize" with greater skill, the test could often reasonably be a "test of ability to transfer (generalize)."

In the science curriculum from which the above lesson plan was adopted (and modified to suit the present purpose), other subsequent objectives in a unit on measurement for kindergarten and first grade children included "linear measurement," "metric measurement," "making comparisons using a balance," and "comparison of volumes." Similar lesson plans for those objectives (Briggs *et al.*, 1966, pp. 60-73) also emphasize the role of real objects, the teacher, and activities of the children as frequently used media to implement the events of instruction.

The lesson plan in Figure 2 assumes group-paced, teacher-led instruction, a conventional procedure for this age level of learners. This is not to say, however, that similar lessons could not be taught by individually paced, automated instruction, such as an audio-tape, to direct the child's activity with objects and pictures of objects. Such methods are widely used for individualized programs in reading and mathematics (Briggs and Aronson, 1975; Talmage, 1975; Weisberger, 1972). In such programs, the voice on the tape can ask the child to "draw a circle around the longer one" of a pair of pictures on a page in a book; after a suitable pause, the voice on the tape provides feedback by saying "yes, the red one," or "yes, the one on the left." Such procedures allow children to work at their own pace; any errors they make are made in private, and the feedback is given privately (*via* earphones). Often periods of individual work with such media are interspersed with small-group work conducted by the teacher for children who have reached a similar stage of progress in the unit.

In summary, for young children, a teacher may *plan* a series of lessons simply by stating the objectives, then drawing a lesson plan for each lesson similar to the plan in Figure 2. For older learners, who can read, great use may be made of printed materials, and more use may be made of motion pictures or television combined with class discussions. For these more advanced learners, the lesson plan may take on a different form, necessitating some additional steps, as seen below.

Step 3: Selecting media for events. There are several different meanings that people attach to the word "medium" or "media." We will list them, and show what usage is intended here:

1. Sense organs acted upon: eye or ear. (We use the term "channel" for this, since the research literature deals with the "auditory" and "visual" channels.)

2. Type of stimuli. Spoken words, still pictures, objects, motion pictures. This is a more general set of terms than our usage of media. For example, "spoken words" does not specify whether by "tape recording" or "teacher's live voice." Motion pictures could involve videotape or 16mm projections.

3. Form or mechanism for conveying the stimuli. This is our meaning of media: books, programmed texts, motion picture films, overhead projections, slide/tape presentations.

4. Equipment. Associated with and necessary for some of the above media are items of equipment such as overhead projectors and motion picture projectors.

In our usage, the *teacher* is a medium of instruction, since the teacher's voice, for example, is a mechanism for presenting spoken words. There is no intent to dehumanize the teacher by adopting this terminology. The intent, rather, is to "upgrade" the other media from an older usage which relegated these media to extensions of the teacher. That is to say, it used to be thought by many that "only teachers teach; media are tools for the teacher."

Our view is that "anything that presents instructional events teaches." Therefore, both the human teacher and the other media provide instruction. This terminology is consistent with the overall view of instruction as presented in this book.

Students find no difficulty in the distinctions among "type of stimuli" and "media" and "equipment" (see the portion of Chapter 16 entitled "Assignment 3").

In Figure 2, the simple lesson plan could be presented in two columns, partly because the teacher and physical objects "carry the burden of the instruction." But when other print and non-print materials are appropriate for the learners, a more complex "worksheet" may help record elements to result in the lesson plan. With older learners, a greater variety of media may be considered as vehicles for accomplishing the various instructional events. Also, the learners can supply more of the events for themselves. Thus, the learners and the media other than the teacher can be heavily involved, especially in the event "presenting the stimulus material." This can give the teacher more flexibility in planning the media, event by event, and objective to objective, thus providing variety; and often, in addition, more than one option can be offered at points in order to adjust to media preferences of the learners.

These media preferences *may be* more highly related to learners' achievements for learners of age 9-18 than for college students. Differences in reading ability among groups in the 9-18 age bracket may account for a reasonably high relationship between preferred media and most successful media, while college students are generally skilled in learning by reading and listening to lectures. It is quite likely that learners are more "media sensitive" at the 9-18 levels than are college students; that is to say, there will be a greater relationship between media preference and amount learned for the younger of the two age brackets. Even if this proved to be the case, however, there is reason to provide more media choices than is often the case in college instruction, due in part to more "open enrollment" policies current in higher education.

Thus, a third step can be to list the media the teacher would like to use for each instructional event (including any options the learner may be offered). Then the teacher would search among available materials to see if the information desired as the stimulus materials is available in the desired media (step 4 in the process being described in this Chapter).

Figure 3 presents a format for a "worksheet" for the first five steps in lesson planning.

Step 4: Selecting materials and activities. Once the teacher has stated the objective for a lesson, and has listed the instruc-

Worksheet for Developing a Lesson Plan

1. Objective:

2. Instructional Events	3. Desired Media	4. Materials and Activities	5. Events in Materials
a.			
b.			
c.			
d.			
e.			
f.			
g.			
h.			
i.			

Figure 3: Sample worksheet for use in lesson planning.

tional events and the desired or ideal medium for each, the search for materials in those media may be made. As mentioned before, filling in those first three steps in the worksheet for an entire series of lessons can enable the teacher to search catalogs of materials for the entire series. Armed with several such worksheets on adjacent objectives (or enabling objectives) for a series of lessons, the materials search can be made more efficiently. Thus, while inspecting one catalog of films, or printed materials, or slide/tape presentations, the teacher can note potential materials for the entire series of lessons. This saves additional time if the needed catalogs are not located in the school.

At the present time, most catalogs of materials list items by title or topic, not by behavioral objectives. Nevertheless, many catalogs carry also brief descriptions of each item listed to help the teacher make a first judgment as to the possible relevance of the items for the list of objectives for lessons being planned. Stated differently, most catalogs describe only the stimulus materials contained in the media covered in the catalog. Such notations speak most directly to the event "presenting the stimulus." Once a teacher decides that an item in a catalog *appears* to present the desired stimulus, the item itself can be examined (previewed) to determine whether in fact the material is relevant, and whether the material also contains the means for providing other instructional events desired.

Suppose, for example, in a unit on heredity, a teacher has an objective that the learners can show how the physical characteristics of different species of animals are passed on to their offspring. For the event "gaining attention," the teacher may hope to find an interesting film showing how animals of various species differ. Perhaps the desired film would have the animals humorously discussing which features are better and how they were inherited. The teacher would have noted opposite the event, "gaining attention," on the worksheet, the entry "animal film." If such a film could be found, the teacher might hope it would also cover the event "informing the learner of the objective." For other events, such as "presenting the stimulus" (the rules of heredity, with examples), and "guiding thinking," the teacher might prefer a self-paced slide/tape or programmed instruction booklet. If located, such media might also "elicit the performance" and "provide feedback." If the search of catalogs for the desired media fails to result in usable materials, the teacher would look next perhaps in catalogs of plastic models (of chromosomes); the teacher may also turn to a book or encyclopaedia.

When the search of catalogs has been completed, and the selected materials are previewed favorably by inspection of the materials, the teacher is ready to complete the lesson plan by summarizing the desired events (teaching steps) that are supplied by the materials, and noting how the remaining events are to be supplied.

Referring to the worksheet (Figure 3), the teacher notes in column 4 the accepted materials located in the catalogs.

The notes in column 5 show the events the materials provide. The teacher might circle the events not supplied in any of the material located. The final step (step 6 in this method of lesson planning) is to complete the lesson plan, possibly in a format as simple as Figure 2, or perhaps more elaborate, as in Figure 5 (p. 254).

It is easy to realize that the worksheet will often be very "marked up" by the time the lesson plan is finished. In some cases, the desired media for some events may have to be changed to other media. In the case of the relevant materials located, the teacher may have noted in column 4 of the worksheet "good only for excellent readers," leaving the task of finding something else for other learners. When the materials finally selected are noted in the lesson plan, the teacher may also enter pupil activities to be undertaken if they are not as obvious as reading a chapter in a book or viewing a film.

Needless to say, this entire process may often be greatly simplified if an adopted textbook is required as the basic material. But, even then, the teacher should consider how each desired event is to be accomplished, so the worksheet is still useful.

Step 5: Events in materials. Perhaps the most typical event provided by materials (in all media) is "presenting the stimulus." But materials vary widely in whether other events are also provided. Some textbooks, for example, provide only the "stimulus"; others also guide thinking; a few list objectives, practice exericses, and tests over the objectives. In some cases, these latter "instructional features" are deliberately omitted, as in the case of this book. The reason for this is given in the Preface.

Unlike a book, in which the student may skim and look both forward and backward, as well as *reading* line by line and page by page in a linear fashion, media such as films and TV are normally presented only once, in linear fashion, to a group of learners *at a fixed pace*. The merits of the more vivid film presentation may therefore often be offset by the merits of a book or a programmed instruction unit because the latter are self-paced. Many programmed texts are intended to be self-instructional (because they provide all the needed instructional events), while most textbooks are planned with the assumption that a teacher is present to direct the learning in whatever manner the teacher desires, with emphasis on whatever content areas the teacher wishes to include in the objectives.

It follows from the above that most textbooks have the advantage of containing stimulus materials that may be used for a wide variety of instructional purposes. In the case of this book, the content may be used for a theory course, or for a "practicum" course, or for both, or even to direct graduate students' attention to needed areas of research which might become dissertation topics for the students. The instructor then needs to determine the purpose before lesson planning centered around the book would begin.

On the other hand, self-instructional materials, such as programmed instruction, being intended for a single purpose, can contain all necessary events of instruction.

Of course, a book could be "programmed" for a *single* purpose—in the instance of this book, for a theory course, a practicum course, or a research course. It would then be more advantageous for the intended purpose, but it would not serve other purposes. It is perhaps clear from the above that most programmed texts are much narrower in purpose and scope than are most textbooks, and hence must be much briefer in order to be economical.

Films often have the characteristics of a "book on a limited topic." That is, they usually contain no events such as "eliciting the performance" and "providing feedback." They suffer from the enforced linearity mentioned earlier, although the advantage of motion is extremely effective when motion is required in the instruction. Other features, such as animation, "slow motion," and "fast motion," are especially effective for specific limited purposes.

In summary, various media typically have their own special advantages, enabling the teacher to use each as appropriate. One seeks both *authoritative content and effective presentation* of the stimulus, along with any other desired instructional events the media may contain. A teacher may choose a book rather than a film or programmed text because the book has more authoritative content as the stimulus; the teacher is then willing to supply the other events not contained in the book rather than sacrifice the authoritative content.

In recent years, research demonstrations have shown that learning from films or TV can be improved by breaking up the continuous presentation of stimuli in order to pose questions, to provide a pause for the learners to think or write their answers, and then to provide feedback. It has also been shown that learning from print material can be enhanced by providing "self-test" questions (based on the objectives) which learners respond to before taking a (different) test over the objectives. Simple chemical or mechanical devices have been designed to make this feedback automatic after each response, rather than requiring the learner to check his answers with an "answer key." The effectiveness of this technique of using self-tests over chapters in textbooks was first demonstrated extensively by Pressey (1950) and his students (Briggs, 1947), and has been confirmed repeatedly by more recent research (Frase, 1970). Pressey coined the term "adjunct auto-instruction" for this technique.

The above research findings suggest that when a required text must be used, a shortcut to lesson planning could be as follows:

1. State objectives for each chapter in the book.

2. Prepare practice tests ("self-tests") and answer keys (or an automatic feedback device) for the learners to use as a part of their study of the chapter (thus focusing the study on the objectives of the chapter).

3. Administer objective-referenced tests over the chapter (see Chapter 6).

4. Conduct generalizing experiences, such as by group discussion of new problems to be solved.

Whatever the media and materials selected for the lesson,

then, the teacher can design a lesson plan so that the learners are not simply attending passively to the total stimulus materials, but are actively focusing on the parts of the material relevant to the objectives. In such techniques as adjunct auto-instruction, just mentioned, several instructional events are provided (presenting the stimulus, guiding thinking, and performance and feedback). The learning so promoted also enhances learning of parts of the material for which no self-test items were presented (Frase, 1970).

Evidence exists, then, that when attention is focused so that the learners' efforts are directed to the explicit objectives reflected in the practice tests, students *learn other objectives, too.* The findings from many investigations of adjunct auto-instruction have been summarized by Hiller (1974, p. 202) as follows: "A set of widely held conclusions is that inserted postquestions may raise the learning of (a) specific details asked about by the questions (Rothkopf, 1966), (b) details categorically related to the questions (Rothkopf and Bisbicos, 1967), and (c) information not directly related to the questions (Rothkopf, 1966)." This phenomenon, by which directed and focused attention stimulates recall of materials not covered on the self-tests, has been called "mathemagenic behavior." Such self-test questions need not be restricted to information learning. An early practice advocated by Pressey led others to construct several self-tests for each chapter—"factual tests," "interpretation tests," and "application tests" (Briggs, 1947). Such sets of practice tests thus can be made into either a "self-instructional delivery system," or the tests can be used primarily to help the learner establish the information base on which group activities can be built. This writer has used them both ways, with resulting learning which was significantly superior to the achievement of matched groups of students who took the same course in a conventional classroom mode of instruction (Briggs, 1948).

A possible interpretation of the "mathemagenic" effect has been offered by Frase (1970, p. 346): "Questions are motivational stimuli. They have arousal and associative outcomes." The degree of such arousal appears to be related to the perceived difficulty of the material and the readability level. It is suspected that the *overt* responding required is most facilitative for more difficult materials, or for learners scoring low in reading ability. Yet the effects also are present for superior students, whether they are studying independently or participating in special seminars for superior students (Briggs, 1948).

Whether it is best to provide the self-test questions before, after, or during study of the material is still under investigation (Frase, 1970). When such details are better understood, textbooks could be published with the self-tests "built in."

A teacher, then, can plan lessons directed to stated objectives as well as watching for and rewarding the attainment of unexpected outcomes. Some of the unexpected outcomes might be of sufficient value to be included when making new lesson plans for the unit.

Step 6: Planning means for the remaining events. When the fifth column on the worksheet has been completed, the teacher is ready to construct the lesson plan. Since column 5 shows which desired events the materials (in the various media) can supply, the remaining step is to note how any remaining events are to be accomplished. It was earlier suggested that after completing column 5, the teacher circle, in column 2, the events not provided by the materials. Then, simply by writing "pupil" or "teacher" and the nature of the activity, in the circled event in column 2, the planning is completed. The results then are recorded in clearer form in the lesson plan itself.

The foregoing discussion has centered on the events that the selected materials can provide, in order to urge the reader to plan to "get the most out of the materials." But, of course, teachers are concerned also with the planning of learner activities other than studying alone. One might think of learning activities in three categories:

1. Learning activities representing effective use of the materials selected for the lesson.

2. Learning activities related to the lesson but which are conducted independently from the materials selected for the lesson.

3. Learning activities directed towards a long-term goal, such as "learning to work together as a group," in which learning of the objective of the lesson is facilitated in addition to attitudes and "socialization" objectives.

These three types of activities will now be described in turn.

Learning activities related to the *materials* selected for the lesson may be as obvious as "reading," "listening," or "watching." However, in some cases, the teacher would need to give *directions*, such as "How to use a filmstrip projector" or "How to study this chapter." Such directions by a teacher can relate both to generalized study habits and to study procedures specific to the selected materials. Thus, both the specific (immediate) objective of the lesson may be enhanced and also the "cumulative objective" that the learner will develop good study habits.

Learners will study some materials alone; other materials will be viewed as a group. The "directions" given by the teacher would vary accordingly.

Learner activities for a lesson may be *independent* of the materials selected. Such activities could either build on the materials already studied, or could represent a part of the lesson plan for which no materials are available. Thus, a teacher may be forced to teach either an entire lesson without supporting materials, or a teacher may need to provide some of the instructional events, or some of the needed "stimulus" not found in the materials available. In this case, the learner activity, beyond listening and watching, may involve group discussion, responding to questions, etc.

The relative *amount* of learner activity independent of printed materials and non-print materials such as TV will, of course, vary by the subject being taught and by teacher preference. A course in public speaking, for example, conceivably could be taught entirely by oral methods. The only "media" would be the teacher, who gives oral instruction, and the learners, who ask questions, give speeches, and discuss the speeches given. A subject such as biology, on the other hand, might use many media for each lesson—books, films, filmstrips, laboratory specimens, etc. The nature of learner activity would be quite different in the two subjects just mentioned, even though the same instructional events are achieved in each case.

Learner activity directed towards *cumulative* (long-term) goals and objectives could often "kill two birds with one stone." That is, a lesson on "automobile emission standards" could be used for the cumulative goal of "peer discussion as a means of arriving at positions on controversial issues" and for the specific objective of "state how automobile emission is measured."

Specifying learner activity, then, becomes a part of the final step in completion of the worksheet and the lesson plan. This topic has been left until last, not because it is less important than the previous steps in lesson planning, but rather because it emphasizes *what the learner does with* all the materials selected for the lesson. In fact, the materials would be useless if the learner did not respond to them in an appropriate activity, whether implicit (thinking) or explicit (overt action).

An unstated but intended purpose of each instructional event is to stimulate learner activity. The events are phrased in terms of what the *teacher and the materials are intended to do*, but without some form of *attending or responding by the pupils*, there is no learning. That is why the instructional events (teaching steps) are often called the "external events," while the internal responses of the learners are called the "internal events" (Gagné, 1970). A related point may be made here: *teaching* may be a group process but *learning* is an individual process. Thus, a teacher or a film may "present the stimulus" in a group situation, but the learning from that external event is an internal matter taking place in the nervous system of the learner. Only individuals have nervous systems; groups do not. Therefore, an advantage of a self-instructional program that is also self-paced, is that the "lesson stops" when the pupil fails to respond. A programmed instruction unit, for example, "stops" until the learner responds to each "frame." Lapses in attention, then, may be less serious in a self-instructional lesson than in a group paced lesson.

With the above points in mind, the reader may wonder why self-instructional materials are not in greater use than they are, except where group interaction is required for the objective. This is not a simple question to answer, but some elements of the answer appear to be:

1. Lack of effective programs for many subject areas or objectives of education.

2. High initial costs of program production, requiring a large marketing effort to provide enough adoptions to defray costs.

3. Teachers' fear of being replaced by the programs.

4. Difficulty of monitoring an individually-paced program in order to keep each learner working on the appropriate objective.

5. Learners' reactions against programs that are too easy or too difficult, or that are not as interesting as other materials.

6. Too much "overselling" in earlier years (1960-1965), when many firms were producing programs, leading to a "backlash" when unrealistically high expectations were not realized.

As a matter of fact, self-instructional materials *are* in rather widespread use in schools which also provide a "delivery system" which gives teachers a way to monitor individual pupil progress. The theory and mechanism for such delivery systems have been described by Weisgerber (1972) and Talmage (1975), and the actual operation of such programs in schools has been described by Briggs and Aronson (1975).

Until such individualized programs are more widely adopted, teachers need to continue to make lesson plans by considering all nine of the instructional events discussed in Chapter 7. When some use is made of self-instructional materials, the teacher needs to inspect them to determine which events, if any, remain to be supplied by other means.

Most teachers tend to alternate between individual study of materials by the learner and group instruction. There seem to be several good reasons for this practice, and it does not conflict with the concept of instructional events. Let us list some of the events that might often be supplied by the teacher, by the materials, and by group discussion (see Table 2).

Table 2 is not intended to be applied in a blind fashion, of course. A teacher would consider the nature of the specific objective, the age and other characteristics of the learners, and the materials available when deciding how to plan for the achievement of each instructional event. (It was assumed, in Table 2, that some self-instructional materials were available. If not, the last two events listed there under "materials" would have to be shifted to another medium.)

One generalization might be made from the above: when self-instructional materials are available, initial learning is best done by individual study. Then, the role of the teacher is defined in the "Teacher" column of Table 2; the role of group discussion is defined in the right-hand column.

The teacher usually also has a role in those group discussions which are designed especially to enhance retention and transfer.

Table 2

Media and the Events They May Provide

Teacher	Media Materials	Group Discussion
Events:	*Events*:	*Events*:
Gaining attention	Presenting the stimulus materials	Enhancing retention and transfer
Informing learners of the objective		
Stimulating recall of previous learnings	Providing learning guidance	(Also to promote discussion skills; to experience "consensus"; to learn of
Assessing the performance	Eliciting the performance	values held by others; to learn that others make mistakes, too;
	Providing feedback about performance correctness	to aid in self-evaluation of progress.)

Such discussions provide review and reinforcement of prior learning accomplished by individual study, and they broaden generalizations. The learners hear how other pupils would apply what has been learned, and the teacher helps stimulate further application and generalization.

A few other purposes of group discussion are noted in Table 2. These refer to some of the broad goals of education that may be enhanced by repeated use of discussion in the context of specific objectives to be learned. Each of those goals deserves attention to a degree that is beyond the scope of this book, and only a few comments will be made about them here.

Even in the individualized programs in schools reported by Briggs and Aronson (1975), pupils spend only a portion of each day in individual work in reading and mathematics. The remainder of each day involves conventional group instruction. But even during the hours for the individualized portion of the program, the teacher may conduct discussion in speaking skills for the total group, and small-group instruction for specific skills for those pupils who are at the same point of progress in the program. Such sessions also may enhance goals related to interaction and socialization skills. The programs observed were conducted mostly in grades 1-6.

What is the role of group instruction for *college* students who are enrolled in a course that is heavily "materials dependent?" Many college courses now provide both self-pacing and self-instructional materials (see Chapters 12 and 13). Why would the students need to meet in the classroom? Experience suggests that the answer to this question is largely to provide motivation and encouragement, and to "keep the students on schedule" (or perhaps, in some cases, to keep them working at all). While there is little direct research on this question, the almost universal experience is that without some class meetings, the materials are not used evenly during the weeks of the school term. There tends to be higher use at first, then a "drop off" period, followed by frantic efforts at the end to "catch up." This results in many "incompletes" or failures. However, this does not apply to all students; some finish earlier on a self-paced program than on a group-paced program.

This writer offers a graduate course that is heavily "materials dependent" (the design course discussed in "Transition to Chapter 16"). Students report that they like to have *some* class meetings, for the following reasons:

1. To meet with other students to discuss problems and to "compare notes" on progress.

2. To lead the instructor to illustrate design principles by describing projects he completed in the past.

3. To be reassured that other students also do not find the course to be a "snap"—to receive moral support from other students and the instructor.

4. To be encouraged (and be instructed) by hearing from the instructor some of the problems that former students in the course have encountered, and how they were solved.

5. To hear reports from the instructor on how professional designers and consultants have designed various "design models" to meet different instructional situations in industrial and military training, as well as in education. (See Part II of this book.)

6. To receive feedback on their work. (Actually, the students refer here to the fact that the instructor provides to them in a class meeting the written feedback on each of their four assignments shown in Chapter 16.)

7. To become stimulated by the attention given by the instructor to current and futuristic ideas concerning instruction for future needs.

The final generalization to be introduced here is that the more sophisticated the student, the more events the *student* is expected to supply for himself. A corollary point is that *fewer* of the instructional events are supplied by the teacher, and *less frequently*. For children, *most events* need to be supplied by the teacher or the materials for *each lesson*. As the learner grows to be a more sophisticated learner, the more *self-directed* his learning is expected to be. Thus, a lesson plan that is appropriate for ten-year-old learners would be "spoon feeding" for college students.

Figure 4 provides a sample worksheet for a lesson, as it might appear just before the final lesson plan is written, and Figure 5 presents the resulting lesson plan.

A Sample Lesson Plan

The sample lesson plan used in Figures 4 and 5 is a modification of a plan reproduced in more detail elsewhere by Briggs (1972, pp. 140-177). This was a design submitted by a student, Carol Robb, who kindly gave permission for use of her project for illustrative purposes. While the basic content of her plan is retained, the writer has modified the form.

This lesson is for a high school course in journalism. A required entering competency is for the student to type well enough to submit his news stories to an editor.

The course objectives: "The student will be able to gather news, write it in acceptable form, and edit the copy for publication. He will employ standard practices in newspaper layout and placement of stories according to their 'newsworthiness.' He will be able to write headlines; to avoid libel; and to formulate a position on the role of a newspaper in our society. He can identify the duties of each position in a newspaper organization.''

In this case, the "unit objectives" were stated as topics, since assessment of performance was to be done for each specific objective under the units. The topics are easily inferred from the course objectives.

For the topic "using notes to write a news story," the following objective is derived: "Given notes on a newsworthy event, the student will *generate* a story, in typewritten form, including a good lead and a 'pyramid' form; the story will meet usual standards of brevity and reader interest."

When a learning hierarchy (Chapter 5) was drawn for this objective, one of the essential prerequisites was the defined concept "lead," which may be expressed: "given a news story, the student will classify the lead by underlining it." This becomes the purpose of our sample lesson plan. As the reader may have expected, the prerequisite of recognizing and classifying leads in stories written by others comes earlier in the teaching sequence than does the *writing* of leads in stories.

Since the entries in the sample worksheet in Figure 4 are in a kind of personal shorthand, as in making notes to one's self, we will "talk through" the designer's intent, using "a," "b," etc., to refer to the instructional events listed in Figure 4.

a. The designer wanted to locate a film that would show a reporter at the scene of action of a story; then, the reporter would be seen typing from notes. The question would be raised, "How many sentences are needed to give a capsule summary of the story?" No such film was located; underlining of the event in Figure 4 (gain attention) means the teacher will pose the same question, describing the action sought in the film.

b. The teacher could use either an opaque projector or slides for the events labeled for projection. Actual newspaper stories are the contents of such projection. The Xs in column 5 mean the events are contained in the materials.

c. The designer decided to relate the concept "lead" to the

Worksheet for Developing A Lesson Plan

1. Objective of lesson: "Given a news story, the student will classify the lead by underlining it."

2. *Instructional Events*	3. *Desired Media*	4. *Materials and Activities*	5. *Events in Materials*
a. Gain attention.	film	(none located)	X
b. Inform students of the objective	teacher and opaque projector	brief news stories with lead underlined	X
c. Stimulate recall	opaque projection	recall "pyramid" and relate to lead	X
d. Present stimulus	opaque projection	unmarked stories	X
e. Guide thinking	teacher	pages 76-80 in textbook	text overlaps with above but that is fine
f. Elicit performance	teacher	both definition and underline real stories	X
g. Provide feedback	opaque projection	students underline leads; correct answers	X
h. Enhance retention	students	home search for material	X
i. Enhance generalizing	students	oral exercise	X
j. Assess performance	newspaper story— ditto		

Figure 4:   *Sample notes on the worksheet for lesson plan.*

prior learned concept "pyramid," since both are standard elements in news stories.

d. "Unmarked stories" means that the leads are not underlined.

e. The teacher would assign this part of the textbook for reading in advance of this class session; the note in column 5 shows the designer is aware of overlap between book and lesson, thus providing two learning opportunities. The designer may have even suspected that some students wouldn't read it or wouldn't understand it. Also, a part of the strategy here is to permit learning by either direct, didactic teaching or by discovery. The concept may be learned either before or after the definition, so both practice and definition are planned.

f. The teacher will ask the students to both underline leads in stories and to define lead in their own words.

g. Stories with leads underlined by students are projected and critiqued.

h. Students are asked to clip short stories from newspapers and bring them in for a review exercise.

i. Generalizing here could include many things, at the teacher's option: Identifying leads in stories presented orally; noting differences between newspaper style and other writing styles; covering a wider range of stories of varying lengths.

j. Assessment would probably consist of a story, duplicated by ditto; the student underlines the lead and gives a definition in his own words. Some teachers might defer formal assessment until after the next lesson on *writing* leads for stories.

Having used the worksheet, with perhaps more "scratching out" than is shown in Figure 4, the teacher now can write the lesson plan. See Figure 5.

An alternate lesson plan could be more prescriptive than the plan in Figure 5. This would require students to identify the *formal criteria* for a lead—who, what, when, where, why, and how.

The designer clearly believed in providing some alternatives for the learner, such as to discover for himself, or wait to be "taught." She also provided options for herself, planning, perhaps, to take her cue for decision from the response of the class. Although no note was made of her alternate plan in case of equipment failure, one can't help suspecting that there were a couple of newspapers in her desk drawer.

Lesson Plan

Instructional Event	Activity	Notes
a. Gain attention	Describe a reporter on a news gathering event; cover typing and rush to editor. Relate the story.	Ask: Who can tell the story in two sentences? What are these sentences called?
b. Objective	Project story No. 1. Discuss underlined lead.	
c. Recall	"Pyramid" and relate to "lead."	Try to let students discover the relationship
d. Stimulus	For variety of examples, use story Nos. 2-6, unmarked stories.	Try covering up the lead and see if they realize it isn't there.
e. Guide thinking	Pages 76-80, text. Have students compare their own definitions with text: "the first part of a story that gives a skeleton outline in the fewest possible words." Guided practice on projections Nos. 7-9.	
f. Elicit performance	Alternate practice and definition	
g. Feedback	For each practice response.	
h. Retention	Assign home search—newspaper.	
i. Generalize	Oral stories; story No. 10; magazine story.	Have students see if there are leads in magazine stories.
j. Assess	Ditto story for a "test in underlining."	

Figure 5: Sample lesson plan.

Note also that while the lesson objective itself required the *underlining* of the lead in a news story, the designer decided, in effect, to add the information objective "give a definition of a lead." If her hypothesis was that the two activities would be mutually facilitating, one could hardly disagree. Note also that some of her students might "discover" the definition, while others would be "taught" the definition. Did you notice that one of the "conditions of learning" for defined concepts, *variety of examples*, appears in the lesson plan?

"How Will I Know I've Arrived?"

Up to now we have discussed the first two "anchor points":
1. "Where am I going?" (The objective of the lesson.)
2. "How will I get there?" (The lesson plan.)

Now we ask, "How will I know I've arrived?" (Reached the objective.)

In the sample lesson plan, the students, as a test, are to underline the lead in a story which was not encountered earlier by the students. As mentioned before, some teachers might rely on the event, "elicit performance," to provide an informal test. Responses to this event provide the opportunity for on-the-spot diagnosis of difficulties and remedial instruction in either a group situation or by individual remedial study and informal quizzing by the teacher. If the teacher is aware of the status of each student through the "elicit performance" event, formal testing may be deferred until a group of lessons on story writing is completed. The eventual goal, of course, is for the student to *write* leads, not merely to underline them. There seems little doubt that correctly underlining (or pointing to) leads in several stories would be convincing evidence of the capability of classifying the concept by use of a definition. This capability, in turn, is a prerequisite capability for learning to *write* (generate) leads in stories. Thus the defined concept is an enabling objective to the total task, writing stories, which requires problem-solving behavior.

Notice that a job analysis (see Chapter 12) would not have revealed the prerequisite, classify leads, because you would only see a reporter generate (type) a lead. It is doubtful that an experienced reporter would recall having ever been asked to *underline* a lead; thus, the necessity for the information processing analyses and the learning task analyses dealt with in Chapter 5. Simply listing in order the steps an expert performs on the job is not a substitute for analysis of the *learning* task, as distinct from analysis of the *job* task.

It may be recalled that the designer must decide which levels of the course organization are most suitable for assessments of learner performance. In our sample lesson plan, assessment is to be done at the level of an enabling objective, although it could have been reserved for the objective itself. It is doubtful that one would defer assessment, in this case, to the unit objective of "writing news stories." There are too many essential prerequisites that may not have been acquired by some students. (Recall, also, that these are high school students, not college students.) One certainly would not defer all assessment until the end of the course, if one is interested in monitoring learner progress in order to avoid failures.

Summary

This Chapter for the teacher as designer is entirely consistent with the design theory presented in this book, even though it omits some details given in Chapter 9 for design teams. One reason for the difference in some details is that the teacher normally *selects* materials, while design teams *develop* materials. But the intent to employ appropriate conditions of learning in the way that the instructional events are implemented is a common purpose in our approach to the design of instruction, whether done by a team or by an individual teacher.

We have not reviewed any research concerning lesson planning because we do not know of any research based on the approach to lesson planning presented in this Chapter. However, research on some of the theory supporting this Chapter has been cited at appropriate points.

This Chapter has covered only briefly the matters of objectives and assessment of learner performance, because those are the topics of Chapters 3 and 6. This Chapter has concentrated on the design of lessons, drawing upon the earlier design stages discussed in Chapter 7.

Instruction *needs to be designed*, whether by the teacher or by the teams that produce self-instructional "modules." The amount of detail in designs may vary according to the age of the learner and the nature of the delivery system (see Chapter 9 for further discussion of delivery systems).

Adult learners are often capable of supplying many instructional events by their application of various skills in study methods and research. These latter skills may appear as objectives in some curricula, or they may be acquired as a result of the learner's own efforts.

Three approaches to lesson planning have been outlined in this Chapter. The first approach is a simple three-step method of applying the three "anchor points" mentioned at the opening of the Chapter. The second approach, in which one merely lists the instructional events to be employed and the method for accomplishing them, was illustrated with an elementary science lesson. The third approach, requiring six steps, was illustrated for a lesson in high school journalism.

References

Briggs, L.J. Intensive Classes for Superior Students. *Journal of Educational Psychology*, April 1947, 207-215.

Briggs, L.J. The Development and Appraisal of Special Procedures for Superior Students, and an Analysis of the Effects of "Knowing of Results." Columbus, Ohio: Ohio State University, unpublished doctoral dissertation, 1948.

Briggs, L.J. *Students' Guide to Handbook of Procedures for the Design of Instruction.* Pittsburgh: American Institutes for Research, 1972.

Briggs, L.J., and Aronson, D. An Interpretive Study of Individualized Instruction in the Schools: Procedures, Problems, and Prospects. (Final Report, National Institute of Education, Grant No. NIE-G-740065.) Tallahassee: Florida State University, 1975.

Briggs, L.J., Campeau, P.L., Gagné, R.M., and May, M.A. *Instructional Media* (abbreviated title). Pittsburgh: American Institutes for Research, 1966.

Dale, E.A. *Audiovisual Methods in Teaching*, 3rd Edition. New York: Holt, Rinehart, and Winston, 1969.

Frase, L.T. Boundary Conditions for Mathemagenic Behavior. *Review of Educational Research*, 1970, *40*, 337-348.

Gagné, R.M. *The Conditions of Learning*, 2nd Edition. New York: Holt, Rinehart, and Winston, 1970.

Hiller, J.H. Learning from Prose Text: Effects of Readability Level, Inserted Questions Difficulty, and Individual Differences. *Journal of Educational Psychology*, 1974, *66*, 202-211.

Mager, R.F. *Developing Attitude Toward Learning*. Belmont, Ca.: Lear Siegler/Fearon, 1968.

Pressey, S.L. Development and Appraisal of Devices Providing Immediate Automatic Scoring of Objective Tests and Concomitant Self-Instruction. *Journal of Psychology*, 1950, *29*, 417-447.

Rothkopf, E.Z. Learning from Written Materials: An Exploration for the Control of Inspection Behavior by Test-Like Events. *American Educational Research Journal*, 1966, *3*, 241-249.

Rothkopf, E.Z., and Bisbicos, E.E. Selective Facilitative Effects of Interspersed Questions in Learning from Written Materials. *Journal of Educational Psychology*, 1967, *58*, 56-61.

Talmage, H. (Ed.), *Systems of Individualized Education*. Berkeley: McCutchan Publishing Corp., 1975.

Wager, W. Media Selection in the Affective Domain: A Further Interpretation of Dale's Cone of Experience for Cognitive and Affective Learning. *Educational Technology*, July, 1975, *15* (7), 9-13.

Weisgerber, R.A. *Perspectives in Individualized Learning*. Itasca, Ill.: F.E. Peacock Publishers, Inc., 1972.

Transition to Chapter 9

This Chapter completes the design process for readers who wish to work as team members in developing instructional materials and other components of the entire "delivery system" for a course or curriculum. Then, we go on to evaluation (Chapters 10 and 11).

For the reader wishing to work as a teacher-designer, only the first half of this Chapter may be needed. Then, again, on to Chapters 10 and 11.

Chapter 9

Teams as Designers

James Carey and Leslie J. Briggs
Florida State University

At this point, the reader should refer back to Figure 1 of Chapter 7 to note those early steps in design which are performed regardless of whether a teacher or a team is to design the instruction. The reader may note also in Figure 1 the differences between the steps taken by a teacher who *selects materials* as a step in design and the steps taken by a team which *develops* the needed instructional materials.

Chapter 7 concluded with the last two steps which both teachers and design teams need to take: (a) sequencing of the enabling objectives *within* each objective, and (b) the selection and design of instructional events (teaching steps).

The purpose of this Chapter is to present the remaining steps that a design team takes, and to show how such teams may be organized and managed in order to design, evaluate, install, and diffuse the entire instructional system.

The steps remaining for the design team to take are as follows:

1. Select the type of stimulus for each instructional event for each enabling objective.

2. Select the media for each such event.

3. Select the desired conditions of learning by which each event is to achieve its purpose.

4. Write prescriptions for how the conditions of learning are to be incorporated into each event; these prescriptions aid the media production specialists in both the content to be presented and how it is presented in each selected medium.

5. Develop and produce the instructional materials and the associated learner activity guides, and tests over the objectives (Chapter 6).

6. Conduct formative evaluation to improve the items listed in No. 5 above (Chapter 10).

7. Assist teachers in the use of the complete instructional system.

8. Assist teachers by monitoring the use of the system to see that all intended products and processes are being used as intended.

9. Assist with field tests, and eventually with summative evaluation of the system (Chapter 11).

10. Assist with diffusion efforts when the system is intended for widespread application.

Not all of the above steps will be taken for each system that is designed, depending upon the plans that led to the development of the system, as discussed next.

Instructional Systems

The term "instructional system" commonly refers to the total "package" of materials, tests, student guides, and teacher guides that is needed to reach the goals for any instructional unit, course, or curriculum, along with all supporting activities and processes required to operate the system as it was designed to be operated.

In the present context, such a system could be as small as a few hours of instruction or as long as a K-12 science curriculum. It is clear that the size of the team and the time and budget for the development of the system will vary greatly. It is not possible here to outline how team operations will differ according to the amount of instruction that is being planned, but later parts of this Chapter will illustrate some realities of team operations.

Related to the amount of instruction to be included in a system is the question of whether the system is designed for a single school or school district, or for nationwide adoption. In the single school case, only the personnel of that school need to be considered when plans are made for how the team will design and help install the system in the school. Frequently, a school or a military or industrial organization will contract with a university or other organization for development of the system. The school then becomes the "client" of the "team"; some school personnel also become members of the team during the design and development phase; all personnel of the school may be involved in the installation and evaluation of the system.

In other instances, a university, for example, may take this initiative in designing a new curriculum. In that case, the university usually forms a "consortium" of organizations, including schools, publishers, and other organizations. The financing for the system development may involve federal, state, and local funds. For such a large undertaking, the planning of the project, from the very outset, includes both development and diffusion plans. In other words, key people from schools all over the country will be on the planning team from the start in order to coordinate the plans for the system design with the intended users. As the system is developed, school personnel are trained in increasingly larger numbers so that the system can be implemented widely. This entire process is a complex one. Since this book is primarily for the design team member rather than for the project director of such an effort, the team operations during system design and development will be emphasized here rather than the efforts needed for teacher training and diffusion.

Delivery Systems

Before returning to our account of the steps in the design process, it is helpful to introduce the term "delivery system." A brief definition of "instructional system" has already been given. In essence, a delivery system is the *form* in which the instructional system will be developed and turned over to the client for installation and use. There are no standard sets of terms by which different delivery systems are uniformly known. Therefore, a variety of examples will be given below.

In a conventional school, the teacher and the book may represent the delivery system for use in a "self-contained" classroom. In another school, books, slide/tape packets, films, and team teaching may be the delivery system in "pods" within the school. In other schools, programmed instruction, earphones and workbooks, and teachers may constitute a delivery system for an individualized instruction program (see Briggs and Aronson, 1975).

In a military situation, technical manuals, teaching machines, training aides, training devices, simulators, and instructors may be the delivery system for either the training of individual technicians or of crews of people (see Chapter 12).

In an industrial situation, a multi-media package of films and programmed booklets, plus an instructor/monitor may constitute the delivery system (see Chapter 15).

Note that the total instructional resources used define the "delivery system," which may include several "media," such as books, programmed instruction, films, lectures, and practice with either automatic feedback or feedback from an instructor.

Note also that in the above examples of delivery systems, only in the first two school examples is the teacher a primary source of the instructional content (the information source). In all other examples a teacher or instructor is the manager of the delivery system, but not the primary source of information.

An advantage of using media other than the teacher as the information source is that the instructional stimuli are *replicable.* That is, they are "captured" in the form of print, films, programmed booklets, etc. They do not "disappear" as does a live lecture or a discussion (unless they are recorded). Therefore, they can be tried out, tested, and revised conveniently, in the formative evaluation process. True, a teacher can keep careful notes on his or her lecture, and attempt to improve the presentation on the basis of reactions from the learners, but seldom does the teacher have the time to relate each part of the lecture to pupil performance on a test.

Because of the non-replicable character of lectures, the process of improvement of the delivery system is most feasible when the instructional stimuli are "captured" in physical forms that can be "played back" repeatedly, as in a videotape recording, and examined minutely, as in checking each teaching "frame" in a programmed booklet against an item analysis of test responses by the students (Chapter 10).

For the above reason, design teams tend to rely heavily upon replicable media as components of the delivery system, thus utilizing largely self-instructional media, replicable films, etc., for the design of the instructional system. Such replicable media not only enable the designers to plan the instructional stimuli with much greater care than in a largely spontaneous lecture, but they lend themselves to improvement through field testing more than do lectures. It has been acknowledged previously, however (Chapters 7 and 8), that live lectures can adjust to unexpected happenings in a way that "pre-designed" media cannot. Our general recommendation, then, is to utilize the replicable media when time and budgets permit; then, a teacher can "override" the pre-designed media by changing schedules, making individualized assignments to different learners, etc.

The general effect of employing replicable media is to improve the quality of the instructional materials and media, and to free the teacher for individual diagnosis and prescription of remedial work for those individual students who encounter difficulties. After teachers become accustomed to using pre-designed, replicable media in an individualized instructional delivery system, they often report that they would be very reluctant to return to conventional methods (Briggs and Aronson, 1975).

Having set the stage for how design teams may employ replicable media in their delivery systems, we return now to the design process itself.

Arriving at Prescriptions for Materials

Recall from Chapter 7 that the design team has accomplished previously the following steps in the design process:

1. Analysis of needs and goals.
2. Organizing the "course" into units or into a curriculum scope and sequence.
3. Stating behavioral objectives.
4. Design of learner performance measures.
5. Analysis of objectives into component parts.
6. Sequencing of the component parts of each objective.

7. Selecting of instructional events for each component part of each objective.

The accomplishment of steps 6 and 7, above, was referred to in Chapter 7 as the design of the "strategy of instruction" for each component of a behavioral objective. (Note that this is very different from the logic that led to a decision that replicable media would be used for the entire delivery system.) We are dealing now with the detailed design of a delivery system chosen to fit the resources and constraints applicable to both the assumed development environment and the assumed learning environment—school, home study, learning center, etc.

The next step in the design process could be called the "tactics" of instruction. That is to say, steps 6 and 7 above should be taken in order to have adequate *sequences* of instruction, and to choose instructional events appropriately. Now the question is *how will the chosen instructional events* be implemented? The answer to this depends upon answers to the following questions:

1. What type of stimuli should be employed—spoken words, written words, still or motion pictures, real objects, live demonstrations?

2. Which media can present the desired type of stimuli—books, films, slide/tape presentations?

3. Which would be the theoretically best media—ignoring expense, ease of use, etc.?

4. How can the appropriate conditions of learning be incorporated into the desired instructional events (in the chosen media)?

While one could simply answer each of these questions "in his head" in order to write the "prescriptions" to guide the media producers in their work, the larger the team involved, the more the decisions made should be recorded in order that the efforts of the members of the team may be properly coordinated and directed.

To serve such a purpose, a standard format can help the "master designer" both to record the rationale for his decisions and to direct the work of more specialized team members. This has the added merit of providing a basis for "peer review" through which the decisions may be examined, discussed, and improved.

One format for this purpose was developed and used in a design course for graduate students (Briggs, 1970). Examples of its use by students appear elsewhere (Briggs, 1972, and Chapter 16 of this book). At the time of this writing, approximately 450 students have used this format in a course at Florida State University; an unknown number of students elsewhere have probably used it due to adoption of the two books just cited.

The suggested format appears in Figure 1. In some cases, one page of the format may be used for the several instructional events for a single enabling objective. In other cases, it may be convenient to use a separate page for each instructional event. Samples of both situations appear elsewhere (Briggs, 1972). The sample shown in Chapter 16 uses one page for each event.

Following the sequence in Figure 1, we will discuss each step in this part of the design process, in turn.

Selecting Type of Stimuli

The process of decision-making for the first three components of Figure 1 has been described in previous Chapters, so we now address item 4 in Figure 1, selecting the *type of stimuli.*

Note first of all that selecting the type of stimulus for each of the events is a more general or basic decision than is selecting the specific media to be used. That is, once one has decided upon printed words, he may next consider whether the words are to be in a book, a chart, or in a programmed text. If spoken words are chosen, these could be presented by a live instructor, a tape recording, or the sound track of a film.

Recall from Chapter 8 that the age of the learner, and his reading ability and other characteristics, are relevant to the type of stimuli chosen. Real objects and direct experiences may be best for young learners, while either written or spoken words may do for the college student.

The nature of the enabling objective (task) being analyzed and the particular event are also relevant considerations. If the learner is only to list the steps (information learning) in a process, printed words may be relevant. But if the learner is to demonstrate the process, live or filmed demonstrations may be more useful. For some tasks, both types of stimuli may be needed.

As to the instructional event being planned, a film may be best to motivate the learner or to catch his attention, while printed words may be best for presenting the instructional stimulus if it consists of a definition.

1. Objective or enabling objective being analyzed:

2. Domain and/or type of learning represented:

3. Instructional Event	4. Type of Stimulus	5. Candidate Media	6. Theoretically Best (or tentative) Media Choices	7. Final Media Selection
a.				
b.				
c.				
d.				
e.				

8. Rationale for Media Selected:

9. Prescriptions for Media Producer:

Figure 1: A format for production planning.

Selecting the Candidate Media

Once the designer has selected the type of stimulus for an event of instruction, it may be useful (for the novice designer at least) to list both the "candidate" and the "non-candidate" media. For example, a conventional book *cannot* present spoken words or real objects in motion, whereas a film can do so. A book can present still pictures but not moving pictures.

Note that at this stage one is not trying to select the best, or the most convenient, or the least costly media. One is simply reminding himself of which media can or cannot present a particular type of stimulus.

Another reason for consciously attending to the candidate media is that often there is no reason to prefer one over the other. If printed words are the selected stimuli, provided that the learner can see them as long as he wishes and whenever he wishes, there is no reason to think that one candidate medium is preferable to another. The teacher, of course, may prefer an overhead projection to a list of the same content on a chalkboard, but it is not clear that one is more effective than the other. But if the printed words can be seen only once, as in a group showing of a film, and if the learner needs to refer to them repeatedly, a printed handout would be better. Also, if the function of the words (event) is only to catch attention, the words in the film would be satisfactory and most convenient in terms of the information to be presented next (for another event).

Often the full potentials of media are not employed, as when a videotape rather than a sound recording is used although the only relevant stimuli are spoken words. A videotaped lecture may be more distracting than a simple tape recording if the words, not the picture, actually "carry the message." Awkward motions or facial mannerisms in the videotaped lecture may render the videotape less effective than sound recording only.

Novice designers should beware of media choices that increase the probability that irrelevant stimuli may be introduced. It is *not* always true that simultaneous presentation of a picture and spoken words is better than either one alone. There is much evidence that *alternating* the audio and visual sense organs is more effective than "dual channel" presentation. (Any assumption that *both* channels must *always* be used may be a result of movies and

TV programs designed for entertainment or propaganda rather than for instructional purposes.)

One should try to insure, then, that the candidate media can be used as desired for the chosen type of stimulus—and nothing more. There is absolutely nothing wrong, however, in using a motion picture for two instructional events in quick succession, but using only one channel for a brief period. For example, if the desired stimulus is spoken words for one brief event, then motion picture plus spoken words for the next event, just *leave the screen blank* for the first event, and introduce the picture for the second one. (This suggestion may make the commercial producer tear his hair out, but our criterion is learning effectiveness.)

Theoretically Best Media

Among the media entered as candidate media in Figure 1, one next may profit from designating the theoretically best medium. Sometimes all the candidate media will appear equally effective—in that case just use the one that is most convenient in terms of media under consideration for adjacent events in the series of events.

Careful thought as to whether there *is* a theoretically best medium, however, is often time well spent. Suppose, for example, that "moving pictures" is the desired stimulus, thus leading you to enter "films" and "ITV" (instructional television or videotape) in the "Candidate Media" column in Figure 1. Suppose further that you are analyzing the event "present the instructional stimulus" for a competency such as "explain what happens when a current moves along a copper wire in an electrical circuit." The required explanation is based on a theory of electricity that cannot be seen in looking at a real circuit. A motion picture of someone designing a circuit would not help with this objective, but an animated film could do the job. Such events as "molecules in motion" lend themselves to film techniques better than do live demonstrations or a videotape of a lecture.

It is not known how often it would be just as well to "toss a coin" to select one of the candidate media, and how often there is, indeed, a theoretically best medium. But as a learning experience for the designer, searching for a theoretically best choice is at least sometimes very rewarding. (In the use of the Figure 1 format with students of design, the quality of the prescription often hinges upon this step in the analysis.)

Final Media Selection

Up to now we have only incidentally alluded to a fact that must be made explicit—one *considers* media for each instructional event in isolation from other events in the series, but the final *media choices* are made by reviewing *all* the events in the series. For learning this method of selecting media, the student reader should consider column 6 in Figure 1 to mean two things: "theoretically best media" and "tentative media choices for each event, considered separately." It is in column 7 that you record the results of your final media choices for the *entire series of events.*

In arriving at final media selections, one not only checks to see where one medium can be used for an entire series of events, but one also seeks this "tradeoff": "Use a medium as long as you can for efficiency, but change media when needed to avoid boredom or to gain effectiveness." A corollary for *all* choices, of course, is to keep within the constraints and resources available.

Rationale for Media Choices

When used for student designers, this part of Figure 1 (rationale) is used as a part of evaluating how well the student can utilize the capabilities of the various media. The requirement to complete this part of the form helps the student to avoid purely fortuitous choices. For learning purposes, the rationale is more important than the media choices entered on the form. When Figure 1 is used in actual team operation, a dual value results: continued evaluation of the work of team personnel, and a basis for team discussion to improve the quality of the overall plan.

This part of the form can be used to discuss the reasons for the decisions recorded in columns 3-7. Used this way, one page for each event is preferable, as in the sample analysis in Chapter 16. Thus, the designer can record why he did not use some of the nine instructional events for an enabling objective; why the types of stimuli were chosen; why the particular candidate media were listed; why the theoretically best medium was chosen, etc. This section of the form can also be used to defend the *prescription*, by showing how the appropriate conditions of learning are designed into the "content" of the prescriptions. For example, if one were designing the event "present the stimulus" for the task of learning the concrete concept "circle," one appropriate condition of learning is "give a variety of examples." The designer, in writing the prescription, could thus state that examples of circles must include large and small circles; circles printed with all colors of ink; concrete objects in the shape of circles, etc. The prescription tells the producer what to produce, and the rationale enables a team leader to check to see that appropriate conditions of learning were employed.

It is in filling in the rationale section that a learner or designer can demonstrate his ability to apply learning theory to the design of instruction. In the use of Figure 1 to train student designers, feedback from the instructor to the student concerning the entries made in columns 6 and 8 are most valuable. This can lead the student to revise and improve the decisions made.

Then, a second review, including review of the prescriptions, can be part of the basis for evaluating the learner's performance. Needless to say, if time permits, this evaluation can be checked against the empirical success of the design by the evaluation of materials produced from the prescriptions.

Writing the Prescriptions

Accomplishing the written prescriptions may be considered the end of the "design" phase and the beginning of the "development-production-evaluation" phases of instructional systems design (see Chapter 12).

The prescriptions, when completed, can be evaluated for adequacy by three means:

1. The team leader can review the prescriptions to see if they incorporate the appropriate sets of conditions of learning.

2. The media producers can read the prescriptions to see if they provide sufficient information to go on into production planning.

3. When the materials have been developed in the prescribed media, formative evaluations of their actual effectiveness can be conducted.

How does a designer know what to include in the prescriptions? By careful attention to the learning task and the nature and age of the intended learners, the designer selects appropriate *content* and *conditions of learning* for *each event* chosen.

In regard to instructional content, there is a gray area as to where the prescriptions leave off and the "script writing" by the media producers begins. What the prescriptions *do not* include are verbatim transcripts of words to be spoken or actual pictures to be produced; nor do the prescriptions tell the media developers and producers what production techniques to use. Team members may go through much trial-and-error in order to learn to obtain a good product with a minimum of friction as to the "territorial rights" of each.

In a small team effort, of course, one person may be both the designer and producer. In such a case, the designer "fills his own prescription," as when a physician dispenses his own medicine. (Some doctoral dissertations in the area of instructional research actually require the student to cover at least these distinct areas: instructional theory and hypothesis development; research design; instructional design, development, and production; and statistical analysis of data.)

Selecting Conditions of Learning

So far in this book, we have referred frequently to conditions of learning. It is now time to deal with them more directly.

As used here, conditions of learning are intended to be thought of as they were originally described by Gagné (1965) and later expanded upon (Gagné, 1970; Gagné 1977; Gagné and Briggs, 1974). Gagné has distinguished between *internal* conditions (within the learner, such as motivation and recall of prior learning) and *external* conditions (supplied by the teacher, media, materials, etc.; see Chapter 8).

In Tables 1-3, an attempt has been made to organize the conditions of learning in a novel manner. The format of those tables represents an attempt to relate three major concepts: *domains of learning outcomes, instructional events*, and *conditions of learning*.

The idea for the format for Tables 1-3 grew out of the need to explain to students how the above three major concepts are related. Similar tables had been made earlier (Gagné and Briggs, 1974, pp. 148-149), but those tables related only two of the three concepts in tabular form, type of outcome, and conditions of learning—with the latter not categorized as to instructional event.

In 1975 one of the authors of this Chapter (Briggs) developed the format shown in Tables 1-3, using only enough examples to fill some of the cells in the table. Soon thereafter, as a project during his final year of doctoral study, Dr. Ralph Vedros expanded the original tables to fill all the cells by retrieving information from books (Gagné, 1970; Gagné, 1974; Gagné and Briggs, 1974), and finally by completing the last empty cells on the basis of his own experience and theorizing.

While Tables 1-3 are no substitute for in-depth study of the sources mentioned, they do, in the experience of students, constitute a convenient guide to use while writing prescriptions. The reader is urged to refer to one or more of the sources mentioned for in-depth study of conditions of learning, using the tables as an organizing framework during study and thereafter as a guide to practice.

Note that the *row* headings in the three tables are the *instructional events*; the *column* headings are the types of learning *outcomes* represented by the objective (or its prerequisite) being taught; and the *intersection* of the two (the cells) are the *conditions of learning* to be incorporated into the instructional events.

In actually designing instruction for an objective or an enabling objective, of ocurse, one simply reads down the appropriate domain column.

The steps which complete the design phase of an instructional design and development activity were presented in the first part of this Chapter. The steps included: selecting stimuli for instructional events, selecting media, selecting conditions of learning, and writing prescriptions for materials development. The remaining steps in a team design and development process would include: developing the instructional materials, field testing and revision, and installing and evaluating the materials in the intended instructional setting. The text will return to a discussion of these three steps later in the Chapter, but now it is time to directly emphasize some team aspects of the instructional design and development process.

The treatment of team design will be broken into two parts for discussion. First, a general framework will be presented for

Table 1

Matching Conditions of Learning to Instructional Events and Types of Learning

TYPES OF LEARNING

Instructional Events	INTELLECTUAL SKILLS			
	Discriminations	Concrete Concepts	Defined Concepts	Rules
1. Gaining Attention	Provide verbal directions, gestures, etc., to direct attention to object or characteristic that is to become the stimulus suitable to the learner. (2)		Highlight verbal statement of the concept. (2)	Set apart verbal statement of the rule from verbal directions that focus attention. (2)
2. Informing Learner of the Objective	Inform learner of objective to be able to distinguish each member of a set. (*)	Inform learner of objective to be able to put things into a class and respond to the class as a whole. (*)	Provide a verbal statement of the general nature of the performance to be expected. (2)	Provide a statement of the general nature of the performance to be expected. (2)
3. Stimulating Recall of Prerequisites	Stimulate recall of individual S-R connections by verbal instructions. (1)	Stimulate recall of discriminations and relevant qualities by verbal instructions. (1, 2)	Verbally stimulate recall of component concepts including relational concepts. (1)	Stimulate recall of component concepts including relational concepts and subordinate rules by verbal instructions. (2)
4. Presenting the Stimulus Material	Present distinctive features maintaining contiguity of stimulus and response. (1)	Present contiguous instances of the class and provide examples varying in non-relevant characteristics. (1, 2)	Present verbal definitions, examples, and demonstrations. (1)	Present a variety of examples through verbal stimuli. (2)
5. Providing Learning Guidance	Provide verbal cues to establish proper sequence of connections or to increase distinctiveness of stimuli. (2)	Provide a set of verbal instructions as cues to identifying attributes. (1)	Provide verbal cues to stimulate formation of component concepts contiguously in a proper sequence. (2)	Provide varying amounts of verbal cues contiguous with recall of component concepts that will lead learner to put rule together. (1)
6. Eliciting the Performance	Ask learner to discriminate distinctive features. (*)	Ask learner to respond to a set of stimuli as a class by observation. (*)	Ask learner to demonstrate the concept. (1)	Ask the learner to demonstrate the rule by stating it verbally and applying it. (1)
7. Providing Feedback	Provide differential reinforcement for correct and incorrect responses. (1)	Provide immediate conformation of correct response to new set of stimuli. (2)	Provide confirmation of correct use of the definition. (*)	Provide confirmation of correct rule application. (2)
8. Assessing Performance	After each correct response to an instance repeat distinctive features by omitting elements responded to correctly. (*)	Learner correctly identifies concept instances. (1)	Learner demonstrates concept by using definition to classify. (1)	Learner demonstrates rule application. (1)
9. Enhancing Retention and Transfer	Provide contrast practice using correct and incorrect stimuli and repeat the situations to reduce interference. (2)	Broaden context of examples by providing variety of stimuli differing in appearance but belonging to a single class. (2)	Provide systematic spaced reviews to include variety of situations. (1)	Provide systematic spaced reviews to include broad range of rule applications. (1)

*   Derived from experience of the author.

1   Derived from *Principles of Instructional Design*, Gagné and Briggs

2   Derived from *Conditions of Learning*, Gagné

3   Derived from *Essentials of Human Learning*, Gagné

Table 2

Matching Conditions of Learning to Instructional Events and Types of Learning

Instructional Events	Problem-Solving	Motor Skills	Cognitive Strategies	Attitudes
1. Gaining Attention				
2. Informing Learner of the Objective	Inform learner of general form of problem solution. (2)	Demonstrate to the learner what the skill involves. (*)	Provide a verbal description of the strategy and make clear the general nature of the solution expected. (3)	Provide instances of the modeling behavior, either real or simulated. (2)
3. Stimulating Recall of Prerequisites	Stimulate recall of relevant subordinate rules and information by verbal instructions. (1, 2)	Stimulate recall of component responses, motor chains, and executive subroutines. (1)	Stimulate recall of variety of cognitive strategies of problem solution and associated intellectual skills. (1)	Stimulate learner to identify with human model and recall relevance information and skills. (1)
4. Presenting the Stimulus Material	Present novel problem situations, real or represented. (1)	Provide for proper timing and ordering of stimulus events within parts and among parts through verbal communications, pictures, diagrams, etc. (1)	Present novel problems without specifying class of solution required. (1)	Present respected human model and demonstrate desired behavior leading to vicarious reinforcement. (1)
5. Providing Learning Guidance	Provide a minimum amount of indirect verbal cues to previously learned rules to achieve a novel combination. (2)	Direct the recall of rules and sequence of required movements and practice by proper prompting. (3)	Provide indirect prompts for a novel problem solution. (*)	Establish respect for the human model and demonstrate or describe modeling behavior with learner observing model receiving reinforcement. (*)
6. Eliciting the Performance	Provide a variety of examples for solution. (*)	Require learner to perform part and total skill within required tolerance. (*)	Learner is asked to attack the problem in his own way. (1)	Provide opportunities for making choices or stating preferences in a real or simulated situation. (3)
7. Providing Feedback	Provide confirmation of correctness of rule application. (*)	Provide immediate informative feedback as to the correctness of the part and total skills. (1)	Provide confirmation of originality of problem solution. (1)	Provide reward for desired choice or action either directly or vicariously. (1)
8. Assessing Performance	Learner demonstrates application of new rule in problem solution. (1)	Learner demonstrates performance of total skill recording to prescribed criteria. (1)	Learner originates a model solution. (1)	Learner makes desired choice in real or simulated situation. (1)
9. Enhancing Retention and Transfer	Provide a broad range of problem situations. (3)	Provide for practice of part and total skills. (1)	Provide opportunities for variety and novelty in problem-solving tasks. (1)	Provide instances for making personal choices or for observing model. (3)

Table 3

Matching Conditions of Learning to Instructional Events and Types of Learning

Instructional Events	Names/Labels	Information Facts	Organized Knowledge (Substance Learning)
1. Gaining Attention	Provide variations in speech or print to direct attention to important features of the communication. (3)		
2. Informing Learner of the Objective	Emphasize what is to be learned. (*)	Suggest the association to be acquired by the fact. (1)	Provide Advance Organizers.
3. Stimulating Recall of Prerequisites	Stimulate recall of verbal chains. (*)	Stimulate recall of organized context of information to which new fact is related. (1)	Stimulate recall of context of organized information to which interconnected facts may be related. (1)
4. Presenting the Stimulus Material	Present name/label prior to or at same time as concept. (1)	Present verbal statement of new information in meaningful context and logical sequences. (1)	Present highly organized information in a meaningful context for effective coding. (1, 3)
5. Providing Learning Guidance	Stimulate recall of previously learned organized structure and provide coding or ask learner to invent his own. (1)	Provide verbal communication, picture, or other cue to stimulate recall of larger body of meaningful information and provide coding for relating facts to larger meaningful structures. (1)	Provide direct prompting to take advantage of prior learning of a related class of information. (1)
6. Eliciting the Performance	Learner is asked to supply the name of a specific object. (1)	Learner is asked to state the fact verbally. (*)	Learner is asked to state the proposition in his own words. (*)
7. Providing Feedback	Identify for the learner what is wrong or omitted in the name/label. (*)	Identify for the learner what is wrong or omitted from the statement of the fact.	Identify for the learner what is wrong or omitted from the statement of the proposition. (*)
8. Assessing Performance	Learner makes verbatim statement of name/label. (*)	Learner restates fact in larger context. (1)	Learner restates new knowledge in context of related information. (1)
9. Enhancing Retention and Transfer	Provide repetition in form of spaced reviews. (3)	Provide time for rehearsal and repetition in the form of spaced reviews. (1)	Provide repetition in the form of spaced reviews. (1)

structuring a team design process. Second, each major phase of the design model used in this book will be reviewed with commentary on implications for team design at each point in the model. It is in this second part of the team design presentation that the text will return to a discussion of the three steps mentioned in the previous paragraph.

Structuring a Team Design Process

One particular utility of a systems design model is found in the structure that the model itself can lend to a team design and development activity. For example, a sequence of steps for designing instruction has been presented in this book. If one accepts these steps as being a logical and practical approach to the design process, then one has already defined a majority of the tasks that must be completed by members of a design team. Simplistically stated, one can approach the establishment and management of a team design and development activity in the following way:

1. Adopt, adapt, or develop a suitable model of instructional design.

2. Detail the substeps (subtasks) involved in each step (task) of the model.

3. Develop time lines indicating tentative dates by which subtasks and tasks should be completed.

4. Make tentative assignments of personnel and resources to the subtasks and tasks.

5. Initiate team activities and monitor the process, making revisions as appropriate.

So as not to be misleading, several reservations must be made about the five activities just presented. First, anyone with design team management experience would protest that the process is just not that simple—and would be correct in doing so. Complications include such things as budget, personnel, facilities, equipment and supplies, and liaison with parent or contracting agency. The purpose of this book, however, is to provide a guide to instructional design, rather than to serve as a primer for R & D project managers. The "business" of managing a design team will thus be discussed only briefly, or when it relates directly to design and development questions. The fact remains, however, that a well-chosen model will provide a design team with a basic structure and sequence of tasks to be completed.

A second reservation is that the five activities are often not applied in as linear a sequence as indicated. For example, a large materials development project might complete activity 1 as a general framework and then work through activities 2 through 5 only for the purpose of identifying needs, establishing goals, analyzing resources and constraints, and organizing the course and the units of instruction. The project could then use the results of this front-end analysis as input for subsequent project planning. The next step might be to work through activities 2 through 5 again, only this time it would be for the purpose of planning actual materials design and development. Later, the process might be repeated for planning field trials and summative evaluation. The factors which determine the sequence question are probably size and complexity. In a large, complex design activity, it may not be possible to predict the output of some of the steps of the design model. Thus, it sometimes becomes necessary to work far enough into a step to start realizing some results before planning can begin for the following step.

A third reservation is that the first four activities may have been completed before the design team begins its work. This is particularly true in the case of funded materials development projects where activities 1 through 4 are normally detailed quite thoroughly in the project proposal. The only steps remaining for a design team leader may be validating the plans contained in the proposal and beginning activity 5—initiating team activities and monitoring the process.

In the next few pages each of the five team structuring activities will be discussed in more detail.

Activity 1: Adopt, Adapt, or Develop a Model

Using an appropriate instructional design model is critically important because it serves a central purpose in team planning. There are many popular models of instructional design, all of which share numerous common steps, but none of which may fit the exact demands of a particular design problem. That is why it may be necessary to adapt or develop a model. If a model is so general that it will fit all design problems, it is probably not specific enough to adequately support team planning.

There are three questions that one must ask in judging the appropriateness of a model: "How much does it cost?"; "What can the design team handle?"; and "Does it reflect the intended instructional setting?" First, the question of cost is based on the ratio of available resources to the anticipated product. If the ratio is high, one selects a detailed model like the one found in this book. If the ratio is low, one selects a less technical model, like the one proposed by Singer and Dick (1974), requiring fewer design and development steps. The key is to select a model which will supply as much precision as one's design budget will support. For example, one-to-one, small-group, and large-group formative trials will obviously contribute to the effectiveness of an instructional product; however, low-budget design teams can't afford the time or cost of such extensive formative evaluation, so a model is chosen which specifies a less precise procedure.

The second question concerns the capabilities of the design team. The Singer and Dick model mentioned above would be an excellent choice for novice teacher/designers spending a summer working on a school district design team. The Briggs model used in this book would be overwhelming; the entire summer would be spent in inservice training. However, one would expect professional design team members to use the Briggs model quite well. A model must be chosen that is appropriate to the skills of the team members; too simple a model means that personnel resources are not being fully utilized, and too difficult a model means that time must be devoted to inservice training of team members.

The third question refers to the setting in which the new instructional system will be installed. This is a straightforward consideration which a few examples should serve to clarify. For vocational or industrial training, one might select a model emphasizing job task analysis, like that by Mager and Beach (1967). The military's Interservice Procedures for Instructional Systems Development (Branson *et al.*, 1975) is a model that is currently available for implementation by all branches of the military. For very specialized design problems, one might wish to design a unique model, incorporating specific peculiarities as separate steps in the design process. For example, expedient administrative reviews or check-offs could be written in as specific steps of the model in a highly political design setting.

For the sake of example, let's create a hypothetical design situation and then see what kind of design model might fit the situation. Let's assume that:

1. An R & D center has received a $200,000 grant for a two-year period from a state department of education.

2. The purpose of the grant is to create 16 weeks (80 hours) of exemplary instruction in some particular subject area.

3. The materials are to be designed, developed, field tested, revised, and installed on a limited scale for summative reporting purposes.

4. The target population is senior high school students.

5. If successful, the materials will be reproduced by the state and distributed statewide.

Looking back at the three questions one would keep in mind while selecting a model, it can be seen that the first two would be easy to answer. First, $200,000 and two years should be sufficient resources for a precision design and development effort. Second, a complex model could be used because professional designers would be available or could be hired at an R & D center. The third question presents a problem. In the hypothetical state, no instructional materials have been designed specifically for state-wide distribution, so it is determined that a sophisticated design model will be adapted for the project. By coincidence, the Briggs model is selected and adapted to fit the project's needs.

The 17 steps of the Briggs model are listed in Figure 2. The only adaption of the model is found in the addition of the three steps with boxes drawn around them. They are labeled, 1-a, 2-a, and 6-a.

There is a sound rationale for why these three steps were added and, indeed, a good rationale for inclusion of 1-a and 2-a in most team design activities.

Teams normally design for large audiences. Team design is usually cost-effective only when the high cost of a team effort can be amortized across a large number of students or trainees to create a reasonable cost per student. Large student audiences

1. Determine needs and goals.

| 1-a. Analyze resources and constraints. |

2. Organize the course and the units of instruction.

| 2-a. Begin diffusion planning. |

3. Write the objectives.

4. Analyze the objectives.

5. Prepare assessments of learner performance.

6. Sequence the instruction within each objective.

| 6-a. Validate the objectives and sequence with representative teachers. |

7. List instructional events for each enabling objective.

8. Select type of stimulus.

9. Select media.

10. Select conditions of learning.

11. Write prescriptions.

12. Develop materials.

13. Conduct formative evaluations.

14. Train field test teachers.

15. Conduct field test.

16. Make final revisions.

17. Conduct summative evaluation.

Figure 2:   *The design process adapted for a statewide project.*

generally mean established institutions like public schools, or military, industry, or governmental agencies. Designing for an established institution means that the new product will be installed in an existing instructional system. Unless one wants to hazard the development of an unusable or unacceptable product, one must include step 1-a and make an assessment of the resources available and the constraints that operate within the existing instructional system. Some examples of the need for careful analysis of resources and constraints will be presented later in this Chapter.

It should be noted that there are cases in highly critical training situations where team design is justified for relatively small student audiences; e.g., airline pilots, surgeons, missile technicians, and demolitions experts. It is interesting that team design is justified in such instances through the same kind of cost-benefit analysis that one would undertake when large student audiences are anticipated. The difference lies in the value that is placed on the training goal. We tend to value a well-trained surgeon far above a well-read third grader.

In most instructional settings, systematically designed instruction is still an innovation. If one accepts the idea that most team designed materials are destined for existing instructional systems, then the problem arises of trying to install an innovation in an established institution. It is believed that the efforts of most design teams should include at least some diffusion activity as indicated by step 2-a. Diffusion activity would not begin and end at the point indicated, but would continue for the life of the project. Resistance to change is one of the most difficult constraints operating against any innovation; diffusion activity is nothing more than an attempt to remove the constraint by creating acceptance.

The validation step added at 6-a is another constraint-removal attempt. Instructional personnel are the individuals who will ultimately say "yes" or "no" to implementing new materials. The possibility of a "yes" is much higher if teachers have early input and accept the technical correctness of the content. One of the persistent teacher union demands is involvement in curriculum policy decisions. Step 6-a is included as a specific design step rather than being viewed as a part of step 2-a, diffusion. This is because the teacher validation step will probably provide actual input to the design process as well as serve to create teacher acceptance.

The hypothetical team design situation and the model found in Figure 2 will continue to be used for discussion in the following pages. To facilitate the discussion, a simplified form of the model is shown in Figure 3. The 20 steps have been combined to form six phases or stages of team activity. The combinations are in no way intended to indicate that the separate steps can be viewed as composite activities. The combinations exist only to simplify the discussion which follows. The arrangement of the six blocks in Figure 3 is intended to illustrate the point made previously that diffusion activity would start early in the process and continue for the life of the project.

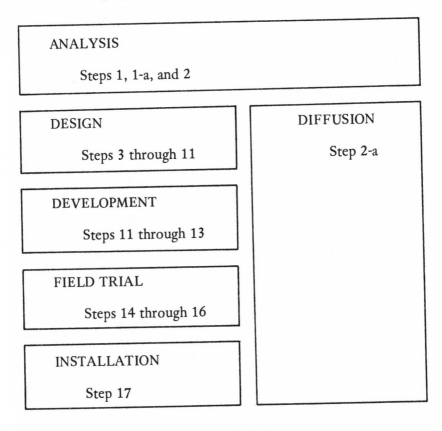

Figure 3: Simplified design process.

This concludes the discussion of the first activity in structuring a team design process—selecting a suitable model of instructional design. The second activity requires a detailed look at the model selected.

Activity 2: Detail the Substeps
Involved in Each Step of the Model

There is some question as to who should complete a detailed analysis of the substeps involved in each step of the model. If the design team leader has experienced professionals available for the team, then this activity could be conducted by individual team members. For example, a team leader need not presume to instruct an experienced evaluator in the details of conducting a needs assessment or a one-to-one formative trial. An experienced mediated materials specialist should be able to prepare his or her own production procedures. On the other hand, inexperienced team members may require extensive details before being able to satisfactorily complete their assigned steps in the model. Regardless of who details the substeps, the fact remains that it should be done. Written details of substeps provide both a guide for ongoing activities and a record for preparing interim and final reports of project procedures.

Examples will not be included here because samples of the detailed substeps required at each point of the model can be found in the preceding Chapters of this book; e.g., Chapter 2 lists detailed procedures for determining needs and goals, and Chapter 3 describes the process of writing objectives, etc.

After detailing the substeps in each step of the model, the next activity in structuring a team design process is developing time lines.

Activity 3: Develop Time Lines

Having carefully detailed the subtasks at each step of the design model, one has in effect created a linear flow of most of the design project activities. Trying to structure even a small team design process along such a linear flow would create two problems. First, the design process is not linear in practice. Many activities occur simultaneously, and one often works one part of a product through a phase of design and then cycles back and begins the same phase again with another part of the product. The second problem with trying to work with a linear flow is that it is difficult to estimate one's status with regard to timely completion of the design process. Time lines indicating tentative dates for timely task completion are indispensable. Knowing how much progress *has been made* at a given point in time is most useful when one also knows how much progress *should have been made* to that point. Summarizing, it is necessary to represent the non-linear relationship among the steps of the design process and to represent the steps within a tentative time frame.

There are two commonly used techniques for representing the steps of a process within a time frame. They are Gantt charting and PERT diagramming. Gantt charting was first used in World War I as a means of comparing promised completion of activities with actual performance. Gantt charting has since developed into a systematic tool for projecting, controlling, and recording operations in a complex system. A Gantt chart is simple in concept, being nothing more than a two-axis chart with time divisions across the horizontal axis and task designations down the vertical axis. A simplified Gantt chart is shown in Figure 4. You will recognize the tasks on the vertical axis as being the major phases from Figure 3, the simplified design sequence.

Figure 4 is intended only to illustrate the concept of Gantt charting. The phases would be too general and the time designations too broad to be of much actual use in project planning or monitoring. It is, however, clear in Figure 4 that the team design process is not a simple linear activity.

Figure 5 is a Gantt chart that was used in preplanning activities for an actual team design project. The time divisions and the tasks are both more specific than those in Figure 4. The Gantt chart in Figure 5 served as a valuable preplanning tool, but when project activity actually began, many of the steps in the activities column were broken down into subtasks and Gantt-charted in more detail before personnel assignments were made.

The process charted in Figure 5 is obviously "light" on front-end analysis and design. That is because needs, goals, and objectives had been developed in a previous project and were available as input to the new project. The project continued for six months beyond the time frame depicted in the chart. The "DIG

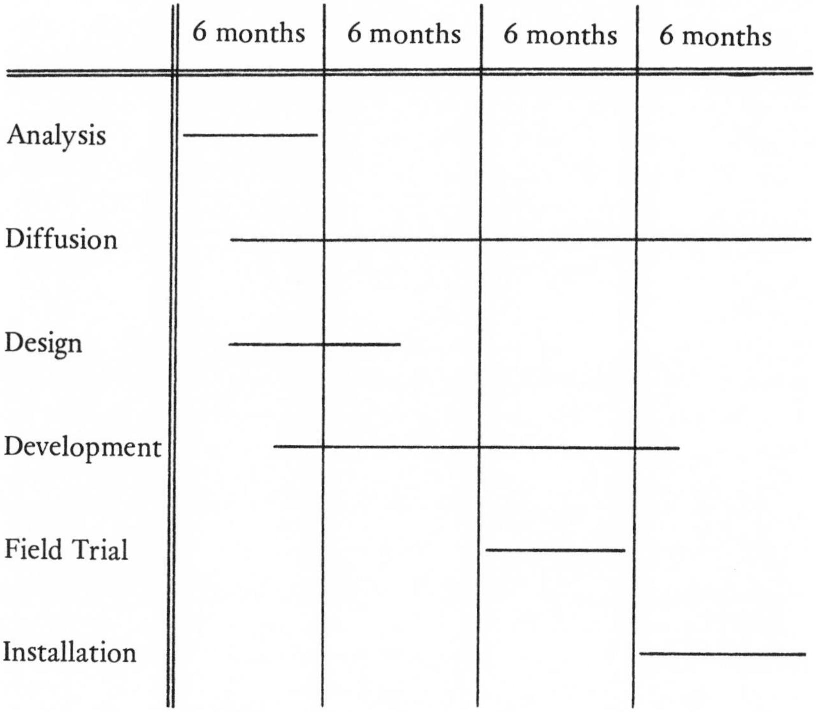

	6 months	6 months	6 months	6 months
Analysis				
Diffusion				
Design				
Development				
Field Trial				
Installation				

Figure 4: Simplified Gantt chart.

Manual" listed in the KEY to Figure 5 was an adjunct reference book that was not really instructional in nature.

Gantt charting and PERT diagramming both provide an information management system function. That is, they both integrate several different types of management information and make it readily accessible for decision-making. Both Gantt and PERT provide a team manager with a running record of design activities. Both flag problem steps that require additional resources for timely completion. They also indicate early task completions allowing diversion of slack resources to other tasks. The two techniques also provide a continuous monitor on team members' performance. For most team design activities, Gantt charting is a sufficient management technique. However, for complex, high-

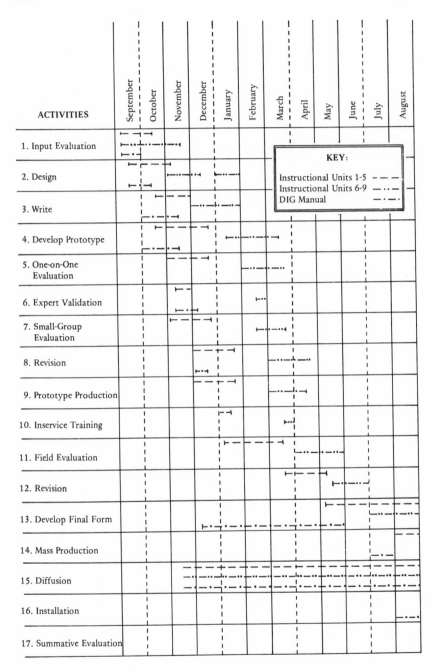

Figure 5: Detailed Gantt chart.

budget projects requiring extremely detailed planning and resource management, it may be worth the time investment to develop a PERT diagram.

The Program Evaluation and Review Technique (PERT) was developed in the late 1950's as a method of planning and managing multi-million dollar space age projects. PERT diagrams are sometimes called networks because of their visual appearance. The elements of a PERT network are illustrated in Figure 6. The activity represented is the same as that in Figure 4.

The circles in a PERT network are called events, and represent the completion of an activity. The solid arrows between events are called activity paths, and represent ongoing work on an event. The times noted above each path indicate the projected time that it will take to complete the activity. There are many ways of using PERT in project management that will not even be introduced here. A complete network for a complex team design effort could require hundreds of events. Such discussion is not really within the scope of this Chapter.

It should be noted that at this stage of structuring a team design process, one is only making tentative estimates of time lines. Tentative though it may be, it is imperative that some kind of management plan be developed. For a more detailed discussion of Gantt charting, the reader is referred to Rathe (1961). Riemer (1968) and Banghart (1969) both provide more detailed introductions to PERT diagramming.

Activity 4: Make Tentative Personnel Assignments

The fourth activity in structuring a team design process is made easier if the third activity has been completed in careful detail. A good Gantt chart provides a team manager with the framework of tasks within which all team members will work. The key to personnel assignment is determining first what skills are required for performance of the project tasks.

Generally speaking, the types of professional skills required are the same regardless of the instructional setting or the scope of the team design project. Different projects may require different levels of skill, but the same types of skills are required. Professional skills normally represented on a design team include:

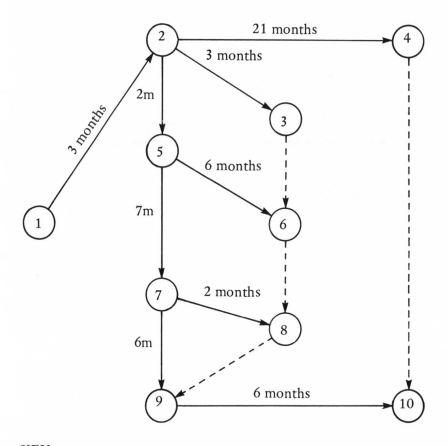

KEY

1. Team hired
2. Needs and goals determined
3. Analysis phase completed
4. Diffusion completed
5. First unit of instruction designed
6. Design phase completed
7. Three-fourths of materials developed
8. Development phase completed
9. Field trial completed
10. Installation completed

Figure 6: A simplified PERT diagram.

educational evaluation, instructional design, mediated materials development, subject matter knowledge, diffusion expertise, and project management.

One problem for the team manager is finding enough flexibility in available personnel resources. This is true because the skills listed above are required in different amounts during different phases of the project. This requires finding multi-talented team members who can readily change roles, or having a pool of personnel talent from which to draw. The latter of these two options is obviously a luxury available in few team design situations. A graphic representation is presented in Figure 7 of how the skills required change as a project goes through various phases. Figure 7 represents the same two-year period depicted in Figure 4.

Fortunately, professional instructional designers usually possess skills in evaluation and materials development, particularly when the materials will be produced in a print format. That provides the leader of a small team with some flexibility in personnel assignment. An instructional designer who is also a subject-matter expert provides a small team with a particularly valuable combination of skills. The hypothetical project in Figure 7 might require the following quantity of professional skill for completion:

1. Project management—24 person-months
2. Educational evaluation—24 person-months
3. Diffusion expertise—12 person-months
4. Subject matter expertise—12 person-months
5. Instructional design—24 person-months
6. Materials development—24 person-months

After determining the person-loading requirements for timely completion of all team tasks, the team leader staffs the project. There are many plausible staffing patterns—the one chosen by a design team leader would necessarily reflect the requirements of each individual design problem.

A useful practice is to write personnel assignments directly into the Gantt chart or PERT diagram. At the completion of this fourth activity in structuring a team design process, the team leader of a small to medium sized effort ends up with a "project on a page." It may indeed be a large page, but at least most of the

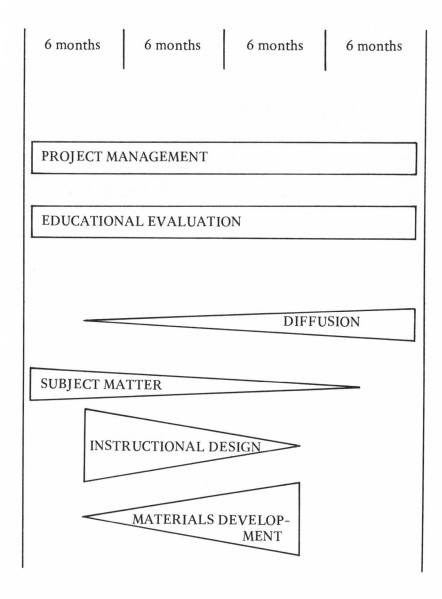

Figure 7:   *Required professional skills through the phases of a team design project.*

information required for day-to-day decision-making is readily at hand.

Activity 5: Initiate Activities;
Monitor and Revise

The fifth activity is basically carrying out the planning that has gone into the previous four activities. Before beginning, a team leader may wish to establish an administrative structure and a management style. The administrative structure will probably depend on the individual project and the configuration of the design team. Each design team leader will have to develop a management style that best suits his or her own personality. For maintaining high productivity and morale in small, labor-intensive processes employing predominately professional personnel, it might be wise to investigate a management-by-objectives approach (Odiorne, 1965; Tosi and Carroll, 1970). Those interested in detailed accounts of project management might consult Cleland and King (1968) or Willner and Hendricks (1972).

Activities 4 and 5 prescribe tentative time lines and tentative personnel assignments. The reason is that one does not know how long a team design activity will take until some experience is gained with the activity. There is a definite implication here both for team management and for the final product that will be produced.

The team process must be monitored. Tentative time and resource projections must be compared with actual accomplishments. If the tentative projections prove inaccurate (and they usually will), the design team leader has decisions to make. The same type of decisions are required whether the projections were optimistic or pessimistic. Table 4 samples some possible revisions that could be made if management projections prove inaccurate. Most revisions would actually be a combination of the suggestions in Table 4.

This completes the discussion of the five activities in structuring a team design process. In the final part of this Chapter, a brief commentary will be presented on how teams approach specific steps in an instructional design model. The commentary will emphasize steps in the Briggs model not detailed elsewhere in this book.

Table 4

Design Process Revisions for
Inaccurate Team Management Projections

Areas amenable to revision:	If deadlines cannot be met:	If deadlines are met ahead of schedule:
Design/Development procedures	revise for efficiency or delete details	revise for more precision or accept original choice
Resources (usually personnel)	reorganize for more productivity or enlarge	redeploy, live with surplus, or cut back
Time lines	look for slack time or lengthen	add or reorder tasks, live with slack, or shorten
Instructional product	look for equal alternatives or accept less	look for better alternatives or accept original choice

Team Approaches to Instructional
Design and Development

The purpose of this final section of the Chapter is to present some of the ways that teams of designers go about accomplishing selected steps in an instructional design model. There are several general ways in which teams do things differently than individuals.

Teams obviously do things on a larger scale; e.g., bigger budgets, more complex models, larger target audiences, more time, and slicker products. Just because everything is bigger, however, does not mean that the design steps are all that different. In fact, the steps detailed in Chapters 2 through 7 and the first section of Chapter 9 are basically the same for individual designers or design teams, differing more in how much is done rather than what is done. Little attention will thus be devoted to those steps already covered in Chapters 2 through 7 and in the first section of this Chapter.

Because a team does things on a larger scale, it must often add two design steps that are of less concern to an individual designer: (a) analyze resources and constraints, and (b) diffuse the innovation. The rationale for including these two activities was previously presented; the following pages will describe how teams accomplish the activities.

There is one more general difference between the way that individuals and teams design instruction. Individuals are likely to use a model in which they review existing materials, select appropriate materials, and adopt or adapt materials for use. This procedure was described in Chapter 8. Design teams are more likely to develop and produce their own materials "from scratch." The following pages will emphasize procedures involved in materials development and production.

The discussion that follows will be organized around the six instructional design phases indicated in Figure 3. Short, general comments will be made about the overall phase, followed by more specific commentary on individual steps within the phase.

Phase 1: Analysis

An instructional design team is often organized as a result of analysis work that has already been completed. Even if needs have already been assessed and goals set, it is appropriate for a design team to take enough time to verify the efficacy of the procedures that were used and validate the results. In a team design activity, the importance of a valid determination of needs and goals cannot be overemphasized. The resources available in team design efforts are often quite substantial, and it is the needs and goals analysis that will determine to what end those resources are expended. An interesting note on team design procedures is that the analysis phase is only the first instance of the heavy reliance that a team places on educational evaluation. In a medium to large team effort, one can trace Stufflebeam's (1971) context, input, process, and product stages of evaluation all the way through the team's activities. Because of the growing recognition of the importance of evaluation, a student of instructional design would do well to prepare in the evaluation field.

Step 2 of Figure 2 is organizing the course and units of instruction. Some might call this a design activity, but it is included in Figure 3 under analysis because one is not really designing units of instruction at this point, but rather analyzing the scope of the entire instructional problem. The output from this step, a tentative course structure, is really input for the unit-by-unit design activities which follow. Procedures for determining needs and goals and organizing the course are adequately presented in Chapters 2 and 4.

The necessity for analyzing resources and constraints has already been discussed in this Chapter; now for some details on underlying concepts and procedures.

The first underlying concept is that resources and constraints must be viewed as affecting the entire team effort and thus should be analyzed with regard to analysis, design, development, diffusion, field trial, and installation. By way of definition, resources are things which tend to support the team's activities, and constraints are things which tend to limit a team's range of acceptable options or directly hinder a team's activities.

A second underlying concept is that the same thing can act as both a resource and a constraint. For example, teachers are certainly one resource that many teams will design into new instructional delivery systems. However, teacher resistance to innovation is a constraint that must be removed through diffusion and inservice training.

A framework for analyzing resources and constraints. In sales training programs, four areas of knowledge are often stressed: Know your company. Know yourself. Know your customer. Know your product. These four considerations will translate directly into four areas in which a design team needs knowledge of resources and constraints.

1. Know your company = analyze the supporting agency or administrative structure within which the team works.
2. Know yourself = analyze the design team itself.
3. Know your customer = analyze the instructional setting in which the proposed product will be installed.
4. Know your product = analyze the proposed instructional system and delivery system.

These four general areas of concern are combined in Table 5 with the six phases of a design effort to form a matrix of possible points of resources and constraints analysis.

Within each block of the matrix, suggested categories of analysis would include:

1. Budget
2. Time
3. Personnel
4. Facilities
5. Equipment
6. Supplies
7. Institutional characteristics

Table 5

*Matrix of Possible Points of Resources
and Constraints Analysis*

	Analysis	Diffusion	Design	Development	Field Trial	Installation
The supporting agency or structure						
The team						
The instructional setting						
The instructional product						

There are 24 blocks in the Table 5 matrix and seven categories in the above list. The categories could even be broken down into hundreds of subcategories. A team trying to account for each topic would get hopelessly lost in detail and redundancy. An individual designing several lessons could mentally cover the whole question of resources and constraints in an hour. A small design team might use the matrix and categories as the basis for an afternoon of brainstorming, then follow up on decisions with brief expert review. A medium sized team with a healthy budget would probably institute a brief, but formal procedure, using the matrix and categories to select topics for analysis that were believed critical to the success of the project. In a large team effort, where major curriculum innovations are being undertaken, a complete context and input evaluation would cover most of the blocks in the matrix, with particular emphasis on the instructional setting and the instructional product.

After analysis is completed, the team must decide how to best integrate resources into the design effort and initiate constraint removal plans. Estimations must be made of which constraints can in fact be removed in time for the project to proceed as desired. Appropriate management decisions can then be made.

Phase 2: Diffusion

Diffusion is really nothing more than a special case of constraints analysis and removal. The constraint being removed in diffusion activities is the natural conservatism of social organizations; i.e., resistance to innovation. The rationale for the necessity for diffusion activity was presented earlier in this Chapter.

Two terms are often used interchangeably: dissemination and diffusion. However, since "dissemination" often refers to communication of information or distribution of products, the word "diffusion" is preferred, because it refers to the process of securing widespread school adoptions of a new curriculum or an instructional system.

There is a body of research that focuses on processes by which information becomes disseminated to schools. Three reviews of such research are: Briggs (1972), Havelock and Benne (1967), and Havelock *et al.* (1969).

The latter two reviews cover mainly the dissemination of information, while the review by Briggs focuses upon diffusion of educational *products* such as curriculum materials.

Much of the research is based on the "agricultural model," in which a county agent provides information to farmers as a means of introducing changes, such as using new kinds of seeds or new farming methods. The agent thus becomes a "change agent" because farmers seek to improve their productivity and profit. Farmers are thus usually "open" to new suggestions.

In the opinion of these writers, the agricultural model is a poor one for education, for two reasons: (a) educational change is brought about more by new *products* than by dissemination of research *knowledge* or by new *techniques* resulting from research; and (b) teachers are not as open to new products or techniques as are farmers. If teachers were paid on the basis of the amount and quality of their pupils' learning, this situation might change rapidly. But measurement of the outcomes of a teacher's performance does not appear to strike people as the same thing as permitting a farmer's profit to be based on the quantity and quality of his products. While much research has been done on methods of evaluating teaching performance, no highly reliable and valid measures have emerged, and there would be great opposition to evaluating teachers by reference to how well their pupils learn.

A framework for team diffusion activities. The following framework will be presented as a series of six general steps that could be followed for planning and conducting a diffusion effort.

Step 1. The first step in any diffusion activity is to identify the characteristics of current practices in the intended instructional setting. The analysis of resources and constraints should already have provided this information.

Step 2. One next reviews the characteristics of the proposed instructional system that is to be installed. Much of this information will also be available from the analysis of resources and constraints.

Step 3. Identify innovations by analyzing discrepancies between current practices and proposed instructional systems.

Step 4. Identify the factors that will interact with the innovations. Examples of such factors are teachers, administrators, the public, facilities, and administrative policies.

Step 5. Classify factors as resources or constraints and determine which constraints can be removed and which must be accepted.

Step 6. Develop a timetable of specific activities designed to support the influence of resources and accommodate or remove the constraints.

Step 7. Implement the diffusion plan.

Most diffusion activities concentrate on the personnel factor in the intended instructional setting; i.e., teachers, administrators and support personnel, and the community. The main reason is that personnel create (or change) the policies that govern most other factors in the instructional setting. Current diffusion strategies emphasize two complementary approaches to preparing personnel for accepting innovation. The two approaches are *involvement* and *gradual change*.

It is important to involve key personnel in the planning of the product. Involvement builds one's investment in a product or procedure—investment in professional status, time, and ego. There are two positive results of involving personnel from the instructional setting: (a) people will accept products in which they have an investment while they might otherwise tend to reject the same products, and (b) an added bonus is that people know their own schools and their students, and can thus help design more suitable products.

Gradual change is a second diffusion strategy. Rogers and Shoemaker (1971) and others hypothesize that people must move through a sequence of steps on their way to acceptance of innovation. First, the person must know about the innovation. Second, the person must be persuaded of the desirability and workability of the innovation. Third, the person must decide to adopt the innovation. Finally, the person's experience in using the innovation must act as a confirmation of the first three steps; i.e., enough of those good promises must come true to keep the person from abandoning the innovation. Dodl *et al.* (1974) developed a detailed diffusion strategy that emphasizes both involvement and gradual change.

An example of innovations that were and were not successful is found in the programmed instruction and teaching machine innovations that began in the early 1960's.

It is interesting that programmed instruction was opposed by teachers partly because it comes in two forms: programmed booklets and teaching machines. Teachers feared being replaced by the machine, whereas they do not feel threatened by a textbook. While one today seldom sees a 1960 model teaching machine in a public school, quite a few programmed texts may be observed. In a study involving visits to 42 elementary schools using some form of individualized instruction, many programmed instruction booklets were seen in use (Briggs and Aronson, 1975).

A variety of strategies was used to achieve an operational individualized instruction system in each of these 42 schools. Some of these programs were developed initially in universities and other research centers. In these cases, some school personnel were a part of the development team. These persons were thus well qualified to conduct early tryouts which could also be observed by still other teachers. Thus, three important ways of introducing teachers to these programs were: (a) as members of the development team; (b) as observers in field test schools; and (c) as workshop participants to learn the theory and techniques required.

Some of these 42 schools developed their own programs. In these cases, the following steps were employed: (a) the teachers received a gradual orientation to individualized methods over a period of a year or more; (b) teachers were then usually asked to state their preference between the old program and the proposed new program; (c) for those interested, summer employment was offered teachers to help develop the program; (d) central office personnel and consultants assisted in both program development and teacher training; (e) in later years, increasing numbers of teachers were offered the opportunity of receiving training for the program; and (f) other schools sent observers who might gradually assist an experienced teacher in operating the program.

It is possible that individualized instruction programs represent the most radical change in teaching method that has been adopted by thousands of schools. This might correspond to the radical change in content that was represented by the SMSG mathematics program. Both these examples appear to represent more radical changes than is the case for other curriculum development projects.

It would appear, then, that *what* is adopted when a school accepts a change in program does make a difference. It is probable that changes are introduced in this rank order:

1. Changes representing adoption of an entire delivery system, including instructional materials.

2. Changes by adoption of materials as single *products*.

3. Changes brought about by special training of teachers in a *technique*, such as team teaching.

4. Changes brought about by disseminating research information to the schools.

Phase 3: Design

An instructional design team follows the same design procedures as presented in Chapters 3, 5, 6, 7, and the first part of 9. The only consideration unique to the team structure is whether the team's designers are also subject-matter experts. When an individual is working alone on a design effort, that person usually is the subject-matter expert. It is difficult, however, to find subject-matter experts who also have the instructional design skills required by a team. The only implication here is that team designers must work closely with subject-matter experts. In the same vein, it is worth noting that if team designers have never taught in the instructional setting for which their product is intended, they would be well advised to familiarize themselves with that setting.

There is one final consideration in the design phase that is not clearly reflected in the model. Because teams usually design exportable products for use in non team-controlled settings, two extra ingredients must be included in the materials package: (a) instructor guidance, and (b) course management materials. The designer of the instruction normally creates both of these ingredients so that they can be produced in the development phase which follows.

In Figure 3, the eleventh step of the model is included in both the design phase and the development phase. It is included in the design phase because writing materials prescriptions often forces the designer to rethink many of the decisions previously made. Writing prescriptions is also viewed as a development step because it is the first time that actual instruction begins to take form. The prescriptions serve to translate the design into something that can be produced and placed in front of a student.

Phase 4: Development

After prescriptions are written, materials development begins. There are two distinct stages of development that concern a team and influence the composition of a team. One stage is writing materials. The other stage is everything that follows writing; for example, editing, filming, recording, printing, etc.

If a team's primary medium is print, then the instructional designers will really be the developers as well. A designer, for example, could not entrust prescriptions for a PI text to an editor for execution. It would simply not be efficient for a designer to write prescriptions so detailed that an editor could create print instruction for them. On the other hand, if the primary medium is nonprint, the team designer would turn prescriptions over to media production specialists for development. It is interesting that during design the media specialist serves as a consultant to the designer, while during development the designer serves as a consultant to the media specialist.

In small team situations, the designer may be forced to be his own developer. On the other extreme, large projects will often employ a full-time materials development staff.

There are many excellent references available on materials development and production, and Chapter 10 provides detailed procedures for formative evaluation and revision. This discussion of materials development will conclude with a list of developmental stages that an average team design project might take.

Develop materials is listed as one step in the model in Figure 2; *conduct formative evaluations* is also listed as a single step. The details below will illustrate how several stages are involved in both of these steps.

1. Write prescriptions.
2. Write instruction.
3. Develop rough draft materials, typewritten with storyboard art.
4. (Optional) Validate materials with teacher consultant and/or subject-mater expert.
5. Conduct one-to-one formative evaluation.

6. Revise materials.
7. Write student and teacher guides.
8. Produce prototype materials, typewritten with low budget mediation.
9. Conduct small-group formative evaluation.
10. Revise materials.
11. Duplicate materials for field trial.
12. Conduct inservice training.
13. Conduct field trial.

Phases 5 and 6: Field Trial and Installation

These two phases are combined for discussion because the field trial can be planned as both a trial of the instructional materials and a trial of the installation procedures. That is because the field trial is actually a small-scale installation. The steps in field trial and installation for a team designed product could be as follows:

1. Conduct inservice training.
2. Conduct field trial formative evaluation.
3. Revise materials.
4. Develop final form materials.
5. Publish or mass-produce materials.
6. Conduct inservice training.
7. Install materials (controlled installation under joint supervision of design team and personnel from instructional setting).
8. Conduct summative evaluation.

Steps 1 and 6 are of particular interest to an instructional designer working as part of a design team. The inservice training component of field trial and installation can be conceptualized as a "mini" instructional design project. As with any other design problem, one would start by determining needs and goals and working right on through a systematic design procedure.

One common mistake in inservice training is that the instruction sometimes concentrates too heavily on the content of the new instructional materials. This may be appropriate in the few instances when the instructional personnel are not already content experts, but that is seldom the case. Carefully determining needs and goals would help one avoid this mistake and focus on the real issues of importance.

The most important issues in inservice training are preparing the instructional personnel to: (a) accept the innovative features of the new product, (b) complete the initial planning for adoption of the new product, and (c) manage the day-to-day utilization of the product. If careful diffusion planning was completed, these three concerns should have already shown up in that phase of the project, and activities may already have begun on preparing personnel to accept innovation.

Details of field testing and revision are covered in Chapter 10, and summative evaluation is treated in Chapter 11. The only thing remaining for discussion here is the actual process of installation.

The final dissemination of a product is usually out of the hands of the design team. This is particularly true when wide distribution will be undertaken. In fact, many instructional design projects are terminated following field testing and final revision. Even when teams do continue on into an installation phase, it is unlikely that team designers would still be with the project. The team manager may even be gone, having turned installation over to a diffusion expert and an evaluator.

The type of installation process that a design team would work in would probably be a controlled installation involving only a portion of the intended instructional settings. The purpose of the team's involvement would be to manage the installation process (usually in conjunction with representatives of the target institutions) and to conduct a summative evaluation. The team would also be busy during this period of time with winding down the project and preparing final reports.

The only point of design interest in the installation process is the inservice training, which has already been discussed. The other part of installation is the establishment of a detailed administrative plan for getting the right things to the right people at the right time. This plan should provide for periodic follow-up and contact with the involved instructional personnel, at least during the early phases of installation. To detail an administrative plan here would not be useful because every installation process will be unique to the institutions involved. It will be left to the common sense of the reader to remember to get the materials there on time.

Summary

Chapter 9 has presented the concluding steps of a systematic instructional design procedure. These concluding steps were discussed from the perspective of a team design and development effort. Chapters 10 and 11 will provide the details of formative and summative evaluation that were not included in this Chapter.

The first part of the Chapter completes the account of the detailed tactics of instruction which flow from the more general strategies of instruction discussed in Chapter 7. (Parallel tactics for teachers were covered in Chapter 8.)

Just as the first part of this Chapter outlines *what* design teams need to do, the second part outlines *how* they are organized and managed in order to do it.

References

Banghart, F.W. *Educational Systems Analysis.* New York: Macmillan, 1969.

Branson, R.K., *et al., Interservice Procedures for Instructional Systems Development* (TRADOC Pam. 350-30 and NAVEDTRA 106A, 5 Vols.). Ft. Monroe, Va.: U.S. Army Training and Doctrine Command, August, 1975.

Briggs, L.J. *Handbook of Procedures for the Design of Instruction.* Pittsburgh: American Institutes for Research, 1970.

Briggs, L.J. *Student's Guide to Handbook of Procedures for the Design of Instruction.* Pittsburgh: American Institutes for Research, 1972.

Briggs, L.J. Development and Diffusion as Mechanisms for Educational Improvement. In H.P. Schalock and G.R. Sell (Eds.), *Research, Development, Diffusion, Evaluation, Vol. III: Conceptual Frameworks for Viewing Educational RDD&E.* Monmouth: Oregon State System of Higher Education, 1972.

Briggs, L.J., and Aronson, D.T. *An Interpretive Study of Individualized Instruction in the School: Procedures, Problems, and Prospects.* Tallahassee: Florida State University, 1975. (Final report for Grant No. NIE G-740065.)

Cleland, D.R., and King, W.R. *Systems Analysis and Project Management.* New York: McGraw-Hill, 1968.

Dodl, N.R., Kibler, R.J., Dick, W., Toomb, I.K., and Rollins, S. *The Florida Assessment and Diffusion Model.* Tallahassee: Teacher Education Projects, Florida State University, 1974.

Gagné, R.M. *The Conditions of Learning,* 1st Edition. New York: Holt, Rinehart, and Winston, 1965.

Gagné, R.M. *The Conditions of Learning,* 2nd Edition. New York: Holt, Rinehart, and Winston, 1970.

Gagné, R.M. *Essentials of Learning for Instruction.* Hinsdale, Ill.: The Dryden Press, 1974.

Gagné, R.M. *The Conditions of Learning,* 3rd Edition. New York: Holt, Rinehart, and Winston, 1977.

Gagné, R.M., and Briggs, L.J. *Principles of Instructional Design.* New York: Holt, Rinehart, and Winston, 1974.

Havelock, R.G., and Benne, K.D. An Exploratory Study of Knowledge Utilization. In G. Watson (Ed.), *Concepts for Social Change.* Washington, D.C.: National Training Laboratories, NEA, 1967.

Havelock, R.G., *et al. Planning for Innovation Through Dissemination and Utilization of Knowledge.* Ann Arbor: Institute for Social Research, University of Michigan, 1969.

Mager, R.F., and Beach, K.M., Jr. *Developing Vocational Instruction.* Belmont, Ca.: Fearon, 1967.

Odiorne, G. *Management by Objectives.* New York: Pitman, 1965.

Rathe, A.W. (Ed.) *Gantt on Management.* Cambridge, Mass.: American Management Association, 1961.

Riemer, W. *Handbook of Government Contract Administration.* Englewood Cliffs, N.J.: Prentice-Hall, 1968.

Rogers, E.M., and Shoemaker, F.F. *Communication of Innovations.* New York: The Free Press, 1971.

Singer, R.N., and Dick, W. *Teaching Physical Education: A Systems Approach.* Boston: Houghton Mifflin, 1974.

Stufflebeam, D.L., *et al. Educational Evaluation and Decision Making.* Itasca, Ill.: Peacock, 1971.

Tosi, H.L., and Carroll, S. Management by Objectives. *Personnel Administration,* 1970, *33,* 44-48.

Willner, W., and Hendricks, P.B. *Grants Administration.* Washington, D.C.: National Graduate University, 1972.

Transition to Chapter 10

It is assumed that either a teacher has selected materials and designed learning activities, or a team of designers has done this. It is necessary now to try out the materials and procedures, and to identify changes needed in them.

Chapter 10 describes how such tryouts may be conducted. More broadly, when an entire delivery system has been designed for a large unit of instruction, every aspect of the system, as seen in operation, needs to be evaluated.

Chapter 10 uses self-instructional materials as the focus for discussion of formative evaluation; but by using ingenuity, all aspects of a delivery system can be checked upon and improved as a result of a field test.

Even a lecture could be so evaluated, if the lecturer kept careful notes on what he said, and how the learners responded. An item analysis of test performance can be related to specific parts of the lecture.

Since instructional theory is still in its infancy, and thus imperfect, and the designers' efforts to apply it may be partly unsuccessful on a first attempt, formative evaluation and revision is a crucial step in the design model.

In a team effort, parts or all of the instruction are designed and tried out before the first regular classroom use of the instruction. But the busy teacher often "designs and teaches" almost simultaneously. Over a period of years, a course may change from a teacher-centered, lecture course, to a materials-centered course, because the teacher keeps at the independent effort year after year. In addition to use of performance tests to spot needed improvements, the teacher may use student comments and written "feedback." Questionnaires used for course evaluation can provide some of the data needed to make improvements.

Chapter 10

Formative Evaluation

Walter Dick
Florida State University

Purposes of Formative Evaluation

It might be said that the purpose of formative evaluation is to correct the mistakes which have been made prior to this step in the instructional design process. Such a definition would not be too far wrong. Formative evaluation may be more precisely defined as a process of systematically trying out instructional materials with learners in order to gather information and data which will be used to revise the materials. The implication of the term "formative" is that the evaluation process occurs *while the materials are still being developed*.

This Chapter focuses on the specific techniques for improving *materials* (print or non-print media) in a largely self-instructional program, in which materials "carry the burden of instruction." Similar procedures can be developed for "teacher-conducted instruction," in which teacher and pupil activity become the "data" for evaluation.

If, in general, evaluation is considered to be the making of judgments based on systematically collected data, then it is necessary to distinguish formative evaluation from other types of evaluation. The judgment which is to be made from the data in formative evaluation is how to effectively improve the instructional materials. There is no judgment with regard to what has been acquired by students beyond their responses to the materials, nor with regard to the relative or comparative effectiveness of the instructional materials. The sole purpose of formative evaluation is to provide the instructional designer with as much information as possible to revise and strengthen the product which is under development. Summative evaluation, on the other hand, may involve comparison of the values of two alternate instructional products or systems.

Use of formative evaluation is not common in the design and development of educational materials. It has been estimated by Komoski (1974) that only approximately one percent of the materials used in the public schools in the United States have undergone formative evaluation. The typical procedure for developing commercial materials involves a subject-matter expert who structures the content in a way which *seems* most appropriate for the target population. The materials are attractively formatted by the publisher and made available for sale to schools. There is little or no attempt to identify the learning difficulties which students may have with the materials.

It is not uncommon for classroom teachers, upon hearing about formative evaluation, to state that they always use this practice in their own teaching. For example, if the teacher makes a presentation to which students do not react particularly well, the presentation is altered the next time in order to make it more effective. The difficulty with this approach to collecting information and revising instruction is that there is no systematic determination of what, in fact, the students did learn from the presentation nor specifically how they reacted to it. Therefore, there is little substantive information to use to revise the instruction.

Why is the formative evaluation process so critical to the total design of instruction? The most important answer to this question is that formative evaluation is the empirical validation of many of the theoretical constructs which are included in earlier components of the instructional design model. If the theory is weak, the product will be less than perfectly effective. Since our present theories and practices are imperfect, we need empirical data as a basis for improving the product. However, the future may be different.

Consider a time in the future when we have perfected our ability to write objectives and design objective-referenced tests, and we can perfectly task-analyze instructional goals to identify the appropriate subskills, and we can identify the perfect instructional strategies which will allow us to teach these subskills. We could use this instructional strategy to design perfect instruction. When, if ever, we reach this stage of perfection, there will be no need for formative evaluation. We can assume that the materials will work perfectly well without any tryout and revision.

However, we have not reached the point of perfection in our instructional design methodology. Therefore, when we are developing instructional materials, it is important at every stage to try them out with students, teachers, and subject-matter experts to identify those parts which are ineffective in reaching the desired instructional goals, and to revise appropriately.

In this Chapter three phases of formative evaluation will be examined, with an emphasis on what the instructional designer does during each phase: Data-collection procedures will be described, with an indication of how such data can be displayed for interpretation; this will be followed by a description of how data can be used to develop a revision strategy.

Succeeding portions of the Chapter will include a brief example of the application of this model of formative evaluation. There will be a review of some of the research studies which have been conducted on the effectiveness of utilizing formative evaluation, and a number of specific issues which surround this topic will be discussed. The Chapter will conclude with a discussion of the contrast between formative and summative evaluation.

Three Phases of Formative Evaluation

Each of the three phases of formative evaluation may be described in terms of its purpose, the requirements to begin the process, the process itself, and the output or results of that process. This section, which describes the three phases of formative evaluation in some depth, will be followed by discussions of the instruments which may be used, and how data may be summarized and interpreted.

Phase I: One-to-One Evaluation

The purpose of one-to-one formative evaluation is to identify the major and obvious problems which exist in a preliminary draft of instructional materials, and to revise the materials accordingly.

In order to initiate the one-to-one process, the designer must have a draft copy of the materials which are to be tested. It should be emphasized that this is not a final, polished version but rather one (for written materials) which may be roughly typewritten, written on a set of cards, or provided in some other preliminary fashion. For non-print media, such as slide/tape presentations, the designer may read the narration and present rough art sketches which are later to become slides. For early work on materials eventually to be placed on film or videotapes, a written script may be presented, or even a "storyboard." The only exception to the acceptability of rough materials at this stage is that any graphics which are *critical* to the understanding of the materials should be in reasonably good form in order for students to interpret them properly.

The one-to-one process is initiated by the selection of one to three students from the target population. These students should be very carefully selected. If only one student can be used, then perhaps selecting one who is slightly below average in ability is preferable. If two or three can be identified, then an average and an above average student should also be selected. During the evaluation of the materials the designer sits with the student and interacts with him or her as the student studies the materials. It is often useful for the designer to follow along with the student in another copy of the materials to make notes on sections in which the student has difficulty, and to describe any help which the designer provides.

One-to-one formative evaluation might best be described as a clinical process in which the designer tries to understand the problems which the student is having and tries to help the student overcome those problems. This understanding can best be gained through talking directly with the student and asking questions as he or she proceeds through the materials. The same process can be used to formatively evaluate any tests which are associated with the materials. It is appropriate to request a student to take the pretests and posttests which are designed for the materials.

However, because so much learning help may be provided by the designer in the one-to-one process, it is not reasonable to interpret posttest performance as an indication of the effectiveness of the materials. The purpose of administering the tests is to have the students identify those items which assess skills which were not included in the instruction, or items which are unclear.

The output of the one-to-one process is primarily a set of comments from the student and observations by the designer concerning major difficulties in the instructional materials. These will include simple typographical errors, verbal or graphic presentations which are unclear, and suggestions on sequencing and formatting of the instruction.

There is one other component of Phase 1 of the formative evaluation process: the review of the materials by a subject-matter expert. Such a person can be invaluable to the designer in all the early phases, from needs analysis to design of the instructional content. The major function of the subject-matter expert is to determine if the materials are accurate, authoritative, and up-to-date. It should be noted that it is not the purpose of the subject-matter expert to suggest revisions in the instructional strategy which has been incorporated in the materials. Such suggestions might be noted and considered later. However, when materials have been designed according to a systematic strategy, they are generally superior to those suggested by a subject-matter expert who does not have a full knowledge of the total strategy.

Phase II: Small-Group Evaluation

The purpose of the small-group formative evaluation phase is to determine if the major revisions made as a result of the one-to-one evaluation are effective, to identify the more subtle difficulties which may still exist in the materials, and to begin to determine the administrative feasibility of using the materials in the environment for which they have been designed. The major input to the small-group evaluation is the revised version of the instructional materials. These materials should now be improved in appearance, such as using a higher quality of paper or binding, but it is not yet necessary to have them in the final, polished format. In the case of non-print media, a "rough cut" film may be used, or a low-fidelity tape recording.

The small-group process of formative evaluation begins with the identification of eight to two dozen students who are representative of the target population. While these students will take the tests and study the instructional materials, it is not necessary that they meet together at one time in one place. The students should be provided with all the tests and instructional materials and be asked to study the materials in a fashion which is similar to that which will be employed when the materials are used in the field.

This phase of formative evaluation may be conducted either by the designer or by another instructor who is responsible for the students using these materials. Whoever is serving as "teacher" should direct the students to work at their own pace. The teacher should help only if major problems arise and a student cannot proceed unless such help is given. At the end of the learning and testing session, students are often given a questionnaire to fill out, and it is helpful to hold "debriefing sessions" in which students are asked to describe their reactions to the learning materials.

The output of the small-group phase of formative evaluation includes test scores, learning time, questionnaire data, and debriefing information. If another teacher is involved in the administration of the materials, his or her comments about the effectiveness and utilization of the materials should also be included. These data are used to make the next major revision of the materials, which will then be ready for the third and final evaluation phase.

Phase III: Field Trial Evaluation

The purpose of the field trial phase of formative evaluation is to determine if the revisions from the preceding phase have been effective and to determine the administrative feasibility of using the instructional materials under normal classroom conditions. Again, it should not be inferred that the field trial must always take place with students in a classroom. If the materials are intended for at-home use, then that would be the environment in which the field trials should be conducted. It is most critical at this phase that the materials be used in the environment which has been identified as the major one for final use following the publication of the materials.

The input for the field trial evaluation includes all the materials which will be used in the instruction, including any teacher manuals, tests, and laboratory equipment. At this stage the materials should be in polished form, very closely approximating the format which will be utilized following publication. All materials should be provided to the teacher who will be responsible for the field trial. In the case of non-print media, one may use an 8mm film later to be "reshot" in 16mm or 35mm to achieve a more "artistic" product.

During this final phase of formative evaluation, the designer withdraws from active involvement in the instructional process and turns the materials over to a regular instructor. The materials should be used by approximately 30 students. The teacher should use the manual provided with the materials to determine how to administer the instruction and how to gather all the test and questionnaire data. The teacher may also make observations of the students while they use the materials. The output of the process is the data from all the various data sources; they will be used to make the final revisions in the instructional materials.

Data-Gathering Instruments

During all phases of formative evaluation there is much information to be collected and a requirement for a variety of instruments which should be employed. The major set of instruments required is the performance tests. It may be assumed that the instructional designer will employ the objective-referenced tests which have been developed earlier to determine the effectiveness of the instructional materials. These tests will be particularly useful in identifying those objectives which have not been met by the students.

The second variable which is sometimes of great importance to the designer is that of learning time—how much time is required by students to complete the testing and instructional components of the materials. No special instruments are usually employed to gather this information. Rather, students are simply asked to write the beginning and ending time on each of the tests and instructional materials which they use.

It is quite common to employ attitude questionnaires in the formative evaluation process. It is desirable to have students indicate their specific reactions toward the instructional method as well as the content which they have received. The designer typically develops his own specific items for the questionnaire to target on his specific product. These items should be carefully worded to ensure that the data received from students will be useful. For example, an item such as "Did you like the instruction?" may provide information which is nice to know, but this provides little direction in determining specifically and with precision what might be done to improve the instructional materials. Therefore, each question which is to be employed on the questionnaire should be carefully designed to provide data which can be specifically used to revise the instruction.

Debriefing questionnaires are also useful during the second and third phases of formative evaluation. The questionnaire is a structured set of open-ended questions which the designer uses while interacting with students after they have completed the instruction. The designer should insure that the items cover all specific parts of the instruction and procedures, in order to obtain a full elaboration from the students on their reactions to the experience.

A final type of data which is often valuable to the designer is the comments made by subject-matter experts and teachers who assist in the implementation of the formative evaluation. While it is possible to simply ask these people for their reactions to the materials, it may be wise to structure an open-ended questionnaire for them, in order that they may respond to the items which the designer feels are most critical to the revision of the instructional materials.

Summarizing Formative Evaluation Data

The use of the formative evaluation process results in the generation of much data, which must be summarized in a meaningful manner. Perhaps the most critical of all data which are available to the designer are those from the various tests which are administered. There are several approaches to summarizing these data, all of which begin with a matrix or chart which lists by name or number all the students along the rows, and the number of each test item at the head of each column. Such a chart is shown in Figure 1. If there is only one test item for each objective, then the objective number and test items are synonymous. However, if two or more items are used for an objective, it is useful to cluster the items by objective on the chart. From this chart it is possible to determine the performance of each student on the test and, more importantly, to summarize the performance of the students on each of the instructional objectives.

Students	Objective I Item		Objective II Item			Objective III Item	Total % Correct
	1	2	1	2	3	1	
S1	1*	1	1	1	1	1	100
S2	0	0	0	0	0	0	0
S3	1	1	0	1	1	0	67
S4	1	0	1	0	0	0	33
S5	1	1	1	0	0	0	50
S6	1	1	0	1	1	1	87
S7	1	1	0	1	1	0	67
S8	0	1	1	0	1	1	67
S9	1	1	1	1	1	1	100
S10	1	1	0	1	1	1	87

Percent correct
per objective

| | 80 | | 60 | | | 50 | |

*A "1" means item passed; a "0" means item failed.

Figure 1: Hypothetical posttest performance for ten students.

It is possible to use several graphic techniques to display the changes in student performance from the pretest to the posttest. For example, a bar graph can be developed in which there are two entries for each objective. The first bar indicates the average performance on each objective on the pretest, and the adjacent bar shows average performance on the posttest. Another approach is to use a line graph on which percentage performance for the group on each of the instructional objectives is plotted for both the pretest and the posttest. Both the bar graph and the line graph can be used to visually identify those objectives for which students have not met a predetermined performance level. See Figure 2 for an example of a line graph. (Two different sets of data are reflected in Figures 1 and 2.)

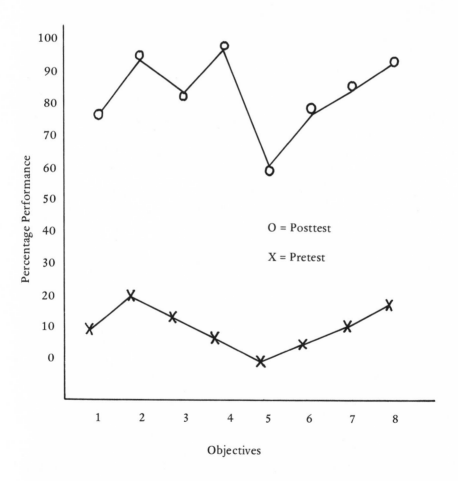

Figure 2:   *Pretest/posttest graph showing student performance.*

The learning time data may also be plotted on a graph, but in this case it is usually desirable to plot the data for each individual student. Such a chart might separately show testing time and learning time. The reason for plotting individual student time is to illustrate the variability in that time and to determine how many students may have exceeded the limits within which it was desirable to have the instruction completed. Any type of average time across students would eliminate this information.

A very different type of data is obtained from an attitude questionnaire. It has been found that the best way to summarize the data from a number of students on a questionnaire is to first determine the frequency of responding, or percent of students responding to each alternative, and then to write these numbers directly on a copy of the questionnaire. It is possible to quickly review the questionnaire and determine the types of responses which have been made by the students.

The final type of data which must be summarized is the comments which are received from teachers and/or subject-matter experts. It is helpful to try to identify the similarities and differences in these comments. It is also helpful to insert various specific comments directly in a set of the instructional materials, to aid in making revisions.

The types of data summaries described above are necessary for the designer to identify the types of problems which may exist within the instructional materials. The next section describes the use of these data to revise the materials.

The Revision Process

When all the formative evaluation data have been summarized, a designer has a good indication of what components of the instructional materials must be revised in order to make them more effective. There is a great temptation to go directly to the materials themselves to start making changes. However, it should be assumed that there may have been problems in the earlier stages of the design process which resulted in the problems in the instructional materials. Therefore, it is suggested that the test data be used to identify those objectives upon which the students have performed poorly. That information may be related to the task analysis chart to determine the interrelationship of those objectives which were not achieved. See Figure 3 for an example. The designer may find a direct relationship between failure to achieve a subordinate objective and failure to achieve later superordinate objectives (see Chapter 5). It may then be hypothesized that not all the instruction needs to be revised, but only that relating to the first objective (in a series) for which the instruction was defective; objective E in Figure 3 would merit close scrutiny; the results for D and F suggest a faulty hierarchy.

After examining the test data in relation to the task analysis, the designer should reexamine the objectives, and especially the test items which have been employed to test those objectives. It has often been found that the lack of effective performance by students is not necessarily due to poor instruction, but rather to inadequate test items which do not, in fact, measure what they were intended to measure. After examining the objectives and the items, the designer should reconsider the instructional strategy which has been employed to determine if there is need for further

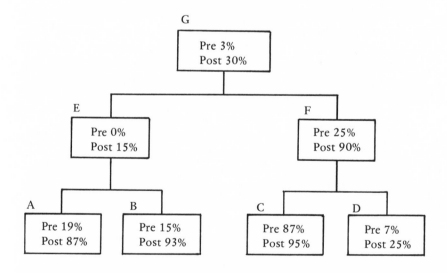

Figure 3:   Pretest and posttest data superimposed on learning hierarchy.

revision. Then, the designer is ready to work with the instructional materials and to note the comments made by teachers, students, and the subject-matter expert.

These revision procedures can be followed after each phase of formative evaluation, but they are most applicable to the small-group and field testing phases. It should be noted that when a particular revision has been completed, it may be desirable to repeat the evaluation rather than continuing on to the next phase. For example, the designer may wish to do as many as six or seven one-to-one evaluations before moving to the small-group stage. Clearly, changes which make materials more effective at an early point will be reflected in savings of time and cost later in the formative evaluation process.

The revision procedures just described are especially effective for adding needed instruction or for improving existing instruction. However, these procedures do not always spot "dead wood" or unnecessary instruction. One safeguard against "dead wood" is to write materials tersely in the beginning, adding items later as needed. Another safeguard is for the designer to always have a copy of the objectives at hand when preparing the materials. A third safeguard is to look for materials not reflected in the tests. Thus, both editorial and empirical measures can be taken to avoid "dead wood."

An Example of the Application of
Formative Evaluation Procedures

The example below is the edited and condensed version of one-to-one and small-group evaluations of a programmed instruction text in mathematics which was systematically designed. Space does not permit the inclusion of phase III field test data, but the write-up for that phase includes basically similar techniques. This description was prepared by Neuza Lindahl, who was a student in an instructional design course at the time of this writing. *The remainder of this section is an edited and condensed version of her report*:

One-to-one. The programmed instruction (PI) was first tested in a one-to-one situation. The first subject was a 13-year-old boy who is a student in the seventh grade. When I asked him to help me with the first evaluation of my program, he told me that he enjoyed studying mathematics, and he would like to experience a programmed text, since he had no experience with PI. His attitude towards the experience was very useful because he gave me many suggestions.

The program was prepared on index cards, one frame per card, with the answer on the back of each card.

Marcellino (the student) and I met for the program evaluation. No interruptions occurred during the time we were working.

Marcellino told me that he had never studied the base-five system of numeration. The pretest was given, and I concluded that he had the required entry behaviors.

He was asked to read each frame aloud and we discussed each answer, as well as the reasons for wrong interpretations, vocabulary troubles, etc. During the evaluation I wrote down all observations and suggestions.

At the end of our session it was obvious that some revisions of the program were needed, but I arrived at some very positive conclusions:

1. There was a smooth flow of material.
2. The reading level of the material was generally adequate.
3. Interest was maintained throughout most of the program.
4. The program was consistent with the objectives and the learner's abilities.

The revisions made are described below:

1. Eight frames were eliminated for different reasons:
   a. Three of them were exceeding the purpose of the program.
   b. Three of them were more "test questions" than required frames.
   c. Two of them contained too large a step.

2. Two new review frames were included in order to give more examples to facilitate the smoothness and the effectiveness of the program.

3. Some words were changed to more appropriate ones: for instance the substitution of the word "uses" for the word

"utilizes" in frame 13. Corrections were also made in some phrases, as in frame five where the original statement "Look at the set of x's" was replaced by "This set is grouped by tens."

Revisions were made and the program was tried again in the one-to-one situation. This time the student was an 11-year-old, sixth grade boy. He was pleased to help me and seemed to enjoy himself during his use of the program. He was a cooperative subject.

The program was again typed on index cards.

The student (Edward) was allowed to take the program by himself. He had never been exposed to the topic, but he had the required entry behaviors. He completed the PI text in 38 minutes, with a very low error rate. He was very successful on the posttest, with 95 percent correct answers. No further revisions were made in the PI text.

The major result of the second evaluation was a revision of the directions for the test item for the final task. It was broken down into two instructions in order to clarify the required performance.

The tested population. The sample for the small-group evaluation was selected from students at a local school. This tested population was composed of 13 seventh grade, low-achievement students with the following particular characteristics as a group:

1. Seven boys and six girls.
2. Eight whites and five blacks.
3. All students were 12 or 13 years old.
4. Low average achievement level.
5. Scholastic record average: B.
6. Reading proficiency test: slow readers.
7. All of them had been "exposed" to the entry behaviors.
8. According to the teacher, this was a well-behaved group, with no evident social problems.
9. According to the teacher, these were self-motivated students, with a positive attitude towards mathematics evidenced in their daily class meetings.
10. The students had very little or no previous experience with PI.

From the above characteristics I concluded that the test

population was a representative sample of the target population.

I found it useful to be present during the small-group administration. It took three days for the complete administration, due to the time limits of the class. The students were given the pretest on the first day, the PI text on the second day, and the posttest on the third day. The students worked under normal daily class conditions and environment. They were instructed on the procedures that they were supposed to follow and on the purposes of the work. They were told not to look at the correct answer before responding to each frame and not to correct their wrong answers to questions in the frames of the PI unit.

Apparently, the students did not enjoy taking the pretest very much. On the second day, though, they seemed to be motivated to work with the programmed text. After the administration, some of the students expressed appreciation for this type of instruction and a desire to keep the program.

The times for beginning and completing the pretest, PI text, and posttest were noted.

From the data I concluded that the program was an effective device and that the learning which resulted was significant. The pretest and posttest data showed a positive difference in the students' performance. A graph of the pretest and posttest clearly showed the students' gain. The change from the pretest average of 28 percent to the posttest average of 80 percent is highly significant.

The frame error rate was low, except for one of the students, who was not able to correctly answer most of the questions. His final performance, though, rose from 12 percent on the pretest to 55 percent on the posttest.

Although I realize that this programmed instructional unit was not sufficiently tested to judge its general applicability, I would say that it is an effective device that could be applied to any population with characteristics similar to the tested population. It could also be tried with normal-achievement students at a lower level, i.e., sixth grade students, to the extent that they have the required entry behaviors for the program. (This ends the formative evaluation report; the report itself, of course, also included tables and figures showing the actual evaluation data.)

Research on Formative Evaluation

While several state legislatures have mandated that all instructional materials sold to the schools must undergo formative evaluation, there is relatively little experimental research evidence which documents the effectiveness of the formative evaluation process. During the 15 years in which systematic instructional design procedures have been developing, almost no funds have been available for research on the development process itself. Consequently, there are very few studies in the literature which can be cited in support of this approach. In addition, it should be noted that it is extremely difficult to conduct research on the formative evaluation process because of the need to involve a significant number of designers in most such studies. In typical instructional research, students serve as the subjects whose data are analyzed; however, in research on formative evaluation, it is necessary to have a number of designers who can be assigned to various experimental treatments.

There are basically two areas of research in formative evaluation. The first is the identification of data which should be collected and analyzed during formative evaluation. A second is the identification of procedures for modifying instruction based on formative evaluation data. Of the studies which are available, most focus on the diagnostic or data-collection question and only indirectly deal with the question of procedures for modifying instruction. The studies which would appear to be of most interest to readers of this Chapter are those which have attempted to investigate the overall effectiveness of employing the formative evaluation process.

Komoski (1974) has argued that designers (and commercial publishers) should try out their materials with *at least one student* and revise based on the information which is obtained. Komoski is not advocating the use of only one student in the total formative evaluation process, but rather he has indicated that revising instruction on the basis of one student is significantly better than not revising the instruction at all. Therefore, the question may be raised, "Is instruction significantly improved if it is tried out and revised on the basis of data from even one student?"

Robeck (1965) designed a study which was directed at this

question. He tried out a programmed instruction text with one sixth grade student and, based on that student's reactions, revised the text. The revised text was tried out on another sixth grader, and based on this information, the text was revised again. There were now three versions of the PI text: the original, the first revision, and the second revision. These three versions were given to matched groups of sixth grade students, and an achievement test was administered after they had completed the instruction. The results indicated that both of the versions which had been revised produced significantly better results than did the original version of the PI text. However, the second revision was not found to be significantly better than the first revision.

While a study such as Robeck's is encouraging in terms of the significance of the difference in favor of the revised version, the question remains as to the generalizability of these results to other designers. Could these results be attributed simply to the skills displayed by this particular designer, and not necessarily to the general process of formative evaluation? Rosen (1968) attempted to bring broader generalization to this area by involving 20 designers in a study of the formative evaluation process.

In the Rosen study, the designers were randomly assigned to two groups. Each group was given a set of instructional materials which had already been tried out with sixth graders. The members of one group also received the test data from the students to use in their individual revisions of the materials. Members of the second group were simply requested to revise the materials based on their own intuition of what was needed. The original materials and the two sets of revised materials were administered to randomly assigned groups of students. Rosen's results indicated that both sets of revised materials were superior to the original set and that, in addition, those which were revised on the basis of the empirical test data were significantly better than those which were revised on the basis of intuition.

Other studies similar to that of Rosen have been conducted by Baker (1970) and Sulzen (1972). Both these studies included the use of a group of instructional designers and both obtained the same result, namely, that the revised instruction produced significantly better learning outcomes than did the original, unrevised instruction.

The limited research which is available supports Komoski's view that it is worthwhile to revise instruction based on only one learner as compared to not trying it out at all. In addition to these research studies, there is less rigorous evidence which suggests that formative evaluation is worthwhile. There are hundreds of instructional designers who have used the formative evaluation process in their design of instructional materials. They have seen the effect that the process has had in helping them to identify faulty objectives and test items, and to improve their instructional strategies. It is the rare case in which any designer using formative evaluation data does not obtain better results from subsequent groups of students. However, this does not serve as research documentation, in that each version of the instructional materials developed by an individual designer has not been simultaneously tried out on large groups, with the average performance of those groups compared. However, the developmental evidence is clear.

Many methodological problems are apparent when one considers undertaking research on formative evaluation. We have not been able to identify the contributions of the specific variables which are measured in the formative evaluation process. In general, studies have emphasized the use of posttest performance data as a key to the revision process. Little research has included pretest data, imbedded test item data, learning time, attitudes, and comments of subject-matter experts and teachers. The relative importance of these various factors has not been systematically investigated.

We have even less research knowledge about the process which should be used to revise instruction based on formative evaluation data. At this point, it would appear that we can only follow the logic of the theories which have been used in the instructional design process.

Issues and Questions on Formative Evaluation

The formative evaluation procedures described in this Chapter are relatively straightforward and can be conducted by the designer without difficulty. There are, however, a number of problems and issues which have arisen over the last few years with regard to the formative evaluation process. In this section we attempt to identify those problems and issues, and to provide a point of view with regard to each.

The first question is whether formative procedures apply to the development of an entire curriculum. It may be argued that these same basic processes can be used for a total curriculum. To do so would require that the curriculum be broken into components or units for formative evaluation, and then integrated as they are completed. Certainly, it is more difficult to find appropriate students who are at exactly the right spot at the right time to take a particular unit. If there is not sufficient time to do this, it may be necessary to first design and then implement instruction in full. When such circumstances arise, it is desirable to collect the same kinds of data which have been described in order that the feedback which is derived may be used to change later components of the instruction—which are still being developed.

Another type of question which may be asked with regard to the formative evaluation process is whether it applies to the development of instruction which will be implemented via complex media such as films or computers. It may be suggested that the same basic approach be applied when such materials are being developed but that a heavy emphasis be placed on the development of a very simple *initial* format for the instruction, i.e., develop simplistic forms of the instruction prior to going to the full medium.

Another question which often arises is "When is the formative evaluation process terminated?" It is conceivable that a designer would continue to revise and revise and never feel that his product is complete. It is difficult to provide a general solution to this problem. Formative evaluation is terminated based almost entirely upon the specific circumstances surrounding the development project. The time which is available to the designer, the staff and resources which are on hand, and the criticality of designing maximally effective instruction are the important factors.

The military, when first developing programmed instruction materials, decided to establish an 80/80 criterion for determining when materials no longer needed to be revised. The 80/80 criterion simply means that when 80 percent of the students achieve 80 percent of the objectives for the unit, then the product is ready for production and use in the field.

Certainly the 80/80 criterion is an arbitrary one and could be easily changed. For example, the criterion of 100/70 could be used, i.e., 100 percent of the students would need to achieve 70 percent or more of the objectives. This type of criterion would reflect a desire to have no students performing at less than the 70 percent level. An alternative would be a criterion of 95/100—95 percent of the students would have to achieve 100 percent of the objectives. Such a criterion would require the perfect performance by almost every student who uses the instruction.

While the criteria listed above offer statistically satisfying criteria for terminating the revision process, it is much more customary for time requirements or funding to determine when the formative evaluation process will be completed. It is critical that the instructional designer attempt to schedule into the development project at least one iteration of each of the three phases of the formative evaluation process.

The Next Step

In most instructional design models there is no step beyond formative evaluation. There are almost always arrows (in flow diagrams depicting the models) from the formative evaluation stage to direct the designer back through the model to revise the previous steps which have been undertaken. That process is then continued until the materials meet the instructional effectiveness criterion or other criteria which have been established for them.

It is quite common, however, for the question to be raised whether an instructional product which has just been developed is *better than* another product. There is very little data from the formative evaluation process which would provide any direct answer to this question. Therefore, in terms of our presentation of the instructional design process, we are including one additional step, namely that of summative evaluation.

In contrast to formative evaluation, in which the emphasis is upon feedback of information to the designer, the emphasis in summative evaluation is on providing data to decision-makers who must determine if certain instructional materials should be used or which of several sets of materials should be selected.

The reader will note that it is possible that some formative evaluation data could be used for a summative evaluation, i.e., for making a decision to continue to use the materials. However, there are many other types of data which are needed for a complete summative evaluation, as will be pointed out in the following Chapter.

Summary

In this Chapter, formative evaluation has been described as a process employed by the instructional designer to collect data in order to revise instructional materials. The three basic phases of formative evaluation include one-to-one, small groups, and field testing. Each phase includes different numbers of students and different procedures. Exmphasis in early phases is on the improvement of the instructional effectiveness of the materials, while later phases emphasize the administrative feasibility of the materials when used in the target learning environment.

Techniques for summarizing and interpreting formative evaluation data have been presented. The designer is encouraged to examine student test performance as a function of the total design process, i.e., the task analysis, objectives, test items, etc., as opposed to just the instructional materials. Therefore, the revision process requires a review of all the design steps to better identify the locus of learning (or testing) difficulties.

A brief review of the research in formative evaluation has indicated that there is experimental evidence to show that the use of this process results in significant improvements in students' performance. However, much research remains to be done in the areas of variables to be measured and specific revision procedures. It has been suggested that formative evaluation procedures can be applied not only to paper-and-pencil instruction, but also to large-scale media-oriented curricula and teacher-led classroom activities.

References

Baker, E.L. Generalizability of Rules for an Empirical Revision. *AV Communication Review*, 1970, *18* (3), 300-305.

Komoski, P.K. An Imbalance of Product Quantity and Instructional Quality: The Imperative of Empiricism. *A V Communication Review*, 1974, *22* (4), 357-386.

Robeck, M.D. A Study of the Revision Process in Programmed Instruction. Unpublished Master's Thesis, University of California, Los Angeles, 1965.

Rosen, M.J. An Experimental Design for Comparing the Effects of Instructional Media Programming Procedures: Subjective Versus Objective Procedures. Final Report. Palo Alto: American Institutes for Research, 1968.

Sulzen, R.H. The Effects of Empirical Revision and the Presentation of Specific Objectives to Learners Prior to Programmed Instruction Upon the Criterion Behavior of Military Subjects. Unpublished Doctoral Dissertation, University of California, Los Angeles, 1972.

Additional Sources

Baker, E.L., and Alkin, M.C. Formative Evaluation of Instructional Development. *A V Communication Review*, 1973, *21* (4), 389-418.

Borich, G.D. (Ed.), *Evaluating Educational Programs and Products*. Englewood Cliffs, N.J.: Educational Technology Publications, 1974.

Gropper, G.L. *Diagnosis and Revision in the Development of Instructional Materials*. Englewood Cliffs, N.J.: Educational Technology Publications, 1975.

Lawson, T.E. *Formative Instructional Product Evaluation: Instruments and Strategies*. Englewood Cliffs, N.J.: Educational Technology Publications, 1974.

Transition to Chapter 11

As will be shown in Chapter 11, the designer's job is often considered to be complete after he has conducted formative evaluations and revisions of the materials and learning activities planned in order to reach the designated goals and objectives for the course.

Notice that the word "project" in Chapter 11 refers to the entire design undertaking, whether accomplished by a teacher or a team of designers. Usually, the full-scale type of summative evaluation described in Chapter 11 would be undertaken only for a team effort in which the "course" or "new curriculum" is to be installed in many schools. Summative evaluation is usually too expensive a process for an innovation carried out in only one classroom. However, in a few cases, single "modules" of instruction have been evaluated economically. It is just that the techniques of evaluation grow out of an assumption of possible widespread adoption of the instruction that was designed.

It may appear to the reader that many of the activities of the evaluator, as described in Chapter 11, duplicate work completed earlier by the design team. This may be so, especially if the design team fails to document its work in detail. If the design process is well documented, the evaluator can use much of it in an economical way to reduce some of his own work.

Note the difference between Chapters 10 and 11 in the scope of the questions raised. In formative evaluation (Chapter 10), one concentrates upon achieving the stated instructional objectives, evidence of which is sought by use of objective-referenced tests.

One is seeing whether *each student* meets the criterion of success set for each objective in terms of performance on the tests over the objectives. Often, when most students reach criterion on most of the objective-referenced tests, we say that the project "met its design objectives." This straightforward approach is one of the strengths of the design procedures advocated in this book. The design team can be congratulated when it meets *its* design objective, as shown by pupil performance (to criterion) on objective-referenced tests.

In contrast to the formative evaluations made by the design team, as just described, summative evaluation takes on a broader perspective. As shown in Chapter 11, the summative evaluator (often called an "outside" evaluator when he has not been a member of the design team), has the duty of taking an "outsider's" dispassionate look at broader questions. He may say: "Of course, I am glad that the pupils scored so well on the objective-referenced tests, but now I must ask how valuable the objectives are before I can say whether the whole undertaking was worth the cost. I must also compare the value of these objectives and outcomes to those of other programs, and I must search for unexpected outcomes not measured by the objective-referenced tests. Also, I want to administer standardized tests so I can compare these pupils' general knowledge of the subject to the level of achievement in other schools. I must be sure the intended processes were followed, so I will know what I am really evaluating. The products (materials) are there for inspection, but were they used according to the intent described in the design report?"

Chapter 11 shows that the instructional materials must ultimately be evaluated, not in a controlled laboratory setting, but in real schools in which the willingness of teachers and pupils to use the products as intended is a crucial consideration. While design teams focus on development of materials, the teacher must monitor the intended pupil activities. Hence, some form of teacher training and process monitoring is a part of successful installation and evaluation. In short, it is the delivery system that ultimately must be evaluated, not just the materials. (Chapter 9 touched further on this point.)

Chapter 11

Summative Evaluation

Walter Dick
Florida State University

The area of evaluation has greatly expanded in the past 20 years. If one reviews the evaluation studies conducted in the 1950's, it can be seen that the typical study used experimental designs which had been formerly employed in psychology laboratories. These studies often compared an innovative process with "the traditional approach." The results almost always indicated "no significant difference" in the learning outcomes between the two groups.

The concept of evaluation has been greatly expanded, and it is now generally agreed that summative evaluation may be defined as a process of gathering, combining, and interpreting data in order to make a decision about a new product. The focus in summative evaluation is on the decision-maker and the amount and type of information which will be needed by him to make an educationally sound decision. It is no longer satisfactory to simply test the statistical significance of the difference in a single learning outcome which indicates the superiority of treatment A over treatment B. A number of other factors need to be taken into consideration by the educational decision-maker.

The purpose of this Chapter is to present several current models of summative evaluation and to identify the components which make up these models. The step-by-step process of doing a summative evaluation will be considered, and several examples of summative evaluation will be discussed. The Chapter will conclude with a discussion of future directions in evaluation.

It should be noted that the summative evaluation process is

not an integral component of the systems approach to instructional design, and therefore it does not necessarily involve the instructional designer. Summative evaluation is conducted *after* a product or instructional system has been completed; therefore, it is not mandatory that the instructional designer have skills in the area of summative evaluation. However, it is definitely to the designer's benefit to be knowledgeable about the process.

It also might be noted that this Chapter does not include a section on research on the summative evaluation process. The question of whether or not to do a summative evaluation is not a researchable question. If it is not done, the information about product effectiveness will simply not be available. The papers which have been published on summative evaluation provide examples of the application of the process, models of summative evaluation, or discussions of various methodological issues associated with the process. There is no experimental research on the effectiveness of this process.

Models of Summative Evaluation

When evaluators reconsidered the whole issue of summative evaluation, they began to look at broader questions than simply the learning outcomes associated with a project. They began to consider the amount of learning time required of students, and their attitudes about the learning experience. Another factor which is critically important to decision-makers is the relative and absolute cost of implementing the innovation; therefore, this must be included in the evaluation. In addition, questions must be asked about whether the objectives for which the instruction was designed are really worthwhile, and whether there are other, unanticipated outcomes that are not directly related to the original learning goals.

In order to look at these factors in an orderly way, a number of evaluation models have been developed. Perhaps the best known of these models is that of Stufflebeam (1971). The four major components of the Stufflebeam CIPP model are Context, Input, Process, and Product Evaluation.

Stufflebeam's CIPP model requires that the evaluator look

not only at the product (outcomes) of the innovative project, but also the context in which the project took place, the input to the project, and the process which is involved in achieving the outcomes. Specifically, *context evaluation* refers to those activities employed by the evaluator to define the relative project environment. This requires an analysis of the goals to be achieved within a project, including the definition of ideal goals and the current level within the target population in meeting these goals. In addition, problems within the environment that prevent project goals from being achieved and factors that could enhance goal achievement are analyzed and described.

Input evaluation refers to those activities that assess the project capabilities and strategies for achieving defined goals, designing plans to implement activities related to project goals, and analyzing alternative plans for achieving goals.

Process evaluation refers to the detection of weaknesses in instruction or procedures through formative evaluation and the collection of information to document materials and procedures which have been employed.

Product evaluation refers to the evaluation and reporting of the operational project objectives, evaluation of criteria for determining success of project activities, the linking of one phase of the project to other interrelated phases, and the reporting and disseminating of data concerning project successes and failures.

These definitions indicate that Stufflebeam believes summative evaluation involves the evaluation of the total project—from the time the original goals are set and strategies developed for achieving certain outcomes, through the implementation of the project activities and the assessment of the project outcomes.

While the model developed by Stufflebeam is meant to apply to all innovative projects, Gagné and Briggs (1974) have used essentially the same model, but have employed terminology which is specific to the instructional design process. Their model has four components: support, aptitude, process, and outcomes. In their model Gagné and Briggs indicate that the support component is composed of the instructional materials that are used in the project, and the climate in the classroom and other more general factors, such as parental attitudes, which will facilitate or interfere with the learning process. These factors should be known in order to assess the value of the learning outcomes that are achieved.

Gagné and Briggs also point out that learner aptitude is a critical variable in any evaluation, due to the significant correlation between the aptitude of learners and eventual learning outcomes. It is also critical that potential adopters of the instructional materials know the ability level of the students who are used in the summative evaluation, in order to determine the similarity between the decision-maker's population and that which was used in the study.

The term process evaluation is used by Gagné and Briggs in a manner similar to that of Stufflebeam. They indicate the importance of carefully documenting the procedures which were used to implement the instructional materials in the learning situation. Similarly, the outcomes of the learning process must be identified and documented in a manner similar to the way in which Stufflebeam defines product outcomes.

Scriven (1974) has employed a different approach to defining the summative evaluation process. He has worked for a number of years to develop a product checklist rather than a model. Such a checklist would be used to evaluate a product which had undergone summative evaluation. The checklist includes consideration of both the quantity and the quality of the information which is available about the instructional product, and thus could be used by a summative evaluator to determine that the data which were being collected would adequately meet the questions that are raised on the checklist.

The first two questions on the list are concerned with the need and the market for an instructional product. Questions are raised about the number of students who will be affected by this new product and the absence of other products which would meet the need. In addition, there is consideration given to the clarity, feasibility, and economy of the dissemination plan for implementing the instructional materials.

The next nine items on the evaluation checklist are directed toward the report of the performance of the students who used the instructional materials. These items consider such questions as these: Was a true field trial carried out? Was the final version of the material used? Was a typical instructional setting used within a typical instructional time frame? Were the data collected from the real consumers of these instructional materials—not only students who would use them, but also teachers, principals, school district officials, state education department officers, and other interested parties?

The report of the summative evaluation is then analyzed to determine whether critical comparisons have been made between this product and other relevant, competitive products which might be employed, such as other textbooks, or instructional materials, or other methods of implementing the instruction. Concern is also given to any indicators of long-term effects, such as a month to a year later, and any potential side-effects from using the instruction.

The report is also examined to determine if there is a detailed description of the process which was employed to implement the instruction in the summative evaluation, and whether the evaluation design which was employed was sufficient to determine that the learning outcomes were in fact a result of the instructional materials that were employed. The obvious question is also raised as to whether there was a significant difference between treatment groups.

The final performance question is a determination of the educational significance, regardless of the statistical significance, of the differences between the performance of the students in the various treatments. Is there any evidence or expert judgment which would indicate that the instructional materials do produce significant educational gains?

The final two items on the checklist are concerned with cost-effectiveness and the support which is required to implement the instructional materials. Questions are raised as to whether a cost analysis has been undertaken and how the costs of the new instructional materials or procedures compare with other forms of instruction. There is also the question of whether inservice training is required of teachers who will use the materials, and if an updating service will be provided to keep the materials from becoming obsolete.

The checklist developed by Scriven is quite extensive. It includes a documentation of the need for the product and the viability of the market to purchase materials that have been produced. It assesses the quality and quantity of the data which are available, and it requires a determination of the cost-effectiveness and educational significance of the materials. The checklist clearly calls for a large number of skills which are needed by the summative evaluator in order to obtain all the information which would be required by the decision-maker to determine whether the instructional product should be purchased for use with a particular target population.

The Process of Summative Evaluation

This section will describe the five most basic steps in the conduct of a summative evaluation. These steps would be followed whether the evaluation was of a one-half-hour, paper-and-pencil module or a year-long, multi-media curriculum in social studies. Each of the steps is complex, but they will be described only in general terms. In order to initiate the summative evaluation process, as described below, the evaluator must have a copy of the instructional materials to be used and some type of report which describes the development of the materials.

Identification of Intended Outcomes

The first step for the evaluator is to identify the basic instructional goals to which the instructional materials are addressed. Hopefully, the developmental report will indicate not only the general learning goals but also the specific outcomes which are intended to be achieved through the use of the materials. If the goals and objectives are stated by the developer, they can serve as the anchor points for the summative evaluation. Much of the instrumentation and design of the study will depend upon these statements. If, on the other hand, goals and objectives are not available, the evaluator, in conjunction with a subject-matter expert, would be required to identify what seem to be the intended outcomes of the materials. Obviously, this is not a satisfactory situation, but sometimes it is the only alternative available to the evaluator.

Identification of Target Population
and Design for the Evaluation Study

The next step, following the identification of goals and

objectives, is to identify those students, representative of the target population, who are available to study the instructional materials. The selection of students will be one of the most critical decisions in the summative evaluation process. Ideally, the evaluator would like to have a significant number of students who are representative of the target population for whom the materials were originally intended. If these students are available, then relatively sound evaluation designs can be established, and the outcomes of the study can be interpreted with some confidence.

It is often the situation, however, that ideal samples of students are not available to the summative evaluator. Therefore, compromises must be made. The extent of these compromises will determine both the design of the study and the extent to which the results may be generalized to other populations.

The ideal summative evaluation design is one in which a large sample of the target population is available. Such students are given a pretest over the instruction to be provided (or students are selected for whom recent general aptitude scores are available). With these data, students can be paired with like students, and one member from each pair randomly assigned to the experimental (or innovative) treatment and one to the control (or alternative) treatment. The two groups can be compared using any appropriate test.

If there are sufficient students for an experimental design of this type, it is possible also to compare the results of each sample group with expected results as determined from the norms for a standardized examination. If a standardized examination is available in the content area of the instructional materials, and if it is relevant to the instructional goals of those materials, it is possible to compare the progress made by an experimental group with that which would be expected from the national norms. For further details, see *A Practical Guide to Measuring Project Impact on Student Achievement* (1975).

A third, and by far the weakest alternative, is to simply establish certain criteria for accepted outcomes on the various evaluation instruments and then administer those instruments to the sample from the target population at the completion of their study of the instructional materials. There is little scientific rigor associated with this approach, and no cause-and-effect relationship can be established with any certainty. However, the summative evaluator can at least describe the instructional setting, the instruments which were utilized, and the outcomes obtained. It is then up to the decision-maker to determine the extent to which it would appear that these results could be replicated with another sample of students.

Development of Evaluation Instruments

It is the responsibility of the evaluator to produce the instruments which will be used to collect data for the summative evaluation. The most critical type of data will be learning outcomes related to the goals and objectives of the instructional materials. Objective-referenced tests may have already been prepared for the instructional materials by the developers. Summative evaluators should determine whether the instruments match the learning objectives for the materials, and whether additional items will be required to evaluate the learning outcomes.

The evaluator will also need to develop attitude questionnaires for the students, teachers, administrators, parents, and others directly or indirectly affected by the implementation of the materials. These instruments should be developed according to sound psychometric principles, and they should include items which assess the reactions of the various groups to both the content of the materials and the method by which the materials were presented.

The third area in which data should be obtained is that of costs. In order to assess the costs associated with the implementation of the instructional materials, it may be necessary to have teachers and students record the amount of time they spend studying the materials. It will also be necessary to determine the initial costs of the materials, as well as any continuing costs which might reoccur over a period of time. These costs should be determined both for the traditional approach and the innovative approach.

Documentation of the Instructional Process

After the evaluator has designed the evaluation study, identified the students who will be involved, developed the assessment instruments, and perhaps administered a pretest, there is still much work to be done. It is the responsibility of the evaluator to document the process which is used in the implementation of the various instructional approaches. It is important to determine that the materials have been used in accordance with the intended instructional plan. For example, if teachers are required to periodically engage in questioning-type activities with groups of students, it is necessary to document that these sessions were held and that questioning techniques were in fact employed. Alternatively, if, at a certain point in the study of the materials, students must have access to certain laboratory equipment, it is necessary to document that the equipment was available and was in fact used in the laboratory studies by the students. Again, it is important that this type of documentation be made for both the innovative and the alternative approaches which are being evaluated. This step is often laborious and difficult, but it is one which must be carried out if the decision-maker is to have data which truly reflect the use of the instructional materials in the way in which they were intended to be used.

A "replicable" item of instruction, such as a programmed instruction text or a slide/tape presentation, is easier to evaluate than is a lecture which is not recorded and hence must be evaluated as a process rather than a product. The lecture "disappears" as it is delivered, while the booklet is available for later inspection. It is also often difficult to evaluate the product separately from the skill of the teacher who determines how the product will be used. But on-the-spot monitoring of use is one aspect of process evaluation.

Preparation of the Summative Evaluation Report

The final responsibility of the summative evaluator is to prepare a report for educational decision-makers. Too often such reports are written as though they were to be read by sophisticated statisticians. They often contain numerous and seemingly unending data tables, formulae, and terminology which are not interpretable by most interested readers. It is imperative that summative evaluation reports be written in a concise, direct manner, and formatted in such a way that they will be attractive and readable to the decision-makers concerned.

The goals and objectives in the project should be clearly outlined and the types of instruments described. Often the instruments might appear in the Appendix of the report. The students who participated in the study should be described, and the design of the study should be clearly and simply presented. There should be an indication of the instructional techniques which were employed, and a brief and concise description of the outcomes should be presented. The Scriven product evaluation checklist, described in the previous section, could serve as a useful outline for a summative evaluation report. The most important point is for the evaluator to remember the audience for which the report is intended—educational decision-makers, not sophisticated statisticians.

The five steps described above may oversimplify the role of the summative evaluator. It must be recognized that there is much interchange between the evaluator and teacher, students, administrators, and parents. The evaluator may also be involved with the staff which originally developed the instructional product. There are often situations which arise in the context of the schools or other learning settings which seem to be designed to destroy the evaluation study. However, experience in working in a specific context will alert the evaluator to many of the difficulties which may arise and provide insights into how evaluations can be conducted smoothly and effectively. The reader is referred to the text by Gagné and Briggs (1974, pp. 247-255), in which is presented summaries of summative evaluation reports on reading and arithmetic curricula as well as a general example of a summative evaluation report.

The Future of Evaluation

At the beginning of this Chapter it was indicated that evaluation processes have changed dramatically in the past 20 years. It may be predicted that changes will continue to occur, and that evaluation will become of greater importance as more and more emphasis is placed on the results of such studies. The era in which bright and creative people were simply provided funds to develop attractive instructional materials would appear to be over.

Accountability for the use of funds in the development of effective learning materials is a growing trend.

The possibility of receiving funds from agencies for an instructional design project which does not include a sound evaluation design will become more remote. Agencies are currently under pressure to support projects which engage in wise planning and clear documentation and evaluation. In essence, these agencies have an investment in the projects that they fund. If projects are to continue, it is critical to have evaluation reports which indicate the total effectiveness of the products. If such projects are to continue to be funded, then accountability must increase.

Perhaps a more professionally appealing reason for engaging in extensive summative evaluation is the obligation of educators to share the outcomes of research and development efforts. Evaluation is an expensive process—not just in terms of hiring a person, but also in terms of the materials and supplies that are involved. In addition, extensive time commitments are required of teaching staff as well as the students who are studying the instructional materials. Numerous hours are required to develop testing instruments, attitude surveys, and questionnaires, as well as to analyze the documentation of the instructional process itself. However, without this information, agencies and educators are left without a dependable indication of whether or not materials are effective in achieving their goals and objectives.

It may be asked if the role of the evaluator will become easier or more difficult in the future. The present trend suggests that the role will become better understood and accepted. It is likely that as more instructional design personnel become receptive to the contribution which can be made by evaluators, the efforts of evaluators will be accepted as an integral part of all projects. In particular, process evaluation techniques will be better understood and accepted in terms of their value in the documentation of the learning effectiveness of materials.

It is likely that in the next several decades decision-makers will become more and more dependent upon summative evaluation reports for the data to make critical decisions about instructional materials and entire delivery systems. As more evaluation studies are conducted, working relationships will develop, and it will be easier to organize, conduct, and evaluate instructional materials. It is also likely that as more evaluations take place, new procedures and evaluation strategies will be developed and implemented, and hopefully, better techniques will evolve.

Summary

The summative evaluation process has expanded in recent years to include assessments not only of a variety of learning outcomes, but also of the needs and the goals of instruction, and the procedures used to implement the instruction.

It is the responsibility of the summative evaluator to: determine intended outcomes and the target population, design the evaluation study, develop all the evaluation instruments, document the implementation of instruction, measure the outcomes, and write the evaluation report.

It is anticipated that the role of the evaluator will be facilitated in the future through the development of new, more effective techniques and the familiarization of teachers and project personnel with the role and functions of the evaluator.

References

A Practical Guide to Measuring Project Impact on Student Achievement. Washington, D.C.: U.S. Government Printing Office, 1975.

Gagné, R.M., and Briggs, L.J. *Principles of Instructional Design.* New York: Holt, Rinehart, and Winston, 1974.

Scriven, M. Evaluation Perspectives and Procedures. In Popham, W.J. (Ed.) *Evaluation in Education: Current Applications.* Berkeley: McCutchan Publishing Co., 1974.

Stufflebeam, D.L. The Relevance of the CIPP Evaluation Model for Educational Accountability. *Journal of Educational Research and Development,* 5 (1), 1971.

Part II

Applications and Illustrations

Transition to Part II
and Chapter 12

As indicated in Chapter 1, Part II of this book turns from the theory and principles of the model (as discussed in Part I) to the application of the model in various organizational settings. Chapters 12 to 14 are similar in that they deal with both the organizational aspects of education and military and industrial training, and with the design processes taking place there.

Chapter 15 is different. It represents a "project report" on how a team designed a specific instructional system. The design techniques recorded there, and the test results for the course, make this a unique Chapter.

Chapters 16 and 17 show what two students did in designing parts of a course. These two Chapters are useful illustrations of the techniques discussed in Part I.

The next Chapter, 12, was placed at the opening of Part II because it compares and contrasts design operations as they take place in education and in military and industrial organizations. It thus serves as an advance organizer for Chapters to follow, although it concentrates most heavily on military and industrial applications.

Chapter 12

Military and Industrial Training

Robert K. Branson
Florida State University

Introduction

Many significant developments in instructional technology have come from the military, industrial, and business communities, and these groups continue to make extensive use of the concepts and tools of instructional technology. In this Chapter, a brief historical sketch of the use of instructional technology in these sectors is traced. Comparisons among these sectors and the academic world will be made in order to show the similarities and differences in their purposes and practices.

Training programs applied in the context of the systems approach may ordinarily be described as having five interrelated but distinct phases: Analysis, Design, Development, Implementation, and Control. Military and industrial training systems also may be considered in terms of their costs and the time required for trainees to go through them. Training effectiveness and efficiency are highly important in the military and industry, and considerable emphasis is given to efforts which are intended to increase effectiveness and efficiency.

Where possible, specific military and industrial examples will be described, and the results of experiments and other studies will be given to indicate how problems are approached and solved. It is important to note that while there is some overlap among the missions and purposes of academic institutions and military or industrial institutions, they have distinctly different purposes and they allocate their resources to their individual purposes accordingly. Sharing of information and practices among all these sectors can probably best be accomplished by trying to isolate analogous problems and solutions to see to what extent they may be applied in the other environments.

Historical Perspectives

There are common historical roots which led to the emergence of instructional technology, even though the applications of that technology may appear different in education than in military and industrial training. Before the 1950's, people were not doing "instructional technology," but rather they were doing research on learning and instruction in psychological laboratories. As the resulting body of research knowledge expanded, the industrial and experimental psychologists employed in the military and in industry began to apply these laboratory-developed techniques for practical and profitable ends.

As has been described in earlier Chapters, we may look at the "things" (hardware) of instructional technology, or the "processes" for the designing of instruction, or the resulting materials (sometimes called "courseware"), or all of these at the same time. Some of the earlier "things" of instructional technology (for example, the motion picture projector) can be traced back to the 1880's. Probably the first device to incorporate a process of instructional technology was Pressey's "testing machine" (Pressey, 1926). (See Figure 1.)

While it is of little value here to trace the history of still photography, motion picture photography, sound recording and transmission, or graphics or television, each of these has its own potential for application in the general field of instructional technology. But it is worthwhile to identify some of the attempts at the application of the *processes* of instructional technology, wherein the things are articulated by the process.

World War II created a sudden need to increase dramatically the effectiveness and efficiency of military training. Large numbers of psychologists were pressed into military service and given the assignment of designing such training. Probably the most interesting of all longer-term training programs is that of air crew

Figure 1:   Pressey Testing Machine (Photo by Angus J. Nicholson).

flight training. As the nature of problems became more apparent, psychologists adapted their traditional laboratory equipment to devise selection tests, after which the equipment was further transformed into various types of training equipment. Throughout this period, the process of instruction and the equipment used for instruction were thought of as integrated.

Shortly thereafter, a variety of special-purpose equipment was designed to train both equipment operators and maintenance personnel for the equipment. Modern versions of this equipment will be described in more detail later in this Chapter.

It was during World War II that the initial research on the use of film in instruction began to identify the actual requirements for motion as well as the differences between subjective and objective views in the film itself. Simple but fundamental discoveries were made during this time. For example, it was demonstrated that trainees learn much better if they are presented with film views as they would see the task rather than as they would witness a demonstration of the task. To achieve this learner-oriented view, the camera was placed over a trainee's shoulder as he learned to tie knots, so that what later trainees saw on the film was much the same as they saw when watching their own hands tie the knots.

Education

Tracing the origins of instructional technology in the academic world is somewhat more difficult than tracing these same origins in the military and industrial environments. While there have always been research examples of innovations in schools and colleges, widespread applications are more infrequent. Some would say that the introduction of hardware into the schools should signal the beginning. But it should be pointed out that while instructional technologies can use television as a part of a system, the use of television does not imply that any kind of *systems approach* was used in the planning of the instruction.

After Pressey's initial research effort, valid applications of instructional technology probably did not occur until the mid-1950's, and then only on a limited research or demonstration basis. Skinner's psychology course at Harvard was one of the earlier applications where students actually received course credit for using teaching machines (Skinner, 1958). Somewhat later, many more projects were undertaken successfully, including Project PLAN (Flanagan, 1968), Individually Prescribed Instruction (Glaser, 1968), and a variety of others.

It is time now to take a specific look at how the principles and practices of instructional technology are approached in the military, industrial, and academic communities.

Analysis

In this Chapter, the term *analysis* refers to the processes of finding out what people do on their jobs, which of these actions require training, how to measure the results of job performance, and selecting the setting in which the training takes place. The crux of analysis is finding out what must be taught and how one knows that it has been taught.

Military

In the military environment, the *validity* of training is paramount to the success of a mission. Extreme care must be taken to insure that there is a direct relationship between what is done on the job and that which is taught in schools and elsewhere. As a consequence, the military spends substantial amounts of money on the "front-end" analysis process—the process of deciding what to teach. Many training courses have been found in which the content of the course did not match the needs of people on the job—they were taught to do things they did not need to know how to do, or they were not taught those things they did need to know how to do.

There are many reasons why the mismatch between what is needed and what is taught can occur. Perhaps the piece of equipment used in training is removed from active service. If training continues on this equipment, the training is wasted. Often, people are taught to a much higher degree of skill than is useful or necessary. If a trainee is given, say, 16 weeks of electronic theory when he is only expected to remove, test, and replace vacuum tubes in television sets, then that theory training has been wasted for this job.

Front-end analysis is a powerful technique for finding out what should and should not be taught. Once those tasks have been identified on which training should not be given, they are immediately dropped from the program. Dropping them from the training program means that no instruction is designed, developed, or delivered on those topics. Since each subsequent function (design, development, delivery) *adds* costs, the elimination of a task from the task list represents probably the greatest opportunity for savings.

By using a carefully planned approach, the Army cut 600 hours of instruction from a Fire Control Maintenance Technicians course. The original course contained a large number of training hours devoted to tasks which were only performed by supervisors—never by technicians. The front-end analysis procedures were almost completely responsible for the savings (Shriver, Fink, and Trexler, 1964).

The correspondence between training and the job is ideally very specific. If people on the job are expected to remove and replace equipment components, they should not be taught the theory and operation of the components, or supervision.

Another reason why training may lack validity is that the custom has been to send experienced personnel to the schools to teach. Each person described his own experiences, and there were often large differences among these people and their experiences—the human memory is not infallible!

In recent years, the military has made important advances in improving the *predictive validity* of training. Predictive validity is ordinarily measured by establishing the degree of correlation between the performance on a test during or near the end of training with a measure of job performance administered on the job. Ideally, this job performance test measures the degree of job performance skills, and it separates people into two groups—those who can perform the job and those who cannot. The required job performance test score becomes the criterion against which training is validated.

Another test, administered near the end of the training cycle, is called the training test. The purpose of this test is to find out whether the students have learned that which was intended in the training program. The training test is much like a final examination in a college course.

There is an analogy between civilian professional schools and certain types of military training. After completing formal training, the candidate must pass the "Bar Examination" or the "Medical or Dental Boards." Generally, these professional exams have performance components.

If the training has been effective in preparing people for the job, there should be a high positive correlation between the training test scores and the job performance test scores. The training test has *predictive validity* to the extent of this correlation. The higher the correlation, the better predictions can be made about success on the job based on the training test scores. People are not sent to the job who cannot do well on the training test. These evaluation techniques are described more completely by Fitzpatrick and Morrison (1971).

In order to improve the degree of this correlation and its predictive validity, important emphasis is placed on the process of job analysis. While the origins of job analysis will be discussed later, the uses of it in the military are important to note here.

In job analysis, an individual is watched for a period of time, and each time that a different action is performed, it is noted on the job analysis forms. After considerable observation, the analyst is able to describe all of the elements that make up the job. When the job analyst has completed detailing all of the components, called tasks, included in a job, it is then possible to analyze them for their interrelationships. Following job analysis, some jobs are further studied by a technique known as the *occupational survey*. This process is important for those jobs in which there are a large number of people, since it permits the analyst to learn which parts of the job are most important.

Most military and a substantial number of civilian occupations have been surveyed. Occupational surveys are extensive lists of job tasks circulated to large numbers of job incumbents who respond to questionnaires indicating whether they perform the task and, if so, approximately how much of their time they spend performing it. These occupational surveys are then analyzed and interpreted according to a process described by Christal (1973). Occupational surveys are the most reliable and valid ways known to discover what it is that people need to know in order to perform a job.

Through careful identification of what can be observed on the job, by watching the incumbent perform, then listing these tasks on a rating form for circulation to as many as 3,000 job incumbents, a great deal of confidence can be placed in the results—these surveys, properly conducted, have extremely high validity and reliability. The computer printouts resulting from the analysis can be set up so that the tasks will be listed in priority order. By using this priority, the training manager can make better resource allocations.

Industry

Training in industry, as in the military, is concerned with people at all levels of the organization—from the top to the bottom of the "pecking order." Some of this training is designed to assist the individual in doing a specific job better, while other training is intended to develop into two rough categories: skills training and personal development training. Skills training will be discussed first.

Military and industrial trainers alike are equally concerned with the identification of the content of a training program. Earlier in this century, Taylor (1947) first conducted his time and motion studies. By using a stop-watch and carefully observing what an individual did on the job, Taylor could then describe methods and techniques for accomplishing the same or greater results with less effort or time. While much of the emphasis was on efficiency in performance, the careful noting of the details of performance also represents an early form of job analysis. This method of documenting a task in detail led to the generation of "efficiency experts" during the next 20 or 30 years.

A common feature of most military and industrial applications is that people are being taught to do something which is very specific. In education, on the other hand, interest often centers on more global, long-term outcomes of teaching, even though specific skills and information are also of interest. Further, careful attention to job detail serves as the basis for job evaluation, which is usually the basic determinant of the rate of pay. Many people would argue that it is the pay system, not the training system, which provides the impetus for job analysis in industry.

Instructional technology is not a necessary counterpart of the elaborate methods employed to determine the content of instruction, if one takes a narrow view of instructional technology. Yet, the skills of the instructional technologist seem to be important in any workable arrangement. For example, it is not necessary to have instructional technologists conduct job and task analyses— these are more appropriately done by those with training in the specifics. On the other hand, the development of the measures of job performance is well within the repertoire of those who have mastered the development of objective-referenced tests. Improving the reliability and validity of the training program through utilizing feedback information from the field, however, should be a responsibility of the instructional technologist.

Academic

The content or subject-matter offered by various educational institutions is determined in a far different way than in the military or industry. For example, it is unlikely that one could identify the content of chemistry or the structure of the subject-matter simply by going into the chemical laboratory and observing what chemists do. Chemistry is a discipline, a body of knowledge, which has its own internal inherent structure. Those who write about chemistry do so in a way which organizes the knowledge in the field. Some chemists write about chemistry for other chemists (in the form of treatises, theoretical books, and research articles); other chemists write about chemistry for *students* of chemistry (in the form of textbooks, workbooks, and similar materials.)

While it is possible that a job incumbent in the military or industrial community could know effectively everything important about the performance of his job, it is totally unrealistic to believe that a single individual could know everything important about the field of chemistry. While it is ordinarily not the job of the instructional designer in the educational community to decide what the important elements of a given subject-matter are, it is frequently the job of the instructional designer to assist the subject-matter experts (chemists, physicists, physiologists, etc.) in describing what their subject-matter is and in agreeing on what needs to be learned and in what order (Gilbert, 1969).

Many disciplines in the academic world have a number of principal theoretical research or development thrusts, and adherence to the point of view held by one group can exclude one from the other groups. Often, these alliances are based upon the influence or position of the great researchers or theoreticians. Since these fields are divided, and often each view is represented on a single campus, it can be difficult to obtain agreement among the faculty on, say, the content of the basic courses. Recent applications of consensus techniques have, however, reduced the time and difficulties previously required to reach agreement.

In an experiment at the U.S. Naval Academy in 1970, an attempt was made to apply approximations of the job analysis technique to the course structure in the physics department. Among other questions, the investigators wanted to compare instructional methods among a number of classes at the school. In order to do this, common agreement among the 19 instructors on the final examination questions and answers was required.

Elaborate plans were made to develop objectives for the introductory course—objectives similar to the types described in

Chapter 3; for each of these objectives there needed to be at least one criterion test item. To obtain agreement on the objectives, a large number of possible objectives were circulated to these 19 faculty members. They were asked to rate each of the objectives on a five-point scale from "critical" to "trivial." The content of the course was agreed to on the basis of the number of objectives rated "critical"; those rated "trivial" were discarded.

Next, the investigators prepared test items (and answers) for each of the objectives, and these were circulated to the same faculty members. They were asked to indicate whether the test items were at the appropriate level of difficulty and if the answers were correct. If not, the instructor was to rework the questions or answers and submit them for consideration.

Agreement was finally reached on scoring the questions—which student responses would receive full credit and which would receive only partial credit.

When it was time to score the tests after the instruction had been given, a serious problem arose upon the discovery that the tests were not being scored as previously agreed. When questioned, the instructors indicated that they were scoring on the basis of what they "knew" the students to know, not solely on the basis of what the student had written on the test. Awarding credit to individual students on the basis of assumed knowledge or skill rather than demonstrated performance is referred to as the "halo" effect, and this is one of the more difficult problems to control in any performance evaluation system. As a consequence of these halo errors, all of the tests had to be rescored by instructors who did not know the students personally before the results of the experiment could be ascertained (Branson, 1971).

Even when faculty members have made a concerted effort to agree on subject-matter, as indicated previously, a significant amount of practice and feedback in using the system is required before the procedure will work effectively. Thus in one sense the subject-matter taught in colleges and universities must have an extremely high degree of *content validity*; the agreement among experts in the field should be high on the subject-matter of any given course. The interrater reliability—a measure of agreement among experts—should be high. On the other hand, in the military and industrial settings, as mentioned earlier, the emphasis is on *predictive validity*.

When agreement has been reached on what should be taught, regardless of whether one is in an industrial, military, or academic environment, the next important step is the design of the instruction.

Design

The instructional designer is analogous to the architect in construction. By taking the "output" of Analysis—the *what* to teach—it is the instructional designer's job to write the specifications for *how* the instruction is to be accomplished. It is the instructional designer who bridges the gap between the job world and the training world in military and industrial settings, and between the content specialist and the instructor in academic settings.

Military

The design of instruction in the military is accomplished in a variety of ways: by military personnel, by civilians employed by the military, and through contracts with universities, research laboratories, and private companies which specialize in instructional technology. It is the designer who specifies the methods and media of instruction, whether training devices, simulators, or computers will be required. The designer also is responsible for making or defending the necessary cost-effectiveness trade-offs based on a number of considerations.

Training programs which are required to support the national defense or space exploration often must meet extremely high standards of human performance. While these standards are specified in Analysis, the designer must consider the alternatives available in order to achieve the specifications. Training equipment used in the military and in industry is usually somewhat more sophisticated than that found in academic environments. These differences are due principally to the wide variations in the missions of these organizations and the degree of risk of human life or equipment that is involved.

Most often, large numbers of trainees are involved in the military programs, and designers must consider the cost and productivity factors in the design of their systems. An instructional design option which might be considered reasonable for 100 students per year may not be reasonable if 3,000 students per year will be served. Instructional designers can vastly improve the total performance of a system if they assist in writing the specifications for technical documentation and training for the system when the hardware is in the design stage. Here, technical documentation refers to the maintenance, troubleshooting, and repair manuals for equipment and machines. These materials can be prepared and revised based on tryout results while the hardware system is being manufactured, greatly increasing the military's capability to maintain and operate the equipment.

Industry

Instructional design in industry occurs in a wide variety of situations and for a large number of purposes. One of the skills the designer must have in industry is that of making a competent analysis of performance problems. Mager and Pipe (1970) have presented a step-by-step procedure that can be learned and followed by designers in this performance analysis. A performance problem, according to Mager and Pipe, typically arises when someone notices that the output of a department is not up to standards, people are not following safety precautions on the job, or perhaps the quality of a product fails to meet specifications. At this point, a manager then requests the training department to conduct training to alleviate the situation.

While it is often possible to design training which would teach the necessary knowledge and skills for the examples mentioned above, the existence of a training problem has not yet been verified. Suppose, for example, that the product quality has fallen because the purchasing department bought drills and cutter blades from the lowest bidder. Suppose, further, that these inferior drills and cutter blades make it impossible for the machinist to achieve the precision and appearance required. In this situation, giving the machinist additional training in the use of drills and cutters would not improve performance. It is often the responsibility of the designer to make judgments of this kind, since the designer is in the key position of translating job performance requirements to training requirements.

Since not every training program is designed in isolation from others, the compatibility of facilities and equipment already owned by the company must be taken into account. For example, in one national company, computer terminals are used in the training program. While it would never have been feasible to purchase a computer and terminals for the training program, it is reasonable to use the computer for training when it has been bought for other company operations. In this sense, the training department is increasing the utilization of the computer, and, presumably, offsetting other costs which would have been incurred had the computer not been available.

Academic

The history and traditions of universities hold that it is the individual professor who is responsible for the design of his or her courses. As a consequence, the instructional design activities in universities are centered around the individual professor. These activities usually take the form of instructional service centers on campuses; centers where professors can go to obtain assistance with their courses. These service centers usually have professional instructional technologists on the staff, who are able to undertake solutions to virtually any kind of instructional problem.

While professors can go there to receive training in instructional design, they may also go there simply to utilize the service on a one-time basis. Usually, it is the internal mission of the service center to try to increase faculty use of their organization and to provide as many professors as possible with the knowledge and skill to design their own courses. Since the service centers normally have access to the campus media centers and libraries, they are usually able to provide the development services which necessarily follow the design activities. In many colleges and universities, there are also "learning laboratories" or "listening-viewing areas" in the libraries where these mediated courses can be taken.

The instructional designer who works at the college or university must also be keenly aware of the costs of design. While it makes good sense to invest heavily in design activities for large-enrollment courses, the same level of effort is unwise for smaller courses. Since academic courses are often seen as a demonstration of the "state-of-the-art," many innovative features are found, such as the use of exotic computer sequences and displays, the use of the computer as a teaching device and computing device in combination, and multimedia sequences which leave strong impressions.

Development

Instructional developers follow the instructions of the designer in putting together all of the materials required to conduct the instruction. The developer actually arranges for the scripts and storyboards, arranges production, writes the test material, selects useful off-the-shelf materials, and conducts the formative evaluation of the instruction before it is put to normal use.

Military

Instructional development occurs in the military in all known ways—in-house productions, contract courses, "turnkey" courses, simple courses, and the most complex courses in existence. In recent years, the Navy has contracted with computer specialists to combine Computer Assisted Instruction (CAI), Computer Managed Instruction (CMI), simulators, training devices, and training aids into a large system training effort for new aircraft. Since it costs approximately $4,000 per hour (in 1974 dollars) to train crews in the aircraft, virtually any kind of effective training costing less than that represents a saving. Projects of this type require the best efforts of specialists over a period of several years before they become fully operational.

The Army recently discovered that the performance of some tasks by soldiers in the field was less proficient than required. Even though the soldiers had reached a high degree of skill during training, the normal course of forgetting caused performance to decline. In conjunction with consultants and contractors, they undertook a massive program to provide individual skills training on the job following resident training.

For example, the Army has traditionally instructed soldiers on the M203 Grenade Launcher using an instructor in a classroom or "platform" situation. Each new group of trainees was presented the same lecture and demonstration, then sent out to practice maintenance and use of the weapon on the range. In 1972, the Army initiated a program called TEC (Training Extension Courses). While the first few of these lessons were developed in-house in 35mm slide/tape format, they soon discovered that the space required to store the slides and tapes was excessive. As a consequence, they contracted for the development of lessons in a super-8 format using film loops capable of full or simulated motion, combined with single frame advance.

The prototype TEC lesson was developed by Branson, Rayner, and McMurtrey (1973). A critical analysis of the learning task suggested that a series of still frame visuals interspersed with short motion sequences would work most effectively. The tape contained approximately 30 minutes of audio narration. During the lesson, the tape would stop at specified points to allow the soldier to view the screen and to practice what had been taught.

In an experiment with Army trainees, Jeon (1976), using three versions of the M203 program (motion, slide/tape, print) found significant differences in the amount learned and significant reductions in time, all in favor of the lesson containing the motion sequences. Furthermore, the print version of the lesson took 37 percent longer than the motion version, and the slide/tape version took 12.2 percent longer than the motion version.

When one considers the number of trainees who must go through this lesson in the Army and National Guard, the potential for savings in training is immense. Here, the investment in short motion sequences was clearly justified.

While there are many important training differences among the military, industry, and education, important to all these is the notion of the "consequences of inadequate performance." If one forgets a line in a poem or reads one's lines badly in a play or makes any one of a number of rather embarrassing but trivial mistakes in an academic environment, rarely does anyone else suffer irreparable damages or injury. While there are many trivial mistakes that one might make in the military or in industry, many highly consequential tasks must be learned to a high degree of proficiency. Normally, there is a high criterion of task performance which trainees must reach for critical tasks before they are allowed to perform in a field situation.

Most training in the military begins with individual skills—the basic competencies that a person in a given job should have in order to do the job correctly. Then, groups or crews are trained together in those areas in which they must work together as a crew or team; each person is dependent on the others' performance for the crew to perform well. This progression from individual skills to crew training is illustrated in the series of photographs in Figures 2 to 7.

In Figure 2 a pilot trainee is seen viewing a videotape on "Crosswind Landings and Approaches." The total "lesson" is composed of a workbook and a series of videotapes on major flight maneuvers. When the trainee has completed this training package, he passes a test which then permits him to go to the next station.

In Figure 3 an instructor watches a monitor as a group of trainees practice on the communications and navigation trainer. This device sets up problems for the trainee to solve; it requires many hours of practice to learn standard procedures of communication and navigation. As training becomes more sophisticated, it also requires more and more individual attention.

In Figure 4, an individual trainee is checked out in the cockpit trainer by an instructor. As the more difficult and critical tasks are more closely approximated, the trappings of the occupation become more regularly used. In the cockpit trainer, the trainer wears his regular flight clothing and oxygen system.

When the trainee has progressed from this system, he is then ready for training in the complex simulator shown in Figure 5. Notice all of the cables and wires necessary for the system to work. This simulator is mounted on hydraulically actuated supports which simulate the actual physical position of the aircraft. Here, the pilot's controls cause the simulator to turn, bank, climb, dive, and fly level, depending on how and where the pilot positions the controls.

To this point, we have traced primarily the development of knowledge and skill of the *individual* trainee. We have not looked closely at the complex training problems brought about by the addition of several people who must work together as a team in a crew-served system, or the coordination of several individuals who must work both individually and in coordination, such as in

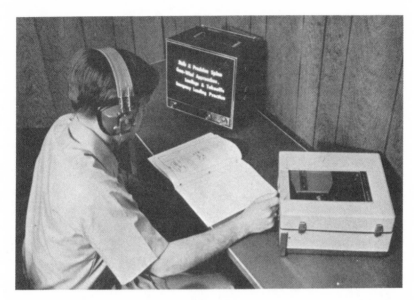

Figure 2:   Pilot trainee with videotape training package (Official U.S. Navy Photograph by H.R. Curry).

Figure 3:   An instructor monitors the progress of students (seen in background) training on the communications and navigation trainer (Device ID23) at Pensacola, Florida (Official U.S. Navy Photograph).

Figure 4:   *Individual trainee in cockpit trainer (Official U.S. Navy Photograph).*

Figure 5:   *Trainee utilizing a complex simulator (Official U.S. Navy Photograph).*

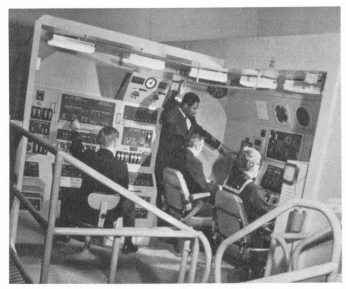

Figure 6:   Submarine ship control trainer (Official Navy Photograph by Saul Fitzgerald).

Figure 7:   Three astronauts at the Apollo Command Module Simulator console (NASA Photo).

aircraft working together in flights and squadrons. While an individual pilot could make an error which could be dangerous and costly only to himself and his aircraft, in many other situations individuals could make errors which would effectively negate the work other people are doing and could endanger the entire squadron.

One situation in which individuals must live and work together for long periods of time is on submarines. In Figure 6, a series of people who must work together are shown in a submarine ship control trainer. Here, the crew must work together according to established standard or emergency procedures in order for the ship to perform its appointed mission. Hours of practice as a crew are required for proficiency. Further, the importance of standard procedures becomes much clearer when it is understood that any member of the crew may be asked to serve with any crew. In a 24-hour day, there are at least three or four shifts (depending on whether the shifts are six or eight hours long). Any member of any team may be asked to work on any crew or team to be sure that everyone can do the work correctly with everyone else. Team and crew training probably represents one of the large differences between military training and academic training. Rarely are teams or crews, as such, trained in the academic environment.

In Figure 7, the simulation and training problem has reached perhaps the highest degree of complexity. Three American prime crew astronauts participate in a debriefing session following a major simulation of a flight exercise. The instrumentation is complex and the risks are high. Here, relatively small numbers of trainees are given extremely complex and lengthy training. While the equipment could be used for the training of large numbers of trainees through time, there is not likely to be a need to have so many people trained in these skills. Such training probably represents the most expensive possible option.

A number of different types of devices have been shown which contribute to the total training effort, each of which has a slightly different name and purpose. These generic names and purposes are:

Training aids. A training aid is a piece of equipment generally used by an instructor to illustrate the working relationships within some kind of hardware or device. For example, pieces of machines are cut away or removed to reveal the inner working parts. Other assemblies or machines may be made of glass or plastic so that their working arrangements can be viewed. In still other cases, an item is enlarged, such as in a large slide rule mockup viewable from all the seats in a classroom.

Training devices. A training device is a piece of equipment on which a trainee practices in a situation where it is intended that what is learned in the training situation will transfer to the job situation. Each trainer may relate to either a small portion of a job or to a large segment of it. Examples of training devices include: gunnery trainers, eye-hand coordination trainers, cockpit trainers, etc.

Simulators. A simulator is a complex training device which tries to capture many significant features of the operational environment with as much fidelity as possible in order to maximize the degree of transfer from the training situation to the job setting. Simulators can range from the simple driver trainer to extremely complete and complex environments. The various devices described above are used in a "training" environment, not in the "job" environment. But the military instructional developer is not restricted to that which can be learned in the "schoolhouse" or that which can be learned in the classroom. Data reported by Lecznar (1972) suggest that the Air Force's on-the-job training program may be equally effective and less costly as compared to other forms of instruction. As a research undertaking, trainees were assigned either to technical school or directly to duty; they were then followed up several months later to see which group performed better. Lecznar found that there were no significant differences in the quality or quantity of output, but he did find that those who had been sent directly to duty were assigned a wider variety of tasks than were the technical school graduates. Since Gay (1974) has shown that costs for formal on-the-job training programs are less than they are for resident technical school programs, a significant opportunity exists to obtain important benefits from careful analysis and instructional development efforts in on-the-job training programs.

Industry

Instructional technology is developed in a variety of ways in industry, depending on the particular jobs that people will be doing and the size of the organization. A common method for the development of innovative instructional materials and procedures in industry is through trade associations. Many trade associations have pioneered the development of innovative instructional materials as a service to their members.

While it is difficult to obtain complete training materials from a trade association which will meet the specific needs of each of the members, there are often enough common jobs among companies to justify the development of job-oriented materials to be used by all. For example, one job that virtually all banks have is that of "teller." And, while each bank has its own specific forms and procedures for tellers to follow, there are enough tasks that tellers perform commonly from one bank to another that general training materials can be useful. The same is often true of life insurance agents. Insurance, regardless of which company issues it, has certain identical characteristics. Learning about insurance and the process of selling insurance occurs in all insurance companies. Thus, materials produced by trade associations can be a cost-effective means for providing training.

The larger the company and the more people in common job classifications, the more likely it is that instructional technology can have cost-effective applications. Specifically, banks which have large numbers of branches will often have the same job classifications in each of the branches with one or more people in that job. Since branches are often separated by some distance, it is inconvenient to assemble all employees in a given job classification in one place.

Consequently, many banks have developed exportable training packages which can be sent from a central training department to the branch officer in charge of training. Typically these materials include instructions on how to conduct the training and how to administer the test. There is also a rather extensive feedback system so that the training department can be sure that new training materials meet the requirements of the branches. Training materials sent out this way typically include audiovisual lessons such as sound slides, films or videotapes, programmed instructional materials, and a fairly large number of practice exercises with worked solutions to increase knowledge and skills of employees.

Contractor-development activities are seen much more often in industry than in other sectors. While the military must deal with extensive turnover problems and be prepared to train many new people each year for both old and new jobs, industry enjoys a considerably more stable set of jobs and a more stable work force, thus requiring less instructional development. Since it is unlikely that most industries would consider maintaining full-time instructional development personnel, they depend on contract services extensively.

Academic

As with instructional design efforts, development activities have normally been the professor's individual responsibility. In some instances, heated controversies can be stirred by suggesting to individual faculty members that someone else should develop their course materials. Such an attitude has been partly responsible for the creation of a paradox. Formative evaluation—determining through student tryouts whether the instruction is adequate—is considered a part of development. Recent trends in universities and colleges have been towards more accountability from faculty members and an increased emphasis on student evaluations of faculty. If instruction is not effective, the faculty member is generally not rated highly by the students—yet he may not personally have the knowledge or skill necessary to improve the instruction, even though he is a subject-matter expert.

In those institutions where there are instructional service centers available, it is often possible for faculty to obtain help in improving course effectiveness. While only a small fraction of the courses in colleges and universities have been carefully designed according to modern principles of instructional technology, the future trend appears to be clearly in that direction.

Implementation

Implementation is the process of putting an instructional technology program or project into place—installing it according to plan. Analysis, design, and development are professional-technical activities which rarely involve difficulties with large numbers of people, or resistance from those people who must use the new system. While earlier efforts may have been principally technical in character, implementation has high components of feelings, politics, and internal organizational rivalries. The magnitude of the implementation effort will in large part be governed by the degree of resistance encountered.

In recent years, a number of researchers and authors have addressed themselves to the problems inherent in promoting organizational change. The interest in this area of study has been stimulated in part by observing the results of large-scale modernization efforts in education. The federal government has sponsored programs designed to improve instruction at local school levels through the purchase of audiovisual hardware and certain kinds of course materials, only to learn that the new materials were not being used. Schaller (1972) contends that efforts of this kind can never be effective unless they are accompanied by a thorough grass-roots awareness of the problem and tentative agreement on the solution.

Implementation of organizational change within an individual's sphere of influence is a much more direct kind of effort. The individual professor can decide to change the way he goes about conducting his course and then implement the plan. Teachers in a single school can agree on a change in methodology or organization and then work together to implement the change. While these efforts are to be encouraged, they are not ordinarily effective in influencing larger organizations. Further, neither individual professors nor groups of teachers in a single school are well enough qualified or have enough background and training to do a complete job of research and development. Each sector has common implementation problems with the others and also unique problems not normally found in the other sectors.

Military

Applications of instructional technology in military settings normally come about in distinctly different ways than in the public schools or the university environment. One important difference, of course, is the organizational structure in which each of these institutions operates. The command and control structure in the military is much more direct and firm than in academic environments. Second, the nature and mission of military forces typically results in a larger pool of effective managers. Thus, except in rare instances, the decision to implement an instructional technology-based program in a military school or training center would follow a careful analysis of alternative solutions and the selection of a single plan to follow. The impact of the command decision is very strong, and, unless the action personnel lack appropriate knowledge or ability, the implementation would go ahead reasonably according to schedule.

Another characteristic of the military which is not typical of public school or university environments is the relatively high turnover of people in given jobs. Normally, a military officer would expect to be in a job assignment for a period not to exceed three years, and many will spend less. Consequently, each new person coming into a management or instructional job in a military service school must be provided with adequate orientation and training in order to do the job.

Most of the work of the military is carried out according to procedures which have been established by service-wide *regulations* or by locally established operating procedures. For example, since 1968, the Army has been operating under a regulation which provides for "Systems Engineering of Training." The prescribed steps in this regulation are spelled out in Figure 8. Notice that the procedure is typical of a number of instructional design models described in the contemporary literature.

In addition to regulations, there is normally adequate "guidance" which provides the methodology by which regulations can be carried out. While a regulation requires *action, guidance* merely provides *suggested* approaches and alternatives. Individual managers are expected to apply the guidance provided in order to comply with and achieve the expected results of the regulations. Recently the U.S. Army and Navy published a new manual which provides guidance in Instructional Systems Development (ISD), *The Interservice Procedures for Instructional Systems Development* (Branson *et al.*, 1975). The ISD model is shown in Figure 9.

Many military applications of instructional technology occur as a result of a single problem which has been documented in a

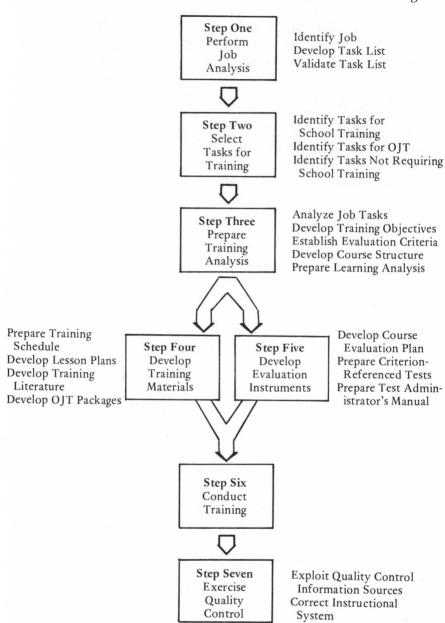

Figure 8:   *Prescribed steps in the Army's TRADOC Regulation 350-100-1, Systems Engineering of Training (from U.S. Army Training and Doctrine Command Regulation 350-100-1).*

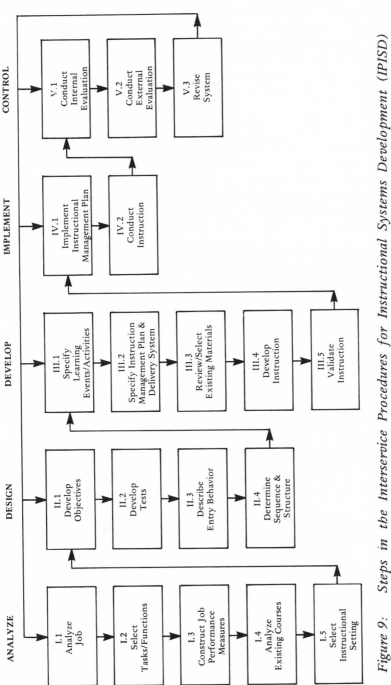

Figure 9: Steps in the Interservice Procedures for Instructional Systems Development (IPISD) Model (from U.S. Army Training and Doctrine Command Pamphlet 350-30 and NAVEDTRA 106A).

local setting. For example, in the early 1970's it was observed that an Army course for field wiremen was having an unusually heavy rate of attrition during mid-course. Analysis revealed that this was a time in which the soldiers were to learn to climb a utility pole. Further, it was noted that the course graduates could not perform all of the required wiring hook-ups and connections according to required job standards. Attrition and poor performance were the problems identified.

The project researchers from the Human Resources Research Organization (HumRRO) devised a scheme that would improve the proportion of trainees who mastered all of the skills required in the field wireman course and, at the same time, they resequenced the course so that the pole climbing module was placed first. By so doing, they saved training time and effort by identifying which trainees could not master the pole climbing tasks. The solution was found in a "peer tutoring" technique in which each trainee served first as an observer, then as a student, and then as an instructor on each of the major tasks that were taught during the field wireman course; see Weingarten, Hungerind, and Brennan (1972).

On a more general basis, the military services must provide for adequate training of those people who are to do the instructional design work. This training is offered to two groups. First, faculty development programs are conducted for individuals who will be new instructors. Second, training is also given to those who will be instructional designers. These courses vary in length from one to six weeks, depending on the level of sophistication required by the students and the assignment they will be fulfilling.

Industry

The implementation of instructional technology in industry is not nearly so difficult as it is in the military or in the academic world. Once a clearly defined need for the training has been established, then the methods for accomplishing the training are considered from their cost and effectiveness aspects and the industry's ability to do the work. There is rarely any large-scale resistance to the introduction of a new training program.

Most industries do not have large pools of instructors and school managers who are in the position of trying to protect a vested interest in the status quo; many instructors in industry would rather return to the field than remain as instructors. Large groups of instructors and school managers do exist in the public schools and in the military training system, and they become an important group in the bureaucracy. As a consequence, the approach taken to get people to accept new training methods is far more important than the methods themselves in the military and university environments.

Academic

Throughout the past 25 years a number of large-scale efforts have been made to implement various aspects of instructional technology in universities. Many of these programs have attempted to increase implementation and utilization in public schools as well. Some of these efforts have been centered around a large-scale media project such as television rather than a true application of the principles and processes of instructional technology.

More recently many community colleges and universities have established instructional support service centers, with the principal function of providing assistance, training, and support to faculty members who wish to employ instructional technology to design their courses. Some of these centers employ specialists in media, computer applications, instructional television, film, instructional design, evaluation, and learning center management. Normally, a professor would go to the instructional technology service center and discuss the alternatives available to him for course improvement. Here, the contact is between an individual professor and a staff member at the instructional technology service center. Occasionally, a department head, or even a dean, might be involved in the discussions, if major changes in the course offering or budget would be necessitated by the professor's plan.

Typically, a professor would begin with the development of one or two modules on selected topics so that they could be tried with appropriate students. If they work well and the professor is satisfied with them, more modules are prepared, and the course is ultimately designed into its final configuration.

From time to time, large-enrollment courses are considered for redesign because of the potential for payoff with them. Here, payoff could mean an increase in the quality of the instruction, a decrease in the costs of instruction, a rearrangement of the time in the course so that the professor has more time to spend with individual students, or some combination of all of these. Such courses are often seen as targets of opportunity by instructional designers, since the potential to realize a payoff in high-enrollment/high-impact courses is so much greater than for courses having smaller enrollments.

Control

Control, in this context, is a short form of "quality control," which implies a methodology to insure that planned objectives are met and that the objectives are valid. Three major functions occur in the context of control: internal evaluation, external evaluation, and revision. Evaluation certainly takes into account the major concepts in Chapter 10 (Formative Evaluation) and in Chapter 11 (Summative Evaluation). Further, the analysis of the data collected in the process is intended to provide ample opportunity for direct, data-based decision-making. Data-based decision-making is one of the features of instructional technology which clearly separates its processes from those of more conventional instruction.

Military

Most military evaluations of instructional technology measure several variables known to be important to the total system. Here, it is possible to look at process variables (to insure that the actual work is done correctly), progress variables (to see that the development work is on schedule), performance variables (to insure that the students are meeting planned objectives), and preference variables (to check on the students reactions to the instruction). The internal evaluation process is concerned with finding out to what extent results are achieved according to plan.

Military organizations present opportunities for good external evaluation procedures. Here, external evaluation refers to following up on the students when they have left the training system to see whether what they learned in the instruction was adequate to meet the expectations. Did they learn well, and was what they learned what they should have learned? Feedback from students who are on the job can be valuable in revising the instruction to increase its value.

Revisions in the instruction occur only after careful analysis of all of the considerations. While in research and demonstration projects, it often makes sense to continue revising until the maximum performance is reached, the same rules do not apply in military situations. Each time revisions must be made, the people who do the work must use time that could have been spent on another project. Management must insure that the people involved are working on the highest-priority effort, not on those programs with lower priorities. If this means using a less than perfect course to work on other, higher priorities, then that is what should be done.

Industry

While considerable effort is spent in industry keeping the content of instruction current, much less effort is spent on the refinements of the methodology. Often this is true because of the small number of people who might use the instruction, and because much development work is done by contract, and so the price of the contract would normally increase with additional revisions.

Complex and high-risk training programs in industry would be subjected to the same kinds of quality control procedures as in the military, and in many cases they would be more stringent. Occasionally, programs which must be used by a large number of people will be refined until they reach maximum efficiency (see Chapter 15).

Academic

Quality control in academic instruction ranges from the minimum possible to very elaborate and exacting standards. Since many instructional technology projects are done in the academic world, one finds a wide variety of approaches and purposes. Since some of these projects become courses in which students must receive grades, additional attention must be paid to the equal opportunity available to each of the students, and to fair treatment for all.

Revisions are frequently required in order to provide additional subject-matter within the same time frame—to make the course cover more material in a fixed time period. Academic environments often have resident instructional technology evaluation specialists who like to improve the state-of-the-art in the process of evaluation and spend time working on these processes.

Only infrequently does the administration or management become involved in the content or quality of instruction in academic institutions. As mentioned earlier, these two areas are normally within the purview of the instructor and are not approached by a department head or dean.

It is rare for academic institutions to be concerned with external evaluation—there is little tradition in this area. Exceptions have occurred, for example, in the area of attempting to determine the relative quality of instruction offered at community colleges and at regular four-year institutions. Here, students who transfer to the four-year institutions are compared with those who did their early work at the senior institution to see whether the preparation received in the first two years was equal.

It would be uncommon for a law, medical, or dental school to consider revising its instruction on the basis of the relative success of graduates on the licensing examinations or in later professional practices. There are philosophical issues involved, particularly in deciding what the expected outcomes of the schools really are. Some teacher-training institutions conduct surveys of their graduates from time to time in order to evaluate their instructional programs. But, for external evaluation to be useful, one must be able to identify the jobs for which people are trained, and the training must be oriented towards those jobs. Finally, those who conduct the external evaluation must be in a position to influence the revisions if the loop is to be closed. It is not infrequent for all of the necessary evaluation to occur and for the information to go unused because the evaluators cannot specify and enforce the needed revisions.

Individual professors who are working on modules for their courses or on their courses as a whole may continue to revise them for a number of years. Postlethwait (1969) originally designed a botany course with a number of elements to serve different purposes. He had laboratory sessions, large-group sessions, and small-group sessions. Student reaction and evaluation results over the years caused him to make substantial changes in the methodology of the course and in the relative emphasis on each of its parts. By continuing this effort through time, one can "fine-tune" a course to a near optimum level for any given type of resources and existing constraints. Many professors do exactly this, but their efforts are not made public, and hence the process is not adopted by others. In contrast, many colleges have adopted Postlethwait's procedures.

This book itself is a first step to define the content for a college course, after which any systems desired for individualized or group instruction could then be designed. See the Preface to this book.

Management and Cost Considerations

In the military and in industry alike, "cost-effectiveness" is continuously sought. Often, this emphasis is translated into slang terms which become clichés, such as "more bang for the buck." While there are many ways to approach cost-"effectiveness" or cost-"benefit" analysis, a brief discussion here should be helpful.

In the military, training *effectiveness* is defined as follows:

Training is effective to the degree that the expected proportion of qualified trainees achieve mastery in the allowable limits of time.

There are technical terms in the definition which must be spelled out further, but the notions of "mastery" (Chapter 6) and "expected proportion" are key. In modern military training, mastery is operationally defined as a test score which a trainee must reach or exceed to be considered a "pass." "Expected proportion" means the percentage of students who should achieve mastery in the course. This is usually estimated from the experience of prior groups.

In Instructional System Development (ISD) there are three principles which have direct impact on the cost-effectiveness of instruction and must be taken into account by the instructional designers:

1. For any instructional problem, there are at least two

alternative solutions, one of which will be the more *effective*.

2. For any instructional problem, there are at least two equally effective solutions, one of which will be *less costly*.

3. For any instructional problem, there are at least two equally effective alternative solutions, one of which will require *less time*.

These principles are important to the designer when analyzing the constraints which will be present in any situation. Sometimes, it is important to select the most effective choice; for example, in training astronauts. Other times, it is important to seek the least costly solution; for example, when contracts are awarded on the basis of price competition. Finally, the most time-efficient solution can be appropriate when one is threatened with imminent disaster or damage where delay cannot be tolerated.

Designing cost-effective training programs is given considerable emphasis in the military and in industry, because training is seen as an "overhead" cost. That is, training is a cost that should be minimized because if an employee is paid to attend a training course in industry, he cannot be productive during the period he is training. He was hired to produce—to make things, to sell things, to provide service.

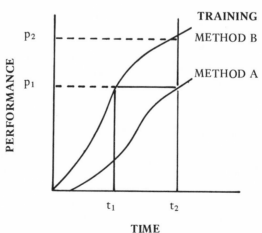

Figure 10: *Hypothetical performance differences as a function of time for two different training methods (from U.S. Army Training and Doctrine Command Pamphlet 71-8).*

In Figure 10, there are two performance curves, for training methods A and B. The rate of progress in method B is much faster than in method A (the slope of the B curve is steeper). At the first point in time (t_1), there is a large difference in performance between the two methods. On the basis of this information alone, it seems that method B would be selected, since it requires much less time. However, Method B may cost more than Method A and may not be justified by the number of trainees who must use it. There are other questions. In some occupations, training is specified in the number of clock hours of instruction required (e.g., barber and beautician training) by a regulatory agency or by law.

Why Training Is Provided

No serious analysis of the cost-effectiveness of training can be made without a clear understanding of why the training is provided. It can be provided by industry or the military as a method of improving job performance, or these same organizations can provide training opportunities to benefit the person.

Up to now, we have discussed only training of individuals and crews for the job. If the job training is successful and the person is able to perform on the job successfully, it is then often in the best interest of the industry or military to provide the additional training desired by an individual.

In many occupations, the amount of relevant training received is directly related to production or the opportunity for promotion, and so training may often affect the rate of pay. Individuals are concerned with the opportunity for promotion and also with pay increases. Further, if individuals do well on the job, it is in the best interest of the industry or military to try to retain them—to keep them from seeking employment elsewhere or leaving the service. The manager of training must make frequent "trade-offs" between the investment of money in "people training" and the payoffs from that training. If it costs more to replace a good employee than it does to provide training for one who is on the job, then it makes good economic sense to invest in those who are now with the organization.

There is a broad spectrum of training in the military and industry. Opportunities for training are brought about for a variety of reasons, and these reasons have a direct impact on the type of training given and the amount of money invested in it.

In universities, it may be less expensive for the *institution* to prolong training even though it may be more expensive for the *individual*. Normally, in those training situations in which the organization sponsoring the training is paying the trainees, economies occur when instructional time can be reduced. Getting the students out in the minimum possible time is not a prime goal of the university. On the other hand, providing an atmosphere in which individual students can accelerate their progress through their courses may be an important goal. Applications of instructional technology and effective management practices can be of great benefit to students in the pursuit of their goals—credit by examination is an area in which students get credit for courses they did not "take." Here, they escape the requirement that they be instructed in areas in which they already are competent.

It would probably be fair to say that in the university setting, the concentration is on the course level, while in business and in the military, most of the concentration is at the job level. The university, or an individual professor, may be interested in improving the quality of a single course or in making it more efficient, although entire faculties are interested in the quality of degree programs. In industry or the military, the manager would be interested in reducing the time required to get the trainee on the job or in reducing the costs of training. Rarely would the manager in business or the military be interested in improving the "quality" of instruction for its own right, while most professors would value a higher-quality course.

It is often difficult to understand the difference in approach of the military or industrial community compared to the academic community unless one understands the differences in purposes, mission, and personnel. It is hard to imagine how a course in, say, poetry appreciation would be directly contributory to the job performance of a college graduate. Yet, it is a strongly held view in the academic community that such courses are a part of the total academic experience. The university is, for the most part, not a direct training institution. Some colleges, such as law, dentistry, and medicine, are more clearly career oriented—those who study medicine have more clearly defined interests than those who take their degrees in English Literature.

How are cost-effectiveness and cost-benefit ideas applied in the academic community? This is a field of study all in itself, but let us look at this problem from a student's point of view. If the student has as his goal the earning of a college degree—for whatever reason he might have selected this goal—then he will invest whatever time and effort that are required to achieve the goal, even if it means staying a year or two longer to get the degree. To the student, will the degree mean an increase in compensation? Perhaps so, perhaps not, based on the conditions of the economy when he graduates; he may not be able to find a job at all. But the benefit of the degree to the student may have been worth the price he paid. That is, he may value a college degree more for its own sake than for its direct effect on compensation.

In the university situation, the student is one of the important decision-makers about what happens to him. The university cannot apply the same cost-effectiveness analysis techniques in general that are applied in the military and industry, in part because students are not compensated by the university for being in school. It is clearly possible that the university could offer the student a degree in six years rather than in four—and save itself money. That kind of saving could not occur in military or industrial situations.

On the other hand, the university can use cost-effectiveness approaches in the design of courses. It may be more cost-effective to invest development time in a large-enrollment course to improve its effectiveness and reduce the time required of faculty to teach the course. Ordinarily, computers, mediated instruction, or television could be used to achieve time savings. When these savings are realized, professors are normally expected to increase the amount of time devoted to research, scholarship, or service to the community.

Summary

As its historical evolution has indicated, instructional technology has grown and prospered in a number of settings. The military, industry, and academia have all made major contributions to the current state-of-the-art and will, in all likelihood, continue to do so in the future.

Instructional technology can be viewed and compared across major sectors of the society in terms of the five aspects of application in the context of the systems approach: Analysis, Design, Development, Implementation, and Control.

Instructional technologists can advance their own knowledge in the state-of-the-art by keeping current in the literature available from each of the sectors. It is common for instructional technologists who work for the military or industry to be familiar with the academic literature, but the reverse is not nearly so true. The short overview provided here should suggest a wealth of additional information sources useful to the professional.

References

Branson, R.K. Formative Evaluation Procedures Used in Designing a Multi-Media Physics Course. Paper presented at the Annual Meeting of the American Educational Research Association, 1971.

Branson, R.K., Rayner, G.T., Cox, J.L., Furman, J.P., King, F.J., and Hannum, W.H. *Interservice Procedures for Instructional Systems Development* (5 Vols.) (TRADOC Pam 350-30 and NAVEDTRA 106A). Ft. Monroe, Va.: U.S. Army Training and Doctrine Command, August, 1975.

Branson, R.K., Rayner, G.T., and McMurtrey, D.B. M203 Grenade Launcher: TEC Lesson. Prepared for the U.S. Army Combat Arms Training Board, 1973. (Contract Number N61339-73-C-0150.)

Christal, R.E. The United States Air Force Occupational Research Project. Paper presented at Symposium, the State-of-the-Art in Occupational Research and Development, Navy Personnel Research and Development Center, San Diego, July, 1973.

Fitzpatrick, R., and Morrison, E.J. Performance and Product Evaluation. In R.L. Thorndike (Ed.), *Educational Measurement* (2nd Ed.). Washington, D.C.: American Council on Education, 1971.

Flanagan, J.C. Project PLAN. In Aerospace Education Foundation, *Technology and Innovation in Education.* New York: Praeger Publishers, 1968.

Gay, R.M. *Estimating the Cost of On-the-Job Training in Military Occupations: A Methodology and Pilot Study* (R-1351-ARPA). Santa Monica, Ca.: Rand Corporation, April, 1974.

Gilbert, T.F. Some Issues in Mathetics: I. Saying What Subject Matter Is. *NSPI Journal,* 1969, *8* (2), 4-19.

Glaser, R. The Program for Individually Prescribed Instruction. Paper presented at the Annual Meeting of the American Educational Research Association, February, 1968.

Jeon, U. *Effectiveness of Image and Motion Variables in Motor Skill Learning.* Unpublished doctoral dissertation, Florida State University, March, 1976.

Lecznar, W.B. *The Road to Work: Technical School Training or Directed Duty Assignment?* (AFHRL-TR-72-29). Lackland Air Force Base, Texas: Personnel Research Division, Air Force Human Resources Laboratory (AFSC), April, 1972.

Mager, R., and Pipe, P. *Analyzing Performance Problems.* Belmont, Ca.: Fearon Publishers, 1970.

Postlethwait, S. *The Audio-Tutorial System* (2nd Ed.). Minneapolis: Burgess Publishing Co., 1969.

Pressey, S.L. A Simple Apparatus Which Gives Tests and Scores—and Teaches. *School and Society,* 1926, *23*, 373-376.

Schaller, L. *The Change Agent.* New York: Abingdon Press, 1972.

Shriver, E.L., Fink, C.D., and Trexler, R.C. *FORECAST Systems Analysis and Training Methods for Electronics Maintenance Training* (HumRRO Research Report 13). Alexandria, Va.: Human Resources Research Organization, May, 1964.

Skinner, B.F. Teaching Machines. *Science,* 1958, *128*, 969-977.

Taylor, F.W. The Principles of Scientific Management. In *Scientific Management.* New York: Harper, 1947.

Weingarten, K., Hungerland, J.E., and Brennan, M.F. *Development and Implementation of a Quality-Assured Peer-Instructional Model* (HumRRO Technical Report 72-35). Alexandria, Va.: Human Resources Research Organization, November, 1972.

Transition to Chapter 13

Following up on the purpose of Part II, Chapter 13 discusses instructional design as it takes place in higher education. The Chapter draws on organizational features of higher education to show the factors that facilitate or hinder design efforts. It also identifies those stages in design that are handled in a special way, and those stages which typically follow the procedures outlined in Part I.

Chapter 13

Instructional Technology and Higher Education

Walter Wager
Florida State University

Resistance to Instructional Technology in Higher Education

The instructional technology movement in higher education started slowly, and it has not progressed as rapidly as some had anticipated. The Carnegie Commission report (1972) cited as a principal deficiency the absence of appropriate instructional software for use in the hardware associated with the new technology. The report also cited other possible causes of the slow rate of progress:

1. Instructional technology is not uniformly welcomed by the academic community.
2. Faculty members who are interested in designing learning materials for the new instructional technology usually are not properly rewarded for their efforts.
3. There is a lack of compatibility between products of different manufacturers.
4. University autonomy works against adoption of other than locally produced materials.
5. Faculty members, in general, do not possess the skills needed to develop high-quality instructional materials.
6. Research, in general, has not shown significant differences between learning from media vs. learning from conventional methods.

Software is the primary product of the instructional design process. It is the materials (text, film, videotape, model, etc.) that contain the instructional stimulus. Anyone who has developed software through the use of an instructional design model knows that it is an intensive, time-consuming effort. However, the systems model does allow us to "do things right" in order to produce effective instruction. Why, then, should there be such a resistance to its adoption in higher education? In addition to the reasons given above, the writer would add (1) the historical foundations of higher education institutions in the U.S.; (2) the perceived role of the faculty member; (3) the funding pattern of educational institutions; and (4) the lack of management systems needed to support instructional systems. These four factors in the resistance to educational technology will next be discussed in turn.

Historical Foundations

The heritage and rapid growth of higher education institutions have gone hand-in-hand with perpetuating a parochial, labor-intensive system of classroom instruction and time-based instructional programs. Graduate instruction was built around the German tutorial mold in which college and university teachers are specialists in their disciplines. It has been taken for granted that if a person could learn, he could teach. Traditionally, the college or university professor learned without the advantage of electronic technology, and he teaches as he was taught.

Techniques such as recitation, lecture, and seminar have a long history associated with the roots of our system of higher education. Along with the practice of these techniques goes the feeling that they are adequate, whether they really are or not. This inertia is one of the most difficult problems in implementing instructional technology, which many faculty members feel is a threat to their credibility as teachers.

Perceived Role of the Faculty Member

The college or university faculty member has lived by the motto "publish or perish."

A university obtains money for doing research. Faculty members who can do research are in demand. Publishing the results of research serves to identify the faculty and bring recognition to the school. Schools with national recognition have attracted the best students—students who could learn in spite of great variance among professors in their ability to teach. Higher education in general has adopted a philosophy of meritocracy, with teaching as secondary to research in priorities. With increases in federal involvement in the past generation, colleges and universities have been called upon for new services they might provide to the public (generally through the sponsoring federal agencies). Without explicating the idea in detail, *service* has become a third function for the university professor; he is evaluated on his *Research, Service,* and *Teaching,* generally in that order.

There are, no doubt, professors who consider their primary role as that of teacher. While this appears commendable on the surface, teaching does not bring in additional external sources of funds, as does research or service; therefore, teaching is generally funded poorly in terms of expense and development money. The professor is the major source for the instructional program, and he is often the only instructional delivery system available to the student. The compulsory classroom contact hours system discourages the professor from being interested in instructional technology, since he is paid on the basis of contact time with students. In order for instructional technology to have any lasting effect in universities, the role of the instructor will have to change. We may now be seeing the beginning of that change with increased emphasis being given to the improvement of undergraduate instruction; but tradition dies slowly.

Junior and community colleges should have less inertia to overcome with regard to changing the role of the instructor. These institutions have sold themselves as being "teaching" centers rather than "research" centers. Their faculties, as a rule, teach heavier class loads than do university faculties, because they are not expected to do research or to publish. However, many of these faculty come from the university mold, and although they do not feel the need to publish, they have not developed their abilities to be better teachers, either. This may be due to lack of knowledge on the teacher's part, to lack of time, or to lack of rewards for doing better. One suspects it is probably a combination of all three.

Funding of Higher Education

Public universities are funded according to formulas relating to the size of the annual student enrollment. Generally, state legislators are happy when many of their constituency find access to colleges and universities. However, they are also aware of the high cost of education, so they are generally looking for ways to reduce annual costs, or to at least hold them stable. In a labor-intensive system, such as the present one, this is difficult to accomplish. Inflated fixed expenses can result in faculty reduction, which leads to threats of fee increases, enrollment caps, etc. Although education professionals talk about instructional technology as a solution to the decreasing resource problem, they seem to take the present system as a fixed "given."

Part of the problem in initiating significant instructional technology efforts rests with the "front end" cost. It takes an initial capitalization to change from the status quo, and the benefits to be effected will probably become evident over a period of several years. Colleges and universities are funded on a yearly basis and thus have little money to devote to an initial capitalization for instructional technology. The problem may be shown as a relationship between "level funding" and "investment funding" (see Figure 1).

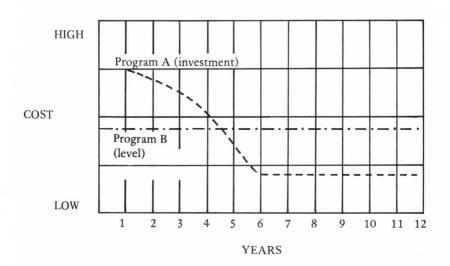

Figure 1:   Relationship between level and investment funding.

It is obvious that a college or university could afford to operate two programs of type B with the same amount of money that would be needed to start only one of type A. Although over the long run the program employing technology might save money, under the present annual funding system there is no incentive to initiate program A.

Lack of Management Support Systems

The development of software, although critical, is only one step in the use of instructional technology. The software often must be used with hardware (equipment), and it must be maintained along with the hardware. Far too often software is developed and adopted only to be useless within the period of two to three years. Videotapes wear out, computer programs need updating, films break, slides get lost, etc. The initial development money is gone, and very often the originator of the materials has departed or has no resources for the maintenance of either software or hardware.

Instructional technology is too costly to do only half way. The problem of revision and maintenance has to be taken into consideration at the beginning stages, and management schemes for dissemination, implementation, and continued utilization must be established if long-term gains are to be realized. It is probable that resources will have to be allocated with regard to systems benefits in order to drive the type of development effort that will lead to cost-effective instruction.

There is currently a great deal of interest in staff and program development at colleges and universities. Schools across the country are seeking out all the information they can find on faculty development. The focus of efforts in faculty, staff, and program development is purportedly the improvement of instruction. It would seem that the success or failure of these programs could have a significant effect on the use of instructional technology in higher education; and, if the use of instructional technology is not addressed in these programs, an opportunity to affect the traditional system will be delayed. What is to be feared, lest the whole concept of systematically designed instruction be considered frivolous, is the adoption of the concept of instructional technology without the policy or procedures of institutional management to support it.

Applications of Instructional Technology
in Higher Education

There are basically two ways in which instructional technology is used in higher education. The first is as a supplement to the classroom instruction by use of adjunct materials.
The reason most often given for use of adjunct materials is
that they provide the student with "another way" to learn the
course material. Sometimes materials are produced to "teach"
a segment of a course that depends upon special techniques in
order to accomplish a goal. An example would be the introduction of a simulation game into the conventional class
curriculum. The simulation game is designed to achieve specific
objectives when used according to the developer's directions,
and it is "replicable" instruction, in that it can be expected to
repeatedly produce the same results.

The second way instructional technology is used is as an
alternative delivery system for an entire course. When employed in this manner, the materials are generally produced in
an audio-visual format that allows for replicable instruction.
The effort in developing this type of course is much greater
than that in developing supplemental materials. Often it is
necessary to implement small sections of a course at a time.
The danger here is that the instructor, either working with a
developer or alone, will not have the resources or the time to
finish the mediation of the course, and the cost savings that
could have been realized are lost.

A common misconception about instructional systems
technology is the idea that mediation of instruction *is* instructional systems technology. Most designers recognize this fallacy
immediately. In a system design model, the production of
instructional materials follows task analysis and the development of evaluation instruments. However, there are many
procedures for developing mediated materials (sound-slide
presentations, videotaping live lectures, etc.) that do not
produce validated instructional materials. The "mediation of
instruction" does not, *per se*, make it systematically
designed.

The Changing College Population

Most students in traditional four-year colleges and universities are more alike than different with regard to their learning skills. They are what might be called "sophisticated, highly verbal" learners who are able to learn from highly abstract media (verbal symbols). This is fortunate, since more than 90 percent of college teaching is oriented to the lecture and the textbook. An argument might be made for not bothering with media by those who see the present system as satisfactory. What they forget (or conveniently overlook) is that the egalitarian philosophy pervading our culture today says that catering only to the very able is simply no longer satisfactory. Schools are now expected to do something with the "less sophisticated" learner, other than fail him out of the system.

Students desiring higher education today are a more diverse group intellectually and demographically than they were 15 years ago, and they expect more from the institutions. They have many different reasons for attending school, and they have more of a voice in structuring their own programs of study. Culturally segregated groups are demanding equal access and equal opportunity under the law. All these factors have implications for the use of instructional technology at a school, and the use of instructional technology has implications for school management. Actually, it is impossible to stereotype contemporary entering students. The role that community colleges, colleges, and universities have assumed for themselves has changed the student population; as a consequence, the "conventional" way of instruction, we are finding, is not adequate to meet their needs. This is a major justification for finding new ways to meet students' needs, among which is the use of instructional technology.

Designing Courses for Higher Education

The design process described and illustrated here includes only the initial phases relating to organization of the course and defining objectives. The closing section of this Chapter discusses the higher education context of all major steps in the design process.

Considering the previously mentioned systems inertia, the funding methods, the diversity of students, and the egalitarian philosophy of much of contemporary higher education, what might instructional technology realistically hope to accomplish? At best, four opinions are offered. First the "course" and "credit hour" will not rapidly disappear, so "classroom instruction" will remain the primary delivery system for the campus resident population. Second, the application of technology is going to be initiated by the individual instructor or small groups of instructors who see a need within a department. Third, unless present systems change, or outside money becomes available, technology will be viewed for short-term rather than long-term payoffs. Fourth, the most probable unit of instructional development is the college "course."

Conventional courses represent units of a broader "program" curriculum, and they might be described as units of definable content. Instructors often talk about what is "covered" in a course, which means the content to which the student will be exposed. In contrast, the questions an instructional technologist might ask are: "What is the student to be able to do with this content?" and "What can he do when he leaves the course that he could not do before he entered?" The answers to these questions should lead to the formation of behavioral statements of objectives. Although the instructional developer might wish to start designing a program or course by investigating the "need" for the course, the need, in most cases in higher education, is established by precedent. It will not help to ask whether there is a need for a college freshman composition course, as the answer of the faculty is obvious. The question quickly turns back to content, and the subdivisions of the course, the course units. For example, a course on teaching might contain units on "student evaluation," "media and methods," and "classroom management." Each of the units has a more or less discrete content component, and taken together, the units lead to the accomplishment of the course goals.

Course units generally have terminal intellectual skills, attitudes, or, in some cases, motor skills objectives. We can approach course design by answering the question, "What should the students be able to do, or choose to do, after studying the content of this unit?" To illustrate how this process has been used, we will mention briefly a unit of a course called "College Teaching" offered at Florida State University.

Please note that the following discussion, including Figures 2-4, exactly parallel the "levels of course organization" discussed in Chapter 4.

The structure of the course was built around the *functions performed* by the classroom teacher, namely, evaluating and grading students, the use of methods and media, lecture-discussion skills, and course management. The first step was to define the course goal or objective from which the unit objectives are derived. The second step was to generate unit objectives and their interrelationships as shown in Figure 2.

The third stage in course development is the specification of specific objectives that are to be learned in order to attain the unit objectives. This step involves a task analysis of the unit objectives. (This is distinct from the analysis of specific objectives as discussed in Chapter 5.) This unit analysis proceeds from the top down by asking the question, "What should the student learn in order to be able to perform this task?" In the case of attitude objectives the question might be, "What would lead the student to choose one course of action over another?" By asking these questions several lower level objectives are produced to support the unit objective, as shown in Figure 3.

It should probably be stated at this point that the terminal objectives that are defined for a unit, such as the one shown in Figure 3, may be arrived at and expressed in a number of ways. For example, one could ask the student to use the taxonomy and the method of writing objectives presented by Gagné and Briggs (1974; see Chapter 3). An alternative would be a combination of Bloom's taxonomy (1956) and Mager's method of writing objectives (1962). Figures 2 and 3 may be called *instructional maps* (Wager, 1976), because they present objectives falling into the learning outcome domains of information, attitudes, and intellectual skills. Again, this is a way of showing relationships *among* objectives, while Chapter 5 deals with relationships of prerequisite skills *within* an intellectual skill objective. The point of this discussion is that the "task analysis" of a *unit* will not be restricted to intellectual skills; therefore, it is different from a hierarchy of skills representing a single intellectual skill objective, which was dealt with in Chapter 5.

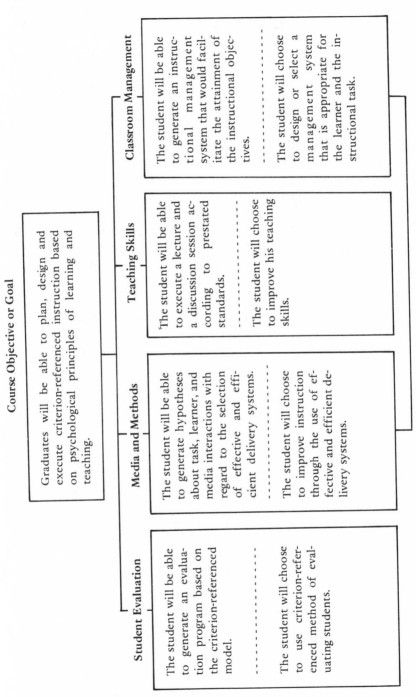

Figure 2: Course goal and related unit objectives.

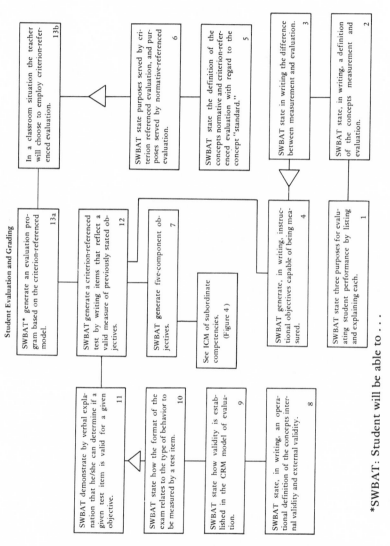

Student Evaluation and Grading

13b — In a classroom situation the teacher will choose to employ criterion-referenced evaluation.

13a — SWBAT* generate an evaluation program based on the criterion-referenced model.

12 — SWBAT generate a criterion-referenced test by writing items that reflect a valid measure of previously stated objectives.

11 — SWBAT demonstrate by verbal explanation that he/she can determine if a given test item is valid for a given objective.

10 — SWBAT state how the format of the exam relates to the type of behavior to be measured by a test item.

9 — SWBAT state how validity is established in the CRM model of evaluation.

8 — SWBAT state, in writing, an operational definition of the concepts internal validity and external validity.

7 — SWBAT generate five-component objectives.

See ICM of subordinate competencies. (Figure 4)

6 — SWBAT state purposes served by criterion referenced evaluation, and purposes served by normative-referenced evaluation.

5 — SWBAT state the definition of the concepts normative and criterion-referenced evaluation with regard to the concept "standard."

4 — SWBAT generate, in writing, instructional objectives capable of being measured.

3 — SWBAT state in writing the difference between measurement and evaluation.

2 — SWBAT state, in writing, a definition of the concepts measurement and evaluation.

1 — SWBAT state three purposes for evaluating student performance by listing and explaining each.

*SWBAT: Student will be able to . . .

Figure 3: Instructional curriculum map (ICM) of unit, "Student Evaluation."

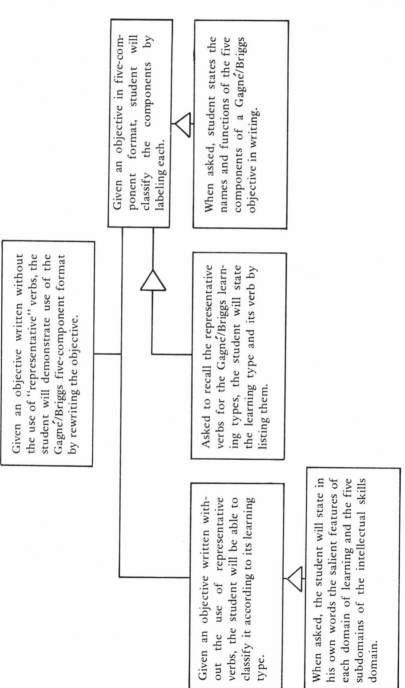

Figure 4: Enabling objectives for Objective Number 7, Unit 1.

As a result of the task analysis procedure for unit objectives, the developer will have a set of underlying specific objectives. These objectives are related to each other as a result of the question-answering process mentioned earlier, e.g., "What must be learned to be able to perform the unit objective?"

After the analysis of a unit, as represented in Figure 3, the designer is faced with the problem of analyzing each specific objective in terms of enabling objectives (Figure 4) and designing of instructional presentations and activities, as described in Chapters 7-9. Note that Figure 4 is also an "instructional map," not a learning hierarchy as defined in Chapter 5, because it contains both information and intellectual skill components as enabling objectives.

Tailoring the Design Steps to
Higher Education

In this closing section we discuss how the institution of higher education often places a different perspective on some of the design steps as they are outlined in Chapters 2 to 11. That is, whereas the steps in the design model correspond to those presented in Part I of this book, the various steps do not receive the same emphasis as in other contexts, nor are the procedures for taking each step identical to procedures followed in other organizational contexts.

Step 1: Needs Analysis and
Job Analysis

Higher education is not directly attuned to needs analysis and job analysis. This is probably due to a division between the instructional and the placement functions. Indirectly, programs in higher education must be aware of the job market, for the potential student will be attracted by career opportunities after leaving school, but there is no one-to-one relationship between job demands and curriculum as there might be in industrial training systems. Needs in higher education are sometimes stated in terms of what will attract institutional funding based on the perceptions of some group such as a state legislature. For instance, if a state is experiencing a shortage of accountants, the legislature may make additional money available for the education of accountants. On the other hand, if there is an oversupply of teachers, the legislature may cut the funding for schools of education. This forces, indirectly, a sort of curriculum priorities analysis. There is virtually no needs analysis conducted specifically for the purpose of developing new delivery systems, or for making present systems more efficient.

Community colleges and technical schools are finding it increasingly necessary to demonstrate success in placement of their students in jobs or in advanced educational systems. In this sense they are being held accountable for developing "needed" curriculum. The move in this direction is being prompted by state level placement/follow-up and accountability studies. However, the systems for accomplishing these studies are not well developed, and there is little evidence that they have elicited true needs assessments.

Step 2: Goal and Learning Task Analysis

In higher education the "program degree" is usually an autonomous instructional unit. Programs are generally represented by their content fields, for example, an Elementary Education Program, or Business Administration Program. Within programs are courses, e.g., in an Elementary Education Program there may be courses in child psychology, teaching methods, art education, music, English, etc., and the courses are said to comprise the curriculum of the program. In a further break-down, courses are generally considered to be comprised of topics, or units, that lead to achievement of an overall course goal. For example, in the "College Teaching" course described earlier in this Chapter, the unit on "student evaluation" is seen as a content entity that contributes to the course goal of producing "better teachers."

It is most likely that if one is going to apply instructional systems technology in higher education it will be at the course level. In this case it becomes necessary to state course goals in behavioral terms. The goal of "producing better teachers" might be interpreted behaviorally as: "In a classroom situation, the graduate will be able to generate and execute plans for changing and evaluating student behavior." Subsequently, the unit level objectives for the student evaluation unit represent component behaviors of the terminal task, i.e., "being able to construct and administer objective-referenced tests" is only a component of the larger, more inclusive course objectives, which include "teaching skills," "course planning," and "course management."

At the unit level it is necessary to recognize the existence of informational, attitudinal, and motor skill objectives, as well as intellectual skills. For example, we do not simply want teachers to know how to use objective-referenced tests—we also want them to *choose* to use them.

The next stage of analysis is breaking down the unit objectives into their component behaviors. This leads to the specification of what might be called "specific objectives." The relationships between these specific objectives might be represented diagrammatically in the form of an instructional map, as mentioned earlier.

Step 3: The Specification of Behavioral Objectives

Behavioral objectives, in higher education, are most often associated with the lesson or individual instructional presentation. An instructor may have some idea from teaching the subject in the past about how much time it will take to learn a certain concept or rule application. This intuition must be tempered with the realization, however, that past instruction was probably not individualized or mastery based, and that the time actually needed for effective instruction might be quite different from the time that was spent (often less time is needed).

There is an important reason for considering instructional time in the case of higher education. Credit for courses is given on a credit/hour basis. This is also the present means of calculating the instructional budget for higher education. A credit hour is defined as one hour per week in contact with didactic materials, for a period of 10 or 15 weeks (depending if one is on a quarter or semester system). Therefore, a three-credit course "meets" for three hours per week over the 10 or 15 weeks. In addition to this, the student is expected to spend two to three hours per week in preparation for each hour of class. One can see that it is difficult to describe the "worth" of a course in credit hours when the instruction is totally individualized.

It is unlikely that developers or instructors will be able to change the funding formula for universities, and so they must learn to adapt to this constraint. This can be done by determining at the outset what constitutes a course (based on traditional content considerations) and by awarding appropriate credit regardless of the time taken by the student in the systematically designed, individualized instruction.

Step 4: Analysis of Constraints and Resources

Obviously, if one has only a dozen computer terminals and a thousand students that need to use them for an average of three hours per week, there is no way that instruction can be provided to everyone in this mode. This is a common example of a resource constraint. Many decisions with regard to "mediating" instruction are made without an analysis of resources and constraints because the project was taken on as a challenge, or to demonstrate high utilization of media. Needless to say, this is not only costly, but also it can make the whole process of developing and using educational media appear frivolous.

Constraints exist in any system, and one must be aware of them in order that the most effective system possible may be planned from the start. Finding out about constraints later in the design process can be costly indeed. It has been shown earlier in this book how a teacher can improve the effectiveness of use of existing materials simply by analyzing the materials, constructing objectives, and developing tests around those objectives. Fortunately, many good source materials already exist in higher education. A systematic process of analyzing and integrating the use of these materials can improve student learning considerably.

In other cases, it might be desirable to design a course as if no materials were available. This complete development effort affords the best chance of designing quality materials that meet the needs of the target population. Before media selections can proceed, it will be necessary to describe and cost-analyze the systems available, or to be developed or purchased.

Step 5: Media Selection

Media selection for most courses in higher education would

have to be described as mostly fortuitous or involving only a slight amount of intuitive reasoning. Actually, for the traditional college student population, the research literature on media selection has shown "no significant difference" in the effectiveness of alternative media. It was mentioned earlier that "traditional" college students are probably more alike than different; as highly sophisticated learners, they can benefit from almost any media. A second consideration is that most college learning is gauged from the paper-pencil test over the "content" of the course. Specified in behavioral terms, it might be estimated that at least 90 percent of the college student's grade is measured from the objectives associated with the verbal information and the intellectual skills domains. For sophisticated learners, text materials for these domains are more than likely adequate.

Before we give up on media selection in higher education and relegate all instruction to the verbal symbolic mode of text, let's take a look at other considerations with regard to the college environment. Media have the capability to provide other than content information. In its broadest sense the classroom is a very special delivery system having elements that can be lost without careful consideration of their presence and the role they might play in student learning. For instance, the instructor is generally a credible subject-matter expert by virtue of the fact that he holds a degree in the field. The instructor is also in physical reach of the student, i.e., there is the capability of instant response and feedback. It might be important that the teacher is real or live rather than "canned," i.e., his presentation is not often polished or edited as in a mediated production, and the students get a chance to see a professional "think on his feet." Indeed, the teacher becomes a role model for the learner to emulate in the learning process, and this is probably a source of attitudinal change. This is not to say that these elements can't be obtained or approximated in mediated systems, or even that they are all necessary. It is just a caution that even if the same cognitive outcomes could be achieved by using books alone, the possible sacrifice of attitudinal outcomes must be considered where a change of media is contemplated.

Another consideration in reinvestigating the role of the media in higher education is the changing student population. Many students with diverse backgrounds are now finding their way into colleges. Many suffer from what might be characterized as learning deficiencies reflected by the simple observation that they don't learn well from traditional methods. On the other hand, there is evidence that given more time, they can learn the cognitive skills expected of them, if they are also given more concrete instructional content. In this context, additional time is supplied by mediated instruction that can be repeated or reviewed at the student's convenience. High-quality materials are a result of a careful task analysis that (a) defines the subordinate skills necessary for mastery of the terminal skills, (b) provides a guide for effective sequencing, and (c) eliminates irrelevant information. Attention to the learner's ability to understand reflects a sensitivity to media, task, and learner interaction that we know all too little about, but have some conceptual frameworks to investigate (Wager, 1975).

Step 6: Designing Delivery Systems

In higher education the primary delivery system is the college classroom. Although innovative instructional methods have appeared here and there, a conservative estimate would place classroom instruction at 90 percent of the total delivery system. Even when mediated materials are used in higher education they are generally considered adjunct to the classroom presentation. Keller, in his article, "Goodbye Teacher" (1968), was one of the first to suggest that the classroom teacher ought to be adjunct to the alternative stimulus materials with which a college student can make contact.

The delivery system will determine the scope of the audience in terms of logistics and level of sophistication. It is obvious that a televised classroom lecture might reach more people than can be reached in a single room in an institution, but the chances are that it will still only be effective for a relatively small percentage of the population that could view it. It is also possible that a cost saving could be made by this relatively simple mediation of a lecture, but it would not necessarily "improve" instruction. The primary question with regard to delivery systems, at any level of instruction, is with the effectiveness of the media for the described target audience. There is little sense in talking about the cost of alternative systems, or other benefits, if the instruction is not effective. Once it can be determined that a system is effective, cost and other considerations discussed earlier in the text become relevant.

Step 7: Diffusion

Higher education is generally characterized by its autonomy. This is not surprising when one looks at the heritage from the English and German universities. Even with the establishment of state university systems, each institution is still, for the most part, responsible for its own instructional affairs. This means that there will be a strong resistance to the adoption of programs developed by other universities or by other producers of educational materials. There is always the identity of the institution that goes along with the education, and the feeling is that each institution is uniquely capable of best meeting the needs of its students through local programming. Although this is most probably an attitude fostered by tradition, rather than by reality, it becomes a powerful barrier to the diffusion of design efforts.

There are at least three reasons that instructional technology is getting attention in higher education circles today. The first is an acceptance of the scientific method of solving problems, including instructional problems. The second is the increasing cost of education and system-wide efforts to find ways of decreasing that cost. A third influence might be our culture's fascination with and dependence on technology regardless of its ultimate cost.

The case for diffusion of systematically designed instruction has not, in this writer's opinion, been made strongly enough. The front-end analysis work involved in applying the systems model is time-consuming and expensive, and it is ridiculously wasteful to repeat it at different institutions for what is, essentially, the same courses. That is, if Purdue has developed a task analysis of what it takes to teach a student to use a microscope, and they have documented the analysis, other schools could use the same analysis. Unfortunately, things are not that simple. Often, development efforts are not documented in enough detail to share with others. It is also often the case that well-developed materials are not available for distribution due to a lack of marketing mechanisms, or possible copyright infringements, or to a professor's desire to jealously guard the use of his materials. Whatever the reason, diffusion within higher education generally takes place as research or development information disseminated through professional organizations and/or publications. Even then it is the idea (e.g., audiotaped lectures supplemented with lab activities) that is adopted rather than the specific materials.

Step 8: Assessing Learner Performance

Higher education is, for the most part, a process- rather than product-oriented system. We give students credit for "attending" classes and "accumulating" credit hours. It would be incorrect to say that the students don't learn anything, but it would be difficult to say with any confidence what it is that students do learn. This situation has been perpetuated for the most part by the norm-referenced testing and grading system, where the student's performance is judged against the performance of other students rather than with regard to the mastery of a set of predefined skills. Again, external pressures are beginning to change this situation. The advent of the College Level Examination Program (CLEP) tests by Educational Testing Service has started to swing sentiment towards credit for performance rather than for attendance or participation. In order to get credit for a course (at a college or university that accepts CLEP) the student need only score at some predetermined level. This level is usually described as the mean of the reference group or what would have amounted to a "C" or low "B" for those who took the course. Of course, the cutoff point for acceptance could be set higher if selectivity is the issue; however, one still doesn't know the skills of the student who has "passed" the CLEP exam, except with regard to its normative referent.

It is not unusual in education, in a case where the standardized test is used as a measuring stick of program or course effectiveness, to "teach for the test." If this is looked at logically it becomes a matter of content and skills analysis (the teacher has to ask, "What do I have to teach in order that my students can pass this test?"). This is one way to promote the idea of objectives (and subsequently the idea of task analysis) in a system not conditioned to accepting this kind of instructional scrutiny.

Ideally, one might conceive of a system where similar

courses, e.g., freshman composition, had similar behaviorally stated competencies that were assessed with objective-referenced tests. This situation might be approximated in some of the lower-level courses within some state college systems, but in reality it would be difficult to get a large number of institutions to accept the same curriculum or a standard criterion level of performance.

Step 9: Designing Instructional Activities

This step of the design process, built around the "events of instruction," is not much different for higher education than for other levels. If there is a definable difference, it probably comes with the ability of adults to work toward long-range goals, and engage in larger "chunks" of instruction. This might lead the developer to group motivational, review, and stimulus presentation events for a number of objectives, instead of treating each one separately. Sequencing considerations are especially important when grouping events, so that important subordinate competencies do not get overlooked or misordered.

As mentioned earlier, adults, in general, are more sophisticated learners than children. One of the most valuable commodities of the adult learner is time, and inefficient learning activities are often seen as worse than nothing at all. Choosing appropriate media, and designing materials for those media, to capitalize on their strengths, is the essence of the design effort. The writer wishes to mention again, at the risk of overstatement, that the instructional activity has attitudinal as well as cognitive effects, and this point should remain in the mind of the designer at all times. For instance, it is possible to design very effective programmed instruction, but many adults object to programmed instruction. The reason might be that they feel it is too time-consuming, impersonal, or tedious. Whatever the reason, if they feel this way, they are not likely to engage the materials enthusiastically, and this attitude might be reflected in decreased learning of intellectual skills.

In designing instructional activities, it will be necessary to avoid the "media trap." The media trap is encountered when one pays more attention to the delivery system than to the objectives of the instruction. This writer suspects that a good amount of design effort goes wasted when the designer turns his media analysis and prescriptions over to production personnel who attempt to squeeze the presentation into their favorite media. Take a design to a television producer and he will put it on television, to a multi-media man and he will "sound-slide" it, to a computer man and he will "program" it. The designer or instructor should be aware of the strengths and weaknesses of the various instructional experiences that can be designed, and he should be in control of the final product that reflects the culmination of the design effort.

Step 10: Formative Evaluation and Revision

There is no reason why this step should be any different for higher education than for other levels. The most important consideration is having a representative target population when field testing the instruction. If the instruction is being designed for students having learning difficulties, it must be tested with such students, not with the existing average college student. It is also necessary to base revision on sound psychological principles of learning.

The biggest problem with regard to formative evaluation is that most development projects get caught in a time crunch. The time for implementation comes up so fast that the instructor is forced to use the materials that are available—often first draft materials produced without the aid of formative evaluation and revision. It is necessary to plan formative evaluation into the project guidelines, so that it will not be neglected because time ran out.

Step 11: Teacher Training

In a system where the teacher (professor) is the implementer, there will be little problem with regard to teacher training, since he or she probably had a great deal of input into the development of materials. However, in a system that utilizes proctors, graduate assistants, etc., a teacher training program is necessary lest the whole development effort be subverted due to a lack of knowledge on how to use it. In Keller Plan systems, there are weekly meetings between the major professor and the course proctors for the purpose of clarifying what activities will take place the following week.

With regard to purchased instructional materials, such as simulation games, the instructor is usually presented with a manual on how to administer the instructional situation. Developers of materials for higher education should plan to produce instructors' manuals if the materials are to be exported or used by other than those who produced them. In a more general vein, institutions of higher education are beginning to provide faculty and staff development workshops to discuss the techniques and advantages of designing and using individualized instruction. Thus, teacher training might be said to exist at two levels—the materials development level and the conceptual or theoretical level; both seem to be important.

Step 12: Summative Evaluation

Summative evaluation is a necessary component of cost-benefit studies that colleges and universities using alternative instructional delivery systems are going to be forced to make. Summative evaluation surfaces in the classical research studies as the dependent variable for comparing programs aimed at the same goals. As mentioned earlier in the text, early planning and thoughtful design are necessary in order to control variables that might give one a false impression of the "value" of one program over another. Not every product will meet all the goals of the designer, and not all programs should be adopted simply because they were "designed."

Summary

In summary, higher education presents some unique problems for designers, due to the nature of the adult learner and the constraints that exist within the system. The design process is basically the same as for other educational levels, and some well-designed instructional systems and materials have made their mark, but change in academia comes slowly. Developers will have to become familiar with institutional operation in order to have maximum impact. They will also have to provide information needed to change management systems.

References and
Suggested Readings

Block, J.H. *Mastery Learning: Theory and Practice.* New York: Holt, Rinehart, and Winston, 1971.

Bloom, B.S., Engelhart, M.D., Furst, E.J., Hill, W.H., and Krathwohl, D.R. *Taxonomy of Educational Objectives: Cognitive Domain.* New York: David McKay, 1956.

Brown, H.S., and Mayhew, L.B. *American Higher Education.* New York: The Center for Applied Research in Education, 1965.

Carnegie Commission on Higher Education. *The Fourth Revolution: Instructional Technology in Higher Education.* New York: McGraw-Hill, 1972.

Diamond, R.M. *et al. Instructional Development for Individualized Learning in Higher Education.* Englewood Cliffs, N.J.: Educational Technology Publications, 1975.

Gaff, J.G. *Toward Faculty Renewal.* San Francisco: Jossey-Bass, 1975.

Gagné, R.M., and Briggs, L.J. *Principles of Instructional Design.* New York: Holt, Rinehart, and Winston, 1974.

Harrison, S.A., and Stolurow, L.M. (Eds). *Improving Instructional Productivity in Higher Education.* Englewood Cliffs, N.J.: Educational Technology Publications, 1975.

Keller, F.S. "Goodbye Teacher." *Journal of Applied Behavioral Analysis,* Spring, 1968.

Levine, A., and Weingart, J. *Reform of Undergraduate Education.* San Francisco: Jossey-Bass, 1973.

Mager, R.F. *Preparing Instructional Objectives.* Belmont, Ca.: Fearon, 1962.

Martorana, S.V., and Kuhns, E. *Managing Academic Change.* San Francisco: Jossey-Bass, 1975.

Meyer, P. *Awarding College Credit for Non-College Learning.* San Francisco: Jossey-Bass, 1975.

Niemi, J.A. *Mass Media and Adult Education.* Englewood Cliffs, N.J.: Educational Technology Publications, 1973.

Postlethwait, S.N., Novak, J., and Murray, H.T. *The Audio-Tutorial Approach to Learning.* Minneapolis: Burgess, 1969.

Reif, F. Educational Challenges for the University. *Science,* May, 1974.

Rosecrance, F.C. *The American College and Its Teachers*. New York: Macmillan, 1962.

Semas, P.W. The Explosive Growth of Faculty Development. *The Chronicle of Higher Education*, November 3, 1975.

Wager, W. Media Selection in the Affective Domain. *Educational Technology*, July, 1975.

Wager, W. Instructional Curriculum Mapping. Paper presented at American Educational Research Association Annual Meeting, San Francisco, California, Spring, 1976.

Wittich, W., and Schuller, C. *Instructional Technology* (fifth ed.). New York: Harper and Row, 1973.

Transition to Chapter 14

Chapter 14 is similar to Chapter 13 in that it deals with higher education, but the specific reference of Chapter 14 is to medical schools. Again, special organizational features of medical schools are used to identify the resources and constraints that often influence the design process.

Chapter 14

Medical Education and Instructional Design

Richard C. Boutwell
Florida State University

The Academic Medical Center

The academic medical center is not the medical center associated with the popular image generated during the early part of this century and perpetuated by the mass media, i.e., the joining of a hospital with a medical curriculum in some simplistic, unstructured tutorial approach. In fact, the academic medical center is a complex set of interrelated institutions—community medical centers, laboratories, satellite branches, specialty areas, family practice, and a basic science curriculum. The educational responsibility of the medical center includes the education of interns, residents, graduate students in the basic and clinical sciences, and postdoctoral fellows. In addition, medical centers provide training for students and technicians in schools of dentistry, nursing, and allied health and paraprofessional careers.

The complexity of bringing about organizational or instructional change in these medical centers is further intensified by their diversity. A topographical analysis of United States medical schools divides them into ten types ranging from small, low-funded schools of little eminence, emphasizing basic sciences rather than clinical clerkships, to large schools with high prestige, stressing clerkships. These different types of schools vary in many ways: (a) kinds of physicians produced, (b) philosophies in admission policies, (c) student body characteristics, (d) curriculum, (e) career direction, (f) federal and local funding, and (g) amount of innovation. The diversity described here does not represent the full range of variables which may complicate the introduction of instructional change into the medical center setting. Other factors include: (a) faculty ratio of basic scientists vs. teaching physicians; (b) two- vs. three-year curriculum, with and without a teaching medical hospital; and (c) the physical and social environment relating to geographical region, such as rural vs. urban settings.

The variability in curriculum is enormous among schools. Typically, the curriculum starts with courses in the basic medical sciences of anatomy, biochemistry, medical social sciences, microbiology, pharmacology, physiology, biophysics, and sometimes pathology. The students are usually, but not always, in a group setting typical of universities; courses are taught on the semester or quarter system, and examinations stress vast amounts of stored information. The curriculum then makes a dramatic shift in the expected student outcomes. When moved into the clinical clerkships, the students are suddenly expected to become problem-solvers. There is a great need for an intermediate kind of instruction to help trainees prepare for the internship—a need that could be met by simulation exercises having to do with the management of individual patients. The student/physician must be prepared to gather appropriate historical and physical examination data, to order needed diagnostic tests, and to evaluate the effects of prescribed treatment. Computer or pencil-and-paper case history simulation could help meet his need.

It might be well to note what a medical school curriculum cannot be. First, it cannot hope to transform a student into a totally competent physician ready to practice all branches of medicine. Second, it cannot hope to turn out a graduate possessing all the knowledge of the basic sciences or the clinical fields. Third, it cannot even pretend to adequately introduce the student to all the branches of medicine. Generically, a medical education must provide the intellectual tools and attitudes essential to the later pursuit in-depth of a large number of specialties. Each of the basic sciences and the clinical specialties has a varying utility for each student, depending upon his/her future role in medicine. Therefore, the medical curriculum must provide two essential tools for any field of medical specialization: the "language" of the basic sciences and the "language" of the clinical sciences. These languages will prepare the student for any of the major clinical curriculum tracks (specialties) chosen during residency. But some general techniques of diagnosis and treatment could be taught as preparation for the specialties. The various types of medical centers, differing in the variables described earlier, should alert the would-be innovator to the danger of overgeneralization. This is especially true in the design and production of curriculum change. Thus, any instructional suggestions made in this Chapter must be generic enough to apply to most academic medical centers and still be innovative enough to make possible an improvement in student performance.

Systematic Design of Instruction

The overall process for the design of new materials and of automated, self-instructional units is basically no different for medical education than for any other instructional need. But there is a need, first, to review the curriculum to be sure that there is a continuity of instruction, from basic science, to medical information, and then on to clinical methods, before the internship itself is faced by the trainee.

We have previously pointed to computer simulation as a potential means for teaching clinical strategies, in the safety of a "simulated patient" environment, before introducing the trainee to diagnosis and treatment of live patients. The less sophisticated hardware items are adequate for earlier phases of training.

The basic process of analysis is the same as that illustrated in Part I of this book. Therefore, the purpose of this section is to highlight the management system by which designers can work with medical faculty to achieve desired results. We refer to our "in-house" effort to improve the instruction in a medical center. Even though "pieces" of instruction may be imported from other schools or agencies which produce medical education materials, the responsibility for assuring the relevance of such materials is with the local design team. Thus, whether materials are imported or newly developed, the design team assures that an integrated whole results from the analysis.

In the remainder of this section, then, we comment only on unique factors in operation within the medical school environment. We do not repeat the basic procedures and techniques found in Part I of this book. The reader may be interested in comparing this account of working in medical schools with the accounts given in other Chapters in Part II, of working within other kinds of organizations and institutions.

Now, we trace some of those unique features encountered by the instructional designer working in the medical school or medical center environment.

Contact with Client

Upon initial contact with the instructional designer, the medical faculty member (client) should define some instructional problems which he thinks need to be solved. This is not to say that the client always recognizes the true instructional problems. It will be the responsibility of the designer as one member of the team to be alert for evidence of other possible troubles as the initial interaction begins. In the dialogue, the instructional designer must attempt to discern the subject-matter content which the client wishes to emphasize. Because the designer needs to have a "feel" for what the client wants to happen, it is essential that the two persons develop a strong and open two-way communication. It may be necessary for the designer to make explicit their respective roles: that is, while the client is relying on the designer for the solution to an instructional problem, the designer must depend on the client to provide insight into the nature of the desired subject-matter. This initial interaction between the faculty member and the professional designer should be a period of building effective communication. It is wise for the designer to demonstrate such communication by skillful use of probing questions, by paraphrasing shared decisions, and by providing a supportive atmosphere. The designer should be sensitive to the impatience of many medical faculty members with behavioral science jargon and phraseology; the designer needs to use a vocabulary understandable to the faculty member.

Defining Needs and Goals

In this component, the overall purposes of the instructional project are discussed. Such considerations might include: choosing content to meet societal needs, educational needs of the learners, needs of the faculty member, resources available in terms of funding, facilities to be used, available materials, and the methodological approach desirable to the client, e.g., discovery vs. guided learning.

The faculty member initiating the request for instructional assistance is asked to indicate the instructional need that the proposed project is intended to meet. Some of the instructional needs identified in prior development projects have grown out of such problems as these: high enrollments in a class, creating specific related problems; present instruction is inadequate in terms of student needs; a high failure rate; or high variability in material covered among sections of a class taught by a number of individuals.

In addition, there may be other information worth gathering before actual project goals become set. Such information may include: evidence that an instructional need exists, and present instructional procedures.

After the perceived needs and anticipated problems have been defined, the members of the instructional team must decide if the project has enough probability of success to justify faculty time and costs. If the answer is "yes," then a time schedule should be generated at this point in order to insure smooth management of the project.

Management Process

After the preliminary project information has been acquired (needs, goals, feasibility, project probability of success, etc.), a preliminary cost estimate is prepared that includes projected personnel time, services, materials, special equipment, and other expenses. Often this figure will not match the final cost of the project. However, it will provide a measure by which decisions can be reached as to the capacity of the faculty member's department, or the instructional designer's department, to support the project. It is at this point that the time schedule becomes valuable, in order (a) to furnish planning personnel with time and sequence aspects of activities and events, and (b) show the interrelatedness of many events.

When the necessary personnel needs and the sequence of events have been decided upon and approved by the funding agency, an instructional development team is formed, usually consisting of the following personnel:

1. *Project Administrator*

   This person is usually an administrator who has expertise in management procedures and staff utilization. Project coordination does not have to be confined to a single individual. Any of the team members could assume this function.

2. *Client (Subject-Matter Expert, Faculty Member, or Physician)*

   This person is usually a subject-matter expert from an academic department in the school/university. Occasionally, another content expert may be called in as a consultant by the joint decision of the project administrator and the client.

3. *Instructional Designer/Developer*

   This team member has expertise in systematic instructional design and development. The competencies usually supplied to the team by this person include: content analysis, learner behavior analysis, and specification of features for instructional materials. This person also usually supplies the development skills of writing objectives, storyboarding, script writing, and preparing preliminary pilot testing prior to full production of the instruction.

4. *Evaluator*

   Based upon the criterion tests, the evaluator measures student performance. In addition, instruments should be prepared to measure student attitudes, product cost-effectiveness and cost-efficiency, and management effectiveness.

5. *Production Staff*

   The medical center usually provides staff drawn from several production departments. The competencies of these members are in the area of photography, art work, lighting, camera angles, and sound recording. In addition, they will probably have experience in scriptwriting and storyboarding techniques.

The task of staff differentiation in team membership and

responsibilities is of critical importance to product development. There are countless instances in which a perceived need remained unmet because of the lack of attention to an individual's strength or to interpersonal processes within the team. The foremost barrier to outstanding team performance in product development is poor communication. Achieving understanding and overcoming misunderstanding are necessary for a team effort. The underlying causes of communication problems are often found in the nature of team leadership. Effective team management comes about because of planned intervention for building sound relationships among members. Measures to avoid misunderstandings include: providing clear objectives that arouse commitment, close cooperation to achieve high standards, and quick response to problems by the team leader.

Identifying Learner Characteristics

In the process of systematically designing instruction, it is necessary to identify the characteristics of the students to be taught. Conducting diagnostic pre-testing as well as gathering background information are convenient ways of assessing the student's previous learning. Pretesting serves as a measure of the learner's entering capabilities with respect to the course content. The results of such tests help the instructor identify specific content areas that each learner must cover in the course. A distinction should be made between diagnostic testing and entry testing. The former is designed to measure the student's past experiences in terms of skills, attitudes, and information. The entry test, however, is comprised of questions taken from all of the levels of the learning task. This test measures the student's specific knowledge of the learning task, and the results might allow him to enter further along in the instruction. If individualized instruction is a viable option, pre-testing can reveal each student's needs. These multiple entry and/or exit points are desirable options if individualized instruction is part of the curriculum. A background information questionnaire, calling for data about the student's prior course work, pertinent readings, reasons for taking the specific course, etc., should also be prepared, prior to the development task.

In order for the content to have relevancy for the student's interest, prerequisite knowledge, and course goals, the following issues must be resolved before development begins:

1. What competencies will the student already possess?
2. What skills must the student have in order to enter instruction?
3. What strategies exist for accommodating to individual differences in learning skills or learning style?
4. Should there be developmental programs (e.g., remedial, motivational, sociological) available to increase learner readiness?
5. Does the learner's readiness suggest a particular presentation form for the instruction?
6. Is individualized or independent study a possibility from the learner's point of view?
7. Are evaluation criteria stated which measure affective as well as cognitive growth?

Finally, there are a number of learner characteristics which might influence the instruction and its presentation form. A few are: age/grade level, socioeconomic background, emotional maturity, special interest, reading ability, sex, attention span, level of motivation, intelligence, and learning style. The usual rule of thumb in most schools is that it is too time-consuming and difficult to obtain the kind of information listed above for most students. Medical schools, in this case, may be the exception to the rule. That is, vast amounts of data are gathered prior to the student's admittance into medical school. Biographical characteristics such as age, race, sex, family background, marital status, residence, personal background, health history, and choice of previous schools are all recorded and placed into a student selection model. In addition, intellectual characteristics, such as grade-point averages, undergraduate major, previous academic background, and performance on certain prescribed examinations such as the Medical College Admission Test (MCAT) are also part of the selection criteria. Some medical schools administer personality tests as further input to selection.

Specifying the Student Mastery Model

A mastery model is a description of the student's expected behavior applied in a real-world setting. In addition, the mastery statement identifies the resources and constraints influencing the performance of those behaviors. The instructional value of such a descriptive statement is that it focuses attention on those personal and instructional needs which precede the operationalized terminal objectives. These terminal objectives of a course are often the cornerstone upon which all content and instructional decisions are made. An example relative to medicine would be the case of an anatomy class whose objectives included motor skills in human dissection. This skill may be completed in the laboratory, but its mastery may not predict skill in surgery with a live patient whose pain and general welfare present a new task component.

The mastery model for the student may be stated as long-term goals and shorter-term objectives (see Chapters 2 and 3).

The nature of instructional design implies a need for flexibility at this point in the design process. For some faculty the objectives become apparent only after the content has actually been outlined and test questions generated. Because of this phenomenon, the terminal objectives may be subject to alteration as the design process progresses.

Task Analysis

Task analysis is the examination of the entire process of content and behavior analysis. The decisions made here establish the basis for the internal conditions that must occur to produce the desired learning outcomes. "Content analysis" is the procedure for identifying the subject-matter structure, as opposed to the instructional procedure. "Behavioral analysis" examines the instructional procedures, i.e., interaction of learner and content taxonomy, and determines the ability levels students will reach in the materials (Merrill and Boutwell, 1973).

The task analysis component is presented in Chapter 5. If the instructional developer and faculty member cannot complete a task analysis, i.e., content and behavioral analysis based on the previous information, they should refer back to the content analysis as well as review the goal definition and the learner characteristics.

Test Questions

Once the task analysis has been properly conducted, then the writing of enabling objectives can begin. This phase translates the long-range terminal objectives and mastery model into more specific prerequisite behavioral objectives. Often the writing of the objectives in behavioral terms interferes cognitively and psychologically with the client's ability to conceptualize the behavioral outcomes of the instruction. The generation of test items serves the same purpose as writing specific objectives and does so with a reduction in conflict. An example of this procedure can best be achieved with the following description. A faculty physician was interested in re-designing the pathology course, but he felt that the writing of "behavioral objectives" limited his instructional techniques. Because the physician viewed the task of defining objectives as disfunctional to re-designing the course, the designer was able to overcome conflict by analyzing the course examination, i.e., test items. Having taken the route of test analysis to define instructional intent and content areas, the writing of objectives was facilitated.

Instructional Strategy

At this point, the client and designer/developer must sit down and talk over all the previous steps. The sequence and structure of instruction deals with the organization of the course. This instructional strategy becomes apparent when the developer and client recall methodological preferences (e.g., discovery versus guided learning), learner characteristics, and content and behavior analyses. The use of diagnostic pretests, branching techniques, or self-paced learning materials are issues to be considered here. Other issues must also be dealt with: whether to have multiple entry points; the flexibility of testing out of (by-passing instruction on) a component; learning for mastery (i.e., flexible time to reach criterion); norm- versus criterion-referenced evaluation, etc. While the initial phases of instructional design are reconsidered during the strategy planning, the terminal objectives and the long-range outcomes must also be given renewed consideration. Should there be difficulty in developing the instructional strategy, the designers should return to task analysis. It has been mentioned that terminal objectives are frequently altered as content analysis becomes apparent; this is an instance where further analysis may, in fact, revise the terminal student outcomes.

Events of Instruction

This component marks the implementation of all the prior planning. How the instructional events are accomplished depends in large measure upon the instructional strategy chosen. For instance, a guided (expository) learning approach might utilize different conditions of learning than would be employed in other approaches. A discovery (inquisitory) method may be introduced with specific examples of the concepts to be learned, from which the students would induce the general concepts and rules rather than receiving them as "givens."

Media Selection

Media are selected to match the characteristics of the learner and the type of interaction with the task which is desired for the learner. There are three generalizations concerning the appropriate use of media and instruction.

1. Select media which maximize the probability that the objective will be accomplished.
2. Select media which can utilize programming variables of proven instructional value, e.g., prompting, motivation, providing learner guidance, small steps, review, attribute isolation, and prompting transfer of learning.
3. Select media to maximize the likelihood that the student will get more out of the task stimulus with less effort.

The selection of the most appropriate media involves consideration of many relationships (e.g., teacher/learner characteristics, school facilities, time/cost, availability, etc.).

Development and Production of Material

The actual materials to be used will be the product of decisions made at each of the preceding steps in design. The medium used in conveying the instructional message (i.e., television, multi-media package, computers, or printed materials) should have been discussed earlier—along with resources and the utilization issues such as large vs. small groups. The media chosen can play a significant role in promoting learning, but they can be no better than any part of the prior decisions. Therefore, it is usually best to review the input materials before actual development can be started. Following the review process, production steps can begin.

The designer, in this phase, becomes a manager and facilitator; in addition, the designer usually helps with storyboarding, script writing, and camera work.

The content and evaluation specialists should also be involved in production to insure compliance with their specialties.

In medical schools, there is a heavy reliance on visual presentations, i.e., slide tapes, films, and/or videotapes.

Evaluation and Validation

These two stages of evaluation are described in Chapters 10 and 11.

One of the key issues in medical schools is interchangeability of instruction. Most schools exchange objectives, tests, and instructional packages upon request. It becomes important to locally evaluate instructional materials for special local purposes, but for "core" instruction, appropriate for all medical schools, cooperative testing can be arranged among schools in order to gather more evaluation data.

Summary

The purpose of utilizing a systematic design for instruction is to bring about a process which effectively operationalizes the ways in which learning is to take place. The alternative is a learning environment which is vaguely goal-directed, unplanned, and haphazard. Allowing instruction to be unplanned, and as some educators suggest "natural," relegates some learners to positions of incompetence. The value of simply providing an environment which is conducive to a nurturing or natural method is to suggest the uncontrollability of shaping forces upon the learner. On the other hand, the process suggested within a systems design model identifies those instructional forces and controls them.

The importance of close cooperation between the instructional designer and the subject-matter expert has been emphasized in this Chapter. Also, the possibility of exchange of materials in core skill areas among medical schools was pointed out.

Suggested Readings

American Medical Association. Medical Education in the United States, 1971-1972. JAMA, 1972, *222*:1053, 986.

The Carnegie Commission on Higher Education. *Higher Education and the Nation's Health: Policies for Medical and Dental Education.* New York: McGraw-Hill, 1970.

Merrill, M.D., and Boutwell, R.C. Instructional Development: Methodology and Research. In F.N. Kerlinger (Ed.), *Review of Research in Education.* Itasca, Illinois: Peacock, 1973, 95-131.

Transition to Chapter 15

Chapter 15, unlike most Chapters in this book, was not originally written for use in the book. Rather, it was originally a "project report," submitted to the client, AT&T, after completion of a contract by the American Institutes for Research in Palo Alto, California, where both Dr. Markle and Dr. Briggs were employed. Dr. Briggs was at that time program director of the Palo Alto Office, and Dr. Markle was project director for the design of the first aid course for AT&T. The title of Dr. Markle's original report was: *Final Report: The Development of the Bell System First Aid and Personal Safety Course*, April, 1967. The report carried a sub-title that is especially significant for the present purpose: "An Exercise in the Application of Empirical Methods to Instructional Systems Design." Some of the "formative evaluation" techniques described in the report greatly expand the concept by showing how *early stages of design* (not just materials development) may be influenced by the gathering of empirical data.

Since the first aid course described in Chapter 15 was completed, it has been used to train several million persons. Data provided by the American Red Cross (which now makes the course available, and trains instructors and instructor trainers), indicates that, from 1970 through 1975, over 2.5 million persons were trained.

These figures show that the cost of expert design is not large when high utilization is assured. On the surface, it may appear unacceptable to spend a quarter of a million dollars to develop seven and one-half hours of training. But when the completed course saves training time while increasing first aid proficiency for several million industrial employees, it is the *benefit* that is impressive, not the cost. The course presumably has also reduced hospitalization time of victims aided by those with this training, and it is not known how many lives were saved.

The original report has been edited and abbreviated for presentation in this book. Permission to reprint was granted by AT&T, the American National Red Cross, American Institutes for Research, and Dr. Markle, who, in his closing summary, gives his present reflections on the project, as seen from a perspective of 10 years.

Chapter 15

First Aid Training

David G. Markle
Communication Research Laboratories, Inc.
Denver, Colorado

Project Objective

The objective of this project was to develop a basic first aid course which would, in seven and one-half hours, produce results at least equivalent to those produced by standard first aid instruction taking ten hours. According to an agreement between AT&T and the American National Red Cross, Red Cross certificates have been awarded following completion of standard first aid instruction given in the Bell System. Thus, the new course was expected to meet Red Cross certification requirements.

Methods

Student performance data were used to support as many course design decisions as possible. A set of test questions, defined as potential course objectives, was pretested on trained and untrained members of the student population to determine the actual objectives. A revised subset of these test questions, without additions, was then used as a first draft of the course. Student performance guided the successive approximation of the final course through gradual alteration of the questions and addition of needed instructional materials. The strategy followed throughout was to add instructional materials to the basic test question sequences only when the need was revealed through student tryouts. Response-time data and error data were used in this process.

Empirical methods were used to develop the motion picture

components of the course, as well as the printed portions. Data gathered from tryouts of brief segments of 16mm black and white pilot footage were used to develop scripts for final filming in 35mm color. The 35mm films were in turn tried out and revised on the basis of student performance.

Results

These instructional engineering methods have resulted in the attainment of the project objectives. In addition to the desired increase in efficiency as a function of decreased time, the new, shorter course is far more effective than the standard courses with which it has been compared. On one wide-range test used for comparisons, untrained subjects achieved a mean score of 85, subjects trained in standard first aid courses achieved a mean score of 145, while subjects trained in the new course achieved a mean score of 270, out of a possible maximum of 326 points. Similar results were obtained with other tests and other subjects.

Subject-Matter Analysis

The final product of the subject-matter analysis phase was a set of performance requirements, couched directly in test question form, for all content the project staff could identify as potentially belonging in a set of objectives for basic first aid. These questions were developed through the review of subject-matter references and the application of several schemes of logical analysis.

Criterion Question Generation

The first step was to generate every reasonable-appearing test question implied by the basic first aid sections of the American National Red Cross First Aid Manual. Passages of an obviously orientational nature, such as a definition of "first aid," were not used to generate questions. Most of the questions were written in open-ended form, so they would simulate reasonably well the problems a first aider might face.

Answers to some of the questions could not be determined from the text, even though the questions had been produced from this source. This difficulty was often caused by the mismatch between the general level of the text and the practical "What do you do in *this* situation?" level of the questions. Ambiguities in the text and alternate interpretations of the problem situations were resolved through consultation with the Red Cross, and through the subsequent analysis in which first aid was treated as a decision-making topic, rather than as one composed primarily of procedural skills.

Decision level analysis. The decisions required of a first aider were classified into five different general types, or levels, according to when they would take place during a first aider's chain of reasoning about an accident situation or victim. Each level was cast in the form of a general question type, to simplify the classification of the questions.

The first level involved basic skills and procedures, and thus produced questions of a "How do you . . .?" or "Describe how you would . . ." type. The higher levels, which involved decision-making that takes place *before* basic skills are applied, included (1) determining what specific action to take, (2) identifying the injury or illness, (3) predicting what is likely to be wrong with a victim under specific conditions, and (4) preventing accidents. Each question that had been generated from the text was assigned to a level of decision-making. Each level was divided into sub-groups according to general question types, such as discrimination, listing, and physical skill performance. Questions on general knowledge that did not fit these levels were assigned to a sixth category.

Sorting the questions by decision-making category provided a natural means of checking for omissions. The questions for each first aid topic (e.g., care for wounds) were examined to see if questions of each level of decision-making were included where appropriate for that topic. This was equivalent to making a matrix with first aid categories along one axis and level of decision-making along the other, then examining each cell for omissions. Many questions were added as a result of this analysis.

Decision Flow Charting

The third stage of subject-matter analysis was to design flow charts for key first aid topics, much as one would design for a computer to follow. Analysis in terms of the strict, binary, yes-no kind of decision-making process followed by a computer typically reveals weaknesses in apparently clear specifications. This application proved to be no different: our first-draft charts revealed many unclear areas.

The major difficulties were resolved through consultation with the Red Cross. As the decision flow charts were completed, it became possible to examine criterion questions from another reference point. The first aider's decisions were distinguished from processes or actions by the flow-charting conventions used. Decision points, for example, involved such questions as "Is it a thermal or chemical burn?" while action boxes involved straight-forward actions, such as "Jut the victim's jaw." The decision points on the charts were compared with the existing set of questions and, where necessary, were used to generate new questions that would require students to make discriminations. The action boxes on the charts were similarly used to evaluate existing questions and generate new questions that would require descriptions or demonstrations of procedures. They also provided a guide to topics that would require demonstration on motion picture film.

In addition to the three procedures described above—production of questions directly from the manual, decision-level analysis, and decision flow charting—a number of other sources were used in the subject-matter analysis phase. Research in the available accident literature led to the production of questions on accident prevention. Some of these questions concerned dangerous aspects of apparently innocuous situations, while others concerned the frequency, hence importance, of specific injuries. Additional draft questions were provided by the Red Cross.

Objectives Summaries

The final set of approximately 500 questions was subdivided by first aid topics, such as "care for wounds," "artificial respiration," and "heart attack." General objectives statements were abstracted from the questions for each topic. These statements might have been produced first, had different procedures been followed. In this case, however, the statements were intended to imply only what was contained in the questions from which they were derived, and are best thought of as summaries. The questions themselves were the basis of the objectives specification.

It would be customary to consider the objectives specification task to be complete at this point, since the conventional procedure is to specify objectives on a logical, rational basis, before engaging in instructional materials development and in empirical tryout and revision. In fact, however, the set of questions and their summary statements comprised only the potential objectives from which the course objectives were to be selected. If this set of questions had been used as the objectives, the resulting course would have been far longer and more inclusive than existing standard first aid courses.

The first aid text alone, not counting the additional sources used to develop the questions, contained more than can be taught, in any strict sense, in the time available. The Red Cross instructor's manual explicitly tells the instructor not to attempt to teach all that is in the manual. The instructor is told to teach critical, important, life-saving points. Students are expected to read the remainder outside of class. Whenever instructional engineering methods are brought to bear on existing course materials, much that is normally "covered" must be reevaluated. Incidental topics which are taken seriously in behavioral terms can expand a course considerably.

The next task was to determine which of the potential objectives, as spelled out in the questions and their summary statements, would be included in the actual objectives. Empirical methods, rather than purely logical or rational methods, were used for this task.

Empirical Specification of Objectives

In this phase, the set of criterion questions was pretested on members of the intended student population and refined on the basis of the data so obtained. There were two basic types of refinement: (1) questions were revised to eliminate difficulties that kept them from measuring the behavior they were intended to measure, and (2) questions were dropped from the set of potential objectives when they were shown by the data to represent material already known by the student population.

Specific Problems Faced by This Project

The time limit of the course made it impossible to specify exact course objectives beforehand, since the amount that can be taught is dependent to a certain extent on time available. The flexibility afforded by "self-pacing," or by homework assignments of variable length, was not available. The task was to adjust the objectives to meet the stated time requirement.

Several different strategies were used to accomplish this. The question, "How many of these objectives should be included?" was changed to the two questions: "Which objectives can be omitted because the students already can do those things?" and "How much of what is left can be taught in seven and one-half hours?" The first of these is properly part of objectives specification, and can be answered to a fair level of confidence with pretesting. The second lies in the area of course design methods. Both are empirical questions, and both are critical to making instruction as efficient as possible.

An additional unknown contributed to the difficulty of saying exactly what should be included in basic first aid. The new course was intended to produce performance at least equal to that produced by standard first aid training. But, at the inception of the project, detailed objective performance criteria did not exist for these courses. The natural solution to this problem lay also in testing.

Field Testing

To answer the two questions, "What do the potential students of the new course know already?" and "What do standard first aid courses teach?," the criterion questions were administered to Bell System employees who had and had not received first aid training.

It was not feasible to administer all questions to all subjects in the field testing, so shorter tests were produced. The questions were randomly distributed into four groups, then tabulated by level of decision-making, within first aid topics. Excessive imbalances in topic distribution were eliminated by redistributing some questions. The tests covered different points, but they were approximately equally weighted by topic and were of equal length. A more desirable procedure would have been initially to distribute the questions randomly within level. It had been expected, however, that overall random assignment would have provided a more uniform distribution of items than was in fact obtained.

Because items ranged across many topics and were scored only qualitatively in order to provide data on needed course content, measures of internal consistency were not computed. Alternate-form reliabilities were computed for test forms that were used later for quantitative purposes.

The tests were administered to approximately 800 subjects who were selected on an availability basis by the telephone company from four geographical areas. Three levels of standard first aid training were represented: no training, just completed training, and training within past five years. Some control subjects used in the later quantitative comparisons were randomly selected from these groups.

Responses were tabulated on an item-by-item basis, so the error pattern of each item could be examined. Items that were seldom answered incorrectly were classed as candidates for omission from the potential objectives.

Laboratory Testing on Automated Time-Recording Equipment

Entirely separate testing was carried out with a total of 94 individual subjects on automated time-recording equipment. This testing, which was an integral part of both the objectives specification and the later instructional materials development, provided the means for incorporating response-time data as well as error data into the development process.

Typically, error data alone are available to the course designer. In most instructional programming systems, student errors on program and test items are taken to indicate revision requirements. The kinds of errors often provide leads on what kind of revisions are needed. Correct answers are reassuring to the programmer, but seldom useful for revision purposes. The addition of time data permits a much finer analysis of the function of the question and makes possible revisions aimed at meeting practical time limits. In order to carry out this type of analysis, the length of time a subject spends on a question is compared with the length of time typically spent on questions that are similar with respect to formal type, reading time, and response-request type. Question-answering time that is considerably shorter than normal reading time for items of that type is evidence that the student was not responding to all elements of the question, whether or not he or she answered it correctly. An excessively long answering time indicates difficulty and/or inefficiency. Often, ambiguities are signaled more by response time than by errors, particularly on items that most students eventually figure out.

The automated time-recording equipment was first used with the same four tests that were administered in the field testing. The questions were presented one at a time on a 35mm filmstrip viewer, in the sequence in which they had been printed for the field testing. Confirmation of answers was not provided. Total read-and-answer time for each item was recorded on a printing counter, in seconds in early stages of the tryouts, and in smaller units as refinement progressed.

Data obtained from this testing were used both to eliminate common knowledge items, and to modify retained items. Items which had become candidates for omission by virtue of few errors in the earlier field testing were omitted only if they produced zero error and non-extreme times in the automated testing. Items that were answered correctly but which required unusually long answering times were not omitted, as the long answer times were taken to indicate either a confusion relating to item design, or difficulty with that topic. Items which appeared defective were revised, while topic-related difficulties were noted as evidence of needed training. Subjective comments, as well as time and error data, were used as a basis for clarifying confusing items. Following revision, all items were resubmitted to the testing process.

Ambiguities and inefficiencies were revealed in a surprising number of the items. Identification of such problems has critical implications for the later stages of instructional materials design, because an undetected inefficient question will lead to the design of concomitantly inefficient instruction. The inefficient question will lead to teaching the student both the critical content and how to answer the unclear question, if not just the latter. When measured performance is equated with objectives, each content-related change in the measurement instrument leads to a detailed revision in the objectives. In this context, it would perhaps be better to distinguish between global, overall objectives, which may remain comparatively fixed throughout a project, and detailed, functional objectives, which are much less stable. Functional objectives remain variable until any instructional engineering task is completed.

Empirical Design of Instructional Materials

General Strategy

Development of all instructional components of the course followed the same general maxim: "Do not add instructional materials until you have evidence the student needs them." The course was approximated successively, starting with the refined set of criterion items and *no* additional material whatever as the first draft.

Development of the Basic
Criterion Question Sequence

The previously described tests were converted into first draft instructional sequences by resequencing items. Items were first grouped according to first aid topic within each test form. Within topic, they were sequenced by level of decision making. Basic skill questions, for example, were placed before questions about which skill to use. Then, within level of analysis, items were grouped in order of increasing response time. This sequencing was carried out mechanically through edge punches in the cards on which the items were typed.

The four newly sequenced versions of the tests were presented on the automated equipment with answer frames alternated with the question frames. Trial subjects would read an item, write an answer, advance the filmstrip to the correct answer, check the answer, then advance the filmstrip to the next item. The equipment recorded read-and-answer time and answer-checking time.

Presented in this manner, sequenced but without additional instructional materials, each test was a remote approximation to an instructional program. Students had the opportunity to check their own answers or to learn from the answers presented. But the major function of the sequenced questions at this point was to obtain data. Time and error data were used to modify individual items and to identify needed resequencing. Four major cycles of such trials and revisions were carried out, with essentially the same purpose of gradual data-based refinement. In later stages, the four separate semi-programs were combined to form the master criterion question sequence for the course. When sequences were combined, redundancies that were indicated unequivocally by time and error data were eliminated.

Up to this point, development of the questions had been separate from the development of the procedural skills films, which was carried out concurrently.

Film Development Methods

Early in the project, we decided that the only topics which could be assigned to film treatment on an obvious *a priori* basis were those whose presentation and performance evaluation should involve demonstration of some sort. The "Demonstrate . . ." criterion items produced in the subject-matter analysis phase were used as a starting point for the selection of such topics, which naturally included bandaging, splinting, artificial respiration, etc. Decisions about the inclusion of nonprocedural topics in the films were delayed until later, when empirical data on the requirements would be available.

As a first step, simple black and white 16mm films of basic first aid procedures were made. They were shot, whenever possible, so that the procedures would be seen from the point of view of the first aider himself. The intent in this filming was simply to show how each procedure should be carried out. No special attempt was made to achieve continuity between scenes, nor to achieve artistic effects.

The films were broken down into short, unnarrated segments and mounted on 100-foot reels. The testing procedure was to project a single reel, then tell the trial students to do what they had just seen done on the film. Their performance was observed and notes were made of errors and confusions. No instruction other than what was contained in the silent motion picture film was presented initially. The experimenter replied parsimoniously to questions only after the student's difficulty with the footage had been tentatively identified. Consistent errors and explanations needed from the experimenter were used as indicators of needed reshooting and/or narration. In cases in which alternate versions of a procedure had been filmed, the more effective versions were identified. Reels dealing with related topics were tested in a variety of sequences to identify advantageous sequencing patterns.

After the more effective films had been selected, the clearly defective films reshot, and narration guidelines developed, the films were assembled into more molar units for tryouts in combination with the criterion question sequences. Short segments of film which had been tested separately in silent form were spliced together, and narration was added where testing had indicated a need. White leader and continuous still pictures were used to fill in where the narration took longer than the related motion pictures. Conflicts between audio and visual channels were avoided by minimizing narration during filmed sequences of critical procedures, and by minimizing potentially distracting visual interest when the narrator had a critical explanation to make.

Combination of Criterion Questions and Films

Films and question sequences were first grouped together by topic. Both films and criterion questions were available at this point for topics which had both substantial procedural and decision-making aspects. Bandaging had only films, since no nonprocedural questions on bandaging remained in the final set of questions. Nonprocedural topics like heart attack had only a sequence of questions, since no films had as yet been produced on such topics.

In cases where both films and question sequences were available for a topic, the filmed demonstrations and coordinated practice sessions were placed first, followed by the printed question sequence. The length of an individual filmed demonstration, hence the number of skills to be practiced in an individual practice session, was determined through a compromise of conflicting requirements. Our general preference was to keep the film segments quite short. Student performance on any one task would clearly be benefited by the absence of other material intervening between the introductory demonstration and the practice session. Poor performance could be predicted on a topic which was presented at the beginning of a long series of demonstrations, if practice was delayed until the end of the series. On the other hand, frequent stopping of the film for practice sessions threatened administrative complications and time-wasting.

In Version 1, the typical film demonstration session presented between one and three procedures, according to their complexity and interrelatedness. For example, techniques for the care of wounds were grouped into two sections. The first film segment treated direct pressure, elevation, and the pressure points, and was followed by a practice session for all three. This was followed by a film and subsequent practice session on the tourniquet. The question sequence on the control of bleeding followed the tourniquet practice session.

The sequence of questions was not changed from their criterion question sequence form as produced in the automated testing. Each sequence was, however, prefaced with a page or two of explanatory text on material that was clearly not covered by the films and practice sessions that now preceded the sequence. For example, the explanatory text that was prefaced to the set of questions on *Care for Wounds* did not contain information on direct pressure, elevation, pressure points, or the tourniquet, as these were treated in the films and practice sessions. It did contain information on care for minor wounds, since this was not filmed. Set up in this manner, the questions functioned as a programmed review and test on the films and on the brief printed text passages. Criterion question sequences for topics which did not have films were treated similarly. The sequences were unchanged, but were prefaced with brief introductory texts. The same general strategy of adding a bare minimum of material, as followed in other stages of the project, was followed here also.

A review unit was constructed for the end of the course by selecting critical questions from each lesson. High error frequency in earlier testing and potential life-saving value of the question were used as criteria for this selection.

It should be noted that at this stage the course was hardly "presentable." It had no introduction, no "motivational" material, and very little apparent continuity. All the refinement techniques applied up to this point had been concerned strictly with student performance, with no attention at all being paid to surface appearance. Certainly, no conventional film producer would have shown the film to a client as an example of his skill, nor could any conventional programming criteria have been used to evaluate the workbooks, which contained the brief texts, the questions, and their answers. These materials bore about the same superficial relationship to the final course as the concrete supports, still encased in their forms, bear to a completed bridge.

Course Tryout, Version 1

Version 1 was administered in Atlanta, Georgia to ten trainees who had received no prior standard first aid training. The instructor was given a brief introduction to the course by project staff and the subject-matter expert, but he received no formal training in administering the course. Neither was he given a detailed instructor's guide for the practice sessions, as one goal of this tryout was to identify administrative difficulties and instructor's guide requirements. No unusual administrative difficulties were identified, other than the instructor's natural difficulty in changing abruptly from lecturing about first aid, as he normally did in his work, to the much more limited and specialized tasks required of him by the new course. Project staff were on hand to help out when necessary.

Total instructional time for Version 1 was approximately 12 hours, with the films taking two hours, practice sessions taking three, and workbooks taking seven. It was obviously hard work for the trainees, who commented freely that "this is sure harder than high school." Mild complaints accompanied the distribution of the workbooks in the last few hours of the course. The films, although hardly exciting, were obviously looked forward to as respite from the workbooks, which could be described as an extreme form of "brute force" programming. The students were observed to adopt a style of working quite different from that which is normally observed with low error-rate programs. They would read a question, puzzle about its answer, make a guess at it (usually part of the complete answer), then study the correct answer given on the next page. Obviously, the answers were not serving the occasional confirmation or answer-checking function they serve in conventional low-error programmed instruction, but were often serving as initial instruction.

The no-instruction control group and the group which received Version 1 of the new course were randomly selected from the same pool of newly hired employees. Several last-minute substitutions in both groups by the telephone company upset the randomness but did not introduce any identifiable biases. The control groups which had received standard first aid training were randomly sampled from the appropriate cells of the earlier administered field testing, and represent a pooling of results from numerous different standard first aid courses. All testing was done immediately on completion of the course involved. The no-instruction control group was tested at the same time as the Version 1 group.

Revision of Version 1

The major goal of the revision was to reduce instructional time from 12 hours to nearer the target of seven and one-half hours without sacrificing the effectiveness of Version 1. Data obtained from the Atlanta tryout included observations of performance in the practice sessions, responses to questions in the workbooks, responses to test Forms I and II, and student comments.

Scripts for refilming all of the procedural skills films in 35mm color were prepared from the black and white films tested in Atlanta. Revisions suggested by the testing, aimed both at improved performance and at achieving a closer interdependence between films and workbooks, were incorporated into these scripts. In addition, scripts were prepared for nonprocedural topics that had been identified in the tryout as being troublesome or worthy of greater emphasis.

It was evident that explicit instructor guides would be required. Practice session guides were prepared for Version 2. These consisted of exact scripts for the instructor to read to the students during each practice session, and checklists on which he or she could check off skill points. The scripts were intended both to help the instructor organize the practice sessions, and to set up the situation so some testing of conceptual material would take place. For example, the instructor was told to say, "The victim has a serious wound on his forearm. Do what you would do first to stop the bleeding" instead of "Now demonstrate direct pressure and elevation for a serious wound on the victim's forearm."

The workbooks were extensively revised, with strong emphasis on time-saving techniques that would not sacrifice instructional quality. Consistent correct answers on a single point within the course, in the review section, and on the final tests were used as evidence of redundancy, and some material on these points was eliminated, as was done earlier when the separate criterion question sequences were combined. Questions that were answered uniformly correctly, but which involved content judged to be of less than critical importance, were converted to statement form in order to eliminate time-consuming response requests. This had the effect of restricting the material on which a student would repeatedly be tested to critical, high-value items. Treatments of points on which consistent errors were made were of course modified to reduce the probability of these errors.

In addition to these data-based revisions, a series of accident vignettes was added to the course. Six situations in which first aid would be required were selected on the basis of frequency and/or instructional value. A filmed montage of these situations begins the course with a bit of drama and sets the stage for first aid. Each situation is carried up to the point where the injury or illness occurs, then the scene is frozen and a critical question is posed. For example, the automobile accident scene ends with a closeup of a bleeding victim and the question "What is the first step in controlling bleeding?" After the six situations and their questions have been presented, the film recycles through the question stills and gives brief answers. The critical "Hurry Cases of First Aid" and several other key problems are introduced at this point. Continuations of each of these situations, in which first aid is given to the victim, are used later in the course to introduce individual lessons.

Course Tryout, Version 2

The newly produced 35mm color films were combined with the practice session guides and the revised workbooks in a manner similar to Version 1. The version was tested on two classes in San Francisco. One tryout was informally administered by project staff; the second was formally administered by a Bell System first aid instructor. Preparation of the instructor for the formal tryout was brief, as it had been in the Atlanta tryout of Version 1. On this occasion, however, the intent of keeping his preparation brief was to enable us to evaluate the function of the instructor's practice session guide, without the confounding influence of additional instruction.

The only major difficulty observed in the formal tryout was with the instructor's guide. The checklists and instructor scripts had been printed separately, which made it difficult for the instructor to keep his place in both at once. This encouraged him to stop using one or the other and carry on *ad libitum*. Mechanical difficulties with the materials have been eliminated by later revisions, but the tendency for the instructor to improvise has not been completely eliminated.

Student performance in the practice sessions was noticeably improved. Most of the procedural skills errors which had been frequent in the tryout of Version 1 were eliminated by the new film. Total instructional time was reduced from 12 to nine hours. This time saving resulted from the greater efficiency of the workbooks, and from the much closer interrelationship achieved between the films and the workbooks in Version 2. Minor changes in narration, which added virtually no time, had in some cases permitted us to eliminate some workbook material, and in others to avoid adding material.

Revision of Version 2

Observation of the practice sessions revealed the need for some renarration and resequencing of the procedural skills films and practice sessions. The treatment of mouth-to-mouth artificial respiration was converted from one to two film sequences, with the practice also divided from one into two sessions. This was done to eliminate confusion between several related procedures. No refilming was found necessary. Instructor scripts and checklists for the practice sessions were combined into one document to minimize the practical difficulties observed in the tryouts, and a detailed time schedule was prepared on the basis of predicted time requirements for each component of the course.

Workbooks were revised according to the same strategies used previously, with further attention to time-saving changes in response requests. Interrelationships between films and workbooks were further refined. Questions on material taught in the preceding films and practice sessions were placed at the beginning of each printed lesson, with the pages of instructional text and their questions following. The pages of instructional text, which had previously been grouped together, were split into smaller sections and distributed more evenly throughout the question sequences. The resulting overall pattern for each workbook lesson was (1) initial question sequence on preceding films and practice sessions, (2) brief page of text on new material, (3) question sequence on new material, (4) brief page of text on more material, (5) question sequence, etc. The format of each question sequence was as before, with a question on one page, the answer on the next. In addition to these revisions, subject-matter changes suggested by the Red Cross were incorporated.

Course Tryout, Version 3

The final version, as published, was tested by the Pacific Telephone and Telegraph Company. The class was administered by a Bell System instructor who had been given fairly thorough preparation, and was completed within the prescribed seven and one-half instructional hours.

Conclusions

Relative Power of the
Developmental Methods

The comparative value of the methods used in this project cannot be assessed with the overall course comparison data that were obtained. A cost-effectiveness analysis of the methods used would require an extensive experimental rather than developmental effort. It is nonetheless worthwhile to comment on some aspects of these methods.

Although the main innovative interest of the project lies in the wide range of empirical methods used, the importance of the initial analysis of first aid in decision-making terms must be emphasized. It is critical not that the analysis was in terms of decision-making *per se*, but rather that the analysis systematically shifted emphasis from content to behavior, crosscutting existing classification categories. It appears that the discovery of an analysis scheme which crosscuts existing content-related classifications is of critical importance to projects of this sort.

Techniques for the elimination of common-knowledge material were undoubtedly major contributors to large differences in scores found between the control groups and groups taught by the new course. Standard first aid instruction contains a large amount of common-knowledge material; thus, wide-range tests show small differences between untrained and conventionally trained students. Because so much instruction in most subject-matters is hamstrung by the reiteration of already known material, this aspect of the empirical specification of objectives deserves wide general application.

The successive approximation of instructional materials, starting from criterion questions alone, eliminated the need for initial judgments about what instruction students would require—judgments which are typically made with inadequate information. This procedure also made it possible to exercise careful control over the material which eventually was included in the course. This control is particularly important when time constraints are involved, and when several media of instruction are to be integrated. Time data further facilitated this close scrutiny, calling attention to poorly functioning components which otherwise might not have been identified. Additionally, of course, the time data provided the means for achieving high efficiency through detailed time-worth estimations.

Design Decision Strategies

It is interesting to note that little attention was paid directly to the question of medium selection. Apart from the *a priori* decision to film the skills demonstrations, medium selection decisions were typically made for very small components of the course, in the context of specific data-based requirements and physical constraints. It appears that the highly detailed empirical work on the basic levels of objectives specification and instructional requirements determination eliminated the need for large-scale decision-making on the medium selection level. Design decisions made at any one level of development have surprisingly far-reaching consequences at other levels—consequences which suggest that the sequence of decision-making alone is well worth further attention, apart from questions of what kinds of evidence are to be used for each decision.

Summary

In the ten years since this report was written, the first aid course has been used widely in industrial settings and by the Red Cross. (The course discussed in this report is called "Multimedia Standard First Aid" by the Red Cross.) Since that time we have designed other instructional systems in first aid. The newer materials have been prepared for various student populations, including school children and adult nonreaders. The institutional objectives have been different in each case, but many content objectives have been shared with Multimedia.

In 1966, when we finished the Multimedia project, a colleague remarked, "You wouldn't go through all that empirical research if you were to do it again, would you?" At the time, I insisted, "Of course." Time and experience have refined that answer. If my current colleagues and I were to develop a new Multimedia course, we would do as much or more empirical work, but we would ask different questions and use somewhat different methods.

Empirical development can be viewed as a process of using data to change areas of uncertainty into areas of comparatively greater certainty. There were many uncertainties in the Multimedia project, especially in defining the objectives and scope of the course. The need to specify certification requirements that would be acceptable to the Red Cross and achievable within the contractually fixed course time limit encouraged us to reduce these uncertainties empirically. As Dr. Briggs noted in his introductory remarks, these early steps are not usually treated empirically.

Different projects have different patterns of uncertainties. For example, in a later project we designed basic first aid instruction for students of fifth grade reading level. A major task in that project was to prepare text that would be adequately self-motivating and easy to read for a wide variety of students, including those in disadvantaged population groups. In another project, printed first aid instruction was redesigned for adult nonreaders. For that course, it was necessary to devise an effective but inexpensive audio-visual presentation format. These design problems were all resolved empirically, but the types of initial drafts and the details of tryout and revision were tailored to each project.

In retrospect, most of the empirical methods that were used to develop Multimedia appear to have been suitable for that project. In particular, the tryouts of pilot films, the large-scale pretesting, and the formal tryouts of the three versions of the assembled course were all essential. However, more recent experience with tailoring language to special requirements has made us sensitive to flaws in Multimedia that neither the data nor our editing identified at the time. We would now supplement the automated testing of the text with some informal "tutorial" tryout procedures. The materials would also be given a more intensive stylistic editing.

A weak point in the empirical methodology used for Multimedia was the lack of unmonitored "implementation" testing. The course was tested only in situations in which the instructor followed the directions. We did not investigate the likelihood of or the effects of instructor variability. In fact, most instructors do administer the course as intended—especially those who do not have a prior commitment to a different teaching approach. However, somewhat more consistent results might have been obtained if implementation trials had been conducted with instructors who used a variety of approaches. Effective variations could then have been accounted for in the final course design, administration procedures, and instructor training procedures. In a period of implementation testing, it would also have been possible to obtain delayed retention data—an important revision tool. However, such testing might have doubled the length of the development effort.

The avid empiricist seems always to want to do "one more tryout," but there is a point when financial, institutional, or temporal constraints terminate the developmental effort. This termination is usually fairly permanent, because revision, reprinting, and redistribution are costly and not welcomed when a course has been introduced and is working reasonably well. We are pleased to report that Multimedia is currently being revised and will get more than "one more tryout." Continued wide usage and changes in subject-matter have provided the impetus for updating the course both in content and in instructional methodology.

Transition to Chapter 16

In Part I of this book you read of the entire process and principles of instructional design, beginning with identification of needs and goals, and ending with evaluation of the instruction that results from the complete process.

Up to this point in Part II of the book, you have read how the design process is adapted to the practical problems of working within the various types of organizations that conduct education or training. In Chapter 15 you read of a course design developed under contract for an industrial client.

In Chapter 16, you encounter a quite different kind of "special application." Chapter 16 is, in fact, a "student product" from an advanced graduate course at Florida State University.

The author, Miss Amy S. Ackerman, was a student in the course, "The Design of Instruction," during the 10-week academic quarter in the summer of 1976. The four "assignments" were completed by the students at approximately two-week intervals. Each assignment was assessed by the instructor, and the assignment was returned, along with written comments by the instructor, to the students.

The four assignments in this particular course were based on the assumption that the student had previously identified needs and goals for the "course" that the student would be using as his or her design project. Therefore, Miss Ackerman's course design opens with only a general statement of the purpose of the course, since she did not need to use the consensus techniques discussed in Chapter 2 of this book. However, her design does utilize the theory and techniques discussed in Chapters 3-9, thus ending with "first draft instructional materials." Due to the press of time in a 10-week quarter, only small samples of first draft materials can be developed. Developing materials for an entire course is impossible in that time frame, especially since reading and study time are also required. Actual production and evaluation of instructional materials are reserved for other courses in the graduate program that Miss Ackerman is pursuing as of this writing.

Presented next are the four "assignment sheets," which serve both to define the requirements of each assignment to the students and also to notify them in advance as to the criteria for assessment of each assignment. Note that each assignment sheet contains three parts:

1. The objective of the assignment.

2. The subordinate parts that make up an adequately-completed assignment.

3. The criteria for evaluation, in which "points" can be converted to letter grades, as required by the rules of the university.

Similar assignment sheets could be used by instructors who wish to use this book for a "skill-development" type of course. Entirely different assignments, exercises, or tests should be designed if the book is to be used for only the theory or research aspects of instructional design, as discussed in the *Preface.*

The reader may wish to identify the specific pages in Chapter 16 which show how Miss Ackerman implemented each required step in each assignment.

Not every student in this advanced course earns an assessment of "A" on the first attempt at completing each assignment, as Miss Ackerman did. If your first attempt is judged by you or an instructor as not quite adequate, you are in good company. The majority of students do earn "A" on the second attempt. The points for "prompting" on the assignment sheet allow the instructor to record the degree of help needed by the student. If the instructor has to directly suggest solutions to problems to the student, it is advisable that the student later repeat that part of the design process for a new objective in order to be assured that he or she can repeat the process independently, without aid from an instructor.

Approximately 450 graduate students have completed this design course from 1968 to 1976. Various materials have been developed or adopted for use in the course during this interval, including Gagné's first two editions of the *Conditions of Learning*, Briggs' *Handbook* and *Student's Guide* and Gagné and Briggs' *Principles of Instructional Design* (all cited elsewhere in this book). Also, videotapes made by guest lecturers are available, as well as conferences, handouts, and former student products, like Chapters 16 and 17. This book, being broader in scope than any of the books just cited, is intended as a composite source to be considered as a major resource in such courses as the one described here. Nevertheless, for deeper coverage, those sources, along with others cited at the close of each Chapter in this book, will often afford materials needed by many readers of this book.

In order that the circumstances of the development of Chapter 16 be represented accurately, Miss Ackerman has noted, for the reader, those changes she made during the academic quarter and those made later. This may assist the reader in setting a realistic level of aspiration for his or her design efforts.

For the undergraduate or beginning graduate student reader, it may be useful to skip to Chapter 17 at this point. That Chapter was written by Ms. Karen L. Medsker while she was a student in an *introductory* course in instructional design, in which the "assignments" required a lesser amount of detail.

The four assignments for the advanced design course are presented next, followed by Chapter 16. Note that the original set of assignments Miss Ackerman submitted totaled about 85 typewritten pages. This was reduced in size for publication here. The deleted portions are indicated at various places within the Chapter.

Recall that this course focuses on design of instructional materials, not classroom teaching skills. Therefore, to keep the students focused upon materials, we required that the instruction be "replicable." The statement given to the students in the course syllabus regarding replicability is reproduced here after the four assignment sheets. See also the emphasis on this in the third assignment sheet.

The local designation for the course is "IDD 630"; this designation appears in the "replicability statement." (The IDD signifies "Instructional Design and Development.")

Assignment Sheet

Assignment No. 1: IDD 630

Objective

Given this assignment sheet	(situation)
the student will generate	(learned capability)
an instructional plan	(object)
by writing	(action)
appropriate levels of descriptions	
and objectives, with accompanying	
tests over the objectives, within	(tools or
the announced due date.	constraints)

Components and Criteria

1. Description of the course: who it is for; what is unusual about the course or the students; how it fits into the overall curriculum. 6
2. Is there an indication of why the course is important for the intended learners? 6
3. Statement of life-long objective; what else is needed to make it realistic? 4
4. An end-of-course objective stated in behavioral terms. Avoid trivial objectives and pure reproductive learning of content. 6
5. State at least 3 unit or major course objectives identified as major intellectual skills and attitudes, or give a rationale as to why unit objectives are not used, due to the structure of the course. 6
6. At least 4 specific objectives, identified as supporting unit objectives (at least 2 must be intellectual skills). 4
*7. Is there an orderly progression in complexity from specific, to unit, to course objectives? Is it clear how these levels inter-relate?.. 6
8. For each of the 4 specific objectives are all 5 criteria met, and labeled? ....
    (a) Situation 4
    (b) Learned Capability 4
    (c) Object 4
    (d) Action 4
    (e) Tools, constraints, conditions 4
*9. Are the 4 tests over the 4 specific objectives congruent with (valid for) the objectives? 12
*10. Are the tests adequate (reliable)? 4
11. Is a scoring key given for each test, or a list of criteria and weights when judgment enters into scoring? 4
12. For each test is there a system for assigning grades, or a rationale for not assigning grades? 4

*13. Is the paper free of major or frequent errors in grammar, punctuation, and spelling? 10

Total 92

Possible

*Indicates criteria, not parts of the assignment. These are instructor judgments, not something the students write.

Points attained	_____	_____
	original	revised
Minus prompting	_____	_____
Final Score	_____	_____

Assignment Sheet

Assignment No. 2: IDD 630

Objective

Given this assignment sheet, the student will generate, in writing, a learning hierarchy for an intellectual skill objective, and will show how it relates to one or more objectives in other domains of learning, by the announced due date.

Components and Criteria

The Intellectual Skill Objective
  1. Write the intellectual skill objective 10
 *2. Is the "size of chunk" of the objective suitable for a complete analysis on about one page? 10
 *3. Does each subordinate competency represent a single type of learning, correctly labeled? 10
 *4. Is the analysis complete and detailed enough to provide the basis for both sequencing of instruction and adequate instruction? 10
  5. Are entering competencies shown, and a line drawn to separate entry skills from those to be learned in the course? 10
  6. Are the skills numbered to show the teaching sequence? 10
 *7. Is there any irrelevant or "dead wood" element in the analysis? 10
                                                                           ____
                                                          Total   70
                                                          Possible

Other Objectives
  8. Write a discussion of the place of the intellectual skill objective in the overall organization of the unit, showing how information or other types of objectives relate to the intellectual skill objective.
  9. If information objectives are relevant to the unit or to the intellectual skill objective, indicate whether the function of information objectives is to:
     a. Serve as advanced organizers
     b. Serve as transfer mechanisms within the hierarchy
     c. Provide information regarding rationale, reinforcement or values for attitude formation
     d. Serve as mediational cues for motor skill learning

* = criteria only   Points attained   _____   _____

                                            original   revised

                       Minus prompting   _____   _____

                       Final Score   _____   _____

Assignment No. 3: IDD 630

Objective

Given this assignment sheet, the student will generate an instructional plan, in writing, meeting all components and criteria within the announced schedule.

Components and Criteria

1. A description of the assumed learning environment (real or theoretical), including resources and constraints upon both development and presentation of the course. 5

2. State the objectives or parts of the objective to be analyzed (it must comprise at least two hours of instruction). 5

3. Are the 9 "instructional events" accounted for in each sub-objective or a rationale given for their absence? 20

4. Are media alternatives congruent with the assumed environment and type of stimuli? 10

5. Are tentative media choices consistent with instructional theory? 10

*6. Do final media choices strike a good balance between the tentative choices and "packaging realities?" 10

7. Are rationales for final media choices reasonable for the intended learners, the nature of the competencies, and learning environment? 10

8. Do the prescriptions show use of appropriate conditions of learning? Are they complete enough that another person could fill them as you intended? 10

*9. Do the prescriptions include degrees of guidance or practice with feedback, as appropriate to the type of outcome? 10

*10. Do prescriptions show continuity between events? 10

*11. Do the prescriptions efficiently utilize the resources of the assumed environment? 10

*12. Is the instruction "replicable?" 20

*13. Adequate labels and writing style. 10

Total   140
Possible

First attempt   _____   Second _____

Minus prompting   _____

Final Score   _____

*Indicates criteria only; all others are both parts of the assignment and criteria.

Assignment No. 4: IDD 630

Objective

Given this assignment sheet, the student will generate verbatim, first-draft scripts or instructional material, in writing and/or using drawings, for enough competencies to comprise one hour of instruction, using at least two media.

1. Do the scripts or draft materials follow the prescriptions from assignment 3, or are reasons given for changes? 10
2. Are the scripts labeled, in the margins, to show where each new instructional event begins? (also list events within events or simultaneous events, or media within media) 10
3. Is the material adequate for the designated instructional events? 10
4. Are appropriate conditions of learning incorporated into the materials? Are the correct amounts of prompting, practice, guidance, and review included? 10
*5. Qualitative rating (ingenuity, creativity) 10
*6. Quantitative rating (amount of coverage) 10
*7. Replicability of the instruction 10
*8. Based on the above, are revisions of assignment 3 suggested? Yes.....; No.....
*9. Adequacy of writing 10

Total   80
Possible

*Indicates criteria only; not components of the assignment.

Score   _____

Minus prompting   _____

Final Score   _____

IDD 630

A Rationale for the "Replicability" Requirement

What Is to Be Taught

In assignment 1, students outline an entire course they would like to design and teach by writing course objectives at various levels specified in the assignment sheet. They may use an "instructional map" to show how objectives in various domains of outcomes are related to the overall course structure and sequence.

In assignment 2, students select one intellectual skill objective for which they draw a learning hierarchy. Then, by use of a more detailed "instructional map," they show how information, attitudes, or motor skills are either sequenced into the hierarchy, or how they precede or follow the learning of the hierarchy.

These first two assignments deal only with *what* is to be taught, *not* how to teach it. The latter, *how to teach*, is the purpose of assignments 3 and 4.

How to Teach

In assignment 3, students choose a medium for each instructional event for each subordinate competency (or parts of objectives). It is recommended that two hours of instruction be analyzed in assignment 3, from which one hour will be developed in assignment 4. The scripts or other materials *specified* in the "prescriptions" for assignment 3 and *actually written* for assignment 4 must lead to "replicable instruction." Replicable means "capable of being used for other groups" of students comparable to those for whom the instruction was designed. It also means that the instruction is mediated—that is, "self-contained, and pre-packaged," in a form that others can use. This rules out lectures, live demonstrations, or discussions, unless these are "captured" by videotape or motion picture. There are many reasons for this "replicability" requirement. These reasons are organized as follows:

*The Goals and Procedures of
the Course*

1. It is not the purpose of this course to deal with

conventional instruction, but rather the purpose is to encourage pre-planned, self-contained, self-paced, self-instructional media when possible. This is not a course in platform performance of teachers; it is a course for designers (not deliverers) of instruction. (Some instructional events may be designated in assignment 3 for a teacher to perform, but events using other media should be selected for assignment 4.)

2. Many 630 students will wish to take their 630 scripts into the production-evaluation course sequence. The production courses offered are radio and TV, computerized instruction, multi-media, and programmed instruction. Some adjustments in script developed to meet 630 requirements will be needed to develop an entire script in a single medium. But at least portions done to meet 630 requirements can be utilized. Students planning to enroll in one of these production courses should show their completed 630 work to the instructor in advance, as scripting should be complete before the production course begins. After the production course, the materials undergo testing and revisions in connection with the formative evaluation course.

3. Former 630 students who ignore the above opportunities fail to apply the theory and skills which 630 offers.

4. It is true that some other courses are largely conducted by lecture. This is because resources are not sufficient to "capture" the entire course at one leap, and such courses are being captured in segments, as time permits. But 630 students are only asked for *one hour* of instruction, not an entire course. The purpose is to learn the skills; whether the materials are ever used in normal practice is not the crucial point.

Systems Design Strategy

1. *Entry skills.* Students need to consider the problems arising from heterogeneous entry skills of learners, as well as their differences in speed of learning, and differences in learning style. These differences simply are not handled adequately by lectures or other group-paced methods. There can be some small- and large-group activities, however, within an individually paced total program.

2. *Instructional strategy.* While there are, indeed, occasions on which problems arise that only a teacher can solve, remember

that thousands of people learn by correspondence courses, independent study, etc. Few valid instances exist when it can be fully shown that "only a teacher can do this." It is even hard to show, in many cases, that the teacher does it better than do other media. Do not perpetuate the myth that individual differences are really provided for by large infusions of group-paced methods. Thousands of self-contained media modules of all sorts are used from the first grade onward to adult learning in many subjects and skill areas. The coming concept is that of the teacher as manager of learning, not the presenter of information. Thousands of classrooms are using individualized programs in reading and math at the K-6 levels.

There could be a few instances in which a brief lecture is prepared, but the instructional events so accomplished must be supplemented when appropriate by learner activities.

3. *Media*. Where many media are considered by students in assignment 3, their rationales make better use of theory than is the case for students who prescribe conventional instruction.

4. *Formative evaluation*. To improve instruction, it must be "captured" in print, tape recordings, or other means, so that it does not "disappear" as does a lecture, which is never done the same again, unless recorded. If the materials "don't hold still," the formative evaluation data are not usable for making improvements.

5. *Individualized instruction*. It is often said that teacher-led, group paced instruction is "tried and true" (of proven effectiveness) while other media are only "aids to the teacher." This idea is now yielding rapidly to recognition of the proposition that the purpose of schooling is *learning*, not *teaching*. Some teachers have even been heard to say "I taught it, but the kids didn't learn it."

The "proven" teacher-led instruction is deceptive because it does not separate the effects of learning achieved by the learner by his own efforts with the textbook and other materials, from the learning resulting from what the teacher did in class.

Consider your own learning: does most of it take place at home in your study of the materials, or in the classroom?

Pupils who frequently experience failure by conventional methods often improve rapidly under an individualized instructional system (see Chapter 8). Such systems seem to work well because they include the following components:

a. *Entry tests*, administered at the beginning of the school year, to determine where in the overall skill sequence (in reading, for example) the pupils should begin to work.

b. *Alternate materials* for each objective, to permit the pupil to learn by the most suitable media and materials.

c. *Self-pacing* of study, by which the pupil takes whatever time is necessary to master each objective.

d. *Frequent testing* or monitoring of progress so that a pupil's problems are detected quickly.

e. *Remedial provisions* for correcting one small failure before it turns into a long-term failure.

f. *Small- and large-group activities* when several pupils have reached the same stage of progress in critical skills.

The outcome of such programs is usually steady progress for almost all pupils, regardless of the *rate* of progress as compared to other pupils. And this progress results from carefully designed self-instructional materials. The success of the system then depends on the materials and on how well the teacher manages the system, not on teacher-led, group instruction.

6. In summary, the skills to be achieved in this course are best demonstrated by making the instruction as "materials-dependent" as possible, and by relying on a teacher to manage the system. Once such a system is operating well, the teacher has *more time* for conferences with students, either to diagnose difficult problems or to provide additional challenges to pupils.

7. Taking 630 itself as an example, the instructor has more time for conferences and written feedback to students than if lectures rather than materials were the primary learning resource. (In 1968 we had to use lectures due to the absence of materials; now we don't.) It took years to develop the materials we needed, and they will require continued updating and revision. But students are doing better now than in 1968. This is *not* because the instructor has learned to talk better. He doesn't even have to be an impressive platform speaker for students to do well in the course.

8. Finally, we can't give group feedback because you are all working in different subject areas; this requires individual feedback, just as most problems that students encounter can better be settled in conference rather than in the classroom.

Chapter 16

Income Tax Preparation

Amy S. Ackerman
Florida State University

The above Chapter title is employed for consistency in style with other Chapters in the book.

However, the original title of the total product of the course was as shown on the following page.

For the purpose of this book, revisions were performed on this product by the author, and are within the Chapter.

How to Pay Taxes With a Smile—
Rather Than Cash!

Assignment No. 1

A.S. Ackerman
IDD 630
July 12, 1976

1. Course Description
This course is a series of non-credit workshops designed to
provide an opportunity for instructors (teachers, professors, and
industry or military trainers) to acquire skills in the planning and
preparation of federal income tax returns. In spite of the differing
settings in which instructors work, they share many types of
activities and expenses in their professional encounters.

Many instructors are unaware of the multitude of deductions
for which they are legally qualified, and thus they overpay their
tax bills. This is in contrast to certain groups of people who are
stereotyped for utilizing questionable "loopholes" and the services
of highly paid accountants in order to pay minimal taxes, if any.
This course familiarizes instructors with the tax codes, and enables
them to develop skills in not only calculating deductions, but also,
in generating them! The focal point, of course, is on that of
educational deductions. The learner will conclude, after completing this course, that training in accounting skills is not a
prerequisite to preparing tax returns.

The course also stimulates the participants to take a closer
look into their daily routines. Since tax planning is indeed a
12-month activity and not only *circa* April 15th, one should
continuously perform self-analysis and evaluation concerning his
or her financial strategies. These self-management practices are
addressed during this course. Recommendations for revisions in
tax planning strategies assist the participants by increasing their
self-management of financial affairs. As is discussed in the life-long

objectives, it is hoped that the learners will transfer applicable tax principles to other areas of life as a means of developing strategies to cope with the complexities of modern life.

2. Importance for Intended Learners

Many instructors, who comprise the target population, are unaware of the tax codes, IRS forms, and techniques for synthesizing them with an individual's expenses in order to obtain maximum legal deductions. This course is important because it enables the participants to apply the tax codes and forms to their personal cases as educators.

Often, people do not desire to maintain accurate records, 12 months of the year, unless they can be shown examples of the many deductions they would forget if they depended on memory. Others take the simplified method and file the "standard form." Their excuse is that they lack the necessary minimum in order to itemize deductions. Often hundreds of dollars would be saved by itemizing, if the learners could be made aware of certain deductions which apply to them. Again, the latter is a major goal in this course.

Many instructors are not in a position to engage the services of an accountant to prepare their tax returns. Therefore, the acquisition of the skills provided by this course attempts to permit instructors an equal opportunity to "avoid" paying unnecessary taxes by taking advantage of maximum deductions to which they are entitled. It should be emphasized that the intent of this course is not to encourage tax "evasion," which is failing to pay a required tax.

Lastly, the course is important because any fees or other expenses related to taking the course are tax-deductible.

3. Life-Long Objectives

The student will
- increase his self-management and reduce dependency upon external resources such as professional services;
- conduct continuous self-evaluation of his life style and habits, making revisions as deemed desirable in planning for the future;
- extend his thinking beyond that which is obvious;

- enhance his cognitive strategies and develop new ones to be used in problem-finding and problem-solving; and
- keep abreast of the tax codes, and apply skills acquired during this course for the remainder of his life.*

It is hoped that as a result of this instruction the student's mind will be stimulated. By engaging in activities which require utilization of one's thought processes in order to originate novel results to relevant problems (one's own tax return), the cognitive strategies of an individual might thus be enhanced. The designer recognizes that evidence does not demonstrate that transfer will take place from self-management of financial affairs to other areas of living and life style, but research does suggest that such "remote transfer" is more likely to take place if the teaching is designed for that additional goal.

4. End-of-Course Objectives

I. The student will generate his personal itemized tax return, encompassing maximum deductions and credits to which he is legally entitled.

II. The student will be able to originate a strategy for money management and tax planning after careful analysis of his most current itemized tax return. He will choose to adhere to the devised strategy including maintaining accurate records and receipts.

III. He or she will develop year-around tax consciousness when making everyday decisions.**

5. Unit Objectives

Unit A: Given a list of qualified and nonqualified educational deductions, and tax guides, the student will state the applicable tax rule and recommended IRS form which could be utilized for completion of the tax return, paying the least amount

---

*The reader should note that this "life-long objective" was suggested by the instructor as an addition. The author concurs with the instructor that life-long objectives should refer to the content of the course itself, as well as to transfer effects.

**This objective was recommended by the instructor.

of tax. References of any nature may be used, except human resources.

Unit B: The student will be able to generate miscellaneous educational deductions and credits for which he is currently eligible, calculate them, and enter them on the appropriate IRS forms. He will also be able to originate strategies to strengthen any educational deductions he has generated which may be considered "grey areas." Resources are permitted, except humans.

Unit C: The student will choose to maintain accurate records and receipts and identify a form which might assist him in doing so.

Note to the Reader

This student product was originally submitted in a unique manner. For purposes of checking congruence of specific objectives with the tests, the author designed "fold-outs" which contained each specific objective. Thus, the reader could analyze each test and specific objective simultaneously, which avoided constant "page-flipping."

The author also designed and produced an overlay transparency containing the five components of an objective as described in Chapter 3 of this book. Utilizing this transparency according to the designated alignment, the reader could also observe the appropriate labeling of the components as required in Assignment 1, while examining each specific objective and its accompanying test.

Due to publishing constraints for the reproduction of this student product, the author has revised her original format to eliminate both the "fold-outs" and the transparencies. Also, to save space here, only the first two of four objectives (and their accompanying tests) written for Unit B are reproduced here. The revised form of the two objectives (see Figure 1) and the corresponding tests are placed next.

Test—Unit B: Objective 1

Directions: Using the "straight-line" depreciation method, calculate each item below to determine the amount of deprecia-

Situation	Capability	Object	Action	Tools/Constraints
Unit B				
Objective 1				
Given five depreciable items eligible for deduction, purchase date, cost, and useful life,	the student will demonstrate the	straight-line depreciation method for depreciating items	by calculating the deduction of each item for the applicable tax year.	Some items must be prorated. Any resource may be used except human.
Objective 2				
Given a list of 10 items, purchased this tax year, their use, and estimated life,	the student will classify	investment-credit items	by entering a "Q" in front of those items that qualify, and by entering an "N" in front of those that do not qualify.	Any available resources may be used except human.

Figure 1: Two objectives from Unit B.

tion deduction to which the instructor (purchaser) is entitled for the 1976 tax year. All items are depreciable and qualify as deductions for this instructor. Note that some items must be prorated due to their purchase date. You may use any resources except human.

Item	Purchase Date	Cost	Useful Life	1976 Deduction for Depreciation
1. Tape recorder	1-1-76	$ 50	5 yrs.	....
2. Books	9-1-76	120	10	....
3. Attache case	7-7-76	30	3	....
4. Desk (Home office)	1-1-76	160	10	....
5. Slide trays	1-1-76	20	10	....

Grading

The student must score four out of five correct answers (80 percent) in order to continue to the next activity. A score of less than 80 percent will direct the student to double-check his work. If the student scores below 80 percent for a reason other than carelessness, he will be branched to a remedial activity.

Test—Unit B: Objective 2

Directions: The following items were purchased by an instructor during the applicable tax year. Enter a "Q" in front of items that qualify for "Investment Credit," and an "N" in front of those items that do not qualify. You may use any resources except human.

	Item	Use	Estimated Life
....	1. Books	Professional reference	10 years
....	2. House	10% Home office	40
....	3. Calculator	Classroom	3
....	4. Suits	Wear to classes	8

....	5. Audio tapes	Classroom	1
....	6. Slide trays	Classroom	3
....	7. UHF TV receiver	Educational broadcasts	10
....	8. Camera	Classroom	5
....	9. Attache case	Professional	2
....	10. Portable room Air Conditioner	Home office	8

Grading

The student must score 90 percent (nine correct responses) in order to continue to the next activity. A score below 90 percent will direct the student to locate the applicable "Investment Credit" rule for each of his incorrect responses.

Note to the Reader

The instructor's feedback regarding specific objective No. 2 of this student product raised questions concerning the type of learning classification of this objective. On one hand, the learner might have to apply rules to complete the test, which would change the capability verb to "demonstrate," rather than "classify" (rule versus defined concept). However, the author originally intended the learner to use definitions emphasizing "estimated life" and "use" of items being considered for "Investment Credit."

As per the instructor's recommendation, the final decision regarding the classification of specific objective No. 2 was deferred until assignment 2. The importance of these iterative cycles should be kept in mind during the design of instruction.

(It is entirely possible that the same test performance could require several domain or type of learning categories for several different learners, due to the differences in knowledge and skills as people enter the course. A performance which requires much conscious effort [problem-solving and rule-using] for the beginning student may be performed almost "unconsciously" by the expert. Thus, the classification of a performance changes for a given person as time elapses.)

Assignment 2

A.S. Ackerman
IDD 630
July 27, 1976

Intellectual Skill Objective:
Unit B—Objective 2
Given a list of 10 properties purchased this tax year, their uses, costs, estimated lives, and a set of IRS forms, the student will generate the amount of Investment Credit (if any), for which each qualifies by calculating the applicable amount. Resources of any type may be used, except human. Some properties included in the list do not qualify.

Note to the Reader

In order to prepare assignment 2 for this publication, several revisions in format were made by the author.

The original analysis appeared in a multi-dimensional format, utilizing transparent overlays. The **static** sheet consisted of a diagram of a "pure hierarchy," which pertains only to intellectual skills; an **overlay** which contained information objectives could be placed above the hierarchy, thus changing its composition to that of an "instructional map" (see Chapters 5, 7, 13), due to the presence of objectives in domains of learning other than intellectual skills. The reader should observe that in this diagram subordinate competencies No. 1, 2, 5, 7 are information objectives, and designated by dotted boxes.

Another overlay was also included in the original product. This overlay "color-coded" each box (subordinate competency) with its corresponding type of learning. Since the color coding is an intentional redundancy, due to the specification of learning types also located in the key to the subordinate competencies (boxes), the reader is not slighted with the absence of the color coding in this publication. However, it is interesting to note that this student's hierarchy does increase in complexity from bottom (concrete concepts in this example), to defined concepts, rules, *and finally, problem-solving at the top of the hierarchy diagram. The color coding did nicely illustrate this progression, and served as a realistic example of the process.*

Concerning the diagram, entering competencies are those which appear below the double dotted line. The competencies which correspond with the numbers and letters are also located in this Assignment, along with each type of learning represented.

The reader may recall some discussion in assignment 1 as to the questionable classification of a specific objective in this product.

Please note the revision of the intellectual skill objective B-2, which is analyzed for assignment 2. This was deemed necessary in order to reclassify the original objective, and to enable the designer to address a more complex objective for this assignment. The role of this objective in the course also appears to be more appropriate than the original objective. In fact, the original B-2 objective presently exists as subordinate competency 9 in the analysis for this assignment. However, the capability verb has been revised in order to acknowledge demonstration of rules which are necessary for the performance of this objective. The designer is aware that the test item for B-2 is no longer congruent, and for course adoption, revisions would be necessary.

Unit B—Objective 2: Learning Hierarchy

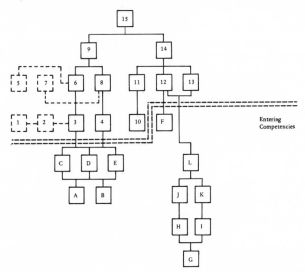

Entering Competencies

At first glance, the number of entering competencies may appear to be quite large; however, one must keep in mind that most of these entering competencies were taught in previous objectives within this unit.

Entering Competencies	*Type of Learning*
A. Classify objects as tangible or intangible.	Def. concept
B. Classify objects that are personal property.	Def. concept
C. Classify properties by useful life.	Def. concept
D. Classify properties as depreciable or nondepreciable.	Def. concept
E. Classify properties relating to professional responsibility.	Def. concept
F. Classify months of the calendar year according to their prorated percentage for purchased items.	Def. concept
G. Demonstrate basic math operations (multiply, divide, add, subtract).	Rule
H. Demonstrate basic math operations using fractions.	Rule
I. Demonstrate basic math operations using decimals.	Rule
J. Demonstrate conversion rule (fraction to percent).	Rule
K. Demonstrate calculation of specified percent when given monetary figure.	Rule
L. Demonstrate prorating a specified amount of time or money.	Rule

Subordinate Competencies (Numbers indicate teaching sequence)	*Type of Learning*
1. State difference and similarities between deductions and credits.	Information Obj.

2. State definition of investment credit. — Information Obj.

3. Classify possible investment credit properties by giving examples which are in accordance with the definition. — Def. concept

4. Classify possible non-investment credit properties by giving examples in accordance with the definition. — Def. concept

5. State the qualifying rules for investment credit. — Information Obj.

6. Given a list of properties, *all* qualifying for investment credit, and their detailed situations, demonstrate qualifying rules by providing the reason why each property qualifies. — Rule

7. State the nonqualifying rules for investment credit. — Information Obj.

8. Given a list of items (properties) that do *not* qualify for investment credit, and their detailed situations, demonstrate nonqualifying rules by determining the reason each property does not qualify. — Rule

9. Given qualifying and nonqualifying properties purchased this tax year, their uses, and estimated useful lives, generate the status of each as an investment credit by determining its qualification or nonqualification. — Problem-Solving

10. Identify the appropriate IRS form for investment credit. — Concrete Concept

11. Demonstrate interpretation of the IRS form for investment credit, by determining the applicable percentage investment credit when given useful life of property. — Rule

12. Demonstrate calculation of portion of cost in percent applicable for investment credit when given purchase date of qualified property.   Rule

13. Demonstrate the calculation of time in percent for which a property is used for professional responsibilities by prorating when given time in fractions.   Rule

14. Given a qualified property, its useful life, and purchase date, generate the percentage of cost for which it qualifies for investment credit.   Problem-Solving

(The above 14 subordinate competencies support Specific Objective 15 as it appears below.)

15. Given a list of 10 properties purchased this tax year, their uses, costs, estimated useful lives, and a set of IRS forms, generate the amount of investment credit (if any) for which each qualifies, by calculating the amounts to which each property is legally qualified. Resources of any type may be used, except human. Some items included do not qualify.   Problem-Solving

The course sequence is designed in accordance with the principle of progressive differentiation. Unit A, an information objective, provides general and inclusive ideas, and serves as an advance organizer. Unit B addresses the general ideas from Unit A, but in a detailed and specific manner. It is within Unit B that the intellectual objective analyzed for assignment 2 is located.

Synthesis and transfer from Units A and B are desirable conditions for Unit C. The events of instruction within a representative objective and subordinate competencies will reveal in assignment 3 the methods for facilitating this transfer. The cases and examples cited hopefully will serve as models for the establishment of the attitudinal objective in Unit C. In addition, after having acquired the necessary intellectual skills from Unit B, the learner becomes cognizant of exactly how he may personally benefit from Unit C (maintaining accurate records and receipts).

The necessity for specific detail of data is clearly observed as a result of the exercises in Unit B. Thus, in order to reduce his tax by increasing his deductions and credits, the learner should choose to maintain records. Additional reasons for record keeping are also addressed in Unit C, such as a means to generate possible deductions/credits, simplify calculations, substantiate data in the event of an audit, and provide a vehicle for self-analysis of money management.

It should be mentioned that this course encompasses additional units and objectives which are not included in the course No. 630 assignments.

After successful completion of the units, including mastery of the objectives, the learner should be able to perform the end-of-course objectives.

Now, for a closer look at Unit B.

Objective B-1 enables the learner to acquire the skill of calculating "straight-line" depreciation, which is a *deduction* applying to personal property relating to one's professional responsibilities. It introduces many of the concepts and rules that are necessary in Unit B, thus these concepts and rules later appear as entering competencies in objective B-2.

Unit B is an example whereby the learning sequence is different from the real-life performance sequence. When completing income tax returns one would first generate possible deductions, and *then* address types of "credits" for which he may qualify. (Credits are subtracted directly from the total tax assessed for an individual, *after* all deductions are included.) However, the intellectual skill analyzed in assignment 2 (Unit B-2) directly follows B-1 and precedes B-3, 4, for these reasons:

1. B-1 serves as an advance organizer for B-2, since concepts (tangible properties, etc.) are addressed with respect to their depreciation.

2. Many concepts and rules acquired in B-1 are then represented as entering competencies in B-2, thus justifying the sequence.

3. The concept of "credit" (versus deduction), is introduced as a "comparative organizer" under which the units and objectives to follow may be subsumed.
4. Acquiring the intellectual skill of calculating investment credit (B-2) is such that it provides immediate feedback and reinforcement to the learner. It is not a long, drawn-out process such as generating the total amount of educational deductions for which one is qualified (the omitted B-3 objective), which is a more complex undertaking. Therefore, this skill acquisition, (B-2), provides self-confidence within the learner due to immediate and observable results. (This is analogous to the rationale for spiral sequencing.)
5. B-2 (investment credit), is often totally unfamiliar to learners (especially instructors, who compose the target population for this course). This, in itself, motivates the student to continue the course in order to learn about additional types of deductions (B-3) and credits for which he may qualify.
6. B-2 provides a vehicle for transfer to the attitudinal objective in Unit C. (Choose to maintain records.) The necessary personal and financial data are such that most likely are not stored in one's memory. Retrieval without records for April 15th would be a nightmare, and would most likely be impossible without a photographic memory.
7. B-2 dovetails with a more complex objective (B-3)—educational deductions—while being subsumed under the comparative organizer of "credits and deductions."
8. B-2, with support from the instructional events, facilitates transfer to the omitted B-4 objective (converting grey areas).

Attainment of the end-of-course and life-long objectives is enhanced via B-2. Again, the instructional events, which are not present in this assignment, describe the manner in which the objective is taught, in order to provide for desirable transfer.

Section 9 of Assignment 2

Information Objectives—Unit B-2 subordinate competencies.

Sub. Comp. 1. State differences and similarities between a deduction and a credit. The anchoring concept of a deduction has been established in the learner's cognitive structure; thus it is hopefully now clear, relevant, and stable. This information objective serves as a comparative organizer in order that the concept of credit be acquired through correlative subsumption. This information objective also functions as an advance organizer for objectives B-2 and B-3.

Sub. Comp. 2. State the definition of investment credit. Due to the fact that this information objective is an example of a previously learned concept (sub. comp. 1), the acquisition of sub. comp. 2 takes place through derivative subsumption. This also serves as an advance organizer and facilitates transfer from the entering competencies to sub. comp. 3 and 4.

Sub. Comp. 5 and 7. State qualifying and nonqualifying rules for investment credit. This prompt leads the learner to recall concepts learned in previous subordinate competencies, and cues the relationship necessary for demonstration of the rules. These information objectives act as transfer mechanisms from the defined concepts 3 and 4 to rule application 6 and 8.

Assignment 3

A.S. Ackerman
IDD 630
August 10, 1976

Learning Environment
Due to the nature of the skills being taught in this course, diffusion may be desirable on a national (and perhaps, international) basis. Instructors employed by the military, industry, or educational institutions are required to file U.S. federal income tax returns, whether they work stateside or abroad. This may constitute a need for an instructional program such as this one, to be offered via remote-access delivery systems. However, as a prototype, this particular instructional unit must undergo formative evaluation stages prior to any type of formal plans for extensive accessibility.

The designer acknowledges the possibility of mass media communications as vehicles for supplying the necessary stimuli for each instructional event noted in assignment 3.

The adult learners who comprise the target population are unable to attend formal classes held at specified times and locations, which eliminates a traditional format, and requires careful consideration of the individual needs of the learners.

The course could, in reality, be designed in a multi-dimensional manner. The following types of offerings might someday exist:
A.   Local—on-campus
B.   Local—off-campus
C.   Remote—mass media communication
D.   Remote—correspondence
The previously exemplified diversity imposes additional criteria and constraints concerning the media being considered for the desired stimuli in each instructional event.

Conditions and Constraints
1.   Remote and local accessibility
2.   Flexible times

3. Flexible branching
4. Live instructors are *not* desired for conduct of lessons
5. Self-instructional packaging—replicable
6. Self-pacing
7. Self-correctional mechanisms with remedial options
8. Exposure to large varieties of media in order to consider application in teaching situations among members of the target population
9. Motivating
10. Alternate delivery systems in the event hardware malfunctions
11. Editing capability to keep abreast of latest tax codes
12. Ease of equipment operation
13. Efficient (when possible)
14. Appropriate to learner (age, education level)
15. Potential for diversified grouping if so desired (small-group, large-group, in addition to individualized instruction)

Current design and production resources are extremely limited for this course. However, the present author speculates that after empirical data are collected from formative evaluations of prototype materials, interest may be expressed by commercial, industrial, military, governmental, or perhaps even educational organizations to support the financing of design, production, evaluation, and diffusion of the course materials.

If funds become available, the original author would supervise the remaining design, production, and evaluation stages.

A major resource which is currently available is the medium of cable television for diffusion. A recent ruling requires that all cable stations provide a channel devoted to educational broadcasts, with no financial strings attached. Additional media, such as communication satellites and networking (telelecture, telenote, telecomputer), enable theoretical plans for diffusion to become a tenable reality.

People often refer to radio as the "hidden medium," and although educational FM stations are currently available for broadcasting, the potential has not yet been realized.

Thus, remote delivery systems are a reality today for this course. Local-access (on-campus) takes place in a state-funded university in conjunction with other noncredit workshops. The local-access environment is such that a learner positions himself at a console, and various media are available to him by merely activating control switches. Perhaps management could be conducted through computers, when funding resources are available for this course.

The unusually large amount of media changes in this program can be justified. The intended learners, who deliver instruction to facilitate learning in their own settings, have expressed an interest in experiencing increased exposure to alternate forms of media delivery systems. The designer has kept in mind that the medium is selected *after* the appropriate stimulus has been determined. It should be mentioned that the entire course is also offered in printed modular format in the event some learners prefer that form of instruction.

Unit B—Objective 2
Subordinate Competency No. 9
Given qualifying and nonqualifying properties purchased this tax year, their uses, and estimated useful lives, students will *generate* the status of each as an investment credit by determining its qualification or nonqualification.

Note to the Reader

Only three of the original nine instructional events are shown on the next three pages. Originally, all nine events, as discussed in Chapter 7, were employed. Events # 3, # 4, and # 7 were chosen for use here in order to illustrate the variety of media chosen, and the different relationships between "theoretically best" media and the final media choices. These three pages also illustrate a simultaneous analysis for two different learning environments— on-campus and off-campus.

Unit B—Objective 2
Subordinate Competency # 9   Type of Learning: Problem-Solving

Instructional Event
3. Stimulating recall of prerequisite learnings

Stimuli	Media Options	Theoretically Best Media	Pragmatic Media Selections	
			Remote Access (Off-Campus)	Local Access (On-Campus)
Verbal (spoken/printed)	CAI/CMI Telenote Communication satellite Programmed materials/audio Telelecture Radio Videotape/disc	CAI/CMI	Telelecture Answer sheet	Programmed materials Audio cassette

Rationale: It is now appropriate (after events 1 and 2, not shown here) to add another stimulus (verbal/spoken), and a medium variation to avoid boredom. CAI/CMI would be the most desirable media, since the necessity for remedial work in any deficient areas could be immediately diagnosed if the learner cannot demonstrate entering competencies. The learner could be branched to a remedial program prior to continuation of this program, and thus augment the deficient areas. The pragmatic selection delays use of CAI until later points in the instructional program.

Prescription: The audio-tape (cassette) is to be designed to prompt the learner to recall relevant Investment Credit subordinate rules and information, while simultaneously serving as an assessment of the presence of desired entering competencies within the learner. Acknowledging the "encoding specificity principle," care must be taken to provide the learner with retrieval cues which are comparable to those used for original encoding and storage of the relevant rules. Questions are to refer to the appropriate concepts, subordinate rules, and their relationship. Remedial work should be available. Direct the learner to the next activity.

Unit B—Objective 2
Subordinate Competency #9　　　　　　　　　　Type of Learning: Problem-Solving

Instructional Event
4. Presenting the stimulus material

			Media Selections	
			Pragmatic Media Selections	
Stimuli	Media Options	Theoretically Best Media	Remote Access (Off-Campus)	Local Access (On-Campus)
Verbal (spoken) Visual (motion) Live visitation	Programmed materials Interview Sound on slide Film loop/sound 16mm film/sound Videotape/disc Communication satellite Field trip Dramatization—case studies	Field trips (Eye witness observations)	CATV (filmloops/sound)	Filmloops/sound

Rationale: Considering the age of the learner, efficiency, replicability, transportation constraints, and such, a field trip is unrealistic. An alternate means to supply the desired stimuli, while presenting novel problem situations (real and represented), is to capture them on film. The medium of film enables instruction to become replicable. Filmloops are self-contained, self-paced, and may be viewed several times, if so desired. Remote accessibility is possible through cable television and a film chain.

Prescription: Stimulus materials are to consist of five filmloops, four minutes each, color super 8mm (cartridge). The "talent" in each filmloop is to be filmed at a slower speed, which creates time lapse effect when projected at normal viewing speed. The filmloops are to depict segments of daily routines of five instructors, (college professor, elementary school teacher, military trainer, industrial instructor, and an administrator in an educational institution).

Unit B—Objective 2
Subordinate Competency #9

Type of Learning: Problem-Solving

Instructional Event
7. Providing feedback about performance correctness

Media Selections

Stimuli	Media Options	Theoretically Best Media	Pragmatic Media Selections	
			Remote Access (Off-Campus)	Local Access (On-Campus)
Verbal (printed or spoken)	CAI/CMI Programmed materials Checklist Transvision insert Audiotape Radio Telelecture Videotape Live demonstration—IRS agent	CAI/CMI	CAI	CAI

Rationale: This is an appropriate point of instruction for use of this medium. Analysis of each situation in instructional event #6 (not shown in this book) should take place, and thus the learner is informed of the correctness of his performance. As a result of the learner responses and his performance evaluation, the computer either directs the learner to the next activity (instructional event #8), or immediately branches him to remedial instruction if diagnosed as necessary. This feedback also provides review of the rules as each situation is once again examined.

Prescription: The CAI program is to reanalyze each situational example in instructional event #6, and ask the learner to respond to questions concerning his performance, decisions, and justifications. In this manner the learner performs a guided self-evaluation. Depending upon the learner's responses, the program provides reinforcement, supplemental information, remedial work, or foundations for future transfer. The learner should be directed to the next instructional event (#8).

Assignment 4

A.S. Ackerman
IDD 630
August 24, 1976

Note to the Reader

For purposes of this book, assignment 3 was reduced to three of the original nine events of instruction, for the competencies being analyzed, with accompanying "rationales" and "prescriptions" for each event, as recommended in Chapter 7.

In practice, next the instructional designer would "fill the prescriptions" for each instructional event by preparing first draft scripts, and then the materials would be produced.

Due to time constraints, assignment 4 requires the students to prepare scripts for only one hour of instruction, which often involves more than one instructional event. To conserve space, only an excerpt from the original eighteen pages of assignment 4 is now presented.

Unit B—Objective 2
Subordinate competency 9. Given qualifying and nonqualifying properties purchased this tax year, their uses, and estimated useful lives, the students will generate the status of each as an Investment Credit by determining its qualification or nonqualification.

Type of learning: Problem-Solving.
Instructional Event: # 4; presenting the stimulus material.
Stimuli: Verbal (spoken) and visual (motion).
Medium: Super 8mm sound filmloop.

As the prescription indicates for this instructional event, the filmloops depict segments of daily routines of five instructors, (college professor, public school teacher, military trainer, industrial instructor, and an administrator in an educational institution). Several of the loops utilize techniques to create the effect of time lapse photography, in order to expedite observations of the daily routines.

The learner may view the loops as many times as he or she deems necessary, and may stop and start the loops as frequently as desired. The filmloops have accompanying videotapes in instructional event # 5 (learning guidance), and in events # 6 and # 7 performance and feedback take place via CAI.

Instructional Event # 4—Presenting Stimulus Material:
Scenario for Super 8mm Filmloop (Sound)

Title: "Are there *meaty* tax breaks without the fear of being *roasted* by IRS?"

Talent:

Pipsqueak stick figures	Used for gaining attention with technique to create animation effect during introduction.
Edward R. Burrow	Interviewer with deep, deliberate voice. Appears as tall, slender, dark-haired character. (Scripted as "Ed.")
John Q. Taxpayer	Tenth grade drama teacher in his mid-forties. He is dressed in shirt, tie, and V-neck sweater without suit coat. (Also wearing checked pants and wing-tipped shoes.) Bald. (Scripted as "TP.") Smokes a pipe.
Spouse of John Q. Taxpayer	Sharp in appearance, pleasant. Teacher with doctorate in education. (Scripted as "Wife.")

Location:

Residence of John Q. Taxpayer

Video	*Audio*
1. Title superimposed over frying pan with stick figures labeled "taxpayers" dancing in it. Stove burner is labeled "IRS." Use	Saran wrap crinkled over microphone to create special effect of fire. Pipsqueak voices are yelling "ooh, ah, it's hot!"

Video

Audio

cable release to shoot series of still frames, moving stick figures each frame in order to create animation effect when projected.

One pipsqueak voice says, "enough of this IRS frying pan jazz, let's get on to the nitty-gritty and a little more serious."

2. Camera dollies out from kitchen through hallway and on out through front door. Use slower film speed when shooting in order to create fast motion when projected. If camera has zoom capability, use it to create same effect, zooming from kitchen through hallway and out front door.

3. Front of house—sunrise scene.

Rooster crows.
Music begins, part from *William Tell Overture*, "Swiss Alps at Dawning"
Music fades.

4. Front doorway of house with Ed walking toward it.

Ed: "Continuing our teacher visitation tours, this morning we begin at the residence of John Q. Taxpayer, a tenth grade drama teacher."

5. Doorbell—Ed pushing it.

Doorbell rings (traditional chime effect).

6. Door opens, wife appears, and smiles as she glances at her digital watch, set for 7:02 a.m.

Ed: "Hi! I'm Edward R. Burrow. Is your husband up yet for our interview?"

7. Camera trucks down hall with wife and Ed walking around corner. Shot of study with TP at his desk.

Wife: "He's *still* up! He pulled another all nighter, but I guess his grad work will be worth it.

8. Camera pans to follow wife picking up sign.

Soon we'll have a new name plate on our front door."

Video   *Audio*

9. Sign—which reads "Dr. and Dr. John Q. Taxpayer."

10. Wife and Ed in doorway, TP at desk.

Ed: "So, there will be two 'doctors in the house'!"

11. Wife walks out of room.

12. TP turns around, stands to shake hands with Ed, and sits again, monitoring for Ed to also sit down.

Ed: "Oh, is this where a teacher spends his work time outside of the classroom? Might this be considered your 'home office'?"

13. TP sits and rocks back on his chair with Ed next to him. (Typewriter is in view.)   A*

14. Typewriter†

B*

TP: "Just sit tightly while I finish typing the cover page of this paper for my grad course. This electric typewriter has been one of the *keys* to my success. It's three years old but I just invested in a complete overhaul and repair to the *tune* of $38.00 (audio chime sounds) and it works like a dream, I want you to *note*.

*The upper case letters refer to items for consideration of investment credit qualification and are analyzed in instructional event # 5.

†The original script included camera angles; however, they have been omitted for purposes of this publication.

End of Excerpt

Note to the Reader

Although the original script was arbitrarily interrupted at this point for presentation here, hopefully the reader grasps the flavor of the content and style in which this student "fills her prescription" for this event of instruction (presenting the stimulus material).

The original assignment 4 script was followed by videotapes, which provide "learning guidance" (event 5) to the viewer by analyzing the content of the filmloop; however, for publication purposes, these have been omitted.

For additional samples of scripts taken from first draft materials, also written by students, the reader may refer to the *Student's Guide to Handbook of Procedures for the Design of Instruction*, by Briggs—cited elsewhere in this book.

The reader, having read excerpts from the four assignments for which this student product was designed, should be reminded that due to the time constraint, a ten-week quarter, which also included reading and study time, the author has only developed *samples* of an entire course.

An ideal situation for completion of the design of this specific product would apply the approach described in Chapter 9, which would utilize a design team, and a great deal of time and resources.

The author of this student product plans to continue her efforts in the design of instructional programs, utilizing the principles advocated in this book.

Transition to Chapter 17

This final Chapter is a second "student product," this time from an *introductory* course in instructional design.

While the assignments for that course do not include all the details required in the advanced course from which Chapter 16 is a product, the reader can see that the same design model was used.

Also, the "assignments" were in "smaller chunks" for the introductory course, so there were more assignments, and they covered a broader scope. Thus, the advanced course (Chapter 16) emphasized media analysis and design of first-draft materials, while the introductory course (Chapter 17) included a simple needs analysis and a *plan* for formative and summative evaluations. The reader will note that the objective is repeated at the opening of most assignments; the students were taught to do this to keep themselves "on target."

No corrective changes have been made; the series of assignments is reproduced here just as Ms. Medsker turned them in during the academic quarter, with the exception that several pages have been deleted to conserve space. The nature of the deleted materials is noted at appropriate points in this Chapter.

Chapter 17

World Hunger

Karen Medsker
Florida State University

Assignment 1: Needs and Goals

The course proposed here is to be designed for use by study groups (for example, by church, club, or other organizational sub-groups) of individuals concerned about the topic of world hunger. It is assumed, for practical reasons, that the format will be a series of approximately four group sessions, based on recommended individual "homework." The target population is composed largely of adults with at least normal intelligence and with at least high school reading level. Hopefully, it will be a course which is adaptable to a variety of learning situations.

The reason for such a course is that among certain people there exists the perceived need to understand the world hunger problem and to learn how to deal with it in an informed and realistic manner. This global problem, as important as it is to today's world citizen, may become even more critical within the next several years. Widespread starvation implies possible redistribution of the world's economic resources, likely to be accompanied by tremendous shifts in power and changes in ways of life. Present world views, economic and social structures, and personal value systems are threatened. While many strive to confront this present and future food crisis, vast numbers of people know (and perhaps care) very little about the causes and solutions. The desired state of affairs would be an informed, sympathetic, and active populace, while the actual situation is far from that ideal.

If time and resources permit, a thorough needs analysis should be done to verify the perceived need for this course and to identify specific requirements in terms of objectives, content, and format. Ideally, a survey would be made of potential users of the course. The general level of public knowledge about the topic should be ascertained. Among others, experts in the fields of nutrition, hunger, underdeveloped nations, agriculture, food science, and public administration should be contacted. Input from these sources could help insure that all the proper questions in this area are identified and addressed by the designed course. Without such a complete needs analysis, however, it is still possible from talking to limited numbers of people and from reading current literature to draw some tentative conclusions about what is needed. For example:

1. The present level of related information is quite low for most people; thus, basic instruction should be provided.

2. Resource material must be condensed into manageable and easy-to-digest form, especially in view of the time constraints of busy people.

3. The instruction should serve as a preparation for direct action, rather than being entirely academic.

4. The only real solutions to world hunger may require attitude and behavior change as well as cognitive learning.

Based on the needs analysis, the course goals are stated as follows:

After participating in the study group, each person will:

1. State the political, economic, social, biological, and psychological causes of world hunger and describe their interrelationships.

2. Identify and evaluate possible solution approaches.

3. Generate new proposals for solutions to the problem.

4. Choose to become involved in personal and public action strategies aimed at combatting the world hunger problem.

The course goals will probably be approached in the order given, although some overlap might occur.

Assignment 2: Behavioral Objectives and Subordinate Competencies

I. Intellectual Skill Objective

Goal 3: To generate new solutions to the world hunger problem. Behavioral objective (problem-solving): Having achieved goals 1 and 2 [omitted in this book], and given appropriate resource materials, the participants will generate a set of specific solutions to the world hunger problem by writing a list of proposed U.S. foreign and domestic policies, using group discussion to obtain consensus within a two-hour period.

The objective has been classified as problem-solving, because subordinate rules and concepts must be applied to the task. While it is possible that some learners may use "creativity" and come up with original solutions, it is expected that the thinking required will occur within the same context as the other instruction in the course, so that problem-solving is the most probable outcome. Since the designer does not wish to specify the exact list of solutions that the group will generate in fulfilling this objective, flexibility will be allowed. However, certain items may predictably be on the list, given the subject matter involved. For example: "The U.S. must put an end to its overconsumption practices." For each solution the group might generate, it would be possible to indicate which subordinate learnings are prerequisite. Due to lack of time and space, only one example will be given, and it is assumed that a similar sequence would exist for the other possibilities. The learning sequence is from bottom to top in the list below.

SAMPLE PROBLEM SOLUTION: The U.S. must put an end to its overconsumption practices.

HIGH ORDER RULE: U.S. overconsumption causes hunger directly and indirectly.

SUBORDINATE RULES: (1) In order to make huge supplies of resources available at cheap prices to the U.S., affluent ruling minorities, usually military dictatorships, keep the people in poor countries from consuming their own resources.

Concepts: economic stratification, affluent minorities, military dictatorships

Related Information: Much of the farmland of poor nations is used to grow cash crops—tobacco, coffee, etc.—for export to rich nations, instead of for food to feed their own people.

(2) With a finite and diminishing supply of world resources, more consumption by the U.S. means less for the world's poor.

Concepts: finite resource supply, consumption

Related Information: According to government estimates, within 10 years, we will be importing 50 percent of our raw materials, almost all of which will come from poor nations. As 6 percent of the world's population, we use 33 percent of the world's resources. If one out of every 5 people consumed at the rate we do, the other four would have nothing. Many of our natural resources will be exhausted within 25-100 years.

(3) Hunger is one product of generalized poverty within a country.

Concepts: hunger, poverty

Related Information: Statistics will be provided on rates of malnutrition, protein deficiency, income distribution, people below poverty level, etc.

It can be seen from the above example that the subordinate rules and concepts needed to solve the problem will have been learned during the first portion of the course, under Goal 1. It is also evident that *much* lower-level learning is merely assumed to be present, due to the nature of the learner population.

II. Attitude Objective

Goal 4: To choose action strategies aimed at the world hunger problem. Behavioral objective: Given the course information on protein waste involved in meat-eating, and given the alternative of a high protein meatless diet, the participants will often choose the alternative diet by cooking and eating meatless meals, using vegetable protein complementarity principles.

There are many types of action strategies which might be chosen by an individual or group studying world hunger. Various political strategies, from letter writing to violent confrontation, are possible. Economic methods, ranging from fund-raising campaigns to the economic restructuring of society, might be undertaken. The completed course outline would specify such categories of action strategies in the form of several behavioral objectives under Goal 4. The particular one selected for analysis here concerns a fairly personal action strategy, one which obviously must involve the changing or strengthening of an attitude set. The observable behaviors of cooking and eating certain foods are taken to indicate that the attitude set has indeed been adopted, although one cannot be sure that there is a direct correspondence between attitude and behavior.

There would be a large cognitive learning component required by this objective. Briefly, such prior learnings as these would be involved:

- *Information* about protein waste, protein content of various foods, a stock of recipes, etc.
- *Concepts* such as amino acids, protein complementarity.
- *Rules* such as how to combine vegetable proteins to obtain maximum useability.
- *Discriminations* among various protein-rich ingredients such as bulgar, nutritional yeast, whole wheat flour, soy flour.

Psychomotor abilities involved in cooking and eating would also be required. In addition, it would be necessary to structure the situation to facilitate attitude change. One way of doing this is briefly outlined here as a suggested learning sequence.

1. Source credibility (perhaps a nutrition expert) is established for the learner.
2. Cognitive dissonance is created in the learner, following consistency theories of attitude change. For example, the learner might be taught to hold two dissonant cognitions simultaneously: "Meat eating wastes protein." "I eat meat."
3. The learner might next be presented with an appropriate communication from the credible source which advocates the desired position (attitude and behavior).
4. The learner might also be presented with a respected model who has already adopted the desired attitude and behavior.

Assignment 3: Delivery System
and Media Selection
Learning Environment, Development Environment,
Resources and Constraints

As stated in assignment 1, this mini-course is being designed for use by an adult study group which is interested in the topic of world hunger. The class will not meet in a regular classroom but rather in a meeting room of a church or other public building, or perhaps in a private home. Meeting for approximately 4 to 8 sessions, the assumed format is group discussion based upon individual research and home study. The course will be on a non-credit basis and will operate very informally. The participant/ learners are presumed to be in various states of information, noninformation, and misinformation. There will be a wide distribution of opinions, and some will conflict with others. Various political viewpoints and life styles will be represented, but the learning group will be largely middle class. They will be relatively flexible as to learning style. They will also be very busy people, involved in work, civic, and other activities.

While there is no deadline for completion of this design and development project, it is assumed that the course is being planned by one individual, possibly with help from a committee of volunteer non-experts. It is being done at home, on the designer's own time, and without compensation. Thus, the amount of time available must necessarily be a limiting factor. In addition to limited development time, it is necessary to realize that instructional time is very short in relation to the scope of the goals and objectives. People will not spend much time on individualized work at home, and they will have a narrow tolerance for attending more meetings within already busy schedules. A further constraint is that no money is available except out-of-pocket donations by participants and/or the designer. Resources, however, include access to certain reference material which has already been collected, the use of duplicating equipment, and minimal secretarial assistance. Basic audio-visual equipment, such as screens and projectors, can probably be made available.

Delivery System

Based on the above assumptions, resources, and constraints,

it seems that the delivery system for the course as a whole should be composed of the following:

1. Materials-centered home study packets, consisting mainly of printed material and including objectives, study and thought questions, brief readings, and self-tests.

Rationale: While technological media might be more effective, the lack of funds prohibits anything more expensive than printed material. Lack of development time and talent precludes anything elaborate. The individual home study packets will enable the busy adult participants to learn at their own paces. Based on this structured method of preparation, the group sessions should prove to be quite productive.

2. Group-centered activities prescribed for study sessions. These might include lecture, discussion, demonstration, multimedia presentations, experiential techniques, or combinations of the above.

Rationale: Since the course objectives fall into many different domains of learning, a variety of media is appropriate. In order to be effective, it will be necessary to maintain as much interest and motivation as possible, and variety should be helpful in this regard. Since the learners will be flexible in their learning styles, they should easily make transitions from one medium to another.

Media Selection

Goal 4: To choose action strategies aimed at the world hunger problem. Behavioral objective: Given the course information on protein waste involved in meat-eating, and given the alternative of a high protein, meatless diet, the participants will often choose the alternative diet by cooking and eating meatless meals, using vegetable protein complementarity principles.

In order to select media for this objective, it is helpful to look both at Dale's and Briggs' models. Dale emphasizes the age of the learners and gives direction as to the types of media one might choose for efficient cognitive and affective learning. It also categorizes media types and organizes them into a hierarchy from concrete to abstract. Briggs' model points to the desirability of classifying each sub-objective by domain, specifying the conditions for that learning type, and selecting appropriate media. Ideally, principles from both models would be used for each objective in the course. For purposes of this assignment, however, only very general aspects of each will be applied.

Assignment 2 discussed the fact that there are cognitive components within the above objective, and these may be seen as subordinate competencies required to obtain the attitude portion of the objective. These two domains will be treated separately for purposes of media selection and instruction.

1. Cognitive portions of objective: information, discriminations, concepts, rules, skills, etc.

Since the learners are adults with at least high school reading levels (as stated in assignment 1), it would be most efficient, according to Dale, to focus at the higher levels of the cone of experience. Thus, *reading and lecturing*, using charts, diagrams, and other *symbolic visual aids*, would convey the subject-matter quickly, and well. According to Briggs, exact learnings are broken down into constituent elements. This will be done in assignment 5, when specific teaching/learning activities are prescribed. It can be foreseen, however, that certain concrete demonstrations, exhibits, etc., will be helpful as supplementary techniques. The primary media, however, will be spoken and written symbols.

2. Affective portions of objective: actual attitude (and behavior) change.

According to Dale, attitude change can best be accomplished, even in adults, by using techniques towards the concrete (lower) end of the cone of experience. *Exhibits* of actual vegetables will be used. *Demonstrations* on how to use the foods in recipe preparation would also be appropriate. *Direct and contrived experiences*, being very concrete in nature, should be most likely to provide affective impact. One social psychological theory states that behavior *causes* attitudes, rather than the reverse. If a person engages in a behavior that is contrary to his/her present attitude, she/he is more likely to change that attitude in the direction of the exhibited behavior. Based on these theoretical notions, it makes sense to use a direct, purposeful, although semi-contrived, experience. If it is a pleasant one, positive feelings would thereby be associated with the alternative diet, and the desired attitude/behavior would be promoted. Such a practical application of the learning should also enhance retention and transfer.

Assignment 4: Assessing Learner Performance
The overall objective used in this assignment was also used in assignments 2 and 3 and is restated below:

Given the course information on protein waste involved in meat-eating, and given the alternative of a high protein, meatless diet, the participants will often choose the alternative diet by cooking and eating meatless meals, using vegetable protein complementarity principles.

For purposes of media selection (assignment 3), this objective was divided into an affective component and a subordinate cognitive component. (Before the learner can *choose* to do something, she/he must be *able* to do it.) The same division will be followed here for evaluation purposes. It will be necessary to state the cognitive portion as a formal intellectual skill objective, as follows:

Domain: Intellectual skills

Subdomain: Problem-solving

Given the course information on protein waste involved in meat-eating, and given the alternative of a high protein, meatless diet, the learner will generate a solution to a meal planning problem by planning and preparing a meatless family meal, using protein complementarity principles.

This problem-solving skill must be achieved first, so it will be evaluated first. Due to the very limited instructional time mentioned earlier as a constraint, not much time should be spent in testing. This conclusion also follows from the nature of the course: a voluntary, non-credit interest group for adults. It seems practical, therefore, to evaluate the learner's achievement of this entire problem-solving objective at once, without necessarily testing each subordinate competency. The hierarchical nature of the subordinate learnings as well as the maturity level of the learners seem to justify this testing procedure. Another pragmatic decision is to make the evaluative instruments a self-test to be placed in the individual home study packet (part of the delivery system described in assignment 2). In this way, the actual practice and performance of the skill can be done in each participant's own "lab" (kitchen), and each person can evaluate his/her own performance. Results can be shared in the group session. Any encountered difficulties or failures, as well as successes, can be shared among the group. What follows is the actual self-test and evaluative criteria that would be used by participants.

Self-test: Using the book *Diet For a Small Planet* and any other relevant resource material and recipes, plan and prepare a meatless family meal that contains at least 45 percent of a person's daily usable protein requirement per serving, by combining complementary proteins.

Evaluate your product:

1.   Can you demonstrate how each person received at least 45 percent of the daily protein need?
2.   Did you combine foods that complement each other in amino acid content?
3.   Are you sure that no meat was used to prepare the meal?
4.   Was your meal a success? Did the family enjoy it?

The overall objective (stated at the beginning of this paper) requires the measurement of an attitude as evidenced by chosen behavior. Since direct observation of the private behaviors of cooking and eating would be almost impossible, it seems that the next most accurate way to assess such learning is through a questionnaire survey conducted some time, say three months, after the end of the mini-course. This "wait" will give the new ideas time to sink in and will give people time to practice with the new behaviors. It will also provide ample time for participants to observe their own behavior patterns in preparation for a self-report test. This questionnaire could be used to measure the attainment of several objectives, in addition to this particular one. However, the questions which follow are aimed, directly or indirectly, at determining attitudes towards an alternative diet.

(*Note to the reader*: To save space here, the questionnaire has been deleted.)

**Assignment 5: Designing Instructional
Materials and Activities**

Following the precedent established in assignments 2, 3, and 4, the objective that is used in this assignment is broken down into two parts: an overall attitude objective and a subordinate intellectual skill (problem-solving) objective. These will be handled separately in the prescriptions for materials and activities.

*I. Intellectual Skill (Problem-Solving)
Objective:*

Given the course information on protein waste involved in meat eating, and given the alternative of a high protein, meatless diet, the learner will generate a solution to a meal planning problem by planning and preparing a meatless family meal, using protein complementarity principles. (It is recognized that subordinate motor skills are required by this objective, but it is assumed that they are present and recalled at the time of instruction. It is also assumed that previous lessons have established certain prerequisite discriminations, concepts, and rules.)

Lesson Plan

Instructional Events	*Media*	*Prescription*
Gaining attention		Dependent upon learner's own will. Audience is adults who should be self-instructional.
Informing learner of objective	Written material in home study packet	State objective in written form.
Stimulating recall of prerequisites		Refer learner to appropriate reading matter, charts, and diagrams used in previous lessons. These include a list of rules for

Presenting stim-
ulus material and
providing learning
guidance

protein complementarity
combinations in foods.

Deductive method will be
used for sake of efficiency. (Rules are given and
solutions are deduced
from them.)

Several exercises are presented to learner in form
of hypothetical meal
planning problems.

Attempt to use a wide
variety of situations.

Examples:
a. What dish could be
   used to complement
   the incomplete pro-
   tein in a bowl of
   split pea soup?
b. If you were baking a
   cake which con-
   tained 1½ cups of
   whole wheat flour,
   what ingredients
   would most effec-
   tively complement
   the wheat and in
   what amount?

Answers to sample prob-
lems should be provided
as feedback.

Examples:
a. Muffins with sesame

		seeds and sunflower seeds.
		b. ½ cup soy flour.
Eliciting performance		Administer self-test (see assignment 4). Provide standard meal planning form with space for recipes, protein content, etc.
Providing feedback and assessing performance	Informal family discussion Home study packet	Feedback on the actual meal is provided by learner and family or friends. Instructions: go over the evaluative criteria (see self-test in assignment 4).
Enhancing retention and transfer	Group discussion within study session	Hold group discussion on successes, failures, and problems encountered in above procedures. Also, see next group activity.

II. Attitude Objective:

Given the course information on protein waste involved in meat eating, and given the alternative of a high protein, meatless diet, the participants will often choose the alternative diet by cooking and eating meatless meals, using vegetable protein complementarity principles.

Lesson Plan

Instructional Events	*Media*	*Prescription*
Gaining attention	Exposition by verbal presentation	Suggest the social activity described below.

Informing learner of objective	Exposition by verbal presentation	Informal statement about "why we are doing this": to build positive attitudes.
Stimulating recall of prerequisites	Discussion	(1) Ask learners to refer to home study packets and the meals they have just prepared at home.

(2) Recall previous readings and discussions on causes of world hunger, especially the protein waste involved in meat eating.

(3) Recall opinions of nutrition experts in reference to a reduction in meat consumption and its effect on overall world food supply.

(4) Re-establish cognitive dissonance between above cognitions and learner's own actions. |
| Presenting stimulus material and eliciting performance | Concrete, direct experience | Learners prepare meatless dishes and bring them to a communal dinner—a social event where all the dishes are shared among the participants. |
| Providing learning guidance | Verbal communication among learners | (1) If possible, highly respected persons or opinion leaders should be in- |

		cluded in this activity as participants. These persons should exhibit positive attitudes to establish "model" behavior.
		(2) During the meal, let people explain how their food was prepared, its protein content, etc.
Providing feedback	Social interaction	Learners socially reinforce each other for participating in the meatless communal dinner.
Assessing performance	Written material	Questionnaire survey three months after end of course. (See assignment 4.)
Enhancing retention and transfer	Concrete, direct experience	Social reinforcement for desired behavior, provision of other human models, and repetition of performance already accomplished at home. Intention is that experience will be pleasant, and a positive affective association will be established with the alternative diet.

Assignment 6: Formative and Summative Evaluation

The characteristics of a course evaluation must be consistent with the nature of the course being evaluated. This World Hunger mini-course is a small-scale operation. It is designed, taught, and attended by interested persons on a voluntary basis, for no credit, and for no pay. There is no budget. It is intended to be loosely organized and informally operated. The learners are busy adults who may have careers and/or families, so that instructional time is quite limited. Due to the relative uniqueness of the subject-matter, the course is not replacing an already existing one, but is designed to fill a gap. In order to be successful, the course must involve and interest people, as well as instruct them. If the participants achieve the learning objectives but find the learning process dull or boring, the course is, essentially, a failure.

These characteristics of the course imply certain features of a realistic evaluation plan. The procedures will of necessity be of a modest scale, i.e., not very technical, extensive, time-consuming, or expensive. The evaluation cannot be comparative in nature, because, presumably, there are no comparable instructional systems. Standardized tests of achievement, ability, or attitudes are not appropriate for the relatively "new" and specific subject matter of the course. The evaluation must include an assessment of the motivational and interest-arousing aspects of the course, in addition to some measurement of instructional effectiveness and efficiency.

(*Note to the reader: A part of the assignment has been deleted here to save space. This was an "enabling objective" requiring the student to draw a diagram of the stages in the instructional design process.*)

Assignment 6A: Formative
Evaluation Plan

The World Hunger course consists of two components (the home-study packet and the group session activities) which require somewhat differential treatment in terms of formative evaluation.

Home-study Packets

I. *One-on-one trials.* At this stage, the materials would be in rough form. They would already be in the ultimate medium, which is paper-and-pencil. The designer would go through the materials with two or more individuals, as time would permit. A draft of the entry skills test and pretest would be administered prior to the actual work on the instructional materials, and a draft of the posttest would be administered at the end. (Pretest and posttest would include attitude objectives as well as information and intellectual skill objectives.) The data obtained from these interactions and used for evaluation would consist of:

(a) *marked-up sets of materials*, with indications of
   (1) spots which need more or less instruction, where difficulties were experienced, or where too much time was consumed;
   (2) ambiguities, wording problems, inconsistencies; and
   (3) omissions of important topics.
(b) *verbal feedback* on specific units and on package as a whole in terms of interest and enjoyability;
(c) *scores on the self-tests* which are imbedded in the materials themselves;
(d) *scores on pretest and posttest* as well as suggestions for revising these instruments.

At least one person selected for the one-on-one trial should be something of a "subject-matter expert," a person who is well-informed and perhaps knows something about teaching/learning. At least one other person should represent the opposite end of the continuum, knowing very little about the subject matter.

II. Small-group try-out. Next, the home study packets would be tested with a small group who would, concurrently, participate in the first trial of the group activities. The designer/instructor would not be as closely in contact with the individuals as they work on their packets as was the case for one-on-one. Therefore, very specific instructions for critiquing the materials would be supplied to the users. The types of data obtained at this stage and used in revision would be:

(a) *marked-up sets of materials*, with the same types of feedback as the one-on-one trial. In addition, users would be asked to indicate time spent on each major section;
(b) *written feedback* on interest and enjoyability;
(c) *scores on self-tests*;
(d) *scores on pretest and posttest* and suggestions for their revision; and
(e) *verbal feedback* (perhaps tape-recorded) on how well the home-study materials correlate with and complement the in-class group activities.

An effort should be made to select persons for this small-group trial who would adequately represent the intended population. Subjective judgment would have to be used here. Volunteers who express interest in participating would be used, as long as the group would not be biased in any obvious way, such as heavily weighted with "experts." It might be necessary to accept acquaintances of the designer rather than total strangers, but it is assumed that these persons will not be any more cooperative nor any less critical than the average participant.

At each stage of the formative revision, it will be helpful to make use of the structured or hierarchical set of objectives developed earlier. Since the tests will measure subordinate competencies as well as ultimate objectives, it will be possible to see where the instruction is deficient and how far down into the structure of cumulative objectives it is necessary to go for revision.

III. *Field Trial.* This trial will be held in the ultimate setting as described in assignment 1. A study group of volunteer adults will be meeting in a church, public meeting room, or private home. Noise will be present as in any normal and unprotected environment. The participants will use the home study packets for individual work and will come together for a series of group activity sessions. Formative evaluation will be conducted on both instructional components simultaneously.

The same kinds of data will be collected as for the small-group trial. In addition, a follow-up questionnaire will be sent out approximately three months after the end of the course. (Some of the purposes and content of this questionnaire have been discussed in previous assignments.) The questionnaire will be designed to measure retention and transfer of the knowledge, skills, and attitudes attained in the course. Particularly in the case of attitudes, the delay is essential in order to provide time for behavior self-observation. It is recognized, however, that some effects may be due to factors intervening after the end of instruction.

IV. *Continuing Formative Evaluation.* It is projected that this course, if successful, might be distributed to more groups, perhaps in other cities. If so, a continuing feedback system will be developed whereby user groups and their instructors can add up-to-date information and new activities to the evolving course, and this input can be passed on to future participating groups.

The group sessions will be evaluated in two stages: the small-group trial and the field trial. Data used in each revision will be:

(a) *verbal feedback* from participants on the effectiveness of each activity (media, instructional procedures, coordination with home-study materials);

(b) *anonymous written feedback forms* following each session; comments on interest and enjoyability, effectiveness; and

(c) *instructor's report* concerning:

    (a) logistic problems of implementation

    (2) interest level of group

    (3) judgment of performance on group objectives.

(**Note to the reader**: *Two pages of sample test questions for the formative evaluation have been deleted from the original materials.*)

Assignment 6B: Summative Evaluation

1. What kinds of summative evaluation questions are appropriate for the World Hunger mini-course?

(a) How much cumulative learning (information, intellectual skills, and attitudes) actually occurred?

(b) To what extent do the learners retain the learning and transfer it to their daily lives?

(c) Have any other courses been designed that do a superior job?

(d) Do participants feel that the objectives are worthwhile?

(e) Do participants find the course interesting and enjoyable?

2. What data are needed to answer the above questions?

(a) A comparison must be made of pre- and posttest results, with the posttest being administered immediately following instruction. It would also be good to have a control group take the pre- and posttests, but probably this is impractical due to the difficulty in getting volunteer adults to take them unless they had been in the course.

(b) The three-month follow-up questionnaire described in

this and previous assignments should be used to determine interest.

(c) Feedback from other users and people interested in the topic of world hunger would be needed, as would a scanning of relevant publications.

(d) Ask participants (in the follow-up questionnaire) whether their time was well-spent taking the course, was it worth it to them, would they recommend it to their friends, etc.

(e) Certain items on the follow-up questionnaire would be aimed at this issue. Also, instructor feedback would be used.

Author Index

Subject Index